D1565554

India and
the China Crisis

INTERNATIONAL CRISIS BEHAVIOR SERIES

Edited by Michael Brecher

STEVEN A. HOFFMANN

India
and the
China Crisis

University of California Press
BERKELEY · LOS ANGELES · LONDON

1990

University of California Press
Berkeley and Los Angeles, California

University of California Press, Ltd.
London, England

© 1990 by
The Regents of the University of California

Library of Congress Cataloging-in-Publication Data

Hoffmann, Steven A.
India and the China crisis/Steven A. Hoffmann.
p. cm.—(International crisis behavior series; v. 6)
Bibliography: p.
Includes index.
ISBN 0-520-06537-9 (alk. paper)
1. Sino-Indian Border Dispute, 1957–   I. Title. II. Series.
DS480.85.H64   1989   89-4672
954.04—dc19   CIP

Printed in the United States of America
1   2   3   4   5   6   7   8   9

For Cheryl,
and for my parents

Contents

Maps and Figures

Foreword

THIRTY YEARS HAVE elapsed since the first dramatic clash of arms in
the remote Himalayan region of the Sino-Indian borderland—ample
time for a creative reexamination of the unresolved conflict. This is
accomplished in Steven Hoffmann's study of India's behavior in the
crisis culminating in the 1962 war. During prolonged and tenacious
research he examined with care the rich documentary and secondary
sources and interviewed virtually everyone involved in the most
traumatic setback to India's foreign policy since independence. For the
principal Indian decision-maker, Nehru, he had the benefit of a wealth
of interviews and biographies by other scholars.

The result is an illuminating book which combines the best of
history and political science. At one level it is a fascinating and
comprehensive narrative. At another it is a perceptive analysis of
India's behavior under stress which also uncovers striking similarities
with the behavior of other states confronting foreign policy crises.

The account of India's attempts to cope with China's persistent
challenge and territorial claims, from the Kongka Pass incident in
October 1959 to the massive attack on 20 October 1962, is full of
insights. The drama of the war phase is effectively portrayed, as are
many of the basic Indian decisions adopted under stress, including the
personal request by Nehru to Kennedy on 19 November 1962 for
immediate and massive military aid to stem the Chinese advance.

Those who are interested in the international politics of Asia will
find much to ponder in this post-revisionist analysis of what led to the
Sino-Indian border war, as well as of the mind-set that led Nehru,
Krishna Menon, and the Indian decision-making group as a whole
to err fundamentally in their estimate of China's intentions and capabilities as the conflict escalated in the summer of 1962. Those with a

special interest in how political leaders behave under stress will learn much from this in-depth case study, for in the last part of his book Hoffmann draws together the principal findings, both in terms of the specific case and in relation to important hypotheses about crisis behavior generally.

These findings focus on coping and choice under stress. They are organized around four crucial aspects of decision-making: information processing, patterns of consultation, decisional forums, and the search for and consideration of alternatives. A few illustrations will be noted here. Hoffmann attributes India's failure to absorb information about the forthcoming Chinese attack to "a certain mental rigidity," the "difficulty in learning from negative results of past decisions," and Nehru's inability to think in terms of a punitive military raid rather than full-scale war for unlimited objectives, for India and China "could do things only on a grand scale."

Consultation, too, suffered from the existence of a Nehru faction with a mind-set shaped by the prime minister. This faction reinforced Nehru's views through a distorted picture of reality, and that situation was compounded by the members' acceptance of Nehru's worldview and his intellectual superiority. Although consultation broadened during the war phase, the change was too little and too late.

Hoffmann is also critical of the decision-making process: "Too much Indian leadership activity was ad hoc in 1962." And the blame for India's military setback, as well as for the flawed information processing, is clearly placed on Nehru; Krishna Menon; B. N. Mullik, the director of the influential Intelligence Bureau; and several generals, notably B. M. Kaul.

Perhaps Hoffmann's most valuable finding is that India's behavior in its crisis with China was remarkably similar to that of other states in foreign policy crises. Thus, Nehru and his associates relied heavily on past experience in interpreting information about China's behavior. They also relied on extraordinary and improvised channels of communication in the prewar phase of the crisis. Their receptivity to new information became increasingly biased, and they became less sensitive to negative feedback.

Many other hypotheses, derived from other crises, were also strongly supported. India's decision-makers became much more concerned with immediate threats than with the long-term future. Their attention narrowed sharply. And, like other ICB studies in this series, this study finds no evidential support for the hallowed view that stress and performance have a curvilinear relationship.

In short, Hoffmann demonstrates beyond doubt that India's behavior in the crisis with China was "normal"; that is, it replicated crisis behavior by other states. And he derives a noteworthy lesson from this discovery: To "become mindful of how easily normal behavior by a nation's decision-makers can lead to tragedy" is a major benefit from this inquiry.

Like almost the entire literature on the Sino-Indian conflict, Hoffmann's is a study of India's behavior, not China's. Nevertheless, it contains many vignettes about the other party. One, relating to the gap in stakes, is worth noting: "India needed the 'historical' border concept [the basis of India's claim was historical] for national identity purposes, just as much as China needed strategic boundaries for security purposes."

If not the last word on the subject, Hoffmann's book is certainly a major contribution to the analysis of a continuing conflict between the two most populous states in the world. It also provides a valuable study of how states behave in foreign policy crises. It is a persuasive narrative. And it is instructive about the high costs of misperceiving an adversary's objectives and power, as well as of the "prisoner of one's past" syndrome. More than a quarter of a century after the end of the crisis and war, the legacy of mistrust and deadlock remains a barrier to normal relations. The promise of close cooperation between India and China remains unfulfilled.

Michael Brecher, Director
International Crisis Behavior Project

Acknowledgments

THIS BOOK WOULD not have been written without great encouragement and editorial guidance from Michael Brecher, director of the International Crisis Behavior Project. The bulk of the research was carried out under the auspices of the project. For all the time, concern, and friendship Michael devoted to this book and its author, I am most profoundly grateful.

My appreciation goes too to Leo E. Rose of the University of California at Berkeley, for his advice and support. Long ago he made me promise to write this book, and he forgave my later doubts and delays. I hope he feels that the promise has been kept properly at last.

I am grateful to all who have stimulated and guided my long inquiry into this and related subjects. Outstanding among them were Norman D. Palmer and Donald E. Smith of the University of Pennsylvania and Walter Filley of the State University of New York at Binghamton. For financial support of the research, I am indebted to Michael Brecher and the ICB project and to Eric Weller, dean of the faculty at Skidmore College.

I also owe a debt of gratitude to the Centre for the Study of Developing Societies in New Delhi, which was a source of friendship and help over many years, although it gave no official support to this project and is in no way responsible for what I have written. Indeed, many of its members will disagree with much of what I have said. Similarly, I express my gratitude to academics, officials, and military officers who gave generously of their time and interest, without expecting that my ultimate interpretations would necessarily adhere to their own views. Such persons include S. Gopal, D. K. Palit, J. S. Mehta, K. Subrahmanyam, and A. Lamb, who were kind enough to comment on portions and versions of the manuscript.

Finally, I thank my wife, Cheryl, and my stepsons, Eddie and Andy, for her proofreading and their support and forbearance.

Saratoga Springs
September 1988

1
THE NATURE OF
THE CONFLICT

CHAPTER ONE

The Sino-Indian Border Problem

DISCUSSIONS OF CONTROVERSIAL subjects sometimes reach a certain
maturity. Debate over the controversy often called the Sino-Indian
border dispute has passed through the requisite preliminary stages,
and the time has come for its contending facts and ideas to be
fashioned into new interpretations.

Since 1959 this boundary dispute has bedeviled the relationship
between the two biggest nation-states in Asia and has generated a
large body of scholarly literature. That literature has offered no
consensus; instead, it has been dialectical. The earliest accounts by
academic authors looked upon India as the victim of Chinese betrayal
and expansionism,[1] and a pro-Indian school of thought was thereby
established. Contrary ideas about the historical-legal side of the
dispute were soon introduced by the British historian Alastair Lamb.[2]
But a more favorable image of China vis-à-vis India did not appear until 1970, when Neville Maxwell's comprehensive revisionist study was
published.[3] Maxwell, a former London *Times* New Delhi correspondent and an Oxford scholar, provided the most detailed and comprehensive treatment of the subject available for many years; and his
views became widely accepted. Accordingly, China was often portrayed as a victim of India's self-righteous intransigence. The 1962
India-China war occurred, or so it was argued, because China was
provoked into practicing a justifiable form of realpolitik.

The two seemingly irreconcilable academic schools of thought still
exist, and each finds adherents among statesmen and diplomats. The
debate remains lively today, especially with the publication of the new
semiofficial biography of Jawaharlal Nehru by the historian
Sarvepalli Gopal.[4] An alarming escalation of tension along the Sino-
Indian frontier in 1986 and 1987, which showed that military con-

3

frontation is still possible, makes the debate more than a historical exercise. Rajiv Gandhi's 1989 visit to China, the first by an Indian prime minister since 1954, indicates that new thinking about the border dispute is taking place in both New Delhi and Beijing.

Ultimately, the academic dialectic should go into its synthesis stage. To help initiate that stage, this book offers a new case study of India's decision-making between 1959 and 1963, the critical first years of the China conflict. This work of synthesis does not simply rely on factual material made available by contending scholars. It draws heavily on interviews and other primary source material gathered during a period of concentrated research conducted in India, England, and North America between 1983 and 1986, and intermittent research under-taken in India and elsewhere during the previous seventeen years. From interviews with Indian officials, military officers, and political leaders (see list in the Bibliography) and from the growing documen-tary record, which includes many memoirs, more of the perceptions and realities of Indian decision-making can now be deciphered than were previously known.

In addition, insights were obtained from the extensive literature on foreign policy decision-making and crisis behavior built up by theoretically oriented political scientists and scholars from related disciplines. A researcher who is attempting to reinterpret the early years of India's conflict with China can make good use of individual concepts taken from that literature and can utilize one of the several available descriptive models that combine those concepts into a larger integrated whole. By using such a model, the researcher becomes aware of questions that are relevant to the study of foreign policy decision-making in general, and not just to one particular case. These are questions that the researcher can answer, ultimately, by compiling many case studies and noting the consistencies among them.

To be appropriate to this particular study, such broad theoretical questions must cover certain specific but crucial historical questions raised by critics of India's 1959–1963 decision-making and by its defenders. Those historical questions are:

1. Why did India's government, and its intelligence community, fail to absorb information showing that China would attack Indian frontier forces in 1962? Before and during the 1962 border crisis, why did the Nehru government fail to deal adequately with information about Chinese intentions and capabilities?[5]

2. Prior to the attack, and during the war, how well were Prime Minister Jawaharlal Nehru and other Indian decision-makers served by their regular consultants—that is, the officials and military officers who provided them with information and advice?[6]

3. Before and during the 1962 war, what were the actual decision-making roles of Nehru; his defense minister, V. K. Krishna Menon; and his main military commander, Lieutenant General B. M. Kaul? How did those roles interact; and for what successes and failures was each person responsible?

4. Did these decision-makers and their consultants escalate the conflict with China to the level of armed confrontation and ultimately war, instead of seeking alternatives such as meaningful negotiations? How open was the Nehru government to considering constructive alternatives in its dealings with China?[7]

These case-specific questions from the India-China conflict can be encompassed by the following research questions of conceptual or theoretical significance. One such broader question, to cover intelligence failure by India's government or any other government, would be:

1. How does increasing stress (among other factors) affect the information processing capabilities of decision-makers and the consultants who serve them?[8]

Information processing can be analyzed by examining its key dimensions. These include (a) the decision-makers' (and consultants') perceived need and consequent search for information, (b) their intellectual and emotional rigidity or openness at particular times, and (c) their receptivity to the specific information they are receiving.

A theoretical question that focuses on the workings of a governmental consultation process, such as that conducted by the Indian government on China policy between 1959 and 1963, would be:

2. What are the effects of rising stress (among other factors) on the ways in which decision-makers consult with advisers and with one another?

Analytical dimensions of the consultation process include (a) the types and sizes of the consultative units involved and (b) the ways in which individuals and groups participate in such units.

A theoretically oriented question on how decision-makers' roles are played, and interrelated, would be:

3. What are the effects of rising stress (among other factors) on
   decision-making forums (i.e., units)?

Two analytical dimensions of that question are (a) the size and
structure of the decisional forums and (b) the authority patterns
within those forums.

A theoretically oriented question on how decision-makers in any
nation-state consider alternatives such as war or negotiation would
be:

4. How does rising stress (among other factors) affect the
   performance of decision-makers and their consultants in perceiving
   alternative strategies and actions, and in choosing among them?

Two key analytical dimensions of this question are (a) the ways in
which the search for and evaluation of alternatives are conducted and
(b) the perceived range of available alternatives at various times.

One political science model that requires its users to concentrate on
such questions is the "crisis" model formulated by Michael Brecher
and his associates in the International Crisis Behavior research project
(ICB.)[9] The ICB model will loosely guide this study.

Briefly summarized, the model specifies that information processing, consultation, the structuring of decision-making roles, and the
consideration of alternatives are "coping mechanisms." These are the
mechanisms with which decision-makers try to cope with perceptions
of an international situation. If they believe that the situation is a
"crisis," their key perceptions will be of (1) high threat, (2) limited
time available for appropriate action, and (3) high probability of
armed hostilities. As they vary and interact with one another, these
three perceptions generate high levels of "stress." But whether or not
the situation is perceived as a crisis, the "coping mechanisms" enable
the decision-makers to formulate a response to the situation and to
implement that response.

Such activity allegedly takes place in the context of the decision-
makers' fundamental worldview (their "attitudinal prism"), as well as
their semipermanent "images" of international and domestic realities.
Moreover, each response produced by the decision-making process
alters that worldview and those images and creates revised perceptions of the international situation. Thus, a response ultimately results
in "feedback," which starts a new round of decision-making. The
model therefore has a "cybernetic" character.

The ICB model is described in more detail in Chapter 17. The reader may either turn to that chapter now or examine it after working through the full presentation of factual material in Chapters 2–16.

This book is organized according to a chronological pattern specified by the model. The pattern divides the material into three periods: pre-crisis, crisis, and post-crisis.[10] In the Indian case the pre-crisis period lasted from 15 March 1959 to 7 September 1962. During this period India tried out a series of strategies (alternatives) designed to deal with China's territorial claims and alleged encroachments on Indian soil. The ensuing crisis period lasted from 8 September to 21 November 1962. It included an Indian effort to force the Chinese out of a disputed section of the frontier, which both sides had recently occupied, and a general Chinese attack on Indian frontier forces. In the post-crisis period, from 22 November 1962 to 28 February 1963, the Indian government sought to recover diplomatically from military defeat and made decisions that would permanently alter India's military-security policies.

One theme pursued in this book does not come from any theoretical source but is derived instead from much familiarity with modern Indian history. That theme is the importance of Indian nationalism. The Chinese failed to understand the role of Indian nationalism in the border conflict, but so has much of the academic literature, whether pro- or anti-Indian. "Indian nationalism" refers to the beliefs, attitudes, and perceptions brought forth by India's struggle for independence from Great Britain and shaped by the long history and culture of the Indian subcontinent. Prime Minister Nehru often spoke of the nationalist influence on the basic worldview and particular images held by his government, but its influence was more subtle and pervasive than even he realized.

Therefore, this study begins with a brief discussion of the Nehru government's nationalist interpretation of the legacy of British policy toward the Sino-Indian frontier. Contrary to later Chinese accusations, Nehru's India did not try to build directly upon British India's frontier policies but instead formulated an interpretation of the British legacy that was far from favorable to the British. That interpretation appeared in the early 1950s and, coupled with the contrary Chinese view of frontier history, did much to direct independent India and China toward conflict with each other.

During the 1959–1963 era, that conflict was a dynamic, escalating process in which each disputant took initiatives and reacted to those of the other side. Because India's decision-making is studied here in depth, whereas China's is not, these pages may sometimes give the unintentional impression that the initiating actions and policies usually came from the Indian government. But the reader should note that China's initiatives, as well as India's, are described carefully as the study proceeds.

CHAPTER TWO

British Ambiguity and Indian Frontiers

BY THE LATE 1940s, when Indian nationalism and other pressures finally induced the British to abandon their Indian empire, and when Communist victory finally freed China from civil war and foreign intervention, no mutually acceptable India-China border had yet evolved. Demarcation of a border on the ground had occurred at only a few places. Two undemarcated frontier regions would later constitute the most sensitive areas of conflict between India and China. One would be the Aksai Chin plateau, situated on the western edge of the India-China frontier (see Map 1). On its three sides the Aksai Chin faces Ladakh (in Indian-controlled Kashmir), Tibet, and Sinkiang. The Aksai Chin is part of the larger region that both India and China call the Western Sector. The other much-disputed area lies at the eastern end of the Sino-Indian frontier, near Burma. This is the Assam Himalayan region (also shown on Map 1), which the government of independent India would call the North East Frontier Agency (NEFA). In 1986 it became the Indian state called Arunachal Pradesh.

There would be still further problems in the "Western Sector" (Ladakh), and along the so-called "Middle Sector" of the frontier (running from India's Uttar Pradesh to the Punjab), but as minor squabbles they need not be subject to detailed treatment in this study. . The same holds true for problems involving the Himalayan kingdoms of Sikkim and Bhutan, both of them under India's diplomatic and military protection.

THE AKSAI CHIN AND BRITISH POLICY

There was no one British policy on the disposition of the Aksai Chin. A high-altitude desert forming an extension of the great Tibetan

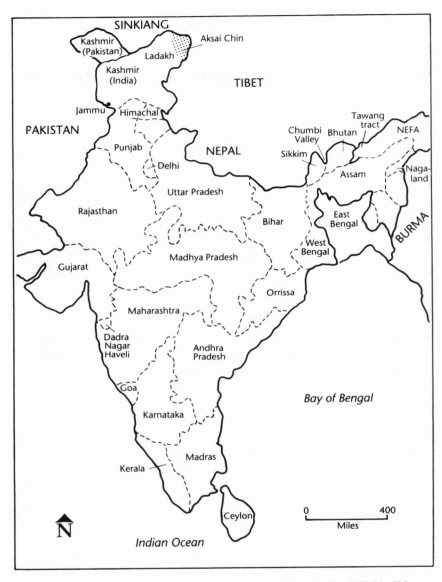

SINKIANG

Kashmir
(Pakistan)
Aksai Chin
Ladakh

Kashmir
(India)

TIBET

Jammu Himachal

PAKISTAN

Punjab

Delhi

NEPAL

Chumbi
Valley
Bhutan

Tawang
tract

NEFA

Sikkim

Assam

Naga-
land

Uttar Pradesh

Rajasthan

Bihar

East
Bengal

BURMA

Gujarat

Madhya Pradesh

West
Bengal

Orrissa

Maharashtra

Dadra
Nagar
Haveli

Andhra
Pradesh

Goa

Bay of Bengal

Karnataka

Madras

Kerala

Ceylon

N

Indian Ocean

0   400
Miles

Map 1.   AKSAI CHIN, TAWANG TRACT, AND INDIA IN
         1961–1962.

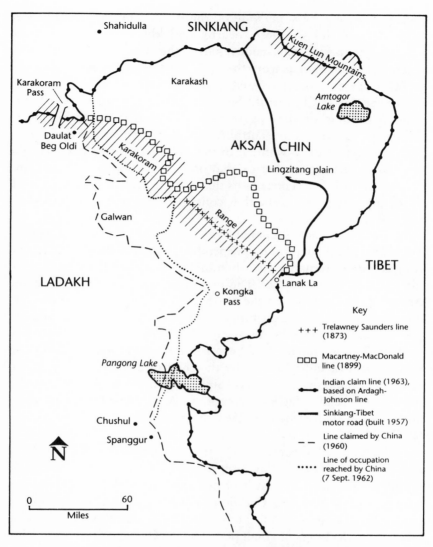

Map 2. BRITISH-FORMULATED BOUNDARIES FOR
        LADAKH.

plateau, and cut by some valleys, the Aksai Chin had no intrinsic value. People did go there; nearby Ladakhi villagers used it for summer grazing and thus made it part of the "Cashmere" wool trade. There was jade mining from the Sinkiang side, and some ancient (if secondary) trade routes crossed it. But that was all.

Yet the Aksai Chin could be strategically important as a buffer zone, depending on developments in the great game of big-power influence and balance in Central Asia. The British, as a major part of their policy, always wanted to have buffers lying between the populated parts of northern India, on the one side, and Russia and China, on the other. The regions that were to serve as buffers, as well as the primary power to be thus contained, varied as British perceptions of threat varied.

According to a note prepared (probably in 1951) by the first director of the Historical Division in independent India's Ministry of External Affairs, three alternative British boundary lines had been formulated for Ladakh.[1] (See Map 2.) The most northerly could be called the Ardagh-Johnson line. On the north and northeast this line touched upon the great Kuen Lun range of mountains. Thus, the Ardagh-Johnson line included the Aksai Chin within the area of British Indian control. This boundary had been formally proposed to the British Government of India in 1897 by the chief of British military intelligence in London, Major General Sir John Ardagh. In dealing with the Aksai Chin and adjacent territories, Ardagh had supported an alignment drawn earlier (in 1865) by the Survey of India explorer W. H. Johnson.

The second of the proposed British borders, usually called the Macartney-MacDonald line, represented more caution. Its most significant feature was that it placed almost all of the Aksai Chin's main section in Sinkiang. Certain localities on the Ladakhi periphery of the Aksai Chin were on the British Indian side of the line. These places were the Lingzitang salt plain and the Chang Chenmo and Chip Chap valleys. Later they too would become subjects of dispute between India and China.

Yet another British idea was to place the Ladakh frontier along the Karakoram mountain range. Any conceivable Karakoram boundary (such as the one drawn by the India Office cartographer Trelawney Saunders for the Foreign Office in 1873) would lie far to the south and southwest of the other (more forward) lines. Thus, it would be favorable to forward movement by the Chinese.[2]

An Indian scholar who helped devise the official view of the Nehru government after independence has argued that by the end of World War I the British Government of India had tacitly accepted a version of the Ardagh-Johnson line as the de facto boundary. He also says that British acceptance of such a line became more explicit in 1936, when New Delhi advised a frontier ruler to abandon practices and rights that were incompatible with observance of that line. The government of independent India then reexamined the whole Ladakh boundary question after 1947, and found that a de facto boundary line had "crystallized" prior to independence.[3] But these assertions must remain speculative as long as many independent scholars do not have access to the records of that period in Government of India archives.

One independent scholar who lacks such access no longer believes that after World War I British India still claimed the Aksai Chin by tacitly or explicitly accepting a modified Ardagh-Johnson line. He has changed his view because in doing research recently he found no supporting evidence in the archives of the India Office and the Foreign Office, and none in nonarchival sources. To the contrary, he believes now that the 1899 Macartney-MacDonald line was the last to receive any measure of acceptance as general British policy, which it did in 1907. Thereafter the British were, in fact, legally and constitutionally bound to the 1899 line, having presented it to the Chinese and included it on an authoritative 1909 map. But they did not explicitly claim a Ladakh border between 1909 and 1947.[4]

The findings of scholars do show that if a version of the Ardagh-Johnson line became the basis of British thinking about the Aksai Chin after World War I, this policy was not made clear on Survey of India (i.e., the most authoritative Government of India) maps. Only after 1945 did Survey of India maps (as had the 1909 map mentioned earlier) imply a claim to the Aksai Chin by the way a broad "color wash" (band of color) was used along the northern and eastern frontier of Kashmir.[5]

That the British considered other possible Ladakh boundaries, as well as the Ardagh-Johnson line, all through the period from 1897 to the 1940s has been proven by recent research in the India Office files.[6] These competing policy directions can be attributed to the institutionalized relationship that already existed between the British Indian government in New Delhi (or Calcutta when, earlier, it was the British capital in India) and the British home government in London.[7] Most heavily involved in that relationship at the London end was the India

Office (Secretary of State for India) and the Foreign Office (the British foreign ministry).

Where frontier questions were concerned, the India Office and the Foreign Office were cognizant of wider considerations than simply the advantages and disadvantages of a specific move in India's border-lands. They had to be concerned with the political and strategic implications for the empire of any boundary agreements concluded with other powers bordering India. Such powers included Russia and China, and relations with them were seen from London as set by such matters as Anglo-Russian dealings in Europe and the Middle East and British interests on the mainland of China. Thus, London tended toward avoidance of forward claims and lines.

By contrast, the Government of India was naturally most concerned with potential and actual threats to India. This concern particularly preoccupied its army and its Foreign Department (after 1914 called the Foreign and Political Department, after 1935 the External Affairs Department, and after independence the Ministry of External Affairs).[8] Influencing Delhi's perception of such threats was a mentality consis-tent with ruling a colonial empire rather than an internally secure nation-state. The coming of any independent sovereign power toward India's frontiers, especially an Asian power, was seen as potentially disruptive of internal stability.[9] A line such as the Ardagh-Johnson boundary would have seemed most preferable, given such concerns.

The different perspectives of London and Delhi sometimes led to what one close observer of this relationship has called "bureaucratic chicanery."[10] Via various stratagems Delhi officials would try to push British imperial policy further in certain directions than the India Office (and the Foreign Office) in London was prepared to allow. Important Foreign Department officials, such as Henry McMahon and Olaf Caroe, acted in this fashion. It is not surprising, therefore, that London documents would generally reflect thinking which favored a cautious line tied to the Karakoram, while Delhi leaned in other directions.

Another reason for the appearance of different and competing strands in British policy was that opinion within the Government of India also varied over time.

Thus, the forward boundary proposed by Ardagh in London was not at first accepted in Delhi when this proposal was put forward in 1897. The then viceroy, Lord Elgin, and his government preferred another boundary.[11] In 1899 the British Indian government initiated discussion with the Chinese imperial government on acceptance of the Macartney-MacDonald line. The Chinese never agreed to it formally, but their provincial government in Sinkiang thought the proposal a fair one.

Among officials in both India and London, during 1907 and 1908, the Macartney-MacDonald line "was regarded in official British circles as the international boundary of British India, a boundary which, again for this limited period, was certainly delimited."[12] But in 1911, when apprehension about Russia was again prompting reexamination of the Kashmir frontier situation, the Indian Army came to look favorably upon the notion of an Ardagh-style line, having opposed it earlier. Aware that the then foreign secretary of the Government of India supported an Ardagh option, the army General Staff stated in a memorandum that "the extended frontier would be an advantage provided we have not to occupy the portion beyond our present frontier by posts, but merely aim at keeping it undeveloped."[13] Accordingly, in 1912 Lord Hardinge, the viceroy, proposed to the Secretary of State for India that the Aksai Chin and adjacent territory be placed within the limits of British India, by using Ardagh's line.[14]

To add to the ambiguity, yet another boundary (not related to the Ardagh-Johnson or Karakoram lines but somewhat related to the Macartney-MacDonald line) was proposed in 1914, when the British delegation to an India-Tibet-China conference attempted to assign the Aksai Chin to Tibet. At the Simla conference of 1914, the British delegation's leader, Sir Henry McMahon, produced a map showing (among other things) the Aksai Chin placed squarely within Tibetan territory. An earlier reference to such an idea had been made by the foreign secretary of the Government of India (Sir Louis Dane) in 1907, and now McMahon was apparently trying it out on the Chinese and Tibetans. The gain being sought in 1914 was to have a Tibetan Aksai Chin serve as a buffer between Sinkiang (then coming under Russian influence) and British India (Kashmir), without giving the Aksai Chin to a China now undergoing revolution.[15] The effort failed when China rejected the conference results for other reasons.

If the British Government of India's policy favored an Ardagh-Johnson boundary after 1936, the General Staff of the Indian Army demurred in 1946. The General Staff had assayed the likely defense problems of an India nearing independence. The map it submitted to the 1946 Cabinet Mission team (sent from London to advance India's progress toward independence) showed no evidence of either Ardagh,

McMahon, or Macartney-MacDonald thinking.[16] Either during 1946 itself, with no obvious threat looming on the frontier, or at some earlier time, the military arm of the Government of India had become reluctant to envisage a forward defense for Ladakh.

THE ASSAM HIMALAYA

If the government of an independent India later had to choose among several competing elements within British frontier policy toward Ladakh, it would find a more consistent but still ambiguous pattern of evolution in British policy toward the Assam Himalaya. The Assam Himalayan region and its foothills contained a population of tribals, and as of 1947 this area was still largely unadministered. But the British Indian government had developed a certain conception of what Indian interests required.

Prior to the emergence of any sense of external threat coming from the direction of the Assam frontier, the tribal belt had been managed via a form of indirect British rule. Starting in 1873, the British had established a series of map lines below the foothills. Beyond those lines incursion and economic activity by Indian and British lowlanders were discouraged. To prevent raids by hill tribes into the valleys and plains below (a practice the tribes had resumed after the last strong Indian regional dynasty had gone into decline), the British had adopted a system of bribes and punishments.[17] Such a system helped limit the British presence in the tribal belt to a few political officers. It required only occasional diplomacy, to negotiate arrangements with tribal leaders, and the equally occasional punitive military expedition.

A crucial exception to this pattern was the north-south strip of territory known as the Tawang tract, which included the monastery town of Tawang itself. Here there had been substantial penetration into the tribal belt by Tibetan political, cultural, and religious influence. Accordingly, throughout most of the nineteenth century the British regarded Tawang as an extension of Tibet, possessing substantial autonomy.

After 1875 the British made a distinction between two parts of Tawang. That part lying north of Se La Pass was thought to be directly ruled from the neighboring Tsona district in Tibet. The section south of the pass mainly contained various kinds of landed estates. Some autonomy was thought to exist here, to the extent that Tibetan rule was exercised indirectly through the Tawang tract's own officials and monasteries.[18] (See Map 3.)

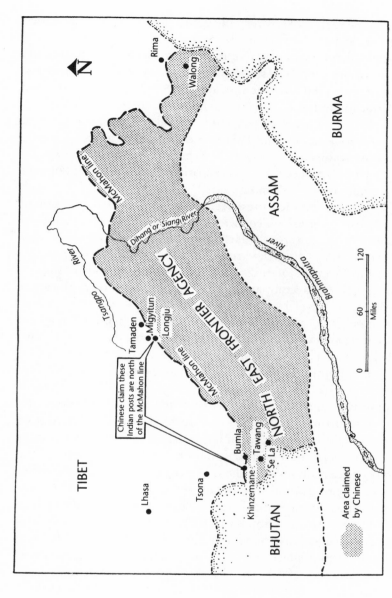

Map 3. BOUNDARY DISPUTE IN THE EASTERN SECTOR, 1959. (From Alastair Lamb, *The China-India Border* [London: Oxford University Press for the Royal Institute of International Affairs, 1964]. Reprinted by permission of the Royal Institute of International Affairs.)

Events in the early 1900s forced the British to reconsider the limited position they had established on the Assam frontier. The last years of the Manchu Empire in China were marked by a sudden, if temporary, increase in China's military strength and activity in frontier regions. Chinese forces in the frontier portions of Szechuan, Yunnan, and beyond came under the overall command of the energetic leader Chao Erh-feng. Not only were eastern and central Tibet under Chinese domination between 1905 and 1911, but during those years a Chinese presence was established along much of the Tibetan side of the Assam Himalaya. Chao's forces even entered briefly into the tribal zone on the Assam side of the high mountains.[19]

Such a Chinese forward presence, as well as a tribal incident in which a British political officer was killed, made the British Indian government in Assam particularly interested in extending direct administration further northward. The provincial (Assam) government, the Government of India, and London all agreed to stage a punitive expedition, accompanied by a new program of exploration and surveying.

This campaign adopted an ambitious objective: to establish a true line of separation between Assam and what was regarded as Chinese-controlled Tibet. The Government of India proposed that this be not just an administrative line but a real political and strategic boundary.[20]

The punitive expedition and its associated activity all along the Assam frontier from 1911 to 1913 transformed British knowledge of the region's topography and population patterns. Far better understood as well were the political situation and the structure of the Tawang tract. Certain areas in the high ranges, however, were either not covered or not examined in detail.

The new information enabled New Delhi to propose a border along the crest of the Assam Himalaya. Discussions with the Tibetans began, as part of a lengthy round of negotiations held during 1913 and 1914 between representatives of British India, Tibet, and the Yüan Shih-kai government of China. The chief venues for the talks were Simla, summer capital of the British Indian empire, and New Delhi.[21] The ostensible role of the British was to mediate some serious disputes between Tibet and China, but security for India was the prime concern of the British chief delegate, Sir Henry McMahon. As foreign secretary for the Government of India, McMahon pursued the goals of making Tibet a buffer state and setting an Assam Himalaya boundary. He did so relentlessly, despite a successful Tibetan uprising against occupying Chinese troops and the collapse of Chinese influence near the Indian frontier.

A set of notes (constituting an agreement) were exchanged between McMahon and the chief Tibetan delegate, Lonchen Shatra, on 24–25 March 1914. Accompanying the notes was a British-drawn map that outlined boundaries and buffer territory between China and Tibet. The notes and the map also delineated a border along the crest of the Assam Himalaya that would henceforth come to be known as the McMahon line. Among its features was the placement of the Tawang tract within Indian territory.

Although Ivan Chen, the Chinese delegate to the Simla conference, was shown a smaller version of the McMahon map during discussions on other issues in April, there is some question whether he appreciated the significance of the new Assam Himalaya line. Neither is it certain that he knew of the separate India-Tibet negotiations that had produced the line. However, he initialed the 27 April 1914 text of the Simla Convention, most likely knowing that his government would repudiate it for other reasons. The Simla Convention itself was initialed again by the British and Tibetan conference leaders in Delhi on 3 July 1914, and they signed a joint declaration pronouncing the convention binding upon themselves, even without Chinese agreement. These actions constituted (inter alia) formal Tibetan acceptance of the McMahon line, or so the British delegation assumed.

McMahon's achievement seemed substantial at the time, but its meaning proved to be ambiguous at best. All the results of the Simla conference were repudiated by the Chinese central government, but not because of the McMahon line per se. The status of the McMahon line was an issue mainly because of China's refusal to agree to the British attempts to enhance Tibet's autonomy. Among their other criticisms of the Simla affair, the Chinese have consistently claimed that Tibet had no right to assume independent treaty-making powers.

In the absence of Chinese acquiescence, and with the onset of World War I, acceptance of the McMahon line by the British themselves (and especially by the British home government in London) became lukewarm and even unsupportive. British policy toward the line thereafter varied according to changing international circumstances (among them the problematical Russian attitude toward the Simla agreement in 1914) and the vagaries of bureaucratic politics in London, India, and Assam itself.[22]

But the McMahon line acquired a strong advocate in 1935 in the person of Olaf Caroe, then deputy secretary in the Foreign and Political Department of the Government of India. That year a diplomatic incident involving Tawang (the Kingdon-Ward affair) prompted a telegraphed inquiry from the Foreign and Political Department in New Delhi to the Assam government and British India's political officer in Sikkim (who also served as a representative to Lhasa). The inquiry, probably written by Caroe, reminded its recipients of the existence of the McMahon line and the 1914 Simla Convention. From the answers that came back (and from consulting relevant files), Caroe discovered that the Assam government had been viewing Tawang as still tied to Tibet and that India's main Lhasa representative had not known that the McMahon line was a real border. Such information induced him to think through the entire question of the northeast frontier.

In subsequent correspondence with the Assam government, with the Indian government's successive representatives in Lhasa, and with the India Office in London, Caroe revealed several concerns. The most important of them were (1) whether the Tibetan government was firmly committed to the McMahon line and (2) whether the Chinese might use the seeming British lack of interest in the line to support the argument that no ratified agreement existed between India and Tibet.[23]

Caroe's main response was to campaign for official British reaffirmation of the McMahon line. Having been led to believe in 1935 that the Tibetans had just made a verbal commitment to uphold the line, he proposed to the India Office, in a personal note (but in the name of the Government of India), that the 1914 Indo-Tibetan agreements be published in the official (Government of India) documentary series known as Aitchison's Treaties. He further proposed that the McMahon line start appearing on Survey of India maps.

As of 1936 the India Office was prepared to concur with the suggestions about Aitchison's Treaties and the Survey of India change, but it set forth certain conditions. Of these the most important was that unnecessary publicity should be avoided; the press should not even be notified of the Aitchison changes. It was agreed that an Aitchison volume should contain a notation indicating that China had not accepted any of the 1914 arrangements but that the other two parties, India and Tibet, considered them binding upon themselves.

The policy change started by Caroe's campaign was subjected to strict limitations in the fall of 1936. Among several Government of India proposals not accepted by the India Office was one suggesting that the Tibetan government give written confirmation of its acceptance of the McMahon line, in view of recent news (to New Delhi) that Tibetan administration and tax collection were still being conducted in Tawang. Another New Delhi proposal opposed by the India Office (and the Foreign Office) was that a protest should be made to the Chinese government about maps (in some recently issued atlases) which portrayed most of the Assam Himalaya tribal area as being Chinese.

Yet another crucial problem appeared in the autumn of 1936 when the Tibetans made clear that their acceptance of the McMahon border was not firm. As a condition for their acceptance, the Tibetans wanted the British to secure Chinese agreement to the Tibet-China relationship specified by the Simla agreements of 1914. Caroe's own department, and presumably the India Office as well, ultimately (in the spring of 1937) came to consider dropping the border as a matter for discussion with Tibet, unless it arose in discussions of other issues that were of greater concern to the British—namely, Tibetan autonomy vis-à-vis China and Tibetan relations with India (as governed by past treaties). No such discussions were held between 1936 and 1939. Instead, an effort was made to persuade the Tibetans to withdraw their administration from Tawang.

The Aitchison changes were allowed to appear in 1938. In order to publish them quickly, and to give a greater sense of authenticity to the new entry without having it attract undue notice, the India Office (and probably Caroe) contrived to issue an amended version of the appropriate 1929 Aitchison volume, without giving it a new publication date. Copies of the original 1929 volume—located in offices and libraries in India, England, and elsewhere—were then replaced by request and discarded. A few were found by scholars decades later, including one at Harvard University, another at the India Office library, and a third in the National Archives in New Delhi.[24]

The Survey of India map changes wanted by Caroe were completed in 1937, after the surveyor-general had made some adjustments to the McMahon boundary, apparently based on more accurate topographical knowledge acquired after 1914. These corrections followed the principle that the highest watershed ridges constituted the border. Left approximate were certain sections of the line that the surveyor-general felt he could not fix on his own, given the information and instructions he had available to him. Some later India-China disputes (concerning places called Migyitun, Longju, and Thagla Ridge) were to focus on two of these indeterminate stretches. (See map 7 in Chapter 7).[25]

The British still did not have an unambiguous policy toward taking control of their side of the Assam frontier. Within India a "forward" school emerged, which favored assertion of British control up to the McMahon line, particularly within the Tawang tract. Members of that school included a British governor of Assam, Sir Robert Reid, and the leader of an expedition sent to Tawang in 1938, Captain G. S. Lightfoot. A more cautionary approach was taken by other officials, including the viceroy in 1939, Lord Linlithgow.

For various reasons, including strong Tibetan reluctance to relinquish their rights in Tawang, Reid and most other concerned officials in India between 1940 and 1945 reached a new consensus about the Tawang tract. They proposed that the Tawang-India frontier be placed at Se La Pass (see Map 3), or even further south, and that no administration of northern Tawang be attempted. They hoped that such moderation would ultimately lead to Tibetan acceptance of the rest of the McMahon Line. In general, British Indian officials were concerned with placing the Assam frontier under India's protection, and with future Indian security from the direction of China during and after World War II. Up to 1944, American support for the Kuomintang's sensitivities about Tibet, the demands of World War II on British resources, and British support for Tibetan autonomy prevented the British from pressuring the Tibetans via diplomacy and on the ground.[26] But substantial pressure was exerted in 1944–1945, even though the British Indian government offered to drop its claim to the northern Tawang tract. The Tibetans were not responsive. In 1945 they reaffirmed their claims, and in 1947 the Tibetan government sent a list of territorial demands to the new government of independent India.[27]

During the last few years of British rule in India, British exploration, trade, and administration had been extended into the tribal areas of the Assam Himalaya and into the southern Tawang tract, although not Tawang itself.[28] Thus, the British Indian government had acted on its cautious acceptance of the McMahon line, but no final provision was ever made for Tawang. The future of the town and the issues associated with it would depend on the evolving decisions of a new India and the policies of the new (Communist) China that took over Tibet in 1950.

INDEPENDENT INDIA'S BORDER DECISIONS

The primary responsibility for determining what kind of border the new Indian nation-state shared with Tibet and China fell to India's first prime minister, Jawaharlal Nehru. He served as his own foreign minister, and the Ministry of External Affairs (MEA) reported directly to him.

Nehru's involvement in the border formulation process was intensive and detailed. Long a keen student of world politics, and practitioner of it for the Indian nationalist movement, he was also an amateur historian. Although he read every line of the historical material the MEA submitted to him (he liked to do the work of officials for them), it was the sweeping political conclusions to be drawn from history that held a fascination for him. Nehru would never know the documentary details as well as his subordinates knew them, but the policy conclusions were very much Nehru's own.[29]

The key person handling the documentary details was the first director of the MEA's Historical Division, K. Zakariah. A former academic and an older man not likely to remain in government service long, he is recalled by his colleagues as brilliant, scholarly, and honest.[30] As part of a long discussion about the northern frontier taking place within the ministry between 1947 and 1954, Zakariah came to be charged with gathering British and Indian records and collating them. Only in 1951 did he start presenting these records to the prime minister.[31]

Alastair Lamb has suggested that the adoption of the Ardagh-Johnson line, as the foundation for the Ladakh border, came just after independence, with the crises then confronting the new Indian government. Contributing to the decision were (1) the trauma of the partition of British India and the sense it left behind of a fragile Indian state and nation, (2) the dispute with Pakistan over Kashmir, (3) the presence of Kashmiri politicians in India able to act as a lobby, and (4) the close ties between the prime minister and other high officials with a Kashmiri heritage.

Involvement in the conflict with Pakistan over Kashmir was especially important, since it required that the limits of the disputed region be defined. Such definition could not offend the sensibilities of those Kashmiris leaning toward India or uncommitted to Pakistan. Questions of subcontinental military defense, similar to those that had exercised the minds of the British, also had to be considered. But some important new elements existed in the Indian strategic perspective.

Among them was the awareness that the subcontinent was now
politically divided between India and Pakistan (and therefore might be
more vulnerable to outside threats) and that Pakistan itself now
constituted a strategic and ideological problem for Indian security
policy.[32]

The process that eventually produced the Indian-claimed border
was surely influenced by some of these considerations. The sparse
evidence presently available, however, indicates that the immediate
cause of India's taking over the remainder of the Tawang tract on the
eastern frontier, as well as the drawing of the Aksai Chin boundary on
the western frontier, was the Chinese military occupation of Tibet in
1950. Only then was the interministerial North and North-eastern
Border Defence Committee (Himmatsinghji committee) created with
participation by the military. The committee probably recommended
that some boundary-defining decisions be taken.

The Nehru government was compelled to act on the strength of
certain China-related strategic perceptions as well. The prime minister
was prepared to accept the consequences of the loss of Tibet as an
autonomous buffer between Chinese and Indian power. Although he
always believed that India had some sort of special political interest in
Tibet and in Tibetan autonomy, he became convinced that instead of a
Tibetan buffer India must have a recognized border.[33]

In addition, Sino-Indian ties had been strained briefly at the time of
the 1950 Chinese move into Tibet. Although no armed attack on India
was expected at that time, Nehru "did not rule out infiltration by
groups or even occupation of disputed areas."[34] Rapid recovery and
improvement of those ties did not entirely erase concern about China's
intentions. It was therefore important to establish Indian border
claims quickly and to leave no question about them.

The prime minister was influenced, too, by his belief in the historic
expansionism of the Chinese state. He told his intelligence chief in
1952 that during a period of internal unity and vigor, like the present
one, China would be aggressive, or so his sense of Chinese history
showed him.[35] Despite his hopes of establishing a friendly India-China
relationship, given the imperative Indian need for it, and despite his
appreciation of the anti-imperialist experience and feelings the two
countries shared, he was still prepared in 1952 to see China as a
potential security threat on a par with Pakistan.

At the initiative of the MEA foreign secretary, K. P. S. Menon, an
Indian political officer (accompanied by an armed party) arrived in

Tawang in February 1951. A general policy of strengthening Indian administration and control in NEFA was undertaken as well.[36] In 1953 a decision was made to reject the Macartney-MacDonald alternative and to regard the Aksai Chin as properly Indian. This decision was part of a larger policy-setting decision to publish official maps showing an unambiguous delimited boundary between India and China.

Essentially, these decisions were Nehru's. Officials advising him could have only limited influence. In 1953 the director of the Historical Division, K. Zakariah, was in the process of retiring and being replaced by J.N. Khosla, who stayed only until 1954. Most of the work of confirming and solidifying the Indian case for the border fell to Khosla's successor, Sarvepalli Gopal, who assumed the director's post in 1954 and retained it until 1966.[37]

THE PSYCHOLOGY OF INDIAN BORDER FORMULATION

In addition to strategic or political considerations, a basic set of attitudes and beliefs, shared by the prime minister and many of his officials, was brought to bear on the process of border formulation. Underpinning them all was the fervent belief that an Indian nation had existed through time—defined by culture, common experience, custom, and geography—long before the British had created and imposed their own state structure on the subcontinent. Nehru's own preindependence writings had dealt with this point at length. Indeed, his major books, such as *The Discovery of India* (published in 1946, only one year before independent Indian border definition began in 1947), ranked among the most eloquent nationalist repudiations of the British view of India. Crucial to that British view had been the belief that India existed as a viable political unit only because of British military and administrative power.[38]

With the Indian belief in a "discovered" India came a corollary: that India's traditional and customary boundaries had long existed and had evolved naturally, since they were based on the activities of populations and cultures and on geographical features such as mountain ridges and watersheds. The British had chosen to reinforce these boundaries, or to deviate from them, for strategic reasons and because their knowledge of Indian geography was not complete. More important, however, was that, when acting as definers of borders, the British were not basing their thinking on historical evidence. That was why they could wittingly or unwittingly sacrifice Indian interests when formulating frontier and border decisions.[39]

It was toward this last conclusion especially that the prime minister and the MEA would have been drawn when confronting the British Indian historical files. They did not have immediately available to them all the India Office records (the London archives were not consulted until 1959), but they could easily have seen documents from the archives in New Delhi. Those archives would have contained most of the relevant (British) Government of India files, much India Office material, and pertinent documents from the British Foreign Office as well.

Accompanying the Indian belief in "historical borders" was the conviction that these borders were necessarily linear. Such a belief would present problems. As Alastair Lamb suggests, known traditional borders in sparsely populated mountain regions, such as those found on the India-China frontier, will usually not be lines but only a series of separate points. They will generally be "located at passes or at the crossing places of streams and rivers."[40] Frontier peoples or states would not necessarily agree on how to join those points together. Moreover, as another student of the subject justifiably points out, inner Asian peoples and rulers traditionally conceived of boundaries as large zones (like the "march" lands of European history) rather than lines. Zones were sufficient to separate populated areas. The concept of linear borders is a modern European invention.[41] Even treaty documents from earlier periods in Asian history (and there were some for Ladakh) would not have distinguished between frontiers (as the term is being used here) and borderlines.

The Indian government's perception, however, was (and still is) that linking historically known border points together in a way sensitive to topography, and utilizing evidence of such regular activities as trade, grazing, travel, administration, and revenue collection, shows the traditional and customary boundaries to which the treaties refer. Not all segments of such borders would have been linked at the time in the mind of any one ruler or mapmaker, but when these borders are given a modern interpretation (something required of the modern nation-state), their linear nature is clear. In addition, the known boundary points were such clear political-jurisdictional markers to the people using them that some awareness of the location of a linear border must have existed.[42]

This point, like many historical, administrative, and topographical

questions, required a deciphering of ambiguity. Most Indian politicians and officials, whether in the early 1950s or later, discounted the
degree of that ambiguity. Ambiguity or indeterminacy was shaped
according to psychological predispositions derived from Indian nationalist thought and experience, so that the evidence appeared more
determinative than it was.

Thus, on the Aksai Chin the Indian government chose to endorse
the Ardagh-Johnson line, partly because it allegedly showed where the
jurisdiction of the Kashmir (Dogra) Kingdom traditionally ended.
This was the Kashmir government's view, supported by the reports of
W. H. Johnson and other explorers. To buttress its claim to the Aksai
Chin, the independent Indian government could later produce "a
regular sequence of official records, stretching over many years," on
"such matters as revenue assessment, police jurisdiction, public works
projects, census returns, control of trade routes and survey and
mapping operations."[43] It also pointed to the findings of British
Indian and Kashmir government explorers, travelers, traders, and
hunting parties. Such evidence came from Kashmir archives and other
documentary sources available to the MEA.

Similarly, one of the Indian arguments concerning the Assam
Himalaya was that Tibetan authority over the Tawang tract had been
only religious authority and implied no political rights. Indeed, at the
particular time when the McMahon line was formulated (1913–1914),
and for decades before, Tawang had allegedly functioned independently of any outside political authority.

More important, the Indian government came to believe that the
McMahon line was not merely a British invention. Political control
over all the northeast tribal region had been exercised, in various
indirect fashions, from the Assam side for centuries before the British
appeared on the scene. Therefore, the McMahon line itself constituted
recognition that the watershed crest of the Assam Himalaya formed
the natural geographical divide between Tibet and an area (the Assam
Himalaya) where Indian states had regularly exercised jurisdiction
while Tibet and China had not.[44]

Gopal of the MEA would later summarize India's attitudes toward
establishing historical borders, in the following pithy fashion:

> To set aside the considerable and varied evidence of tradition,
> custom, and administration stretching over centuries and look solely
> at some odd maps of the last hundred years is to miss the wood for
> some of the nearest shrubs. To assume that nothing mattered in India

before the arrival of the British, to revel in the details of policy-making during the raj and to recommend compromise alignments whose sole aim to consideration is that they were suggested by Englishmen is to exhibit intellectual shallowness.[45]

INDIAN BORDER REASONING AND ITS COSTS

Before the 1962 border war, official Chinese critics of India's border claims would take issue with the accuracy and/or interpretation of Indian evidence. After 1962 independent scholarly critics would do so as well, and with more effect. Most telling would be their successes in showing that various points of evidence could be interpreted in other ways.

Space limitations do not allow analysis of these evidentiary controversies here.[46] But, contrary to the argument of one scholar, there is no evidence that Nehru's officials ever deceived him about the definitiveness of India's border case. Nor did Nehru seek to deceive his country, contrary to the view of another scholar.[47] From the comments of Nehru and his officials, especially those comments made in private,[48] it is clear that Nehru and his consultants instead shaped ambiguity primarily according to their attitudinal prism—that is, the basic screen through which evidence had to pass.[49]

Moreover, the weight of all the evidence amassed by the Indians, rather than just the individual pieces of it, made for a plausible case. Critics could not have appeared to puncture that case so easily if Indian spokespersons had merely shown its strength relative to that of the Chinese. But to the extent that India claimed absolute rather than relative worth for its border case, by holding that linear borders had been conclusively "delimited" by history and "discovered" through documentary investigation, the Indian case became vulnerable. Discoveries of flaws in it created the false but natural presumption that if India's claims were not absolutely correct, then they were absolutely unjustified. After 1962 that presumption would cost India dearly (and unnecessarily) in the court of scholarly opinion.

Even more important, the Indian view of border formation became extremely costly in that it adversely affected India's relations with China after 1959, just as China's views ultimately alienated India. By 1959 China was publicly evolving an entirely different approach to border formation—one more sensitive to ambiguity about exact

borderlines but less sensitive to ambiguity about past Chinese contact
with places such as the Aksai Chin and the Assam Himalaya.

Peking's post-1959 approach was based on the belief that the
historic China was defined primarily by the centralized and powerful
governmental (i.e., state) structures which have ruled Chinese empires
in the past. Frontier regions (such as Tibet and Sinkiang) were
therefore thought to belong within that portion of the world that is
historically Chinese because of the past exercise of centralized Chinese
state power over them. These regions have sometimes acted autono-
mously or even independently, and have been threatened by foreign
powers (such as Britain and Russia), especially when the Chinese state
was internally weak. But the inability of a Chinese state structure to
maintain effective sovereignty over frontier territories, and deal with
threats to them, has historically signified the infirmity and increasing
illegitimacy of that state (e.g., a dynasty or one of the post-1911
governments). Such incapacity has even contributed to the overthrow
of that structure by forces originating inside or outside China.

Now that the Chinese revolution has made China strong, any
Chinese government worthy of being granted legitimacy by its own
people would be required to control such territories, especially since
they are vital to China's defense and security from American, Soviet,
and other forms of "imperialism." The precise placement of borders
around these regions is less important than the use of such borders,
and small tracts of land encompassed by them (e.g., the Aksai Chin),
to ensure that regions such as Tibet and Sinkiang remain controllable
and free from foreign influence.[50]

If China's neighbors are friendly, or so the present Chinese
government has reasoned, negotiating new borders with them is the
most desirable course of action. Such borders will then have been
delimited via acts of national self-determination, and not bear any
taint from past imperialist adventurism by Britain or other Western
powers. But if the friendliness of a neighboring state is in serious
question (as India's was thought to be after 1959, and possibly earlier),
using armed strength to secure important frontier tracts has been
thought proper.

If such a tract is vital from the standpoint of defense, it should be
built up militarily. But if it is not now fully controlled by China,
and/or is not needed for permanent defensive use, it can be employed
as a bargaining chip in dealing with neighboring states. The Aksai

Chin, in which the Chinese after 1950 began constructing an all-weather road system linking. Tibet and Sinkiang, became a tract having considerable defensive value. In the spring of 1960, the Assam Himalaya, where the Chinese had established only a limited presence, was offered as such a chip.

In all, after 1959 China's determination to delimit new *strategic* borders, using both diplomatic and military methods, would conflict sharply with India's post-1947 determination to have *historic* borders. The two conceptions of proper border delimitation have never been reconciled.

CHAPTER THREE

The Path to Conflict

IMMEDIATELY AFTER THE Chinese invasion of Tibet in 1950, a group of
Indian cabinet members and top-level officials became concerned
about India-China relations. The decision-makers in that group were
Nehru and another of the "tall leaders" of the nationalist movement,
Vallabhai Patel, who in 1950 was the Deputy Prime Minister and the
Minister for Home Affairs. Their most important official consultants
were the ambassador to China, K. M. Panikkar; the secretary-general
of the Ministry of External Affairs, G. S. Bajpai; and the director of
the Intelligence Bureau (IB), B. N. Mullik.

The IB issued a note on "New Problems of Internal Security," and
Patel sent a lengthy letter to Nehru warning of likely problems from a
hostile China. An immediate result was the November 1950 decision
to form the temporary North and North-Eastern Border Defence
Committee, under the then Deputy Minister for Defence, Major
General M. S. Himmatsinghji. Officially appointed in February 1951,
the committee contained representatives from the defense, communications, home, and external affairs ministries, and from the IB, the
army, and the air force. The two parts of its report were submitted in
April and September 1951, and a final version was given to the defense
ministry in early 1953.[1]

On the committee's advice a road-building program was initiated in
frontier areas, frontier constabularies were expanded and redeployed,
and the Indian administrative network was expanded in NEFA.[2] The
Indian intelligence system was reorganized so that most intelligence
functions came under the IB's control.[3] All these steps reinforced and
extended various directives that Nehru had been issuing since 1947.[4]

In 1953 IB director Mullik was permitted by Nehru to establish
contact with an elder brother of the Dalai Lama who was residing in

India. Mullik was instructed to maintain regular contact with the Dalai Lama's brother and other refugees and to help the Tibetan refugees in order to keep up their morale, draw on them as sources of intelligence about Tibet and China, and prevent machinations by them against the Chinese. A year later (May 1954), after learning of the refugees' shocked and bitter reaction to the Sino-Indian Treaty of April 1954, Nehru decided that even if Tibetan expatriates in India were helping their countrymen to resist the Chinese within Tibet, the Indian government would take no notice. Unless Tibetan activities became too blatant, New Delhi would not entertain any protest from Peking.[5]

This was a strange and risky decision, coming at a time when the Indian government had succeeded in establishing good relations with China (1954). But all through the 1950s Nehru was trying to strike a balance between his sympathy for the Tibetans and his dealings with the Chinese. Moreover, he did not expect in 1954 that Tibetan resistance activities would be as effective as they ultimately came to be, and that they would be greatly assisted from the mid-1950s onward by the U.S. Central Intelligence Agency (CIA). Indeed, Nehru's basic attitude was that the Tibetans should not mount a violent resistance effort against Chinese occupation, because such resistance would only result in their being crushed.[6]

India's northern border was deliberately not militarized, despite a 1952 report submitted by a military committee headed by Lieutenant General Kulwant Singh. The Kulwant Singh report was a preliminary assessment of the measures that would have to be taken if an anti-China defensive posture proved necessary. Although a small Indo-Tibetan border force was established at its recommendation, the report was shelved, presumably at the cabinet level, and the matter was not raised again until the autumn of 1959.[7]

Border militarization was not thought necessary because other approaches to frontier security were being taken. Tibet was the major subject of India-China talks held between 1950 and 1954. They were aimed at removing all remaining obstacles to friendly relations. The two most senior officials of India's Ministry of External Affairs in late 1951, Secretary-General Bajpai and Foreign Secretary K. P. S. Menon, sought to extend these talks to cover the border. They even recommended that India should refuse to withdraw its garrisons in two Tibetan trading centers (holdovers from the British period) until China's recognition of a border was secured. Instructions to Ambas-

THE PATH TO CONFLICT

sador Panikkar to make clear India's interest in affirmation of the northeast (NEFA) portion of the boundary (the McMahon line) and the rest of the India-Tibet frontier were approved by Nehru in January 1952.[8]

Those instructions were set aside by Panikkar, who found Chou En-lai reluctant to discuss the matter. Panikkar himself preferred to stress India-China friendship and the widening of trade and other interchanges as better guarantees of Indian security. Moreover, both he and the Prime Minister may have taken too seriously the general Chinese assurances about the absence of territorial questions between the two countries.[9]

It is still not fully clear why Nehru eventually chose to favor Panikkar's point of view, although intellectual affinity between the two men was surely involved. Nehru generally found Panikkar's intellectual style of geopolitical argument to be closer to his own than were the styles of more narrowly focused officials such as Bajpai and Menon. Nehru had also appreciated Panikkar's dispatches and role during the Korean War.[10]

The rationale for Nehru's decision was explained by Panikkar to Bajpai (now retired from the MEA and serving as governor of Bombay) in 1952. If India raised the border issue with China, wrote Panikkar, the Chinese would be forced either to accept the Simla agreements, in which the McMahon line had been set down, or to refuse such acceptance but offer to negotiate. Peking's adoption of the first option was unlikely. The second would not be advantageous to India. However, if China raised the issue of the border, "we can plainly refuse to reopen the question and take our stand... [already taken by Nehru in a public statement] that the territory on this side of the McMahon line is ours, and there is nothing to discuss about it."[11]

In 1954 Nehru made clear that this contingency plan would cover India's entire northern border, rather than just the NEFA section. In a memorandum to the appropriate ministries on the recently concluded treaty with China concerning Tibet and related matters, Nehru wrote that the northern frontier "should be considered a firm and definite one, which is not open to discussion with anybody. A system of checkposts should be spread along this entire frontier. More especially, we should have checkposts in such places as might be considered disputed areas."[12]

These instructions reflected the fact that the 1954 agreement had not included explicit Chinese acceptance of a border; therefore, compensating action was required—namely, a further hardening of India's public stand on such a border's existence. But the instructions also reflected a belief that no further negotiation would be necessary, since border security had been assured primarily through friendship with India's northern neighbor. Establishing that friendship, which had required Indian surrender of all British rights in Tibet via the 1954 treaty, had seemingly strengthened China's desire to avoid making frontier claims. Such was Nehru's view, reinforced by the publication by China of a small-scale but acceptably sketched map in 1954 and by the wording of sections of the 1954 treaty.[13]

Among those sections was the preamble of the 1954 treaty, which contained a list of five broad principles of international behavior allegedly agreed on by both governments.[14] Those "Five Principles" (or "Panchsheel," as they were called in India) were subsequently hailed by both India and China as constituting the foundation of the harmonious bilateral relationship that seemed to have come into being.

Beyond the 1954 Sino-Indian treaty were other reassuring events of the mid-1950s, including the visits of Nehru and Chou to each other's countries in 1954, and the 1955 Bandung Conference (a conference of nonaligned states), at which Nehru informally helped China gain admission into this group of nations by supporting the diplomacy of Chou En-lai. Chou En-lai paid three visits to India in 1956–1957, when Tibet's Dalai Lama and Panchen Lama were in India too.

During the several months of the Dalai Lama's 1956–57 stay in India, however, an incident occurred that might have severely damaged that new India-China relationship. With rebellion already having begun in Tibet, the Dalai Lama indicated that he did not want to go back to Lhasa. He was considering remaining in India to speak out on his country's behalf. Prime Minister Nehru personally persuaded him to return to Lhasa.[15] The Dalai Lama's defection, especially while Premier Chou En-lai was present in Delhi, would have embarrassed the Chinese and Indian governments most acutely. Concern about a possible defection by the Dalai Lama continued, despite Chou's 1954 assurance (to Nehru) that China's government understood that India's government would have to grant asylum to the Dalai Lama if he ever sought it.[16]

By the late 1950s a series of events began to give rise to apprehension on the part of Indian officials concerning the future of the Sino-Indian relationship. One such event was the effort to resolve a dispute over the tiny Bara Hoti grazing ground on the Uttar Pardesh–Tibet frontier (see Map 6). The task of settling the matter (which had lingered on since 1954) had been assigned to Indian negotiators meeting secretly with their Chinese counterparts in New Delhi during April and May 1958. Leading the Chinese delegation was the Chinese ambassador, Pan Tzu-li, while Foreign Secretary Subimal Dutt of the MEA participated as official leader of the Indian delegation. But the intensive contact with the Chinese delegation was carried on by middle- and junior-level personnel of the Indian team.[17]

The inflexibility and sloganeering of the Chinese team at these talks left Indian participants upset and suggested that the Chinese were mindful of an unsettled border.[18] Foreign Secretary Dutt came away with the impression that the Chinese were unwilling to negotiate seriously over a very minor point of dispute or to deal with other points that would have been addressed had this conference succeeded.[19] The Chinese seemed unsure about the frontier alignment and did not want to commit themselves to a definite line of demarcation in the Bara Hoti area. They also left the impression that they were still studying the records of the previous Tibetan government before deciding to lay their claims to specific areas. But such claims would stand apart from the McMahon line, about which they already had sufficient information.[20]

Another event was China's announcement about the Aksai Chin road (see Map 2). The IB had known since 1951 that the Chinese were using the Aksai Chin, but the army had not regarded such activity as a security threat or as a matter that it could act on, given its meager resources and the geographical problems involved. Officials of the MEA did not want to disrupt relations with China over a physically unenforceable claim and were not certain of the usefulness of the Aksai Chin to India. Nor were they certain whether the Chinese had done anything more than improve an old existing international trade route. Therefore, they may not have brought the matter to Nehru's attention, or he may not have wanted to make an issue of it.[21]

But by 1957 the MEA officials who had committed themselves to establishing the close India-China relations of the 1954–1956 period were in posts abroad. More important, the Aksai Chin road could no longer pass unnoticed by the world outside the Indian or Chinese governments when, in September 1957, the Chinese newspaper *People's Daily* published news of near completion of the road. The item was noticed by the Indian embassy in Peking and passed along to New Delhi.

As a result of a subsequent (June 1958) New Delhi meeting
involving the MEA, the army, and the IB, two Indian patrols were sent
to the area in the summer of 1958. One of those patrols was taken into
custody by the Chinese. The patrol was not released until an inquiry
into its whereabouts was made in an informal note (dated 18 October
1958) handed to the Chinese ambassador by the Indian foreign
secretary. That note's main purpose was to protest the Aksai Chin
road's presence on what was alleged to be Indian soil.[22]

Although several earlier border incidents had taken place since
1954, India had not taken them seriously, because they appeared to be
local matters reflecting the zeal of Chinese officials and border
troops.[23] But the capture of the patrol, following China's public notice
about the road, was a matter too striking to be ignored.

In addition, by October 1958 the Chinese were allegedly making
efforts to contest the Indian presence in several localities along the
middle sector (Uttar Pradesh–Tibet) of the frontier. One of those
places was Bara Hoti.

On 3 November the Chinese Foreign Office replied unsatisfactorily
to an Indian inquiry, sent the previous August, about a new Chinese
publication containing what the Indian government said was an
inaccurate map. The Chinese 3 November note, taken in the context
of all that had transpired in the last few months, produced a lengthy
letter sent by Prime Minister Nehru directly to Premier Chou En-lai
on 14 December 1958.

The purpose of the Nehru letter was not to commit the Chinese to
the Indian-drawn border. Instead, it was to have the Chinese confirm
that their conception of the border was still not fixed and that they
were not making real territorial claims. Previously, the Chinese had
been vague about possible claims and, when questioned about their
maps, had indicated that their thinking was open to revision. Now
the Indian government hoped to hear again that a friendly China
was not committed to holding the Aksai Chin or to claiming the
boundary lines suggested on its maps.[24]

Since Nehru's 1958 letter reveals India's attitudes and perceptions
on the eve of the border conflict, it is worth examining in more detail.
The main subject was the fact that Chinese official maps had persisted
in showing large tracts of allegedly Indian frontier territory to be parts
of China. The letter made clear that India would no longer accept
previous Chinese statements that these were Kuomintang maps and
that the Peking government had not yet had time to revise them.

Nehru pointed out in the letter that Chou had on two occasions given assurances to Nehru personally. One such occasion came during a visit to Delhi by Chou in 1956. China's premier had told Nehru that, although the McMahon line had been established by the British imperialists, China had accepted it in recent dealings with Burma and was prepared to recognize it with India too. It would do so, after consultation with the Tibetan authorities, because of the friendly relations existing between China and its neighbors: India and Burma. Another map and a troubling Chinese statement had been issued since that time, so Nehru now confessed to being puzzled. He wanted to make clear that, as far as India was concerned, there had never been a boundary dispute, and there was no question of "large parts of India being anything but India." The boundaries were fixed and well known.[25]

Not mentioned in Nehru's note were still other sources of apprehension and pique, which had appeared by the latter part of 1958. Foremost among them were (1) China's indefinite postponement of a planned visit to Lhasa by Nehru, even though a formal invitation had been issued by the Dalai Lama and forwarded by Chou En-lai, and (2) an unseemly delay by the Chinese government in granting Prime Minister Nehru a visa, so that he might cross a piece of Tibetan territory (the Chumbi Valley) while taking the only existing route to Bhutan (see Map 1). Although Nehru was personally irritated by the Chumbi Valley matter, such nuisances were attributed on the Indian side to growing rebelliousness being encountered by the Chinese in Tibet and to China's displeasure over the activities of Tibetan refugees in India.[26]

For some years China had been protesting Tibetan émigré and foreign-agent activity along the Indian frontier. Nehru responded in August 1958 with assurances that these activities would not be tolerated, and he backed these assurances with instructions to the Bengal state government. This action continued a general policy, in evidence since January 1958, of curbing the actions of Tibetan refugees. Although the government refused a Chinese demand to expel from India the Dalai Lama's brother (who was now an important Tibetan resistance organizer, linked for some time to the American CIA), those Tibetans abetting guerrilla activity from Indian soil would (until 1962) encounter interference from the IB.[27]

Nehru was dropping his earlier policy of having the Intelligence Bureau abet or overlook Tibetan émigré activity, but this decision would eventually make little difference in the real situation on the Tibet border. It is unclear how much India's government knew in 1958 or 1959 about the major CIA program, started in 1956, to assist a growing Tibetan resistance movement. Some CIA operations involved Indian territory, as did ongoing activity by Taiwanese agents. A close observer of the CIA-Tibet connection after 1961 (U.S. ambassador John Kenneth Galbraith) believes that, whatever the IB may have known, "the Indian government as a whole, and particularly Nehru, was not aware of this operation."[28] Nehru would not have acquiesced to CIA actions implicating India, given his attitude towards American intervention in the non-Western world (see next chapter) and his conviction that violent Tibetan resistance to China was suicidal.

But independently of what he knew or did, the Chinese now had reason to believe that they had a serious security problem involving Tibet's southern frontier. From 1958 onward, China's government would also find it difficult to distinguish between India's policies, the activities of Tibetan émigrés in India, and the role of the CIA and the Taiwanese.

The year 1959 began with an event that strengthened the vague feeling in the Indian government that territory along the northern border might be less than secure from Chinese encroachments and claims. This was the receipt of Chou En-lai's 23 January reply to Nehru's letter of the previous December. Now the Chinese prime minister said clearly that, in the view of his government, the Sino-Indian border was not a settled matter and that "border disputes do exist between China and India."

The note was friendly, but the Sino-Indian boundary, wrote Premier Chou, had never been "formally delimited," either by a treaty or by an agreement of any sort between the Chinese and Indian governments. The matter had not been raised at the 1954 negotiations, or at any other time, "because conditions were not yet ripe for its settlement and the Chinese side, on its part, had had no time to study the question." Chou added that China did "not hold that every portion of this boundary line is drawn [on Chinese maps] on sufficient grounds." But for China to make changes in them at this moment would be "inappropriate," since no surveys had been conducted and no other countries had been formally consulted.

Although the Chou En-lai note reaffirmed the Chinese government's willingness to take a "more or less realistic attitude towards the McMahon Line," and assured Nehru that a "friendly settlement"

could eventually be found for "this section of the boundary line," the
implication was that the entire border was negotiable. As for maps,
Premier Chou remarked that, with an undelimited boundary, discrepancies would unavoidably appear between the boundary lines drawn
on the maps published by the two sides, and incidents would occur. In
order to avoid such incidents, he proposed that the two sides maintain
the status quo, "that is to say, each side keep for the time being to
the border areas at present under its jurisdiction and not go beyond
them."[29]

The Indian interpretation of this note was not alarmist.[30] The
Chinese were not claiming the Indian territory covered by their maps.
China had said, however, that disagreements about the status of the
border did exist, and this was a cause for further uneasiness.

Judging from the next step that he took, Prime Minister Nehru
thought it necessary to try to persuade the Chinese side that the border
was a settled matter. He apparently hoped to prove his point by
reviewing the historical-legal evidence for the Indian contention that
the border had been properly delimited in the past. Nehru's next
formal note to Chou, dated 22 March 1959, sought to initiate such a
review. The MEA's Historical Division (headed at this moment by
Gopal's deputy, K. Gopalachari) was now called on to supply the
historical information to be used in a brief presentation of the Indian
case.

Like all of the more important diplomatic notes sent by the Indian
side in 1959 and 1960, this one was the work of both Nehru and
Foreign Secretary Dutt. Dutt either wrote the first draft or reviewed
Nehru's draft, although the prime minister had the final say on the
language used. In accordance with normal procedures, Dutt and
Nehru relied on the appropriate territorial division within the MEA
(in this case the Eastern Division) to gather, check, and integrate
material from the Historical Division and other sources. Within the
Eastern Division most of the China work fell to a deputy secretary,
and a veteran of the Bara Hoti talks, named J. S. Mehta. Both Mehta
and Gopal of the Historical Division sometimes helped Dutt with
his drafts.[31]

The 22 March 1959 note began by saying (inter alia) that Nehru
found himself "somewhat surprised" to learn that the Sino-Indian
frontier "was not accepted at any time by the Government of China."
The Indian historical argument was then described in some detail.
Included in the letter was a request that the two sides not only

maintain the status quo, as Chou En-lai had already suggested, but also rectify the situation where any territory had recently been seized unilaterally. This theme (to become prominent in Indian policy hereafter) now referred to the Bara Hoti area, which the note said had recently been occupied by the Chinese. The theme seemed to apply to the Aksai Chin as well, although the region was not mentioned explicitly.[32]

No further diplomatic action seemed to be needed at the moment. Some post building in Ladakh was being undertaken at the urging of IB director Mullik (see Chapter 6), but the army was reluctant to comply and neither Foreign Secretary Dutt nor Nehru wanted to create tensions. Therefore, it was decided not to open posts too near the Aksai Chin road.[33]

2

THE PRE-CRISIS PERIOD:
15 MARCH 1959 TO
7 SEPTEMBER 1962

CHAPTER FOUR

The Pre-crisis Decision-Makers and Their Psychological Setting

THE ROLES OF THE DECISION-MAKERS

SINCE THE 1920s Jawaharlal Nehru, nearly alone among the important nationalist figures, had taken an active interest in international politics and had firmly established his expertise and influence in that sphere. As a result, even those leaders of the post-independence Congress Party who opposed him over numerous matters of domestic policy usually bowed to his judgment on foreign affairs. By the early 1950s Nehru came to be regarded both at home and abroad as a statesman comparable to the leaders of the great powers, as well as the most prestigious spokesman for the part of the world just emerging from Western colonial rule. As such he frequently traveled abroad on missions of the highest international significance.[1]

Nehru's authority in foreign affairs came not only from expertise and world fame. He also held the pivotal position in the Indian political system. He was leader of the Congress Party, its best vote getter and most effective public orator, member of its authoritative committees and bodies, head of the primary governmental institution for economic planning (the Planning Commission), and the chief spokesman of the government (cabinet) in Parliament.

His place at the center of India's institutional network was in turn derived from his stature as the most important surviving leader of the Indian independence movement. Jawaharlal Nehru was Gandhi's anointed heir and a major architect of India's new political institutions. He was the foremost legitimizing symbol of those institutions, and his willingness to accept the limits imposed by a constitutional framework distinguished him from many other charismatic Third World leaders of the day. Even when India's bicameral parliament

43

became a source of intense pressure upon his China policy, Nehru continued to play the role of the Western-style parliamentary head of government. He did so from a deep devotion to democratic traditions and from the part of his personality that resembled an old-fashioned Edwardian gentleman.

A drawback to Nehru's stature was that he was never held responsible by India's cabinet as a collective body. He made decisions on most domestic governmental matters in consultation with the cabinet minister in whose jurisdiction or area of expertise the problem lay. But even this method of consulting the cabinet was not used in the realm of foreign affairs. Nehru himself was minister for external affairs, in keeping with the fact that no other cabinet member (with the possible exception of Krishna Menon) could match his experience, expertise, and sophistication. When foreign policy was discussed in a meeting of the cabinet or by the cabinet's Foreign Affairs Subcommittee, he did most of the talking. Usually he either lectured to his colleagues on a particular subject or sought to convert them to his point of view.[2] Such conversion was not difficult.[3]

Nehru kept the Foreign Affairs Subcommittee closely informed on China-related matters from the autumn of 1959 to the spring of 1960.[4] But from then until the 1962 crisis itself, the subcommittee was again relegated to the background as far as China policy was concerned.[5]

Some recent critics have said that under Nehru there was no institutionalization in the process of making foreign policy, because of "limited institutional differentiation" in "newly independent India."[6] But such an analysis is not entirely accurate. Institutions within the Indian administrative system were already developing their own bureaucratic routines, drawn partly from the administrative structures and processes of British India.[7] Still lacking, however, was the full range of procedures, checks, and degrees of bureaucratization associated with institutions that have lives of their own. Thus, foreign policy could easily be based more on "projection of national character as interpreted by Nehru" than on "national interests as conceived by professionals."[8]

Other cabinet members could influence the making of India's China policy during the years 1959–1962. Besides the controversial defense minister, V. K. Krishna Menon, an active role was taken by the home minister, Pandit Govind Ballabh Pant.

Krishna Menon has been called "the Adjunct Minister of External Affairs," consulted on almost every issue.[9] His importance was derived mainly from the fact that he and the prime minister shared the same overall worldview (attitudinal prism), although there were some important differences.

Nehru admired Krishna Menon's brilliant mind,[10] and Krishna Menon was highly useful in that he could convey Nehru's thoughts and policies to the outside world in a forceful and organized manner. Krishna Menon acted as a "trouble-shooter," a "roving ambassador," and someone who "relieved Nehru of the onerous burden of day-to-day decisions in many spheres." Engaged as he was in frequent discussion with the prime minister, there was often a "fusion of ideas"; and Krishna Menon's suggestions frequently would be "taken up by Nehru and unconsciously adopted as his own."[11] Krishna Menon had the more analytical mind, while Nehru's was more intuitive. Thus, Krishna Menon could "rationalize Jawaharlal's instinctive, often emotional ideas"[12] and act as Nehru's vibrant intellectual companion.[13]

There was, too, an emotional bond of thirty years' friendship between two lonely men. They had been in touch since the early 1930s, but their relationship had been forged in 1938, when Krishna Menon accompanied Nehru on his last European tour before World War II. Nehru appreciated the sacrifices that Krishna Menon had made in the cause of India's independence, serving for many years as a penurious semiexiled spokesman for his country in London. Krishna Menon also carried out some literary tasks for Nehru, such as editing certain of Nehru's famous books for publication in America.[14]

For Krishna Menon the bond with Nehru would come to contain elements of psychological and political dependency.[15] Within India Krishna Menon had no domestic political strength of his own, since he had lived so long abroad and had never established an organizational base anywhere. He personally antagonized many of the Congress Party leaders, while becoming a member of the numerically weak and poorly organized left faction of the party. Nehru intervened to protect Krishna Menon's political career at certain crucial junctures.

During the several troubled years after India became independent, Krishna Menon was India's controversial High Commissioner (ambassador) to Britain. He then (1952–1956) achieved international prominence and some popularity at home as India's leading spokesman at the United Nations and other international forums. Between 1952 and 1957 Nehru had MEA officials consult closely with him on all foreign policy questions. Krishna Menon joined the cabinet in

1956, despite fierce resistance from a senior cabinet member (and Nehru's personal friend), Maulana Azad, and became defense minister in 1957. From 1956 on, he was also a member of the Foreign Affairs Subcommittee of the cabinet, but his impact on foreign policy was exercised "more behind the scenes than in meetings of the committee."[16]

With the emergence of the China problem in 1959, Nehru deliberately did not bring Krishna Menon into cabinet-level discussions on the subject, although the defense minister knew how those discussions were going. Apparently, Nehru wanted to shield Krishna Menon, and himself. The prime minister knew that, because of Krishna Menon's reputed softness toward the Communist world, any proposal emanating from him would be regarded as suspect by senior members of the cabinet, such as Pandit Pant and Finance Minister Morarji Desai. Moreover, in the mood then prevailing in parliament, there would be still further controversies.[17]

As defense minister, Krishna Menon worked faithfully to achieve the goals that he and Nehru shared. But in that role (as in others) he proved something of a liability. His thin and hawklike features mirrored a personality easily given to disdain and dismissiveness, and his sharp tongue could cause personal and group alienation. As a nationalist who had suffered for the independence movement, Krishna Menon had distrusted MEA officials when he first came into contact with them after India's independence. He was able to overcome that distrust, but he never overcame his distrust of army officers.

Krishna Menon was by nature conspiratorial and prone to complain about persons he took to be enemies. At times Nehru or someone else in the foreign policy or defense spheres would have to remonstrate with him over some public statement or private behavior. He could make amends, however, with considerable courtesy and charm, especially to those whom he considered loyal to himself or to Nehru.[18]

Krishna Menon's only rival for influence over Nehru's China decisions was Pandit Govind Ballabh Pant. As home minister, Pant took a keen interest in the formulation of China policy and was closely consulted from the spring of 1959 until his death in March 1961. He took a special interest in the historical-legal evidence and its implications.[19]

Foreign Secretary Subimal Dutt would take to Pant drafts of diplomatic correspondence with the Chinese and get his reaction, usually at Nehru's request. Possible alternative moves vis-à-vis the

Chinese could be informally discussed with him.[20] Pant was generally appreciated as well by Mullik, whose Intelligence Bureau lay within Pant's Ministry of Home Affairs.[21]

That Pant could make his views well known, and have them figure in Nehru's and Krishna Menon's deliberations, is understandable given his service in the nationalist movement, his standing in the Congress Party, and his personality. A large, calm, and plain-spoken man with a marked stoop and a walrus mustache that made his face seem sad and introspective, Pant had a sharp lawyer's mind and a well-founded reputation for integrity. He habitually wore the Gandhian clothing of the independence movement and had sacrificed his health for the nationalist cause when he was permanently crippled by the blows of police *lathis* (long steel-tipped truncheons) across his back. He had served time in British Indian jails, sometimes as a valued prison companion to Nehru.[22]

Pandit Pant had long been the dominant figure (although not a machine boss) in the Congress Party apparatus in the huge north Indian state of Uttar Pradesh.[23] After joining the Nehru cabinet as Union Home Minister in 1955, Pant also became deputy leader of the Congress Party in parliament. From the cabinet level he continued to mediate and arbitrate occasionally in the politics of his home state, and he became deeply involved in such momentous national problems as the Nehru government's dealings with the Communist cabinet in the Indian state of Kerala.[24]

In his overall political standing in the cabinet and the party, Pandit Pant was second only to Nehru. He was also one of those conservative leaders of a Congress Party establishment that differed with Nehru in philosophy and policy. For these reasons he could have constituted a political threat.[25] Yet Pant and Nehru were reluctant to oppose each other and were able to influence each other,[26] and Pant never would have aired publicly any specific disagreement between himself and Nehru.[27] Indeed, because he would never do anything to hurt Nehru,[28] he never really posed any danger. The relationship between the two was mutually loyal, respectful, fond, and even reverential.

THE ATTITUDINAL PRISM OF THE DECISION-MAKERS

An "attitudinal prism" or worldview is the lens through which foreign policy makers filter and structure information, and thereby perceive the world. Thus, their attitudinal prism contains their fundamental psychological predispositions, drawn from such sources as ideology, tradition, culture, history, and individual personality and idiosyncrasy.[29] From the interaction of information and the attitudinal prism, their psychological environment becomes defined. That environment includes images of other nations and their roles, the domestic political situation, and those problems requiring decisions and actions.

One set of basic Indian beliefs and attitudes through which information was being screened during and after 1959 pertained to the role that India should play in the world. That role was supposed to reflect the fact that India was a new nation-state. But India was not a new nation, if the term *nation* is used to define a people and community with its own sense of identity and uniqueness. An Indian nation, defined by its culture and history, had existed from time immemorial.

Political independence meant not only control by the Indian nation of its own state structure but also the opportunity to express India's national uniqueness, identity, and spirit. In his famous speech made on the evening before independence day in 1947, Nehru said that "at the stroke of the midnight hour" India would "awake to life and freedom" and that the "soul of a nation, long-suppressed," would find "utterance."[30]

An India that had achieved independence under one of the great nationalist movements of the non-Western world had to preserve its independence of action. India had not secured independence simply to become a camp follower of one of the Cold War power blocs and to accept the limitations and restrictions on national interest that such a position entailed. Nehru's policy of nonalignment between the two sides in the Cold War was thus partly the projection of Indian nationalism into world affairs.

Nehru further viewed India as an Asian country with enormous potentialities. India may have been weak militarily, but India counted in world affairs because "she" was not "some odd little nation somewhere in Asia or Europe." Potentially, India was a "great nation and a big Power."[31] As Nehru put it in 1949:

> in regard to any major problem of a country or a group of
> countries of Asia, India has to be considered. Whether it is a problem
> of defense or trade or industry or economic policy India cannot be
> ignored. She cannot be ignored, because ... her geographic position is
> a compelling reason. She cannot be ignored also, because of her

actual or potential power and resources. Whatever her actual strength may or may not be, India is potentially a very powerful country and possesses the qualities and factors that go a long way to make a country grow strong, healthy, and prosperous.[32]

By the late 1950s and early 1960s, Nehru and those advising him saw India playing far more than a merely neutral role in Cold War politics. Active diplomacy was enabling India to serve as a communications channel, go-between, and occasional mediator between the power blocs. Although not a great power, India was a highly responsible player on the world stage, where questions of world war and peace were decided. This view of India's role was not merely an Indian self-perception; it had gradually come to be shared by other governments involved in the Cold War, especially during the Kennedy-Khrushchev era.

One key Nehru belief was that a bipolar world, in which relations between the superpowers were based mainly on balance-of-power calculations, was a world in which nuclear holocaust had become highly likely. India and other countries should therefore stay out of the Cold War and should act to reduce the dangers of superpower confrontation by fostering communication, engaging in constructive diplomacy, and publicly judging each action of the United States and Soviet Union on its merits.

Nehru also believed that the nonaligned role his government had established for India in world affairs was closely attuned to Indian national interests. A nation such as India, which had economic development as a primary goal, needed peace; and nonalignment could help avoid world war. Lesser international political upheavals, such as the Suez crisis of 1956, affected the Indian economy; and so India should help to avoid them as well. Nonalignment also allowed India to receive development aid from as many countries as could be persuaded to contribute, whatever their Cold War leanings.

India could not afford to expend resources on a large defense establishment, which would be necessary if India took sides in the Cold War. An India aligned with no Cold War power bloc would avoid alienating such nations as China and the Soviet Union, both neighboring countries and vital to India's security. As the prime minister said to his intelligence staff (with some hyperbole) in 1952, a hostile frontier with China alone would mean expenditure of all Indian resources just to defend it.[33]

India's place within the international politics of the Asian region was an adjunct to the leadership role adopted by Nehru (and Krishna Menon) in trying to create a worldwide group of nations that stood apart from the Cold War—the "area of peace." The area of peace ideal was first broached by Nehru in the early 1950s, when he began to deal with Asian, African, and Middle Eastern countries then emerging from colonial rule. As he explained to the Lok Sabha (the lower house of parliament) in 1953, he was not trying to create a "third force" to compete with the Cold War power blocs, but rather "an area where peace might, perhaps, subsist, even if war was declared. That would be good, of course, to the countries there, but would be good for the world too, because that area would exercise some influence, when a crisis came, on avoidance of war."[34]

That an association of nonaligned states did come into being testifies to the appeal of Nehru's vision, along with that of his two major foreign colleagues of those years, Nasser of Egypt and Tito of Yugoslavia. China, though formally aligned with the Soviet Union, was seemingly drawn into the area of peace at the Bandung Conference in 1955.

An Indian journalist once said that the Indian political elite, in their attitude toward India's role in international affairs during Nehru's time, manifested a "great power complex."[35] Although that label is too extreme, there was present in the exuberant early days of India's independence a self-image entirely at odds with acceptance of bullying or loss of territory to anyone. Not just Nehru but most of the other Indian decision-makers and consultants as well were convinced by the end of 1959 that China was unable or unwilling to understand any of the sources of that self-image, particularly Indian nationalism.[36]

CHANGING IMAGES
HELD BY THE DECISION-MAKERS
Nehru

In addition to their basic attitudinal prisms, foreign policy decision-makers form less basic but quite complex composite "images" of nations, governments, other international actors, and even international situations and trends. These images change over time, but sometimes not easily.

Although the Sino-Soviet split was not fully perceived until 1963, Nehru and the MEA were already recognizing the first signs of Sino-Soviet dissension by the late 1950s.[37] Since Nehru had made it a fundamental tenet of Indian foreign policy to treat China and the Soviet Union as separate powers posing two different sets of problems, there was, especially now, no reason not to forge the friendliest possible relationship with the Soviet Union. Despite his rejection of Marxism-Leninism, Nehru had sympathized with and sometimes admired the Soviet Union since the days of the Indian nationalist struggle. After the death of Stalin in 1953 and the end of any perceived Soviet connection with rebellious Communist activity in India, Nehru came to view relations with the Soviet Union as existing on an entirely different plane from his government's dealings with the Communist Party of India. He could have high regard for Soviet leaders and disdain for Indian Communists at the same time.[38]

The Nehru government's set of images gave the Soviet Union an advantage not only over China but also over the United States. One biographer of Nehru traces the origin of that advantage to events of the 1920s and 1930s in Europe "and the analysis of them by intellectuals of the British left, especially those grouped around the political scientist Harold Laski and the socialist journal the *New Statesman*."

> From them he [Nehru] acquired a superior attitude to the United States, too rich, too powerful and essentially "immature," and a tendency to give the Soviet Union the maximum benefit of any doubt. Nehru never lost his view of the Russia of the inter-war years, embattled and revolutionary, and its post-war imperialism was always somehow less offensive to him than the pre-war imperialism of the west.[39]

Relations with the United States, in Nehru's view, could be kept constructive and could be improved upon once the Americans overcame their suspicion of nonalignment—a suspicion based on their anti-Communist phobia. Part of the trouble now was that America remained determined to align new non-Western nations against the Soviet Union via pacts and other means. That attitude ran counter to the concept of the "area of peace," as did the American tendency to perceive the Soviet hand in unstable situations everywhere in the non-Western world. The relationship between India and the United States was further constrained by the American policy of arming Pakistan militarily (thereby threatening India's security) and favoring Pakistani sentiments concerning Kashmir.[40]

As a result of a momentous postindependence decision, primarily Nehru's and Krishna Menon's, India had taken a positive view of, and had accepted membership in, that remnant of the British Empire—the

Commonwealth. The Commonwealth tie was perceived as ensuring that, despite nonalignment, India would never be completely isolated. It would be given a channel of communication with the West and with other Third World countries that were Commonwealth members; as a result, Indian diplomatic influence would be enhanced. India's continuing reliance on British military equipment and organizational methods, as well as India's continuing concern for overseas Indian communities in the former British Empire, made Commonwealth membership even more valuable. Other reasons for membership included trade and the possibility of economic assistance.[41]

Beyond the practical reasons for having good relations with Britain and other Commonwealth countries, there were ideological and personal considerations. Indian nationalists under Gandhi had championed the idea of bearing no bitterness toward the British after their final departure, or so Nehru believed. With Britain (and the West generally) there were also ties of culture, ideals, institutions, and personal relations, which Nehru did not want abandoned for small-minded reasons.[42]

All his adult life Nehru remained an admirer and a practitioner of much that was British in taste and manners.[43] As an Indian nationalist and associate of Gandhi, he had rejected the racism, exclusivism, arrogance, and brutality inherent in his image of British and other imperialisms, as well as the British penchant for using force against subject peoples. But he would not reject the English culture he had imbibed when young. He would remain sensitive to gentlemanly behavior and negatively predisposed to discourtesy, arrogance, vulgarity, and attitudes of cultural superiority, even if they came from an Asian source, such as China.

In the post-1959 view of India's leaders, China's insensitivity toward India's nationalist heritage contrasted sharply with Indian sympathy for the Chinese revolution.[44] Prime Minister Nehru, Defense Minister Krishna Menon, and Ambassador Panikkar had seen the Chinese revolution as part of the reemergence of Asia, Africa, and the Middle East during the twentieth century. Like India, China had been a historic nation suppressed, exploited, and degraded by Western imperialism, even though it had never been made a formal colony. In an age when many nations were discovering their identities (or rediscovering them), while throwing off foreign domination and placing themselves back into the mainstream of world history, the

Chinese revolution constituted a major historical event. China's achievement was therefore something to be welcomed.

Accustomed as he was to thinking in sweeping historical terms, the prime minister could think romantically and rhapsodically of past relations between the cultures of India and China, and the two thousand years of friendship they had supposedly enjoyed. His largeness of mind led him to hope that this tradition could continue in an era of Indian and Chinese national reassertion.[45]

Nehru never thought that China's position in the Communist world constituted a problem for India. He was determined to prevent the Soviet Union and China from ever combining against India,[46] but he was certain that the Chinese, like the Russians, were acting on the strength of their own national foreign policy interests and imperatives. China could only be a problem for inherently Chinese reasons, having to do with the Chinese national character, recent Chinese history, and the outlook generated by the Chinese revolution. As he once wrote in a private letter:

> Chinese psychology, with its background of prolonged suffering, struggle against Japan, and successful communist revolution, is an understandable mixture of bitterness, elation, and vaunting confidence to which the traditional xenophobia and present day isolation from outside contacts have added fear and suspicion of the motives of other powers. For inducing a more balanced and cooperative mentality in Peking, it is essential to understand those psychological factors.[47]

These points were made in 1950, during the time when India-China relations had briefly become strained over the Chinese military seizure of Tibet. Nehru elaborated on them two years later, when describing China as an object for study by India's Intelligence Bureau. In a briefing he told IB officers that during past centuries Indian and Chinese cultures had contested for supremacy in Central Asia and Tibet, as well as in Burma and other places in Southeast Asia. Thus, conflict between India and China had never been direct, but there had been intense indirect competition nevertheless, and it was continuing.[48]

Furthermore, throughout its history China had shown a tendency to be "aggressive." That tendency would now be magnified by an aggressive political philosophy held by leaders who for the past twenty years had waged an unceasing and ultimately successful war. As soon as China had achieved a certain amount of economic and political stability, the Chinese could be expected to seek some form of influence, leadership, or even supremacy in Asia. Their biggest obstacle would be India. To achieve their ends, they might attempt to prove their superiority over India in the political and economic fields; they even might decide to occupy some Southeast Asian countries. Alternatively, they might provide help for Communist parties struggling to take over these nations. China's purpose in doing these things, however, would be to further China's culture and national interest rather than Communist internationalism. The Communist Party of India might be used to create a strong lobby supporting the Chinese cause in any dispute with India's government.

From the prime minister's standpoint, China's emergence from the bonds of Western imperialism could release negative political and national character traits, not just positive ones. India would have to be vigilant, especially on the northern frontier. China had (in 1952) no immediate intention to recognize the India-Tibet border formally, Nehru reportedly said, and China would try to extend its influence over frontier territory once the Chinese position in Tibet had been consolidated. That was why India had to develop its frontier administration, including the placement of posts right up to the frontiers themselves.[49]

Nehru's belief that China tended to be an expansionist nation was repeated in various contexts, including private letters sent in 1954.[50] Throughout most of the 1950s, however, other beliefs received more emphasis, both publicly and privately. Indeed, the basic assumption of Nehru, Krishna Menon, and high officials in the MEA was that a friendly Sino-Indian relationship could be established if Tibet was removed as an irritant and if China was brought out of isolation into a world of emerging and reemerging nations. China should also be admitted to the United Nations and thereby placed within the world of international power politics.

Nehru personally remained keenly aware of the implications of Sino-Indian friendship for peace and stability in Asia. He thought that the future of Asia depended on it;[51] therefore, it outweighed his concerns about Tibet. The bedrock Nehru belief about Tibet was that it was part of China, although it should be allowed as much autonomy as possible. India had formally recognized China's rights in Tibet, and after 1954 was bound to do so by treaty (the 1954 Sino-Indian trade agreement). For the Tibetans to resist Chinese control was useless, and so was violent rebellion against the social changes being introduced into the country. In a meeting with the Dalai Lama on 24 April 1959, Nehru told him that "the whole world cannot bring freedom to Tibet unless the whole fabric of the Chinese state is destroyed."[52] Tibet's only alternative was to pursue the goal of autonomy by peaceful means.[53]

There did not have to be any basic conflict between India and China for the foreseeable future, although there could be an element of competition. Nehru had returned from his 1954 trip to China impressed by Chinese revolutionary vigor and by the new China's economic and social achievements.[54] Even before 1954 he was concerned that India should compete effectively with China; that is, India should regard China as a standard for comparison, not as an open rival.[55] India would follow its own unique strategy of economic development. That strategy called for government-directed economic planning, a government-controlled public sector of utilities and industries, and a cooperative but independent private sector.

As far as Nehru was concerned, the transition from Sino-Indian competition to conflict came in the autumn of 1959, when China's behavior, as filtered through Nehru's attitudinal prism, led him to alter his image of that country. The final and most serious border incident, in a chain of them, completed a cumulative process whereby Prime Minister Nehru reluctantly adopted a particular set of beliefs concerning Chinese motives for having initiated the border conflict.

Those beliefs and the composite image they formed were: (1) China was "arrogant" and imbued with feelings of superiority. (2) China was a revolutionary and unsatisfied power, in an aggressive mood. (3) The Chinese state historically tended to be expansionist when strong internally. (4) The fundamental Chinese attributes now influencing policy toward India were Sino-centrism and nationalism, abetted by China's version of Communist ideology. (5) These traits had been reinforced by the recent isolation imposed on China by the West. (6) In general, and on the subject of India, the Chinese were paranoid and possessed of a one-track mind. (7) They were therefore not interested in the kind of border settlement that India could accept.[56]

Thus, his ultimate image of China was that of a "hostile" country, predisposed to harm India on the strength of deep-seated emotions. The border dispute was but a surface manifestation of fundamental Chinese motives.

Krishna Menon

On subjects such as nonalignment, the area of peace, and the position of India in regional and world affairs, Nehru and his defense minister were entirely of one mind. But V. K. Krishna Menon derived his images of China and the Sino-Indian conflict from information filtered through an attitudinal prism that was in many ways different from Nehru's.

Nehru had used concepts from Marxism and Leninism as analytical tools in his preindependence thinking and writing, but he had gradually abandoned those concepts. Krishna Menon, never an "unqualified adherent" of Marxist ideology either, had been more strongly influenced by "Laski's neo-Marxism" of the 1930s. Thus, he retained a basic acceptance of the Leninist theory of imperialism.[57] Imperialism to Krishna Menon was an outgrowth of capitalism. It therefore belonged to the Western bloc of nations, who bore more of a responsibility for the world's ills than the Eastern bloc did. The "central place in Menon's assault on Imperialism" in the 1950s and 1960s was assigned to the United States, the major Western power and a country strongly inclined to intervene in the affairs of the non-Western world. In India, for example, the United States had promoted a pro-American lobby that was hostile to the Nehru government's ideals.

Krishna Menon's images of India's neighbors also were influenced by his deep-seated distrust of imperialism and capitalism. He regarded Pakistan, not China, "as the principal threat to India's security, values, and institutions."[58] To him Pakistan represented a hollow and artificial nationalism, being fundamentally a remnant of British imperialism. After independence Pakistan had become tied to the new American imperialist system via treaty and the receipt of military aid. As an American client Pakistan weakened the area of peace and served as the primary instrument whereby imperialism could threaten India's security.

Pakistan further represented the negation of India's nationalist ideals, especially secularism. In Krishna Menon's eyes Pakistan differed from India fundamentally in embracing religion as the basis for nationhood. He argued that Muslim Pakistan wanted to gain control of all of the empire that the British had taken from Muslim rule. Pakistan was an antimodern throwback to outmoded eras of history, a military competitor with India, and a country with an unresolvable grievance against India (Kashmir). By refusing to accept the 1947 partition of the British Indian empire, Pakistan even challenged India's right to exist.

In contrast, Krishna Menon's image of China was quite positive. Although he rejected totalitarian methods anywhere, he "viewed the New China as a progressive State, secular, socialist, and modern. It was a revolutionary movement in the best sense, pursuing with vigor the noble ends of economic development and social change."[59] Krishna Menon also felt a form of "spiritual kinship" with China. As two great civilizations India and China had just come to assert their national independence after suffering foreign domination for a century or more.

When India-China relations soured after 1959, Krishna Menon regarded China's sensitivity over the security of Tibet as the major motive for its subsequent aggressive actions along the frontier with India. Border incidents, he reasoned, probably arose from China's suspicion that the Tibetan refugees in India might return to Tibet and start another rebellion.[60] Other Chinese motives underlying the border problem, to which Krishna Menon alluded in public statements during the autumn of 1959, were (1) a certain Chinese "despondency" over internal economic problems and (2) the youthful, aggressive fervor of the Chinese revolution.[61]

After 21 October 1959 (the date of the final and most serious 1959 incident), Krishna Menon on one occasion denied that Tibet was the cause of the border troubles, but he did not indicate definitely what the real causes might be.[62] In March 1960 he pointed to several elements in Chinese behavior, including blunder, an effort to intimidate, anger at India's Tibetan policy, and historic Chinese expansionism.[63]

All through the pre-crisis period, Krishna Menon believed that frustration caused by the international isolation imposed on Communist China had helped shape Chinese attitudes. "He believed the Chinese were in the position of a man in solitary." They had to show their strength and energy.[64]

Krishna Menon remained certain, too, that the Chinese mistakenly saw India as representing a threat from the imperialist West. India was too close to the United States and was meddling in Tibet, or so the Chinese thought. As Krishna Menon would remark in 1964, "I am not even now sure that the Chinese did not think we were much more powerful than we were [in 1962]—that the whole of America would be behind us with the threat to invade China from its underbelly. It may have been a foolish idea—but there it was."[65]

On the question of how to deal with the Sino-Indian conflict, Krishna Menon in late 1959 and early 1960 became the leading proponent of a particular school of thought. To that school the territorial disagreement between China and India was genuine, and not a reflection of deeper Chinese hostility. Therefore, a political settlement with the Chinese could be reached and might even have to include territorial compromise. Fascination with historical evidence should not be allowed to restrict Indian diplomatic flexibility.[66]

He did not want India diverted from a "progressive" stance on world affairs, and he wanted to let the Chinese know that if by their actions they had hurt India, they had hurt themselves more, and the world still more. As he told Chou En-lai when they met in 1960, "you have strengthened every reactionary element in this country and the forces of tension in the world."[67]

Krishna Menon did not include Chou himself among the culprits, considering him a decent person and basically open to reason. But others behind Chou had to be persuaded to become more reasonable by diplomacy and, if necessary, by demonstrated Indian control of disputed territory.

Pandit Pant

A lawyer, an Indian nationalist, and a man of moral stature, Pandit Pant also possessed a "towering intelligence."[68] His image of the border dispute was the opposite of Krishna Menon's. Pant's image was based mainly on historical and legal evidence. From Pant's standpoint India was not making a baseless case for its territorial claims, since the Indian evidence was strong. He reached this conclusion by delving into documentary materials more deeply than either the prime minister or the defense minister had. For instance, he carefully read the lengthy diplomatic cables sent back to Delhi from the Peking session of the Sino-Indian officials' talks of 1960. Just before he died in 1961, he became familiar with the "Officials' Report," in which the Indian evidentiary case was presented in great detail.[69]

Pant and Nehru shared a concern for historical propriety. They also shared feelings of unrequited friendship toward China and disappointment at Chinese actions.[70] The key point of difference between the two men was over the emphasis to be placed on such feelings. Nehru did not want parliament to become so excited about the loss of the Aksai Chin that it would pressure his government to change foreign policy fundamentals, particularly nonalignment. He thought

that the China border was just one front, among others, and that India
would still remain secure by staying nonaligned and nonhostile.[71] But
Pant focused on the wrongs the Chinese had done to India. While he
would publicly and loyally support Nehru on China policy, privately
he was a hardliner, particularly on territorial questions.[72] Accordingly, between 1959 and 1961 Pant loomed as an obstacle to consideration of ideas that Krishna Menon favored.

THE INDIAN PERCEPTION OF THREAT

During a "pre-crisis" period such as this one, there is invariably a
conspicuous increase in perceived threat to basic values.[73] But was
Prime Minister Nehru's definition of India's problem with China,
during and after March 1959, colored more by his perception of threat
or by his sense of injury? One scholar has argued for injury as the major factor. He writes that Nehru resented China's failure to give "due
weight to India's importance in the world." Moreover:

> All of India's foreign policy was an extension of Nehru's political
> personality; but no part of it was more markedly associated with him
> personally than India's friendship with China. He had long been
> under attack for it from his domestic critics; now they were gleefully
> reminding him of their past warnings. To this humiliation,
> weakening to his own political position, must have been added the
> sense of betrayal by the Chinese, and particularly by Chou En-lai.[74]

Largely for this reason, or so this argument continues, Nehru suddenly
reversed the policy of friendship with China in late August and early
September 1959.

The evidence suggests, however, that the change came only in late
October and was mainly sensitive to threat perception. That perception, in turn, was heavily influenced by Nehru's belief that China had
become hostile to India in a fundamental and permanent way. Certain
stimuli were required to make him adopt that belief. Among those
stimuli were Chinese ideological statements, as interpreted by officials
in the Ministry of External Affairs.

In March and April 1959 Nehru and his MEA officials were trying
to understand the behavior and language adopted by the Chinese as
they complained of alleged Indian complicity in the 1959 Tibetan
uprising. Articles and editorials appearing in China's press and
elsewhere went beyond specific allegations concerning Tibet and dealt
with the nature of India's political, economic, and social systems. A

lengthy Chinese article, first published in the newspaper *People's Daily* on 6 May 1959, exemplified Chinese ideological thinking and lack of restraint.[75] Entitled "The Revolution in Tibet and Nehru's Philosophy," this article was a reply to a speech given by Nehru in parliament on 27 April. The article not only sought to rebut Nehru's version of events in Tibet but also went on to recall the unpleasant period of 1950 as another case of Indian interference in Chinese internal affairs. Such interference, the article concluded, was not "fortuitous."

> The Indian big bourgeoisie maintains manifold links with imperialism and is, to a certain extent, dependent on foreign capital. Moreover, by its class nature, the big bourgeoisie has a certain urge for outward expansion. That is why...it more or less reflects, consciously or unconsciously, certain influences of the imperialist policy of intervention...[For] historical reasons India's big bourgeoisie has inherited and is attempting to maintain certain legacies from the British colonialist rulers.[76]

Distressing language also appeared in a note delivered by China's ambassador, Pan Tzu-li, to Foreign Secretary Dutt at a meeting between the two officials on 16 May 1959. The meeting had been requested by Pan. The note that he delivered to Dutt contained memorable lines and brought some Indian officials "up with a start."[77] After alleging that India had encouraged the Tibetan rebels in an "objective" sense even if not subjectively, it added:

> On the whole, India is a friend of China, this has been so in the past thousand and more years, and we believe [will] certainly continue to be so in one thousand, ten thousand years to come. The enemy of the Chinese people lies in the East—the U.S. imperialists have many military bases in Taiwan, in South Korea, Japan and in the Philippines which are all directed against China. . . . Our Indian friends! What is your mind? Will you be agreeing to our thinking regarding the view that China can only concentrate its main attention eastward of China, but not southwestward of China, nor is it necessary for it to do so. . . . Friends! It seems to us that you too cannot have two fronts.[78]

India's austere and cautious foreign secretary did not draw conclusions about basic Chinese motivation from such words, beyond thinking that the Nehru government had been warned about the possible price to be paid for expressing opinions, and acting independently in other ways, concerning Tibet. He thought, too, that India was being warned not to help create a dispute along the China frontier, because then India would have to deal with diplomatic pressure from China and Pakistan simultaneously.[79]

Other officials were prepared to go further. They believed that China was trying to intimidate India. With its talk of "two fronts," the Pan letter threatened that India would be treated as an enemy, and that the Chinese would make common cause with Pakistan, unless Indian policy on Tibet changed. On the basis of the crisis-like atmosphere created by the unrestrained Chinese use of abusive language during April and May 1959, and the content of that language in written documents such as the *People's Daily* article and the Pan Tzu-li note, these officials concluded that the Chinese were now motivated in their actions toward India by a militant ideology made up of Sino-centrism and nationalism.[80] China had become fundamentally hostile.

By late 1959 the MEA's main China analyst, J. S. Mehta, came to believe that the Chinese had always felt an ideological antagonism toward India. That antagonism—more readily perceived from dealing with them over minor issues between the two countries in the 1950s than from dealing with them on the level of general policy statements—had been a problem in embryo. The problem had now developed more fully because of Chinese suspicions about Indian involvement in Tibetan affairs and because of China's need to explain the Tibetan revolt without admitting fault or failure. Thus, the emerging border dispute was a product of China's aggressive mood after the Tibetan revolt, China's defensiveness over the damage to its image, and a fully revealed political antagonism toward India that transcended ideology, although ideology was a part of it.[81]

Prime Minister Nehru knew of these MEA images of China. But he found it hard to accept them, with all their threatening implications. Thus, his outlook through the spring, summer, and early fall of 1959 was ambivalent, and he still entertained the optimistic view that Tibet was uppermost in Chinese thinking and that the Chinese government's "excitement" would eventually pass. Present problems, or so he hoped, stemmed from the Peking government's extreme sensitivity over Tibet, what with India's having recently given political asylum to the Dalai Lama and thousands of refugees. They also arose from China's conviction that émigrés in India were being allowed to play a commanding role in the Tibetan uprising. Once the Tibetan revolt had ended and receded into the past, Chinese anger at India would subside.[82]

Nehru began to lose such hope with the receipt in September of a

Chou En-lai letter, which put forward large-scale territorial claims for the first time. The letter came just after the 1959 series of border incidents had begun. Bombarded by the Indian press and parliament for a definitive public explanation of China's motives, Nehru sounded uncertain about whether the Tibetan revolt was still crucial or whether more fundamental motives were involved.

While discussing China's motives, he made the following comment: "[Just as] certain Western nations, not now but throughout the 19th and half of the 20th century, in their pride and arrogance, ignored the rest of the world—they thought they were the leaders of the world and the rest of the world should follow them—so also there is a tendency in some of these Far Eastern countries to forget that there are other parts of the world which count."[83] With statements such as this, Nehru revealed that he was starting to link Chinese behavior with several related concepts that had been part of his attitudinal prism for some time.[84] One was the concept of imperialism as practiced by the West against India and many other countries. Another was his pre-1959 belief that China tended to be aggressive and overbearing when strong.[85] The prime minister also referred to ideology as a Chinese motive, but he stressed his longstanding conceptual distinction between China's historic worldview and communism in general.[86]

Nehru's ambivalence about Chinese motives, and the level of threat they implied, came to an end after the Kongka Pass incident of 21 October 1959 (see Map 4 and chapter 6).[87] During the weeks following the Kongka Pass clash, a hardened line of thought (similar to that already prevalent in the MEA) emerged. The Tibetan revolt, he now said, had acted as a catalyst, bringing Chinese pressure on India sooner than expected. The rebellion not only had brought Chinese troops to the border for the first time but also had led the Chinese to press previously formulated territorial claims now, rather than in the indefinite future. The basic source of the threat to India's territorial integrity, however, was China's expansionism, which he called "traditional, typically Chinese,...the urge made stronger by two factors." One was China's "growing strength"; the other, a communism "more Chinese than Communistic."[88] Nehru elaborated on these ideas during the late weeks of 1959. At the same time, he was developing his highly elaborate image of a hostile and therefore threatening China.

CHAPTER FIVE

Strategic Decisions, 15 March to 21 October 1959

TIBETAN REVOLT, 15 MARCH TO 23 JUNE 1959

WHEN NEWS WAS received in early March 1959 of the spread of revolt throughout Tibet and the start of fighting in Lhasa, Indian press reports indicated that the Nehru government was undecided over what to do if the Dalai Lama and large numbers of refugees sought to enter India. Unknown to the public, the policy in force at that time was to provide medical assistance for the wounded and sick at India's frontier outposts but not to allow refugees to cross the border.

On or about 15 March, the prime minister ordered that an exception be made for the Dalai Lama himself, perhaps in the knowledge that the Dalai Lama might leave Lhasa. Shortly thereafter, appropriate "overtures" were made to the Indian government on the Dalai Lama's behalf. The Nehru government decided to grant the Dalai Lama asylum if he requested it. He crossed into India on 31 March, by which time most other refugees were being admitted as well.[1]

From the Dalai Lama decision evolved a strategy designed to deal simultaneously with the irate Chinese and with anti-Chinese sentiment in India. Its immediate purpose was to renew polite and appropriate discourse on all sides. Restraint on the Chinese side would be needed, and India and China would have to separate the Tibetan affair from larger policy considerations.[2]

A number of actions were taken as part of this strategy. Most of these steps did not involve elaborate decision-making but were reflexive actions consistent with past policy and with the Indian attitudinal prism. Some actions of the Nehru government required a degree of choice, however, and on that basis can be called decisions.

After the decision to give refuge to the Dalai Lama, the prime minister further chose (between 29 March and 2 April 1959) to reject a private suggestion from the president of India, Rajendra Prasad, that he (Nehru) publicly denounce China's "new colonialism." The reason given was that such action would cause a "rupture of diplomatic relations with China." Later, in a meeting with the Dalai Lama on 24 April, Nehru further chose to turn down a request to recognize "a free Government" of Tibet.[3]

This last decision was not publicized as such, but the Nehru government's policy toward Tibetan activity on Indian soil was well known, and in fact the government was being criticized in parliament and in the Indian press for having shackled the Dalai Lama. At the same time, the Chinese were particularly incensed by a published statement issued earlier by the Dalai Lama, when he settled temporarily in the Indian mountain town of Mussoorie. The Chinese also were angered by Nehru's having openly journeyed to Mussoorie to hear the Dalai Lama's views.

Given the feverish atmosphere, especially within India, Nehru and the MEA officials working with him decided, on or about 25 April, to have the prime minister make an official policy speech in parliament upon his return from Mussoorie. This was not a major decision, since such statements were issued any time Nehru thought there was something of interest, in keeping with what he felt was normal parliamentary practice and a prime minister's constitutional obligation. However, parliament was thought to be demanding some kind of statement at this emotional juncture.

Nehru's 27 April speech was drafted initially by J. S. Mehta of the MEA and delivered from a prepared text. Its major import, from the government's point of view, was that India was not pleading for the independence of Tibet.[4] But it did call the spread of the Tibetan revolt a "nationalist upsurge" caused by fear that the Chinese intended to sinicize the country rather than allow it much autonomy. Like some earlier Indian statements, this one rejected the Chinese claim that the Tibetan revolt was caused by upper-class reactionaries assisted from across the border and supervised from the Indian border town of Kalimpong.

One key item in the speech was an outline description of the Indian government's multifaceted approach to all the issues raised by the Tibetan revolt. That outline was repeated again by Nehru on 4 May, in precisely the same language. He said (in part):

> our broad policy [is] governed by three factors: (1) the preservation
> of the security and integrity of India; (2) our desire to maintain
> friendly relations with China; and (3) our deep sympathy for the
> people of Tibet. ... [We hope] that nothing will be said or done
> which endangers the friendly relations of the two countries which
> are so important from the wider point of view of the peace of
> Asia and the world.[5]

It seemed, thereafter, that the Chinese neither noticed nor appreciated the effort made by the Indian government to act with discretion.
Such discretion was shown not merely in the language used but also in
the restrictions placed on the political activities of the Dalai Lama and
all Tibetan refugees. Nor could the Chinese comprehend India's
parliamentary system,[6] in which free discussion was the rule, or
understand the Indian government's unwillingness to curb what was
being said about China and Tibet.

The Chinese would show no restraint; their accusations continued,
highlighted by the Pan Tzu-li note of 16 May. Among other things, the
Pan note claimed that the Dalai Lama had been "abducted to India by
the Tibetan rebels," but the note also criticized Nehru personally for
welcoming and meeting with the Dalai Lama, who (if acting on his
own volition in India) was himself a "Chinese rebel."[7] The assumption in Delhi was that the Pan Tzu-li note had been approved at the
highest level of government, just as Indian notes were.[8]

In response, it was decided to issue a formal written reply in the
name of the foreign secretary, but the draft was Nehru's.[9] The reply
objected to the "discourteous" language of the Pan Tzu-li missive and
made clear that the Indian government would neither discard nor
vary its views under outside pressure. Nor would the right of free
expression of public opinion be abridged, whether in the Indian
parliament or at large, despite Chinese objections to what was being
said in India. The Indian note also implied that the Chinese were
forgetful of past and present Indian friendship.[10]

With the apparent success of China's suppression of the Tibetan
revolt by late May, the excitement on both the Chinese and the Indian
sides began to abate. The most salient matter then became alleged
recent mistreatment in Tibet of Indian trade and diplomatic personnel,
as well as other Indian nationals. Between late May and early August,
the Indian government did not protest strongly over this issue, but it

displayed a definite sense of grievance in correspondence with the Chinese. The exchange of notes on the subject became more frequent and less polite, and the matter became a subject for parliamentary questioning and debate.[11]

Partly because of policy implementation difficulties on the Indian side, the Tibetan revolt continued to be a problem, even after the border itself became the primary issue during the next phase of Indian decision-making. The Nehru government was never able to control the organizational and recruitment activity of the Tibetan guerrilla movement within India, although several factors ensured that after 1960 the main CIA-Tibetan infiltration route via land would run from Nepal (Mustang) into Tibetan territory. These factors included the American government's reluctance to continue airdrops into Tibet after May 1960, Indian restrictions on Tibetan émigré activities, the militarization of the Assam-Himalaya frontier by the Chinese, and opposition to the CIA operation by the Kennedy administration's new (1961) ambassador to India.

Not until 1960 were the leaders of the Indian government told that the CIA's air supply route from Thailand crossed NEFA on the way to Tibet. This information was supplied by the Chinese, but Nehru and Krishna Menon may not have believed them.[12]

In June 1959 the Dalai Lama issued another inflammatory statement and had to be cautioned by Nehru. More decisions were required because in late August 1959 the Dalai Lama wanted Tibet's case taken to the United Nations, and he came to Delhi in September to plead for Nehru's support. It was refused, but the Dalai Lama would not accept Nehru's cautionary private and public advice and succeeded in having a motion raised in the General Assembly. When the motion came up for a vote in October, India was among the minority that abstained.[13]

BORDER CLAIMS, 13 AUGUST TO 21 OCTOBER 1959

The next phase of Indian decision-making began with a discussion in the Indian parliament on 13 August. The prime minister was asked to comment on reports that the Chinese were now threatening the security of Bhutan, Ladakh, Sikkim, NEFA, and therefore India.[14] Nehru dismissed the matter casually but was questioned again later in August on a report that the Chinese authorities in Tibet were promising that Bhutan, Sikkim, and Ladakh would be liberated. This time Nehru made a stronger statement, pointing out that Bhutan and

Sikkim had treaty relations with India and "we are responsible for their defense."[15]

On 13 August parliamentary questioning also was directed toward securing information about whether China had recently denied the historical validity of the McMahon line and no longer accepted it as the international boundary. Still trying to maintain a longstanding government policy of public silence about border problems, Nehru stretched the truth and denied that the Chinese had rejected the McMahon line in principle. The impression he gave now was that only some minor territorial disagreements existed between India and China.

This was no major revelation, since the Bara Hoti problem had been well known. But by now Nehru was revealing to the parliament and press some impatience with China over another border-related issue—the publication of incorrect Chinese maps.[16]

By the end of August, the subject of China's border activities had developed into a furor, as border incidents between Indian and Chinese forces became known via government and newspaper information. Nehru and his advisers realized that parliament was angry and that its members thought they might have been deceived. Many members of parliament felt that the Nehru government had not been sufficiently perceptive and vigilant where China was concerned and might not have fully disclosed necessary information. The most sensitive item was the existence of the Aksai Chin road, which seemingly implied alienation of Indian territory.[17]

The prime minister responded to the parliamentary mood by making detailed statements in the Lok Sabha about the India-China border. Besides recounting recent events, he reported (on 28 August) a decision to turn responsibility for the NEFA border over to the army (instead of the Assam Rifles frontier constabulary). But more important, in response to a 28 August request made from the floor of the house by A. B. Vajpayee of the (right-wing) Jana Sangh Party, he agreed to the release of a white paper detailing all recent developments concerning border problems with China.[18]

The full details of the white paper decision were worked out in the following week. Whether Krishna Menon or Pandit Pant, or both, were involved in determining what the document would contain is unclear. But this decision of Nehru's marked a turning point in the India-China conflict.[19] As part of the cost of having earlier revealed nothing about border difficulties with the Chinese, the Nehru government now committed itself to issuing a sizable pamphlet containing every Nehru letter sent to Chou En-lai since 1958, as well as every letter received from him since that time. The white paper would further include all major and minor notes, statements, memoranda, and agreements that had passed between the two governments on border and related questions, dating back to April 1954.

After the first White Paper was issued on 7 September 1959, a second one came on 16 November, probably in response to the receipt of Chou En-lai's important letter of 8 September 1959, and all that it portended for the Nehru government, both internationally and domestically (see below). Other white papers were to appear steadily thereafter.

The effect of Nehru's white paper policy was to limit his government's foreign policy options. While the lag between any particular exchange of correspondence and its revelation in a white paper allowed for some immediate and private flexibility, it was now imperative for the Nehru government to adopt only those policies that could conceivably meet with approval from an emotionally aroused parliament and press.

From Nehru's public comments (starting prior to the white paper decision) and from the first White Paper, Indian and Chinese perceptions of a number of incidents along the Sino-Indian frontier in recent months became widely known. On 23 June 1959 the Indian embassy in Peking had received a Chinese protest note about one of these incidents. The note alleged that in the Eastern Sector (the Assam Himalaya—that is, the NEFA frontier) hundreds of Indian troops had intruded into and temporarily occupied a place called Migyitun as well as several other positions further to the northeast (near where the Indians would soon say that they had a post called Tamaden). Migyitun had allegedly been shelled, and in both the Migyitun and Tamaden areas Indian troops were supposedly acting in collusion with Tibetan rebel "bandits."[20] (See Map 3.)

The Indian government denied that such actions had taken place. But India protested the arrest of an Indian patrol by alleged Chinese intruders into southeastern Ladakh on 28 July. Another Indian protest was made against a confrontation which had allegedly occurred on 7 August 1959 at a NEFA location called Khinzemane. According to the Indian accounts,[21] the small Indian police patrol at Khinzemane had been physically pushed back (without shooting) by a much larger force of Chinese to a position several miles to the south.

Actual fighting had broken out around an Indian NEFA post called Longju (near Migyitun) on 25 August, said India. One Indian rifleman had been killed when an Indian patrol had been fired on and captured, although most of its members had managed to escape. One day later Longju post itself had been attacked and its personnel forced to withdraw. The Chinese version of the Longju affair was that the Indians had again intruded into the Migyitun area and opened fire. China's border guards had fired back.

Although the situation may not have been fully clear to the government or parliament or the press at that moment, Chinese and Indian personnel were now meeting for the first time along a frontier made highly sensitive by the Tibetan rebellion and by the flight of the Tibetan refugees. The Dalai Lama himself had crossed the McMahon line to reach Tawang, and the Chinese were still operating against Tibetan rebels near the Khinzemane-Bumla area forward of Tawang, driving hundreds of them into India.[22] The Indians had decided to strengthen their presence along the NEFA frontier, but the Chinese were engaged in militarizing it. The Indian-claimed border was undemarcated, and Chinese troops were convinced of links between the Indians and hostile Tibetans. Therefore, incidents were bound to occur.

Compounding the problem was China's opinion that Tamaden, Migyitun, Longju, and Khinzemane were on the Chinese side of the McMahon line. In fact, the Indians had gone beyond the original version of the McMahon line when setting up some of their posts in the summer of 1959. Thus, it was technically true that certain Indian positions were on the Chinese side of the line, as that line had been drawn on an eight-miles-to-the-inch scale map in 1914.[23] From the Indian perspective McMahon's line had made poor topographical sense in some places, because of limited knowledge of the terrain in 1914. At those places it did not adhere to the highest watershed line of ridges, the principle on which it was supposedly based. Nor did it adhere to other distinguishing features, such as rivers. So the Indians had fixed the boundary to the proper ridges or other salient features nearby and had planted some of their posts accordingly.

Indian officials have called this practice "rectification or rationalization" of a boundary.[24] It may be a common international practice, but it is dangerous if a country uses it without consulting the state that shares the boundary. The danger can become extreme if the other side is as truculent as the Chinese were in the summer of 1959.

The Indian political officer in charge of the NEFA frontier at the time felt that the Chinese "wanted to beat us up." The Chinese political commissars and border officials to whom he talked at length, while his men and theirs confronted each other, were polite but patronizing and had a menacing "swagger" to them. The Indians were no less determined and were prepared to go beyond specific orders so as to hold their positions.[25]

The Indian decision-makers thought the Chinese actions wholly unprovoked. Nehru told the Lok Sabha on 28 August that "there is no alternative for us but to defend our country's borders and integrity."[26] Generally, the threat was seen as limited, since the incidents seemed to arise from minor differences in the interpretation of an unmarked border and from the zeal of local Chinese commanders.[27]

Nehru took considerable care to define in public precisely those Chinese actions he considered harmful to Indian goals and possessions, as well as the actions he did not consider harmful. Intrusions and border incidents, he pointed out in response to hard parliamentary questioning, did not mean "any kind of a fixed occupation" of Indian territory. He sharply distinguished between incidents along the McMahon line, which he labeled a "clear case of aggression," and the situation in Ladakh, where he seemed ready to concede that there might be some bona fide disagreement over title to the Aksai Chin. He urged restraint on feelings of injury by government officials and members of parliament alike, and he mentioned the emotional control that he himself was exercising when reacting to all the current difficulties.[28]

To prod the Chinese into revealing their longer-term thinking, an Indian note of 28 August 1959 included another reminder of their offending maps; and Nehru said publicly that the Chinese had recently maintained a "strange silence" about them. The note also showed concern that Nehru had received no reply to his letter of 22 March 1959.[29]

That silence ended with the arrival of Premier Chou En-lai's reply, dated 8 September. Now Indian decision-makers were confronted with a document emanating from the highest councils of the Chinese government. This document, as the Indian officials perceived it, maintained that the Chinese maps were substantially correct and claimed most of the Indian territory shown on them. The Nehru government was now made to understand how China presently viewed the boundary issue as a whole. Chou's letter said that the entire border was subject to settlement only by a process of formal negotiation. It implied that the Chinese were still inclined to accept the McMahon line as the NEFA boundary as a reality, but this would be a bargaining concession on their part and one not necessarily assured to an unfriendly India.

This revelation should have been less surprising than Nehru's sorrowful and injured reaction made it seem. The Indian prime minister argued that neither Chou's January 1959 letter nor subsequent events had prepared him for the idea "that the People's Republic of China would lay claim to about 40,000 square miles of what in our view has been indisputably Indian territory for decades and in some sectors for over a century."[30] But what had actually been confirmed were his fears rather than his hopes. Thus, the Chou note "added to the gravity of the situation and highlighted certain aspects which were perhaps under a shadow."[31]

The Chinese were thought unlikely to secure their claims by infiltration or invasion. Nehru made this point in parliament when he said that "the real danger at the present moment is not of armies pouring in" but in the words being issued from Peking.[32] What was actually feared, in the military sense, was perhaps best stated in Nehru's 26 September reply to Chou En-lai. He hoped that reports of "large-scale movements of Chinese forces in the Tibetan frontier areas . . . do not signify a new policy of actively probing into Indian territory along the whole length of the Sino-Indian frontier."[33]

Among the other troublesome aspects of the Chou note, mentioned by Nehru openly, was the fact that Chinese territorial claims were still somewhat vague. Having said that their maps were not completely accurate, pending a complete survey of the border, the Chinese had left open the possibility of extending their claims further.[34]

The response to the new situation was primarily diplomatic; there was no major effort to reinforce the border militarily. At the end of August, the Chinese had been informed that "the Government of India have issued instructions to their frontier posts to maintain their territorial integrity and use force on the trespassers if necessary."[35] However, as shown by a memorandum dated 13 September, Nehru decided that civil and military personnel were not to fire unless fired upon.[36] In that memorandum, to senior MEA officials, Nehru ordered that frontier personnel stay on the Indian side of the border, instruct any trespassing Chinese party to go back, and then contact Delhi for further orders. In addition, Nehru said, no action would have to be taken regarding the Aksai Chin or the Chinese road across it, for the time being. He also said that Indian officials should be prepared to engage in talks about minor deviations from the Indian-claimed border but not about any major changes.[37]

Toward the end of September, Nehru decided to reject the services of Prime Minister U Nu of Burma, who had offered to go to China. There the Burmese leader would have tried to create a suitable political climate for talks. Nehru's position was that any such effort might harden the Chinese position by suggesting Indian panic and anxiety. No Indian government would accept the "absurd" Chinese claims in any case.[38]

Publicly, Nehru still inveighed against mutual hostility between India and China. He wanted to avoid a "war psychosis"—that is, a "growing feeling of estrangement, irritation and sometimes anger, on both sides."[39] By early October he was helped by the cessation of debate in parliament because of a recess. With street demonstrations and press criticism having ended for the moment, Nehru toured the country, urging both vigilance and calm. Since there were no further incidents along the border, there was also a lull in the exchange of recriminations via diplomatic correspondence.

Certain Chinese actions further improved the atmosphere, including Chou En-lai's cordial response to Nehru's cable of good wishes on the tenth anniversary of the founding of the People's Republic of China. That reply referred to the recent difficulties as only "an episode" in an "age-old friendship." The message was welcomed cautiously by Nehru as "friendly" and an "improvement" over Chou's note of 8 September, but he refused to speculate on it further.[40]

In the middle of October, the Chinese took another significant step by withdrawing from the Indian post at Longju, which they had occupied since the end of August and for which Nehru had proposed demilitarization. The move may have been a response to the Indian decision some time during the preceding weeks to withdraw the Indian post at Tamaden, after it was determined that the post's placement was not justified. With the Chinese still present in force nearby, the Indians did not reoccupy Longju either.[41]

Yet arguments were still being carried on over minor matters, such as the continued harsh treatment of nonofficial Indian nationals in Tibet, propaganda issued by the Chinese embassy in India, and alleged intrusions by Indian ships into Chinese waters near Hong Kong.[42]

This sort of petty friction would persist throughout the years of the Sino-Indian conflict. Some of it would end only when the 1954 India-China treaty lapsed in 1962, and the Indian trade agencies in Tibet (as well as China's trade agencies in India) were shut down.

On the main issue (the border), the Indian government took a diplomatic hard line in September–October 1959. As a precondition for any talks, it demanded immediate Chinese withdrawal from the places they had occupied in NEFA and Ladakh.[43] Talks themselves could lead only to insubstantial territorial concessions made along an otherwise fixed border. Speaking in parliament on 4 September, Nehru allowed that if the Chinese accepted the McMahon line, he would be prepared to discuss any minor interpretation of that line with the Chinese government and to "have any kind of conciliatory, mediatory process to consider this," or arbitration "by any authority agreed to by the two parties."[44]

Nehru, in his 26 September letter to Chou En-lai, included a list of posts from which the Chinese were being specifically asked to withdraw. He was seeking reciprocity for India's withdrawal of the Tamaden post. But available evidence suggests yet another reason why Nehru's letter placed more emphasis on removing posts than on China's withdrawing from the Aksai Chin region.

At the time, Nehru was reexamining in his own mind the worth of maintaining India's claim to the Aksai Chin. In parliament and elsewhere, starting in August, he described the Aksai Chin as a barren area, devoid of population or even vegetation, thereby implying that it had no particular value for India. Nehru had seized upon the idea that the Aksai Chin was without even "a blade of grass" after the idea was casually mentioned to him by the deputy director of the MEA Historical Division, K. Gopalachari.[45]

Nehru even raised questions about the historical validity of India's claim to the Aksai Chin. The area, he said on 12 September 1959, "stands by itself" (i.e., apart from NEFA and the McMahon line as well as other areas along the frontier). "It is a matter for argument as to what part of it belongs to us and what part of it belongs to somebody else."[46] In August, September, and October, Nehru also pointed out that the Aksai Chin boundary had not been conclusively delimited in the past; that the historical, geographical, and legal evidence pertaining to this boundary should be jointly considered by the parties concerned; and that, although elsewhere he would agree to discuss only minor adjustments along an otherwise established line, greater leeway could be allowed for the Aksai Chin. Indeed, the prime minister hinted that an Aksai Chin border could possibly be delimited anew, as if for the first time.[47]

These were just ruminations on Nehru's part, which he mentioned aloud both publicly and privately. They were not formal proposals.[48] But with Nehru not yet committed to the Aksai Chin as much as he was to other parts of the border,[49] a Chinese proposal calling for some mutual territorial concessions might have been received with interest at this moment.

CHAPTER SIX

Strategic Decisions,
21 October 1959 to 29 July 1961

IN SEPTEMBER AND most of October 1959, India's prime minister
thought that the Chinese were willing to make huge claims but were
not likely to take over large pieces of disputed territory. His thinking
changed just after the Kongka Pass incident of 21 October 1959. The
apparent ambush of an Indian police patrol in the Western Sector
(Ladakh frontier), as well as a series of Chinese statements issued
immediately after that action, produced new Indian conclusions.

China's perceived general objective in the Western Sector was to
come further into Ladakh than the Aksai Chin plateau and to establish
control over a far larger area (perhaps all the Western Sector territory
shown on Chinese maps) by setting up posts and attacking Indian
patrols. China's specific purpose in using violence at Kongka Pass was
to prevent the Indians from sending patrols any longer through the
Chang Chenmo Valley to reach the Indian-claimed border at Lanak
La.[1] (See Map 4.)

Discounted was the fact that the Kongka Pass incident had also
originated from IB director Mullik's determination to block Chinese
advances in Ladakh. Back in December 1958, primarily in response to
confirmation of the existence of the Aksai Chin road (but before
public knowledge of it), he had urged the opening of a series of posts in
Indian-claimed territory west, southwest, and south of the Aksai
Chin. These posts, including two located near either end of the
Chinese road, were to forestall development of a more complex
Chinese road system in the area, which the Chinese seemed intent on
adding to their already existing route.

In January 1959 Mullik had encountered stiff resistance to his
suggestion from the Chief of Army Staff (COAS), Lieutenant General
K.S. Thimayya, and Foreign Secretary Dutt. They did not consider the

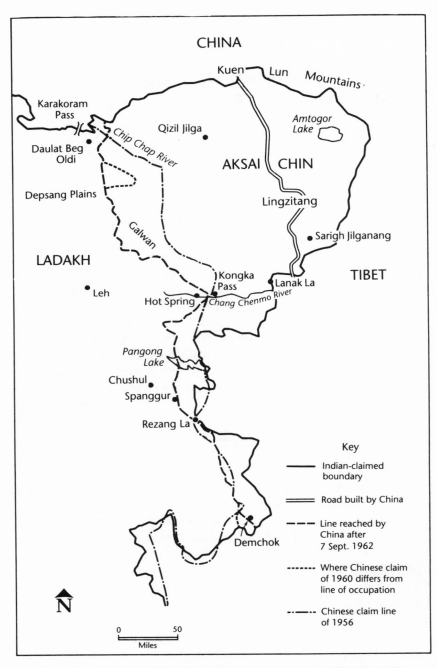

CHINA

Kuen Lun Mountains

Karakoram
Pass

Qizil Jilga

Amtogor
Lake

Chip Chap River

Daulat Beg
Oldi

AKSAI CHIN

Depsang Plains

Lingzitang

Galwan

Sarigh Jilganang

LADAKH

Kongka
Pass

Lanak La

TIBET

Leh

Hot Spring

Chang Chenmo River

Pangong
Lake

Chushul

Spanggur

Rezang La

Key

Indian-claimed
boundary

Road built by China

Demchok

Line reached by
China after
7 Sept. 1962

Where Chinese claim
of 1960 differs from
line of occupation

Chinese claim line
of 1956

N

0   50
Miles

Map 4.   AKSAI CHIN AND LOCATION OF KONGKA PASS.

Aksai Chin strategically important or logistically maintainable, and Dutt thought that these new posts would be unnecessary and provocative. But after further protests from Mullik in February 1959, the prime minister agreed to most of the posts Mullik wanted, but not the two near the Aksai Chin road.[2]

Yet even placement of the remaining posts, including one at Hot Spring near Kongka Pass, proved difficult for bureaucratic reasons and could be accomplished only by bureaucratic sleight-of-hand. Obstacles raised by home ministry officials during the spring of 1959 made it necessary for a desperate Mullik to bypass the ministry during the late summer and early fall. Major border incidents had already occurred; and Mullik—convinced that the approaching end of the good-weather season would delay installation of Indian posts for another year—turned to the Kashmir state government for help. The release of a company of Central Reserve Police then stationed in the Kashmir Valley, and its transport to Leh (in Ladakh) by the air force in late September, allowed another company of police, previously positioned at Leh, to move forward.

This company was commanded by the most experienced Indian patrol leader in Ladakh, one Karam Singh, who (the previous June) had taken a patrol through Hot Spring, Kongka Pass, and then forty miles further to Lanak La. No sign of a Chinese presence had been seen then, but this time (October 1959) the situation would change. After two Indian posts were opened, one of which was at Hot Spring, a small detachment (led by Karam Singh himself) got into a shooting incident with Chinese troops on 21 October. It happened two miles west of the pass, on the banks of the Chang Chenmo River.[3]

The Chinese viewed Kongka Pass as a border pass. In a diplomatic note sent on 25 October, the Chinese stated that they had been patrolling as far as Kongka Pass ever since the "liberation" of Sinkiang and Tibet.[4] Moreover, in a Foreign Office statement issued on 26 October, the Chinese said that if the Indians persisted in sending patrols into Chinese-held territory in Ladakh, China would have the right to do the same in NEFA.[5] Although the Indian decision-makers did not take this notice as an ultimatum, they judged it together with other Chinese references to NEFA and saw a larger meaning being conveyed by veiled threats. That meaning, as Nehru interpreted it in a memorandum to Indian ambassadors abroad, was that the Chinese would start trouble on the northeastern frontier unless India made a territorial concession on the northwestern frontier.[6]

In addition to the Indian perception of threat, the Chinese actions and statements reinforced the Indian perception of injury that had existed since the Tibetan affair of the previous spring.[7] Accounts of the Kongka Pass incident coming from the two sides naturally differed, but the fact that the Indians suffered nearly all the casualties gave credence to the Indian version. In demonstrating their control over the territory and their intention to keep it, the Chinese had deliberately opened fire from ambush, killing a number of Indian policemen and capturing the rest. Actual figures released at the time varied, but the final account seems to have been five killed, four wounded, and ten taken prisoner.[8]

There was also the matter of the treatment accorded to the captured Indian policemen. Considerable public attention was drawn to Indian government statements that the prisoners had been subjected to various forms of maltreatment, including prolonged interrogation, extremely primitive housing, and denial of medical care. Finally, they were forced to sign false confessions before being handed over to an Indian receiving party in Ladakh on 14 November. The policemen had not been treated according to international standards on war prisoners, when it might have been expected that their treatment would be substantially better. Indian diplomatic notes spoke of the "inhuman" treatment meted out to the prisoners, and the "shock" of the Indian government. It was made clear that the Chinese were lying about the treatment of the prisoners as well.[9]

The most important reactive decision on the Indian side was to give the army responsibility for the entire border, and not just NEFA. The army and the Ministry of Defense had resisted any such responsibility up to this point but now the army wanted to control IB activities along the China frontier. The decision was made at a meeting chaired by Nehru on 23 October. Present were the defense minister, the Chief of Army Staff, and representatives from the IB and the Ministries of External Affairs, Home Affairs and Defense.[10]

Reinforcement of the border was to be part of a long-term strategy. Required as part of that strategy, Nehru told parliament and the press, would be a program of strengthening Indian defenses and building up military capabilities. At the proper time, and if peaceful methods failed, India could undertake whatever defensive or offensive operations proved to be necessary. Recovering or protecting individual bits of territory was not the most urgent matter; instead, it was far more important to accelerate India's basic economic development so as to provide the industrial base for military strength. The impression given was that the construction of India's defense-related industries would be accelerated, and every effort would be made to overcome the obstacles posed by the sluggish Indian political system and governmental bureaucracy.[11]

If the government's military thinking was mainly long term, there was also what one military officer later called a "compulsive" and "hasty" movement of troops into NEFA. Contrary to the public impression given on 28 August, regular Indian troops had not been moved into the area to supplement and supervise the Assam Rifles already there. But now the army's Fourth Division (hereafter called 4 Division) was "rushed from the plains of the Punjab to Assam for deployment in the North East Frontier Agency. This Division was organized, equipped and trained for warfare in the plains—i.e., open country. Its transport and artillery were unsuitable for mountain warfare. In fact much heavy equipment was left behind in the foothills and useful manpower was wasted in maintaining this impedimenta. The officers and men were not acclimatized for high altitudes."[12] The division was moved despite the fact that winter was already setting in within NEFA, preventing movement of the troops much beyond the foothills until early 1960. There was little coordination with the civil NEFA administration, then under MEA jurisdiction.

In Ladakh, where similar haste was being shown, the army had to coordinate with the IB and with the Central Reserve Police units under IB control. One difficulty was that the army at first joined with the MEA in regarding the IB's recent placement of posts and patrols in northeast Ladakh (i.e., the China frontier) as irresponsible and provocative, and wanted a halt to any further activity by armed police without army clearance.[13]

Mullik had installed his Ladakh posts in the confidence that Nehru would support him if his initiative was seriously questioned. On 26 October his confidence proved justified when Nehru agreed that managing the IB posts all along the frontier, together with their communications, should remain an independent operation. Only the movements of armed police based in those posts would be controlled by the army.

Despite a change by Thimayya to a more cooperative frame of mind, the IB's operation in northeast Ladakh continued to constitute much of the Indian presence for a year longer. Although two battalions of Jammu and Kashmir militia were placed in northeast

Ladakh by early 1960, the army was not to station a regular battalion there until the summer of 1961. Mullik chafed at being restricted from ordering patrols sent out. He regarded the new policy as effectively immobilizing the Indian side, while the Chinese added to their Aksai Chin road system and occupied more territory.[14]

Yet, curiously enough, the Indian side rejected a Chinese proposal ostensibly designed to ease border tension, in part because the Nehru government would not agree in principle that Ladakh patrolling should be suspended. In a note dated 7 November 1959, Premier Chou En-lai reiterated a proposal that both the Indian and the Chinese governments had made earlier. It was that, as an interim measure, everywhere on the frontier "the status quo should be maintained and neither side should seek to alter the status quo by any means."[15]

Only with respect to NEFA and the Middle Sector of the border did Prime Minister Nehru intimate that both sides should stop forward patrolling. Chou questioned this idea in his note dated 17 December, but he told Nehru that after the Kongka Pass incident all frontier patrolling had been stopped by the Chinese side—a statement the Indians could hardly consider credible. Nehru too claimed to have halted patrolling, but only in the Eastern Sector.

Maintaining the status quo had been just one part of Chou's 7 November initiative. His key proposal was that, in order to create an atmosphere conducive to a friendly settlement, keep the frontier tranquil, and preserve the status quo, India and China should each withdraw their frontier forces a distance of 20 kilometers. In the Eastern Sector that withdrawal would be from the McMahon line. For Ladakh he proposed that each side withdraw 20 kilometers from the "line up to which each side exercises actual control." Neither side should send armed patrols into the areas from which they would withdraw, and neither side should create military posts in those areas. Only unarmed police and civil administrative personnel should be maintained in these places.[16]

The disadvantages to India if it were to accept these ideas were many. To accept would signify willingness to equate Indian control of NEFA with Chinese control of the Ladakh territory they had occupied, the extent of which had been fully revealed by the Kongka Pass attack.[17] From this time onward the Indian government would refuse to recognize any such equation. Moreover, the Indian government was determined not to grant legitimacy to the concept of a Chinese "line of control" in Ladakh. Such a concept had no historical validity, nor did it represent reality on the ground.

Another problem was that of terrain. Chinese possession of higher ground in both the Eastern and Western sectors, and their ability to move forward, backward, and laterally upon the barren Tibetan plateau, meant that after a withdrawal the Chinese could return to their former positions more easily than could the Indians, who would have to traverse difficult ridges and passes. Indeed, a 20-kilometer withdrawal in NEFA would take the Assam Rifles down to much lower altitudes and make any possible return much more arduous. Caught in the north-south valleys of NEFA, thick with vegetation, they could hardly move. Construction of a new line of posts in the Eastern Sector would also be easier for the Chinese than the Indians.[18]

The consensus in Delhi was that the Chou proposal was a trick.[19] Instead of rejecting it outright, however, and in order to get out of the defensive diplomatic position in which he had been placed, Nehru wanted to make a counteroffer. He then decided to permit the Chinese to "utilize the area in Aksai Chin across which they had built a road." This gesture did not imply a diminution of Indian sovereignty, in his view. However, no such Indian offer was made, because of opposition by Pandit Pant.[20]

Therefore, another idea (about the Western Sector) was presented to the Chinese in Prime Minister Nehru's 16 November (1959) letter to Chou En-lai.

> The Government of India should withdraw all personnel to the west of the line which the Chinese Government have shown as the international boundary in their 1956 maps. . . . Similarly the Chinese Government should withdraw their personnel to the east of the international boundary which has been described by the Government of India in their earlier notes and correspondence and shown in their official maps.[21]

Earlier in his note Nehru put the Longju area on a special footing, saying (as he had done previously) that it should simply be demilitarized. At a press conference he suggested that the Aksai Chin road could be used by Chinese civilian traffic but not military traffic, pending a final settlement.

If the Indian counterproposal had been accepted by the Chinese (and it was not), it would have involved their evacuating about 20,000 square miles and relinquishing their control over the Aksai Chin road.

For India it would have meant evacuating a section of about 50 square miles only, although important Indian positions in Ladakh would have been sacrificed. The Indian government had also made clear that there would be no agreement to move away from the McMahon line in NEFA or from positions anywhere outside of Ladakh, although India would agree to stop forward patrolling in those regions. In NEFA, where Indian and Chinese posts were not even within sight of each other, a cessation of patrolling by both sides would serve to avoid clashes, or so the Indian government believed.[22]

The Indian counterproposal had also embodied one precondition that the Nehru government had set earlier for any talks with the Chinese: Chinese withdrawal from disputed areas. This demand was now clearly and unambiguously extended to the Aksai Chin and all other recently seized parts of the Western Sector. A new and second precondition was that the two sides further expound their respective historical-legal positions to each other before any actual negotiating took place. This precondition was implied in Indian demands that the Chinese respond to the historical views and facts set forth in Nehru's 26 September note to Chou En-lai and in a note sent by the MEA on 4 November.

With the dispatch of the MEA's note, the entire border alignment claimed by India in the Western Sector was described in detailed terms for the first time.[23] Only a limited section of this border had been described to the Chinese previously, and it had not included the Aksai Chin.[24] Here was another sign that the official Indian position on the Aksai Chin had hardened.

Behind such signs was a process by which Prime Minister Nehru abandoned his doubts about the historical case for the Aksai Chin. That process had begun after the release of the first White Paper in September, but it was accelerated by the Kongka Pass incident and his conviction that the Chinese had become fundamentally hostile. Yet Nehru would not be satisfied until he had thrashed the matter out thoroughly with the MEA's director of the Historical Division, Sarvepalli Gopal.

In late 1959 Gopal had just returned from several months of documentary research in London. That same year he had also consulted the Kashmir archives in Srinagar and Jammu. Certain that the Indian case for the Aksai Chin was sound, Gopal was able to influence Nehru. He found the prime minister, after the Kongka Pass affair, in a receptive frame of mind—a "malleable mood." Nehru wanted to be convinced; his general attitude was one of defiance and resistance against the idea of handing over the territory to the Chinese.[25]

Yet the historian in Nehru still believed that historical evidence should provide the basis for any decision. Only in February 1960 did Gopal take him completely through the evidence (in a three- to four-hour session at Nehru's home) and finally convince him that India's claim to the Aksai Chin was sound. The prime minister then told a cabinet meeting that he was persuaded. But not until the publication of the massive Officials' Report in February 1961, containing both the Indian and Chinese cases covering the entire border, did Nehru tell parliament that he considered the Indian case almost "foolproof."[26]

Whatever Nehru wanted to do, the aroused parliament and press had by now placed severe pressures on his government. He had resisted demands, from critics in his own party and in the opposition, that India stage military reprisals and break off diplomatic relations with China. Nor would he agree to ask for military aid from the West.

Yet Nehru was no longer (nor did he consider himself) the uninhibited master of India's foreign policy he had once been.[27] Whether a determined Nehru could have kept open the option of a compromise settlement with the Chinese if he had chosen to do so, despite the public clamor, is difficult to gauge. In any event, this was no longer an option he considered seriously, given the conclusion that the Chinese had become permanently hostile.

Instead, he turned to both the West and the Communist world to add to the diplomatic pressure India was placing on the Chinese. In public Nehru pointedly and openly contrasted the peaceful intentions of the Soviet Union and the aggressive nature of the People's Republic of China.[28] In so doing, he not only indicated his belief that friendly relations with the Soviet Union could be maintained but also strengthened his efforts to show the Chinese how alone they were in their hostility and aggressiveness toward India. However, he did not expect the Soviets to want to influence the Chinese directly, or to be able to do so.[29]

Relations with the United States were also featured in this international drive. Improved ties between India and America were demonstrated by the visit of President Eisenhower to India in December 1959. The acute India-China tension and the anti-Chinese sentiment helped make the visit successful and gratifying for the Americans; hundreds of thousands turned out to greet the president in

New Delhi. Although the American government would not declare support for the Indian historical-legal position on the border dispute, it had already (in November) endorsed India's peaceful efforts to settle that dispute. There had also been American condemnation of China's use of force.[30]

In order to maintain India's own direct pressure on China, Nehru was at this time determined to refuse a bid from Chou En-lai for summit-level talks. In his note of 7 November, and again in a letter dated 17 December, Premier Chou had urged Nehru to agree to a meeting, so that tensions could be eased and agreements on "principles" could be reached "as a guidance to concrete discussions and settlement of the boundary question by the two sides." To make his proposal concrete, Chou in the latter note suggested 26 December as a possible date for a meeting in China, although he declared himself willing to come to Rangoon if Nehru found coming to China inconvenient. He was further prepared to consider any other date Nehru might suggest.[31]

The Indian side would not come to talks on 26 December unless its previously stated preconditions were met. Nehru did not rule out talks at some later time, and he publicly stated his willingness to talk, as a matter of principle. But he made clear that the suggestions he had made on 16 November (see above) for relieving frontier tension should be considered first. Moreover, the implicit Indian position was that no discussions could be predicated on the idea that the entire border was undelimited and therefore open to bargaining. The border was historic and traditional, and discussions should be a matter of comparing India's and China's differing claims to a fixed boundary line. For such discussions to take place, India would need a clearer idea of the line claimed by the Chinese.[32]

The policy followed by the Nehru government at the end of 1959 was therefore a policy of pressure on the Chinese to change their minds, but a subtle and "heavily nuanced" policy rather than a crude one. Talks had not been ruled out, but there would be "no yielding on the basic issues."[33] Recovery of territory was not yet a goal, so that patrolling for that purpose was prohibited, and border police and troops would only serve for the moment to prevent further losses.[34]

In late January 1960 India finally acquiesced to Chou En-lai's request for a summit meeting. Nehru made the decision in close consultation with the Foreign Affairs Subcommittee of the cabinet on or about 31 January.[35] Among his reasons for doing so were that in

January a high-level Soviet official delegation was paying a visit to Delhi and Premier Khrushchev was expected shortly (he passed through twice in February). In the context of considering the interests of the Soviets, who were trying to balance their relationships with China and India, the Nehru government could see some merit in trying to talk with the Chinese.[36] The Indians adopted this view despite the fact that the Sino-Indian border dispute was not discussed with the visiting Soviet delegation and was barely mentioned in the private talks held between Nehru and Khrushchev.[37]

In part the decision reflected Nehru's own self-confidence. He hoped that even at this late date he could move Premier Chou to see that wrong had been committed by the Chinese side and that some attempt to repair relations should be made. Ever the optimist, Nehru wanted to make what might be called "the gambler's last throw."[38] Influencing him to some degree was a recent Chinese note, which calmly and reassuringly denied that China wished to expand and expressed a desire for a reasonable settlement of the dispute.[39]

A summit meeting would also fit well with Nehru's belief in always maintaining communications, even between international enemies. But, as Nehru made clear when defending himself publicly against charges of inconsistency, these "talks" would be held to ease tensions; they would not constitute "negotiations" in the sense of bargaining sessions.[40]

What the Chinese prime minister was likely to say at the forthcoming summit could be anticipated from the contents of diplomatic notes and other sources. One of those sources was Chinese diplomatic activity between January and April 1960. In January China and Burma had come to a boundary settlement, in which the Chinese had accepted a section of the McMahon line. But Burma had been required to concede that the border had never been properly delimited and that the new line was the result of fresh negotiations. In March the Nepalese and the Chinese agreed to work toward resolving discrepancies in their conceptions of the Nepal-Tibet border. In dealing with both Burma and Nepal, the Chinese obtained agreement to use joint boundary commissions for survey work and for dealing with minor territorial problems.

Plainly, this was an appropriate and reasonable way to delimit a border, in the Chinese view. But for an Indian government determined not to declare the entire 2,000-mile border open to new delimitation, a more sinister conclusion was drawn from China's dealings with Nepal

and Burma—namely, that China was trying to isolate India, preparatory to forcing on India a boundary settlement based on China's
extensive claims. The same interpretation would shortly be made of
China's dealings with Pakistan. China's effort to secure nonaggression
agreements as well, aimed at keeping Burma and Nepal removed from
any possible hostilities between China and India, was perceived in
New Delhi as illustrative of the real aims of Chinese diplomacy.[41]

The Indian government's intense preparatory activity for the April
talks included the writing of briefs, many of which were used not in
April but at later talks by Indian and Chinese officials.[42] Such
preparation was itself part of a continuing process of examining
alternatives, which took place among Indian decision-makers and
their consultants during the second half of 1959 and early 1960. At this
time several senior MEA officials who favored a political solution to
the Sino-Indian border problem, rather than one based on the
historical evidence, were making their views known either in Delhi or
from abroad.[43]

The prime minister had already made up his mind not to trade
territory with the Chinese, as can be seen from his remarks at a private
meeting held at "the turn of" 1959–60. One of those present recalled
him saying: "If I give them that I shall no longer be Prime Minister
of India—I will not do it."[44] He did not just mean that public and
parliamentary attitudes would be a problem. He also felt that
bartering would be a wrongful act on the part of an Indian prime
minister after the way China had simply seized territory along the
frontier.[45]

From most accounts of the summit meetings in New Delhi on
20–25 April, one of Chou En-lai's gambits was to hint that a barter
arrangement could be devised. Chinese claims to NEFA would be
abandoned in return for India's forgoing any claims to the Aksai Chin
and to all other parts of the Western Sector already under Chinese
control.[46] Chou made at least two public allusions to this offer: during
a press conference in New Delhi on 25 April and in a written statement
issued at the press conference, wherein "six points" of alleged
commonality or proximity between the positions of Indian and
Chinese governments were listed. But the fact that Chou was cautious
and elliptical in his public remarks, just as he had been in private,
suggested that the offer was tentative and could be withdrawn.

The Indian rejection of the entire Chinese approach was unequivo-
cal. Behind that reaction was the sense that India was being asked to

accept the clandestine and forceful seizure of parts of its territory, in return for a worthless assurance that another part of the frontier would not be menaced. Moreover, the Chinese were trying to induce India to abandon the argument that the border was a traditional one, delimited by custom, treaty, and geography. If the Nehru government acceded to this ploy, India's entire northern border would be placed on the bargaining counter, and future negotiations would involve debate with the Chinese over purely arbitrary and changeable claim lines. In the end the Chinese might demand a high price in Ladakh in return for suspension of their claim to NEFA.[47]

Nor was the Nehru government in a domestic position to respond with interest to the Chou probe. The April talks had occasioned public protest, including a massive demonstration led by an opposition party and staged in front of the prime minister's residence.[48] Nehru received the leaders and pledged firmness with the Chinese. The Indian press in April was printing fairly accurate information about the contents of the talks, as they were taking place, and parliamentary questioning was insistent.

The prime minister agreed with what he took to be public opinion.[49] He rejected publicly what he came to call "barter" and "horse-trading" and favored the historical approach to border delimitation.[50] He informed parliament that he had rejected a Chinese argument that they had "constructively" occupied the Western Sector for the last two centuries, in contrast to India's having occupied NEFA effectively only during the past few years. Apparently, he had insisted to Chou En-lai that India had exercised continuous jurisdiction over all of Ladakh, whereas the Chinese had only recently come there. Nehru reported that the Chinese were looking upon the Eastern and Western sectors as if they could somehow be "equated" for the purposes of a settlement.[51] To that he could not agree.

The response to Chou's ideas at the summit meetings in New Delhi was influenced by the intense perception of injury held by his Indian hosts. From the moment Chou En-lai, Foreign Minister Chen Yi, and their party had arrived at Palam airport, and even at ceremonial functions, Indian treatment of these guests was meant to convey the widespread sense of grievance felt throughout the Indian government and nation, and the need for certain things to be undone. Chou En-lai (and members of his delegation) had met not only with Nehru but also with Pandit Pant, Finance Minister Morarji Desai, Defense Minister Krishna Menon, and Vice President Sarvepalli Radhakrishnan. Some

Indian officials and lesser politicians were present at these discussions too. Pant and Desai each lectured the Chinese on the wrongs they had committed.[52]

Clearly, the April 1960 prime ministers' meetings were a failure. Any real chance for acceptance of what Premier Chou was offering had been forfeited months before, as a result of the Kongka Pass incident. Prime Minister Nehru's rejection of the Chinese position during the April talks brought to a final decision the Indian process of considering alternatives, which had started the previous August. This was perhaps the most important Indian decision of the pre-crisis period, and it was fully supported by Pandit Pant and by the officials who advised both Pant and Nehru. One may assume, too, that there was support from the rest of the Foreign Affairs Subcommittee of the cabinet, with the exception of Krishna Menon, who was still seeking a political settlement.[53]

Only one positive decision was made jointly by Nehru and Chou En-lai during the talks. In keeping with the pattern established by China with Burma and Nepal, Chou raised with Nehru the possibility of joint border commissions going to the frontier. The Indian prime minister, acting consistently with his view of the India-China border as already delimited and needing only minor adjustments at best, countered with the suggestion that Indian and Chinese officials meet to examine the documentary evidence. After Chou remarked that his Chinese delegation had come to Delhi to deal with principles rather than details, the two agreed to have meetings held, in the immediate future, between teams of officials from both sides. At the meetings these officials would try to determine the facts of the boundary alignment by examining the relevant documentary material and would ultimately prepare some kind of report.[54]

The decision to hold the officials' talks represented a concession by Chou En-lai. Instead of a joint Sino-Indian survey team trying to delimit the border on the ground, the respective historical-legal cases of the two countries would be examined.

Indian and Chinese officials met from June to December 1960. One conference was held in Peking from 15 June to 25 July; the next, in New Delhi from 19 August to 5 October; and the last, in Rangoon from 7 November to 12 December. The Indian team contained many of the MEA officials who had been advising Nehru and Pant for the last year or so. The team leader was J. S. Mehta, then director of the China Division. He was closely supported by S. Gopal, director of the

Historical Division. The other members were T. S. Murty, who had been political officer in Tawang during the time of the 1959 border incidents; V. V. Paranjpe, a China expert who had been assisting Mehta; and G. N. Rao, a specialist on the historical-legal side. There were other informal advisers as well.[55]

The Indian officials did not have much hope that the Chinese would be converted by exposure to all the historical material supporting the Indian case, although one of them thought that by the end of the talks some persuasion had taken place.[56] As a matter of strategy, Mehta sought to have the Chinese record their Western Sector claims on an authoritative map or a list of map coordinates. That way the conferees could see what the discrepancies between the claims of the two sides actually were. But Mehta's basic idea was that, once the Chinese specified a precise line, they would have admitted the existence of a traditional border in Ladakh—a border formed by a historical process that was legal (i.e., legitimate) even without a formal delimiting treaty.[57]

Under Indian pressure the Chinese officials did produce a new map of the entire China-India border, and it would thereafter take precedence over the smaller and less distinct 1956 map previously mentioned in China's diplomatic correspondence. The Chinese did not think they had an untenable argument, however, since they had already agreed that there was a "traditional customary line." Their version of it was generally based on the Karakoram range in the Western Sector, the main Himalayan range in the Middle Sector, and the southern edge of the Himalayan foothills in the Eastern Sector.

Like the Indians, the Chinese claimed that their boundary had a long historic past. But the Ladakh portion of it had probably been drawn by arbitrarily linking together geographical points that had only come under their control in the 1950s and 1960s.[58] They rejected the idea that the China-India border was delimited and sacrosanct. Their argument was that the line primarily reflected administrative practice and usage—that is, this was the line up to which the two sides had exercised actual control. The Chinese did not think it important that every detail of the line be known. Formal, legal, and final delimitation of territory by means of a precisely drawn border could be done only via contemporary negotiation between the two governments concerned.

The Indian team sought to display its massive store of historical evidence. But the Chinese—because their store of documentation was relatively small, and given their argument that the boundary remained undelimited—relied heavily on "negative evidence," or loopholes in Indian evidence and reasoning, to disprove Indian contentions.[59] Nonetheless, the relationship between the two teams of officials was sufficiently cordial to permit them to put together a lengthy report describing the evidence each side had presented and the conclusions each side had reached. It was not really a single document; each team had compiled its own report. The entire package was completed in December 1960 and published by the Government of India in February 1961. Although it was later shown to contain some errors, the Officials' Report came to be regarded as the most authoritative version of the Indian historical-legal case. Certainly it was the most exhaustive.

The report confirmed Nehru's growing conviction that the Aksai Chin case was sound; he presented copies to visiting diplomats as part of his effort to enlist international support for India.[60] He also hoped that the report, and its historical meaning, would make the Chinese uncomfortable enough to admit error and voluntarily change their policies.[61] "Does not Hon. Member realize," Nehru later asked in a parliamentary debate, "the pressure on the Chinese Government which is being constantly exercised by the facts, by India's attitude supported as it is by all these facts?"[62]

To probe Chinese reactions to the report and to Indian publication of it, the MEA's secretary-general, R. K. Nehru (Jawaharlal Nehru's cousin), was sent to talk to Chinese leaders during July 1961. For both diplomatic and Indian domestic reasons, the meeting could not look like a specially staged event; the scenario presented publicly was that the secretary-general was returning from a visit to Mongolia by way of China and supposedly paying a courtesy call on certain Chinese leaders. As a former ambassador to Peking, he knew them well.

R. K. Nehru was a member of the earlier generation of Indian officials who had helped to forge the close India-China ties of the 1954–1958 period. Like some of them, who perhaps felt that their achievements should not have been so transitory, he believed that a negotiated solution to the border conflict could be reached. At the back of his mind in 1961 was the idea of India's giving up the Aksai Chin and getting in return Tibet's strategically important Chumbi Valley.[63] (See Map 1.) He may have hinted at this suggestion during his China talks, raising false hopes in his Chinese listeners. One Chinese official reacted to R. K. Nehru's later description (in India) of his China mission by accusing him of prevaricating and of abusing Chinese hospitality. The secretary-general's impression of his meetings with Chou En-lai and Chen Yi, however, was that the two sides had merely repeated their cases "with a smile."[64]

The prime minister's assessment of the R. K. Nehru mission was that, although Chou had agreed to examine the Officials' Report, the Chinese position had not markedly changed.[65] Nehru thought that the Indian and Chinese governments, either separately or jointly, should give further consideration to the Officials' Report.[66] This would remain his view until the outbreak of war in 1962.

CHAPTER SEVEN

Strategic Decisions, 29 July 1961 to 7 September 1962

THE "FORWARD POLICY" DECISION

DURING THE LAST part of the period preceding the 1962 crisis, India's decision-makers were persuaded that the Chinese were taking over even more Indian territory in Ladakh. Their response, developed at the urging of their closest official consultants and based on past policy trends, was to add a form of military pressure to the Indian government's evolving list of tactics. A definite decision to do so was made on 2 November 1961. No real military threat was posed to the Chinese; the Indian military effort was mainly symbolic. Nevertheless, by September 1962 the Indian government thought that it had achieved some success in safeguarding territory claimed by China but not yet taken, and in recovering some territory previously lost.

One source of the new policy was the map that showed the 1960 Chinese claim line, that is to say, the map that the Chinese delegation had presented at the officials' talks. It indicated that the Chinese had substantially enlarged their claims to territory in the Western Sector (see Map 5). Another source was the increasing commitment of the Nehru government, starting in the winter of 1959–60, to a policy of maintaining an adequate physical presence along the frontier. Although Nehru had long wanted to have a network of border checkposts,[1] it was only from 1959–60 onward that a line of Indian posts came to be placed ahead of the Chinese advance. In the Western Sector it was assumed that Indian patrols could readily go into the no man's land between the two sides (20 to 50 miles wide, except near the Indian position at Demchok). But, in order to avoid the possibility of clashes with the Chinese, no program of patrolling had been undertaken.

Indian policy evolved a step further at a meeting chaired by Krishna Menon in May 1960. One of its concerns was establishing a military

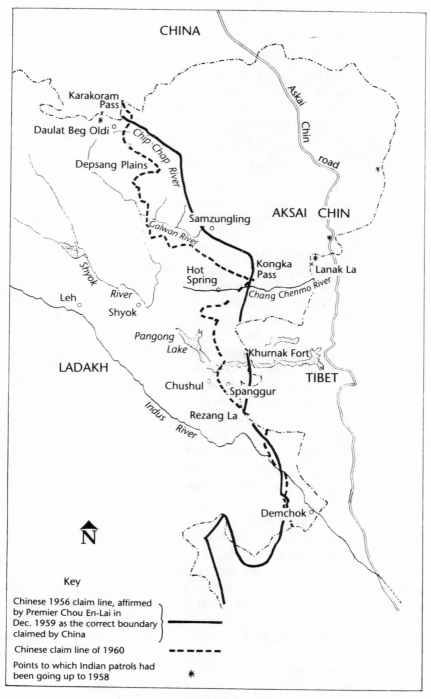

CHINA

Karakoram Pass

Daulat Beg Oldi

Chip-Chap River

Depsang Plains

Askai Chin road

AKSAI CHIN

Samzungling

Galwan River

Hot Spring

Kongka Pass

Lanak La

Chang Chenmo River

Shyok River

Leh

Shyok

Pangong Lake

Khurnak Fort

TIBET

LADAKH

Chushul

Spanggur

Rezang La

Indus River

Demchok

N

Key

Chinese 1956 claim line, affirmed by Premier Chou En-Lai in Dec. 1959 as the correct boundary claimed by China

Chinese claim line of 1960

Points to which Indian patrols had been going up to 1958

Map 5. CHINESE CLAIM LINES OF 1956 AND 1960 IN THE WESTERN SECTOR.

presence along the old trade route to Sinkiang, which ran through Karakoram Pass. At the meeting it was decided that

> the Army should establish itself on the old trade route running north from Shyok, and set up a post as near the Karakoram Pass as possible. When this had been done the possibility of patrolling eastward up the Chip Chap Valley would be explored. In the meantime, unoccupied areas were to be patrolled; but the troops were to avoid clashes and, if they encountered Chinese, to report their position without attempting to dislodge them.[2]

A proposal that Indian posts, and not just patrols, be placed in unoccupied territory across the Chinese claim line was contained in a memorandum signed by Foreign Secretary Dutt later that same month (29 May 1960).

For logistical reasons, however, and because of its reluctance to provoke a Chinese reaction, the army (then still led by General Thimayya) resisted any thought of becoming more active in territory claimed by the Chinese. Therefore, at the end of the summer, despite pressure on the army from civilian officials, Army Headquarters in New Delhi issued orders providing only for patrols into Chinese-claimed (but not yet occupied) areas. The final say on even this decision was left to Western Command Headquarters in Kashmir.[3] General Thimayya had also made clear to Western Command in June 1960 that forward posts should be established only to prevent further Chinese infiltration and strengthen existing Indian defensive positions. The army's main mission in Ladakh, he wrote, was to guard the main approaches to Ladakh and to make certain that Leh, the major town, was defended.[4] Whatever the civilians might want, Thimayya would not sanction the construction of posts simply to occupy territory.

The major reason for continued civilian pressure on the army was that the IB had provided a flow of information showing forward movement by the Chinese. In May 1960 the news from the IB was of Chinese "reconnaissance, probing, surveys, and road-building much beyond the line claimed by them in 1956."[5] Both the central and southern parts of the Ladakh front were thought to be under threat. Other IB reports followed in September and November 1960, the second of which occasioned another meeting chaired by Krishna Menon. The army chiefs, Mullik, and the foreign and defense secretaries were all present.

Krishna Menon wanted to prevent the Chinese from moving west beyond their new circular road. Nor were the Chinese to be allowed to extend that road toward Hot Spring or have troops enter the territories south of the Chang Chenmo (see Maps 4 and 5). An army detachment was based at Hot Spring and other measures were taken, but the year ended with only the Hot Spring area and the populated southeast part of Ladakh considered safe from encroachment.

The question of what step to take next came up at a meeting of the cabinet's Foreign Affairs Subcommittee, held at Pandit Pant's house sometime in January or early February 1961. In the presence of Nehru, Pant, and other cabinet ministers, Krishna Menon brought up the idea of "zigzagging." If the Chinese were placing their posts in Indian territory, the Indians could place posts behind them and closer to the Indian-claimed border. When Pant had him elaborate further, Krishna Menon demonstrated by tapping his walking stick on the floor to show how posts might be patterned ("like this, Pantji").[6] MEA officials were present as well, and one of them recalled (in 1983) that the proposal was accepted. Other events would occur, however, before it actually was accepted.

One such event was the appearance of a new command team at Army Headquarters during the spring of 1961. Thimayya was being replaced as Chief of Army Staff by Lieutenant General P. N. Thapar, and the new Chief of General Staff (CGS) was Lieutenant General B. M. Kaul. Both of the new men proved to be more cooperative with Krishna Menon and Mullik on the matter of positioning troops in Ladakh. Accordingly, the post near Karakoram Pass (Daulat Beg Oldi, established by the IB in the spring or summer of 1960) was reinforced. Army units went elsewhere in Ladakh as well, either to already existing IB posts or to new posts of their own, while still more posts were implanted by the IB independently or jointly with the army.[7]

In early 1961 the IB noticed frequent Chinese patrolling along the Ladakh frontier. After May 1961 road construction by the Chinese was also taking place along much of the frontier, including NEFA and northeastern Ladakh (where it was extending toward the Chinese 1960 claim line).[8] In September 1961 the army discovered that the Chinese had established a post in the Chip Chap Valley, barely four miles east of Daulat Beg Oldi. Furthermore, a motorable road was discovered leading to the Chip Chap post, and Chinese troops attempted to encircle an Indian patrol.[9] On the basis of this informa- tion, the Ministry of External Affairs (presumably the China Division and the foreign secretary) concluded that the Chinese were attempting

to move up to their 1960 claim line in some strength. It was a new foreign secretary, M. J. Desai, who then took the initiative by raising the
matter with Army Headquarters.

Normally, the foreign secretary would have dealt with General
Kaul, who as Chief of General Staff held the second most important
post at Army Headquarters. But Kaul was abroad, so M. J. Desai dealt
with the officiating Chief of General Staff, Major General D. N.
Misra, and the recently appointed Director of Military Operations
(DMO), Brigadier D. K. Palit. As Palit recalled later, Desai was
thinking that "one of the most effective methods of stemming the
Chinese policy of gradually creeping westwards across our borders in
Ladakh would be to give them an occasional knock during these
chance encounters within our own territory and to engage them in a
short offensive action aimed at inflicting casualties and for taking
prisoners."[10] Among the results of these discussions was a request for
a written evaluation from the IB.[11]

The IB agreed with the MEA's assessment and sent a note on 26 September 1961, which made two salient points: (1) The Chinese wanted
to come right up to their 1960 claim line wherever the territory was not
under Indian occupation. (2) But "where a dozen men of ours are
present the Chinese have kept away" (that is, the Chinese have kept
away even when the territory was under only token occupation).[12]
Having described Chinese incursions and other activities since June
1959, the IB note urged the army to fill the Ladakh vacuums that still
existed, and to do so as soon as possible with tokens of Indian
possession. A similar request was made for NEFA, where gaps along
the McMahon line needed to be filled. The IB note gave the impression
that all this Indian activity was not likely to produce a major reaction
from the Chinese.[13]

These ultimately erroneous conclusions and recommendations
would dominate Indian decision-making up to the start of the 1962
war. But in 1961 they were natural ones for the IB to make, not only for
logical reasons, based on prior information, but also for reasons of
bureaucratic politics. Despite increased cooperation by Army Headquarters, IB director Mullik still regarded the army as a hindrance,
because its logistical incapabilities required withdrawal of some
Indian posts during the winter. So intense were his concerns for
Ladakh that Mullik proposed to have IB posts remain for the coming
months even without army protection. The army changed its mind
and decided to increase its support for the Ladakh posts after the

Chinese Chip Chap post and other Chinese activities were discovered. But apparently there was still resistance to Mullik at Army Headquarters. Army Chief Thapar thought that it was impossible to determine when the Chinese Chip Chap post had been planted.[14] Thapar's assumption was that if the post was not new, it did not signify an enhanced Chinese threat. Mullik therefore had to show that his conclusions were correct and win ultimate approval for the program he wanted.

Fortunately for Mullik, he had an ally in Defense Minister Krishna Menon, who held meetings with Thapar and his Army Headquarters staff during October, mainly "to heckle Thapar about the Army's 'inactivity' on the borders."[15] Krishna Menon was probably concerned about the hard questioning that the government was facing in parliament over China policy, and would encounter again over the new Chinese advances.

Mullik was also making his larger concerns about Ladakh known to Home Minister Lal Bahadur Shastri (Pant having died) and Prime Minister Nehru. He had three lengthy meetings with Nehru, using maps to show the "extent of Chinese penetration...since October 1959, and the areas where gaps existed into which the Chinese might intrude any moment as they were then poised all along our frontier."[16] After a fourth such meeting, held on 2 November 1961, Nehru invited Mullik to come to a general discussion session to be held at Nehru's house that day. Among those attending were Krishna Menon; Lieutenant General Thapar; Lieutenant General Kaul; Brigadier Palit; M. J. Desai; the defense secretary, O. Pulla Reddy. The session was to be another important turning point in the Sino-Indian conflict. The official minutes of the meeting contained the following directives:

> (a) So far as Ladakh is concerned we are to patrol as far forward as possible from our present positions towards the international border. This will be done with a view to establishing our posts which should prevent the Chinese from advancing any further and also dominating from any posts which they may have already established in our territory. This must be done without getting involved in a clash with the Chinese, unless this becomes necessary in self-defense.
> (b) As regards U.P. [Uttar Pradesh—i.e., the Middle Sector] and other northern areas there are not the same difficulties as in Ladakh. We should, therefore, as far as practicable, go forward and be in effective occupation of the whole frontier. Where there are any gaps they must be covered either by patrolling or by posts.

(c) In view of the numerous operational and administrative difficulties, efforts should be made to position major concentrations of forces along our borders in places conveniently situated behind the forward posts from where they could be maintained logistically and from where they can restore a border situation at short notice.[17]

The order to patrol as far as the international (i.e., Indian-claimed) border, with a view to setting up posts, was the key feature of the directive. But important too was the use of the word *dominate*. It was a military term, understood by any commander to mean "observe and cover."[18] The idea was that an Indian post should be better situated tactically than an opposing Chinese post. When applied in Ladakh shortly thereafter, the "dominate" concept would mean being in a position to threaten the lines of communication and supply to Chinese posts wherever possible.

According to accounts of the 2 November meeting, objections were raised by the military personnel over the various problems involved. The prime minister was told that numerical and logistical obstacles would prevent the Indian side from keeping up in a race with the Chinese. Eventually, Chinese posts could not be matched in numbers, and Chinese resources could make the positions of Indian posts untenable.[19] Thapar pointed out that new posts could not be given logistical or tactical support. Brigadier Palit noted that the term *tactical support* means the ability to reinforce and resupply an Indian post caught in a firefight with a Chinese patrol that is superior in fire power or numbers. These warnings were not made too strenuously, in the face of Nehru's assurance that he did not expect any firefights.[20]

Army Headquarters did not transmit the new orders to Western and Eastern Commands until 5 December. The point about forward positions being supported by concentrations of troops further back was not mentioned at all. This omission has been explained in various fashions.[21] One of the more compelling, derived from recently revealed information, is that Army Headquarters did not feel entirely bound by the minutes of the meeting. That document came not from Nehru's somewhat rambling instructions but from subsequent drafting by the MEA secretary-general, R. K. Nehru, who may not have been in the room on 2 November. The directive about establishing bases had never been mentioned at the meeting; from the army perspective it was "an afterthought" of the MEA bureaucrats "seeking to hedge their bets."[22]

Moreover, Army Headquarters perceived the task of siting new forward posts and the need to build up a defensive capacity in Ladakh as two separate matters; one was not necessarily dependent on the other. Whereas new forward posts were supposed to establish an Indian administrative presence as close to the border as possible, the establishment of bases behind these posts was supposed to provide for the security of the country against military intrusion or even invasion. Such security would not exist if large army formations were stationed in frontier positions without adequate logistical support. The army had only agreed to man the forward posts because it had been so ordered, and for civilians to urge a larger buildup behind them was merely gratuitous advice—especially since the army had made clear at the meeting on 2 November that it could not send reinforcements to Ladakh until a road link was completed between Ladakh and India proper. The government had also been told that the army was not capable of strongly supporting posts "forward of Leh and Chushul airfields because of lack of roads, mules and porters. Airdrops were the only method of resupply—and this alternative was restricted both by weather conditions and because of lack of sufficient aircraft."[23]

It was Kaul who decided, in consultation with Palit, that the offending paragraph in the MEA draft could be omitted from the instructions to Western Command.[24] The implication was that Western Command's major defensive mission was still to guard the approaches to Leh, although the new patrolling and post-building program would have to be pursued as well.

Although there was no perception of specific time limitations in implementing what soon came to be known (both inside and outside of government circles) as the "forward policy," there was a sense of urgency. Indian troops were sent forward to patrol and establish posts in Ladakhi valleys under winter conditions, with inadequate clothing and logistical support. The usual altitude was approximately 14,000 feet, but patrols went up to 16,000 feet at the passes.[25] Behind this effort was Kaul, who wanted plans speeded up so as to induct more troops into Ladakh in 1962. He expected increased allocations of aircraft for the stocking of posts in both Ladakh and NEFA. "We had the whole winter to plan in, he said, and it would be wrong to assume from now that we would lack operational capacity in Ladakh in six months time."[26]

No overall plan for the "forward policy" in Ladakh was ever formulated by Army Headquarters under General Kaul's direction. Instead, a series of orders were issued, some written and some verbal, covering specific areas and often dictating the establishment and siting of particular posts. These orders were formulated by Kaul personally, along with his staff members, in close consultation with IB director Mullik and his deputy. Nehru, Krishna Menon, Thapar, and Foreign Secretary M. J. Desai also took part in formulating these orders. All this was highly unusual for the Indian Army or any other army, since small-unit troop dispositions are generally left to the discretion of the area commanders. Equally unorthodox was the Army Headquarters practice of naming routes that patrol and reconnaissance parties should take.

Kaul and his staff sometimes communicated directly with corps commanders, thereby bypassing their superiors in charge of the army's Western and Eastern Commands. One reason this last activity was undertaken was because of the known reluctance of Lieutenant General Daulat Singh, the new commanding officer for Western Command, to agree to forward policy actions he considered risky.[27]

After December 1961, when the policy was applied to NEFA as well, resistance came from the commander of XXXIII Corps, Lieutenant General Umrao Singh (rather than from the commanding officer for Eastern Command, Lieutenant General L. P. Sen). At a meeting in Gauhati in February 1962, Kaul sought to browbeat the NEFA commanders into submission.[28] Partly because of that, and partly because Kaul and Umrao Singh were old friends, Umrao was pushed into implementing what Delhi wanted, although some modifications suggested by Umrao were accepted. The new NEFA posts began to be placed in April.[29]

Perhaps the most unusual feature of the forward policy decision was its predication on the assumption by Indian civilians that Indian military capabilities would allow the army to acquit itself well if the Chinese unexpectedly overreacted to Indian activities. Public assurances provided by the prime minister, starting in late 1959, and information provided privately by other government spokesmen, gave the press the impression that the army was capable of defending the borders against any known threats, although more so in NEFA than in Ladakh.[30] The military realities, as they certainly should have been known to Indian decision-makers, were very different. Military contingency plans, forged in the winter of 1959–60, had never been implemented. The reasons for this lapse require some explanation.

A contingency defense plan for NEFA had been offered in October

1959 by the then commanding officer for Eastern Command, Lieutenant General S. S. P. Thorat. The central concept of Thorat's paper was that an inner-line defense be adopted, wherein major defensive positions would be placed well to the rear rather than in the high ridges close to the border. An invading Chinese army would be forced to stretch its supply routes over those ridges, and would thus arrive at the Indian line at a distinct logistical disadvantage.

Thorat's plan became army policy in early 1960. That policy envisaged a front line of forward posts on the border, backed by two other tiers of military strongpoints. The first line of posts would be of the flag-flying variety—that is, symbols of territorial possession and early-warning beacons. The second line would consist of more substantial posts, which could slow down the advancing Chinese and increase their logistical problems. At the last line the Chinese would be stopped, and from there counteroffensives would be launched after Indian reinforcements had arrived. This line would necessarily be located at various tactical strongpoints, such as important passes. These strongpoints were to dominate the strategic north-south valleys of the NEFA terrain.

The NEFA plan was tested in an elaborate sand-model war game, staged at Eastern Command Headquarters in Lucknow in April 1960. The results showed that the plan could not be implemented with less than a division of four brigades (most Indian divisions contained three brigades). In an emergency more troops (approximately one division) would be brought up from nearby Nagaland (see Map 1) to reinforce them.[31]

In early 1961 the Chief of General Staff, General L. P. Sen, raised the minimum requirement for NEFA's defense to two divisions (six brigades) and urged the posting of the needed second division. But only one division was assigned to NEFA before the outbreak of the 1962 war. That division, moreover, was not maintained at its (1960) recommended strength. Instead, 4 Division was deprived of one of its three brigades when Army Headquarters decided to strengthen the force engaged in suppressing the then festering rebellion of the Nagas. Only one brigade (7 Brigade) was on hand in the Tawang-Bomdila (see Map 7) area at the start of the 1962 crisis. Another brigade was stretched out to cover the rest of NEFA.[32]

Ultimately, the three-tier plan was abandoned. In its place a "defense line" was projected, made up of positions that were to have been on the third and rearmost line, but including positions further forward (most important, at Tawang) to guard against Chinese incursions.[33] Even this plan was never implemented.

There were several reasons for the failure to implement plans for the defense of NEFA.[34] Foremost was the fact that the army's General Staff (first under Thimayya and later under Kaul and Thapar) did not press them on Krishna Menon and Nehru and allowed them to lapse. After 1961 a vacuum in military planning for NEFA was allowed to develop, into which the civilian-led government would intrude, starting with the development of the "forward policy" and continuing with further steps in the fall of 1962. Another reason was that the plan to expand the Indian Army, proposed in January 1961, was not carried out because insufficient funds had been allocated for the purpose. Therefore, by September 1962, 4 Division had not received new troops, although the army expansion plan (only partly implemented by now) had called for them. The 1961 expansion plan was abandoned in September 1962 (just before the onset of the 1962 crisis) in favor of a new and more ambitious ten-year plan.

A critical obstacle to the army's expansion program was the inability of domestic Indian production to supply the equipment needed for additional army units. The rate of development of the defense industries, nearly all of which were in the public sector, had been slowed by difficulties experienced by Krishna Menon. As the leading advocate of domestic defense production, the defense minister had problems involving technological lag in India, bureaucratic inertia, his own antipathy toward the private sector, and antagonisms created by his own prickly personality. Since an antagonistic relationship had developed between him and Finance Minister Morarji Desai, the finance ministry was allowed to be obstructive.[35] The situation was further complicated by the fact that the army was engaged in an equipment modernization plan and was not prepared to recommend increased production of obsolete types of critically important equipment. Nor were Nehru and Krishna Menon prepared to spend precious foreign exchange to purchase modern weapons and logistical equipment from foreign countries, believing that foreign suppliers were bound to be politically motivated, expensive, and unreliable. As a result, the army not only was restricted in size but also was condemned to fight the well-equipped Chinese in 1962 with outmoded equipment of all kinds.[36]

During and after the 1962 war, Krishna Menon was often blamed for India's military unpreparedness; indeed, he was accused of misleading his cabinet colleagues, including Nehru.[37] But since India's budgetary priorities ultimately were set by Nehru, such sweeping condemnation of his defense minister is unfair. Those financial priorities were in keeping with the Nehru government's continued commitment to basic economic and industrial development, without undue diversion of resources for military use.

Responsibility must also be shared by the army, despite the substantial effort undertaken by Kaul, Palit, and Thapar to make Nehru and Krishna Menon aware of army problems, especially in the spring and summer of 1962.[38] These warnings, given mostly by Kaul, were focused on army capabilities generally, and seem to have been too broad to make the prime minister and the defense minister look specifically at the state of NEFA defenses.

Financial caution gave rise to other problems as well. For example, there was a delay in constructing adequate road systems and logistical facilities in both the Eastern Sector and the Western Sector, and poor service was provided to forward troops by the overworked air transport system.[39]

In the Western Sector the army by the summer of 1961 had only three battalions (i.e., approximately one brigade). Two of these battalions were from the Jammu and Kashmir militia (which was to fight very well in 1962) and one was from the regular army. In contrast, by the end of 1960 the Chinese were thought to have an entire division, "with some armor." The Chinese troops were highly mobile, thanks to the already developed Chinese road system and motor transport capability. To meet a threat of that magnitude, or so Western Command told Army Headquarters, a full Indian division (which usually included three brigades plus auxiliary strength) would be required.[40] But Army Headquarters knew that, because of the logistical situation, such a requirement could not be met.

Such problems notwithstanding, the army began to implement the forward policy. In March–April 1962 posts were placed in the Depsang Plains and the Chip Chap Valley in Ladakh to prevent further Chinese incursion. No territory already occupied by the Chinese was yet involved.

On 30 April, however, the latest in a series of Chinese protest notes announced the resumption of their forward patrolling in Ladakh, and warned that Chinese patrolling would extend to the entire border if Indian movements persisted. In reply the Indians repeated a long-standing assertion that such patrolling had never stopped, whatever the Chinese government had pledged in the past, and indicated that the Indian side expected aggressive Chinese movement all along the frontier. The Chinese were also expected to "precipitate clashes."[41]

During the spring months Indian and Chinese posts came into close proximity to one another. With Indian posts sometimes set up overlooking or behind their Chinese counterparts, and near or astride Chinese lines of communication, the Chinese answered in kind. Several times there were exchanges of fire between troops of the opposing sides.

Although the Indians had brought a fourth battalion into the race to build posts in Ladakh, the Chinese retained their advantages in numbers (more than five to one) and logistics, and they were able to threaten Indian positions by building around them and occupying higher ground. Indian troops, dependent on airdrops, were still confined to the valleys where dropping zones were available. The Chinese were free to position themselves wherever their ground transport system, based on trucks, enabled them to do so.[42]

Another type of action was adopted by the Chinese on 6 May 1962, when Chinese troops moved toward an Indian post in the Chip Chap Valley, giving every indication that they intended to attack it but not following through. Western Command's request to withdraw the post was turned down by Nehru. At a meeting held in New Delhi, attended by Nehru, Krishna Menon, Thapar, Kaul, and Palit, it was decided that the Chip Chap post should hold firm and not submit to the threat of force. The Chinese eventually withdrew.[43]

The two sides came closest to a major clash in July, during the Galwan affair. Some time earlier, Nehru, who had been making regular inquiries about filling up gaps, had convened a meeting with the defense minister and the army chief to point out continuing gaps. At that meeting he had identified the Galwan Valley (see Map 6) as a place that needed to be occupied quickly if possible.[44] The implantation of a platoon-sized Indian post there, on 5 July, cut the line of communication to a small Chinese outpost further down the valley. The situation became more tense when the Indians held up a Chinese supply party.

The Chinese reaction on the ground was to repeat their May tactics (with the Chip Chap post), this time using more troops. The Galwan post was effectively placed under siege. Besides surrounding and moving close to the post in a menacing fashion, the Chinese positioned themselves in such a way that the post could not even be supplied by

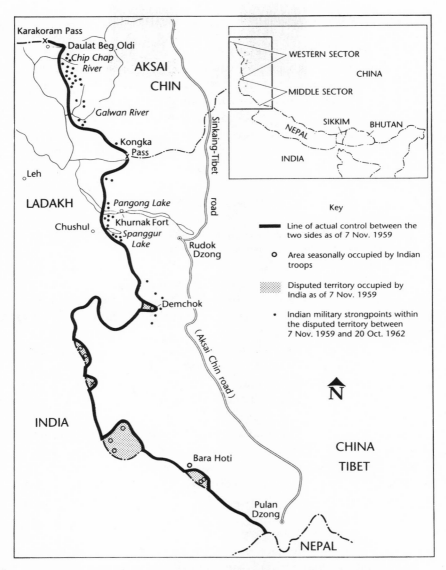

Map 6.   INDIA'S FORWARD POLICY, A CHINESE VIEW.
(From Allen S. Whiting, *The Chinese Calculus of Deterrence* [Ann Arbor: University of Michigan Press,
1975]. Reprinted by permission of the University of
Michigan Press and the Peking Review.)

air. Following the Chip Chap precedent, the Indian platoon at Galwan was told to hold firm. But this time the Indian troops were ordered to open fire if the Chinese came any closer.

The siege of the Galwan post eased on 14 July, when the Chinese pulled back some distance from the post and permitted it to receive support by air. But the Indian side had threatened wider retaliation of some sort if the Chinese attacked Galwan. A subsequent effort to relieve the post via land was ordered by New Delhi, but it failed when the Chinese would not let the relief party pass. At the urging of Western Command, which reported that relief of the post was beyond its resources and was in any case likely to touch off hostilities, the matter was left in limbo until the post was overrun at the start of the 1962 war in October.[45]

The Galwan affair was considered serious enough to occasion consultation with the Defense Subcommittee of the cabinet, and it received major play in the press.[46] But the real decisions were undoubtedly made by Nehru, Krishna Menon, and Army Headquarters. The press conveyed the feeling apparently prevalent within government circles—that a signal victory had been won because Indian troops had stood firm.[47]

As the forward policy continued, certain rules of engagement seemed to be evolving. From May onward the Indian side lodged protests only after a confrontation or firing, rather than after each minor contact between Indian and Chinese troops. To avoid inflammatory publicity, the two sides delayed publication of notes until the other side had received them. Chinese efforts at fraternization on the ground in Ladakh were met with Indian smiles and silence. Chinese actions during the Chip Chap and Galwan episodes seemed to indicate the worst that the Chinese would do. Nehru told the army that it was necessary not to withdraw these posts in order "to study the 'behavior pattern' of the Chinese."[48]

Yet, when a series of shooting incidents broke out in July and it became clear that in some places the Chinese were setting up posts so that Indian posts were virtually surrounded, an order issued by Army Headquarters (surely with higher-level approval) gave commanders in Ladakh the authority to fire if the Chinese came too close, without waiting for the Chinese to fire first. This was an extension of the orders given to the Galwan post; they now covered the entire Western Sector.[49]

Chinese intentions at the time were considered complex. A well-informed Indian source reportedly told an Indian press agency that the government had been aware for some time of possible Chinese moves to harass Indian border troops. The assessment made by the Indian embassy in Peking was that the Chinese were apprehensive about the growing Indian strength along the border and would try to "contain" the forward movement of Indian troops.[50]

According to the same news source, other perceived Chinese goals were (1) to create border tensions for propaganda purposes, especially for the benefit of East European Communist countries hitherto unsympathetic to the Chinese case; (2) to impress the Soviets with the merits of the Chinese case and to change the Soviet attitude toward India, particularly as it applied to a recent Soviet offer to sell MiG fighters to the Indians; and (3) to malign India at the moment when a world peace convention was being held in Moscow.

The Galwan and other Ladakh incidents left the further impression that things were "drifting badly," as Nehru put it in parliament.[51] Partly from this concern, and apparently in the hope that the increased tension in Ladakh was having some effect on Chinese thinking, the Indian government's diplomatic activities increased during the spring and summer of 1962.

In May 1962 the Indian government offered to permit Chinese use of the Aksai Chin road for civilian traffic if the Chinese would withdraw from Ladakh. The offer was part of a larger proposal, in which the Indian government suggested that in the Western Sector each side pull back behind the claim line set down by the other. This proposal, which repeated Indian suggestions made in 1959, carried little hope of acceptance. As Nehru himself admitted, the proposal would have required "a very small withdrawal for us ... a large withdrawal for them."[52] The entire idea was quickly rejected by the Chinese, who noted Nehru's remark about the size of the relative withdrawals. They commented that China needed no permission to use "its own road on its own territory" and made clear that China was not a "defeated country."[53]

Refusing to be deterred, the Indian government in its note of 26 July declared that it was prepared to enter into further talks with China on the basis of the Officials' Report.[54] Such talks could only be held, however, when tensions in the Western Sector had eased through implementation of the Indian proposal for mutual withdrawal. Despite the setting of this precondition, this note marked the beginning of an exchange of letters with the Chinese government regarding meetings between the two sides. China agreed to hold talks but demanded that they be convened without any preconditions. If the Indian troops in Ladakh would simply stop advancing, tensions would be eased and the proper climate would appear. The Indian response to this proposal (in a note dated 22 August 1962) was negative, but India nevertheless declared itself ready to receive a Chinese representative to discuss tension-easing measures, including (mainly Chinese) withdrawals.[55]

Other important diplomatic steps taken during the summer were Nehru's meeting with China's ambassador, Pan Tzu-li, in New Delhi and Krishna Menon's discussions with China's foreign minister, Chen Yi, during the 1962 Laos conference in Geneva. Krishna Menon, Chen Yi, and their delegations negotiated seriously. They were prepared to issue a joint communiqué proposing further talks, but their initiative was thwarted by Krishna Menon's difficulty in contacting Nehru from Geneva to secure authorization and by the negative reaction in parliament to the Geneva meeting.[56]

The ultimate goal of these diplomatic moves, as far as India was concerned, was the same as that of the forward policy. It was to have the Chinese withdraw from Ladakh as part of a general settlement based on the historical findings of the Officials' Report. The Chinese interest in the Aksai Chin road could be accommodated in some fashion, without ceding Indian territory.

It was in this context that Nehru sought to transcend the limitations placed on him by domestic politics. For the first time in three years of parliamentary debate, Nehru informed his parliamentary opponents that he wanted "freedom of action." Naturally, he said, he would be keeping parliament informed, and certainly he would agree that nothing be done "which in the slightest degree sullies the honor of India." But beyond that he wanted a "free hand."[57] These remarks were specifically directed against attacks being made in parliament against the government's diplomatic efforts. But it is doubtful that he would have used such language unless he thought some diplomatic progress was possible.

Meanwhile, the forward policy was now also being implemented in NEFA under the code name Operation Onkar.

The Assam Rifles were expected to be manning posts all along the McMahon line by July 1962.[58] (For a view of the Eastern Sector as of 7 September 1962, see Map 7.)

Although no criss-cross of Indian and Chinese posts was anticipated

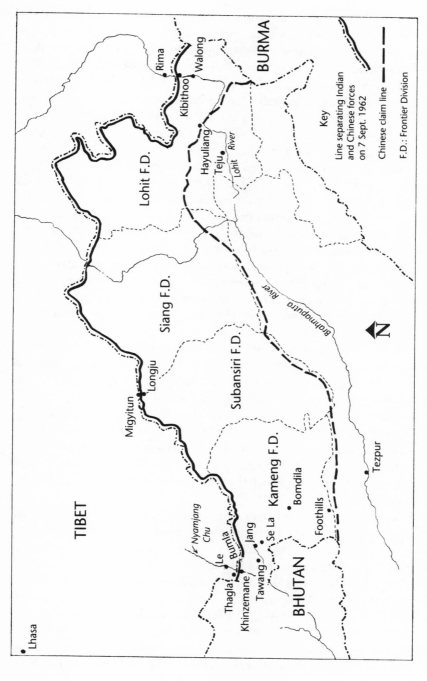

Map 7. EASTERN SECTOR AS OF 7 SEPTEMBER 1962.

Key

Line separating Indian
and Chinese forces
on 7 Sept. 1962

Chinese claim line

F.D.: Frontier Division

TIBET

Lhasa

BURMA

BHUTAN

Rima

Kibithoo

Walong

Hayuliang

Teju

Lohit River

Lohit F.D.

Siang F.D.

Longju

Migyitun

Subansiri F.D.

Brahmaputra River

Kameng F.D.

Bomdila

Foothills

Tezpur

Nyamjang
Chu

Le

Bumla

Jang

Se La

Thagla

Khinzemane

Tawang

N

on the NEFA frontier, a certain rashness was demonstrated by the placement of an Indian post in an area near the Bhutan-Tibet-NEFA trijunction. It was located in the valley of the Namkachu River, below a ridge called Thagla (see Maps 7 and 8). The post would be called Dhola, after a pass lying further to the south.[59] In 1959 and 1960 the Chinese had shown themselves to be quite sensitive about this area, since they differed with the Indian interpretation of how the McMahon line was situated in it. The Khinzemane incident of August 1959 had occurred not far away.

An Assam Rifles platoon, led by an army officer, created the Dhola post on 4 June. The officer, Captain Mahabir Prasad (1 Sikh Battalion, 7 Brigade, 4 Division), was bold enough to question the siting of the post, perhaps because he was the nephew of his division commander, Major General Niranjan Prasad. Upon his return to his base, he not only contacted division headquarters about the position of the Dhola post but also signaled that local IB sources had given him other disconcerting bits of information. The Chinese knew of the Dhola post, did not recognize the territory as Indian, and "would occupy that area as soon as instructions from their government are received."[60]

The division commander referred the question of whether the territory was properly Indian to higher echelons in the army command chain, and two weeks later (after questioning his nephew in person) asked for permission to occupy the Thagla Ridge preemptively. Before any reply was received, he learned that the Chinese had recently carried out military exercises in the Dhola area and had already constructed brigade-strength (but not permanently occupied) defensive positions on Thagla Ridge. To Prasad this news precluded Indian occupation of the ridge, since the Chinese could now move onto it at short notice.[61]

Prasad's immediate superior, Umrao Singh (commander of XXXIII Corps), had also raised questions about this section of the McMahon line during the past few months and had received no reply. No response to Umrao's or Prasad's inquiries came until the Director of Military Operations at Army Headquarters, Brigadier Palit, visited both 4 Division Headquarters at Tezpur and his old command in NEFA (7 Brigade) on 14 August 1962.[62] Prasad raised the whole issue with Palit and gave him army maps on which a straight-line border ran from Khinzemane to Bhutan, well south of the Dhola post. Palit then sought to have the matter clarified at Army Headquarters in New

Delhi. Hearing no satisfactory answer, he eventually lodged a question about the status of the area with Sarvepalli Gopal of the MEA Historical Division.[63]

Gopal was puzzled by the query, since Army Headquarters had been informed two years earlier that the proper border feature in the area was Thagla Ridge. Moreover, Army Headquarters had been sent the minutes of the officials' talks of 1960, as well as the final Officials' Report, in which this issue had been addressed.[64] During the officials' talks the Chinese had also been told of the Indian view on correcting a map-drawn line; that is, the need to correlate it with the actual features on the ground. If a feature such as Thagla Ridge had not been explored when the map was issued, and if the map-drawn boundary was supposed to be set by the watershed ridge, then the line lay on the watershed ridge despite the error on the map.

Gopal now supplied this information to Army Headquarters, but no message or orders reached Prasad in NEFA before the outbreak of the crisis on 8 September. Therefore, the unresponsiveness of higher echelons to the questions raised by Prasad (and Umrao), the need for personal intervention by Palit, the referral to the MEA (Palit to Gopal), and the fact that Army Headquarters did not respond to Gopal's information with a clear decision (the Gopal information may not have arrived until after the crisis began)[65]—all served to prevent a preemptive Indian move. The Chinese were allowed to occupy Thagla Ridge first, starting on 8 September.

OVERVIEW OF THE PRE-CRISIS PERIOD:
MARCH 1959 TO 7 SEPTEMBER 1962

In the period leading up to the 1962 crisis in India-China relations, the Indian government produced a series of "strategic" decisions. They were "strategic" in that they were "broad policy acts," of considerable "significance for the state's foreign policy system as a whole."[66]

The series began during the months of the Tibetan revolt (March–August 1959), when the Nehru government decided to follow a strategy aimed at stabilizing relations with China without being bullied by Chinese demands and without being unduly influenced by aroused press and parliamentary opinion within India. Next (during August–October 1959), the Indian government moved on to a strategy of persuasion and argument over the emerging boundary question.

But in the period following the Kongka Pass incident (21 October 1959 to 29 July 1961), persuasion and argument were supplemented by diplomatic pressure of various kinds. In the autumn of 1961, another strategic step was taken when the Nehru government added a form of nonviolent military pressure (the "forward policy") to diplomacy. This strategy remained in force from November 1961 until the 1962 crisis erupted.

Feedback from each successive strategy encouraged Indian decision-makers to try the next one. Thus, Indian decision-making took on a circular but progressive character.[67]

Each of the individual strategic phases contained important "tactical" (i.e., implementing) decisions.[68] During the Tibetan revolt phase, there was the decision to give refuge to the Dalai Lama. Some less significant tactical decisions made during that phase were the prime minister's refusal to allow the formation of a Tibetan government-in-exile and his rejection of the Indian president's suggestion that Chinese policy in Tibet be condemned as colonialism.

During the strategic phase of persuasion and argument (August–October 1959), the most significant tactical decisions were (1) to respond to the growing apprehension about frontier security by releasing the white papers, (2) to place formal responsibility for the NEFA border in the hands of the army, and (3) to start a dialogue with the Chinese through diplomatic correspondence. These decisions were supposed to arrest a decline in domestic political support and to guard against further Chinese encroachment, so that constructive diplomacy would be possible. Such diplomacy would have been predicated on a line of thought that preoccupied India's prime minister but never matured into a tactical or strategic decision. It was to make some arrangement with the Chinese over the Aksai Chin, especially if Indian historical claims proved not to be well founded. By failing to recognize a moment of opportunity, and by occupying Western Sector territory preemptively, the Chinese may well have lost an opportunity to achieve a negotiated settlement.

During the third pre-crisis phase, which followed the Kongka Pass incident of 21 October 1959, the key tactical decisions were (1) to militarize the border from the Indian side and (2) to refuse the barter offer seemingly being made by the Chinese during the Chou-Nehru talks of April 1960. That refusal constituted the most crucial tactical step taken by the Nehru government during the pre-crisis period. Another (lesser) decision followed it immediately: the decision to hold the officials' talks. For the Indian side the officials' talks constituted a form of diplomatic pressure on China even if persuasion could not be achieved.

In the last phase of pre-crisis decision-making, the key tactical or operational decision was made on 2 November 1961: the adoption of the forward policy. As a decision designed to institute a new form of conflict management, it was flawed in several ways. In the first place, it was based on the prediction that the Chinese would not respond by the use of force. That prediction might well have been accurate in late 1961 and early 1962 but not later. Just as problematical was allowing the forward policy to gain an escalating momentum of its own, on the strength of its apparent success. Still another main shortcoming of the November 1961 decision was the failure to provide requisite military strength to support it. Earlier plans for creating an adequate defensive posture along the frontier should have been implemented, in case the Chinese eventually behaved differently than predicted. Finally, existing Indian military capabilities vis-à-vis the Chinese should have been gauged more accurately by Indian decision-makers. A policy of nonviolent military resistance to Chinese encroachment, and nonviolent pressure on the Chinese to relinquish occupied territory, was not really feasible unless both sides knew that the Indians had a capacity to use force.

Can it be argued, as has been done elsewhere, that perhaps the greatest error in Indian conflict management all through the pre-crisis period was a persistent refusal to negotiate?[69] It is more accurate to say that by 1962 India and China had developed two different conceptions of the proper subjects for negotiation. From the Indian side the most immediate and pressing subjects were the method and timing of Chinese withdrawal from occupied territory, so that border claims could then be considered again, in the light of historical evidence. From the Chinese perspective the most pressing need was to negotiate a halt to India's forward policy. The Chinese then would try again to create a new Sino-Indian border by means of a barter arrangement that took account of the military realities the Chinese had created on the ground.

Even more basically different were the two national psychologies involved. Just as Nehru dismissed the border psychology of the Chinese, believing that the Chinese were motivated mainly by hostility and expansionism, China never understood the psychological dimension of India's handling of the border dispute. Few self-respecting governments would consider a 2,000-mile border open to barter, even if they were assured of a favorable negotiating outcome and no expansionist designs on the other side. Surely, that was too much to expect of the Nehru government, which perceived in the Chinese negotiating stance an attempt to denigrate the historical authenticity of the Indian nation. A true nation would not, in the Indian view, be asked to negotiate its historically evolved borders. That request or demand could come only from a neighbor who (like India's former British rulers) regarded the Indian nation as an artificial creation.

3

THE CRISIS: PREWAR PHASE,
8 SEPTEMBER TO 19 OCTOBER 1962

CHAPTER EIGHT

The Prewar Decision-Makers and Their Psychological Setting

INDIA'S 1962 CRISIS—which began on 8 September, when the Chinese placed pressure on the Dhola post—contained two phases. The prewar phase lasted until 19 October and featured a series of decisions taken for the purpose of relieving the Dhola post and removing Chinese troops from nearby Thagla Ridge. The war phase, 20 October to 21 November 1962, featured India's responses to the Chinese military offensive of 20 October and 17 November in NEFA and Ladakh.

THE ROLES OF THE DECISION-MAKERS

During the prewar phase of the 1962 crisis, three men played the key decision-making roles. Two of those men were Krishna Menon and Nehru. Lieutenant General Kaul became the third decision-maker in early October, after his return from leave in Kashmir. For a time he was in control of the effort to solve the problem of the Chinese incursion into NEFA; full military authority was entrusted to him.

General Kaul was not ideally suited for the assignment, since he was a political soldier rather than a military leader. Before independence and immediately after, he had been one of the few regular Indian Army officers with pronounced nationalist sympathies. Early in his career his nationalist views, and the fact that he was a distant relative of the Nehru family, enabled him to become an acquaintance of the prime minister's. Subsequently, Kaul also received favorable notice from Krishna Menon. Although he never commanded a military unit in combat during World War II or in the Kashmir war of 1948, he was still promoted to choice army assignments.

General Kaul was articulate, intelligent, charming, dapper, and a person with interests ranging far beyond the parochial sphere of military affairs. He was someone whom political intellectuals like Nehru and Krishna Menon could find interesting and credible. Krishna Menon, who distrusted army officers generally, trusted Kaul, although the relationship between the two men was sometimes argumentative.[1]

Kaul and Krishna Menon were decision-makers, but they were also consultants to Nehru. By September 1962 the relationships between Nehru and the persons immediately around him had coalesced into a certain pattern or structure. The structure was that of the Indian political faction—the major type of informal grouping found in Indian domestic politics. As is true of factions in many political systems, this one crossed formal organizational lines.

The distinctive structural features of an Indian faction exhibited by this group were (1) the presence of a leader-teacher thought to possess a unified worldview (i.e., a broad perspective beyond the immediate grasp of his followers); (2) the existence of an inner circle immediately surrounding the leader, and a number of competing outer subcircles, each with its own leader; (3) values and preferences that create nearly impermeable boundaries around the core circle and each outer subcircle within the faction, making each a primordial (emotionally based) support group; (4) competitive coalitional (as well as hierarchical) linkages between the subcircles in the faction.[2]

The members of the circle closest to Nehru in 1962 were Krishna Menon; the IB director, B. N. Mullik; Kaul; and the MEA foreign secretary, M. J. Desai. All were conscious of Nehru's highly developed and broadly consistent philosophical perspective on world affairs, and they revered him for it. They felt that both in political and personal matters Nehru was beyond pettiness, narrowness, or obsession with minor details; instead, his thoughts were focused on the great issues and trends of history and world affairs. Toward the members of his inner circle, he was personable, warm, and even humorous, and they responded with warmth and loyalty of their own. Since their time with him was considered a privilege, and since their careers depended on his continuing patronage, they prized their access to him.[3]

All members of the inner circle (with one exception) were themselves leaders of subcircles. Kaul's subcircle fell within the confines of a particular organization—the army; but he had developed his own support group within it. Members of Kaul's subcircle (mostly junior officers) were labeled "Kaul's boys" by detractors. Although senior officers working with Kaul at Army Headquarters in 1962 did not regard themselves as members, they were perceived as such by other people. These senior men included the deputy Chief of General Staff, Lieutenant General J. S. Dhillon; and the Director of Military Operations, Brigadier D. K. Palit. The army chief, General Thapar, while nominally superior to Kaul, and possibly even disliking him, could be counted within Kaul's support group as well. Toward these immediate friends and followers, Kaul could be generous, warm, and sympathetic, although one has written that "like many egocentrics, [Kaul] was not empathetic by nature; he gave his sympathy and support explicitly as largesse rather than as subtle and understanding gifts."[4] Nevertheless, ties with him were more than simply a matter of obligation incurred from political and professional patronage, just as was true of ties with Nehru.

Krishna Menon had support from civilian officials in the Ministry of Defense. He could also secure assistance and agreement on particular issues from some MEA officials and from certain cabinet members, such as the petroleum minister, K. D. Malaviyya. These relationships were based more on ideology or patronage than on personal warmth, and they were unstable.[5]

Mullik's subcircle lay within the IB, an organization that he had practically created.

Only Foreign Secretary M. J. Desai lacked a personal support group. His subordinates within the MEA were longtime professionals who liked and respected him but were not attached to him by bonds of personal loyalty.[6]

Each subcircle leader could act ruthlessly toward members of other subgroups, whether those subgroups were inside or outside the overall Nehru faction. Mullik would do so in pushing policy ideas against the army, even after Kaul and Thapar took over. Kaul was a fierce opponent of other factions in the army, and was even prepared to persecute prominent individuals (including the now-retired General Thimayya). M. J. Desai, acting on the strength of his commitment to implement Nehru's thinking, was to be a source of pressure on the hapless General Thapar in the fall of 1962. Krishna Menon had a well-deserved reputation for divisiveness and factional strife.[7]

Within the Nehru faction as a whole, however, there was a common worldview, a common set of images, and a reluctance to deviate from them. During the 1962 crisis this mentality was evidenced most strikingly by Kaul, whose activities in NEFA made him aware of realities that he could not reconcile with the group consensus in New Delhi. IB director Mullik exhibited it when he provided factual confirmation for the group's predictions. Foreign Secretary Desai also promoted "groupthink" by making himself an enforcer of the general consensus against dissent.[8]

Among the factors allowing groupthink to become an influence on decision-making was the state of Prime Minister Nehru's health. He had suffered the first major illness in his life (kidney malfunction) in April 1962, and it had taken its toll on his energy. One official, who later described Nehru's activity in the last months before the 1962 war, recalls that Nehru still had "flashes of hard work and incisiveness. But slowly the malaise was setting in."[9]

Nehru became more dependent on those around him, particularly on Krishna Menon for political (i.e., ideological) guidance and on M. J. Desai for note drafting and other details. He had always possessed a temper, although an outburst would pass quickly and persistent individuals could get their points across without untoward consequences. Instead of displays of temper, however, Nehru since 1960 or 1961 had been responding to an unpalatable fact or opinion with prolonged silence. Now, in 1962, officials who knew about those silences or his temper, and out of genuine veneration for him, sought "areas of agreement" with Nehru and tried not to tread "on thin ice."[10] Only the war itself would produce in Nehru an intellectual activeness and openness reminiscent of his old self.

THE ATTITUDINAL PRISM OF THE DECISION-MAKERS

Shaping the Nehru group's decisions and actions was the Indian attitudinal prism developed after March 1959. The elements of it most influential in 1962 were (1) the belief that, unless checked, the Chinese were prone to infiltrate further into Indian border zones and occupy Indian territory; and (2) the prediction—made with greatest conviction by Nehru, Krishna Menon, and Mullik—that the Chinese would not react violently to India's forward policy measures. Underlying these elements was the fundamental conviction that China was hostile (i.e., basically predisposed to do harm) to India and that the border dispute was largely a surface manifestation of that hostility.

Another belief, held by Nehru and his MEA officials, was that China was competing with India for influence in Asia. By reaching border settlement agreements with states neighboring India, the

Chinese were extending their influence and trying to isolate India.[11]
Thus, in their dealings with Burma, Nepal, and Pakistan, the Chinese
had sought to demonstrate their reasonableness and portray India as
"bloody minded."[12]

One factor thought likely to limit what the Chinese could do in the
immediate future was China's domestic situation. China's ills included the failure of the "Great Leap Forward" of 1958, drought
between 1959 and 1962, and the continuing effort to subjugate Tibet.
These problems seemed serious enough to preclude external adventurism on China's part.

Possibly reinforcing that estimate was a trove of intelligence
material captured by Tibetan rebels who had ambushed a Chinese
road convoy in 1961. The Tibetans transferred these materials to the
Taiwanese, who shared them with the Americans. This "batch of
Chinese political-military documents relating to the period of 1
January to 26 August 1961" indicated that China's domestic difficulties had produced extremely low morale and physical fitness in the
People's Liberation Army.[13] The United States and/or the Tibetans
may have shared this material with India. In any event, a tendency
to denigrate the quality of Chinese troops in Tibet became a part of
Indian thinking.

Indian decision-makers and their consultants viewed the Dhola
intrusion of September 1962 within the context of the political and
military decisions that India had previously undertaken. The gradual
Indian military deployment along the frontier, as well as the forward
policy, had created the attitude that further Chinese advances did not
have to be permitted, either in Ladakh or in NEFA.[14] The general
impression among key civilians was that in NEFA, unlike Ladakh,
India could do something militarily if necessary. Some persons at
Army Headquarters thought similarly. The Operational Instruction
(i.e., standing orders) covering 4 Division in NEFA by the start of
September indicated that the division should support the Dhola post if
it got into trouble.[15] In all, those making decisions in Delhi in
September and October 1962 believed that they were merely extending
and developing policy made earlier, rather than creating it anew.

Another part of the Indian attitudinal prism at this time was the
belief that India's forward policy and other military actions were not
ends in themselves but, rather, should be aimed at talks. Indeed, in his
debates with those persons in parliament holding far more hawkish
opinions, the prime minister had made it an article of faith that

resolving the border conflict via constructive talks was the highest goal of his policy toward China.[16] To him this goal represented taking a modern, civilized, and peaceful approach suited to international conflict resolution generally. One part of this approach—the part that allowed the use of physical but nonviolent pressures to alter the thinking of the other side—most likely was drawn from the Gandhian dimension of the Indian nationalist struggle, as Nehru perceived it.

Nehru spoke publicly of his impression that the Chinese government would like a settlement with India, but what settlement they had in mind he could not say.[17] The key question in the summer and early autumn of 1962 was how to reach agreement soon on what subjects the next round of talks should cover.

CHANGING IMAGES HELD BY THE DECISION-MAKERS

Nehru

Nehru left for the annual Commonwealth Prime Ministers' Conference on 8 September, before news of Chinese pressure on Dhola arrived. He was subsequently kept informed through the Indian High Commission in London. It is inconceivable that the September decisions could have been taken by Krishna Menon and his consultants without Nehru's approval, although he was not consulted on day-to-day developments. When he returned, on 2 October, Nehru fully endorsed all that had been done and was being planned.

That Nehru would stay abroad until October, and even pause briefly in Egypt on his way home, testified to his belief in the link between the Indian frontier situation and the global political system. The prime minister was accustomed to seeing such linkages and making projections from them. In his view two trends in international relations were enhancing India's security against China: the easing of Cold War tensions between the United States and the Soviet Union, and the widening of the rift between Russia and China.

Thanks to eased Soviet-American relations, and the Soviet Union's own problems with China, India could now explore the possibility of countering China by drawing closer to the United States without alienating the Soviets. The Indian image of the United States was affected by the election of John F. Kennedy to the presidency in 1960. Kennedy gave the impression of being particularly friendly toward India, and tolerant of nonalignment, while trying to correct the bias toward Pakistan in America's South Asian policy. The Nehru government felt let down when the United States delivered F-104 jet fighters to Pakistan, and both governments were disappointed when Nehru's visit to Washington in November 1961 did not go well. A cooling of relations occurred when India seized the Portuguese colony of Goa in December 1961. But the Kennedy administration's friendliness and generosity with economic aid still left open the possibility of a new Indo-American relationship. So did announced United States support for India in the border conflict with China.

One of the Indian perceptions was that Kennedy in 1961 appeared "insecure in his handling of power."[18] Nehru also felt less comfortable with Kennedy personally than he had with Eisenhower. Nehru was not inclined to agree with the deepening involvement of the United States in Vietnam, and he refused to ally India with the United States in any way in South and Southeast Asia. American relations with Pakistan remained a sensitive issue. Yet, under Nehru, India would now work for closer relations with the United States.

During his Washington trip Nehru expressed the belief that it was in the Soviet Union's own interest to help restrain Peking and that Khrushchev saw India as a future bulwark against China.[19] This outlook was reinforced in early 1962, when the Soviets agreed to sell to India more of the high-altitude transports and helicopters they had already been supplying. Such equipment, along with American helicopters being acquired by India, would obviously be of use along the Himalayan frontier. In August 1962 India and the Soviet Union signed an agreement calling for the delivery to India of twelve MiG-21 fighter aircraft. The agreement, which had been concluded despite objections from Western governments (and counteroffers from Britain), further obligated the Soviet Union to assist India in developing the capacity to produce MiG-21s on its own. Another Indo-Soviet agreement, concluded in July 1962, called for the licensed manufacture in India of Soviet engines for an Indian-designed supersonic aircraft—the HF-24. All this activity was taking place in the full glare of international publicity.[20]

According to Nehru, China was rational enough to foresee the global consequences of a war with India. To attack India would threaten world war. "[Local] wars do not take place, are not likely to take place," he had said earlier (22 December 1959), "between two great countries without developing into big wars and the big wars without developing possibly—not certainly—into a world war." His point was that warfare between countries having the size and military potential of India and China would become protracted warfare, in which neither side could defeat the other. In such a conflict the likelihood of great-power intervention was high, and therefore so was the danger of world war. But ultimately neither America nor the Soviet Union would allow India to be grievously harmed. The Soviets would be forced by the danger of world war to pressure the Chinese into halting their military adventure.[21]

With such an image of the international situation, and given his personal lack of military experience or inclination, the prime minister was unable to imagine that a Chinese military move in NEFA or Ladakh could be something less than an invasion but more than another border incident. He did not speculate on the range of options open to Chinese ground forces, options that might preclude great-power intervention.

Drawing from the experience he did have, the prime minister focused on his impression that the Chinese were still maneuvering so as to negotiate advantageously. At the same time, his historical-mindedness led him to perceive a slightly less militant China. On 14 May 1962 he pointed out in parliament that, perhaps because of the great economic setback in China during the past several years, traditional Chinese culture (which he had long praised as calm and courteous) was reappearing. "Even Confucius is talked about now." He cautioned that there had been "no political reaction or political relaxation" in China, but "nevertheless, there is a certain relaxation in life, generally.... This may change again, of course."[22]

With the start of the crisis on 8 September, Nehru thought that the Chinese wanted to use the Dhola intrusion to bring NEFA within the scope of talks that would otherwise deal only with the Western Sector. He felt strongly that the Chinese should not be permitted to bring the McMahon line into the discussions as a negotiable item. To allow them to do so would equate India's forward policy in Ladakh with China's incursion into NEFA, and would again raise questions about bartering India's claims in the Western Sector for China's claims in the Eastern Sector. Furthermore, the Chinese should not be able to use a familiar tactic successfully: seize territory and then ask for talks about it.[23]

Krishna Menon

As of September 1962 the Indian defense minister still saw the India-China conflict as a border dispute, rather than an expression of any deep-seated Chinese hostility. His convictions had been reinforced during his July discussions with Chen Yi at Geneva. "He returned to report to the prime minister that he had long private conversations... with Chen Yi who assured him that there may be skirmishes between forces of the two countries along the border, but full-scale hostilities were unthinkable."[24] For Krishna Menon Pakistan—not China—was the enemy to guard against.[25]

Krishna Menon discounted the military threat posed by China, but he remained a strong advocate of forward policy movement on the ground.[26] With India's defense expenditure being kept "within the limits of our economy," he favored "building posts, showing the flag and so on, largely depending upon our hope that good sense would prevail. We expected negotiation and diplomacy to play their part."[27]

Prior to 8 September 1962, he opposed any idea of having the Indian Army stage a limited military engagement somewhere on the frontier.[28] But once the Dhola situation emerged, he did not want to allow further intrusions by the Chinese. He was convinced that Chinese forward movement had to be met at the border itself and that the Chinese should not be allowed to come any distance into NEFA. Furthermore, he thought at first that Chinese troop strength in the Dhola-Thagla area was quite limited, making the problem militarily manageable. His general conclusion was that the Chinese should be removed from Thagla Ridge by force.[29]

Kaul

Until he was sent to NEFA in October 1962, and was persuaded by the situation there, General Kaul thought that the India-China conflict had been well managed under the prime minister's overall direction. Along with his immediate associates at Army Headquarters, he believed that the forward policy was succeeding and that the Chinese were unlikely to react in any massive way.[30]

Both Kaul and Thapar, however, wanted to avoid a general war with China. They were convinced that the army was not ready for one. In view of the army's weaknesses, Kaul had been heavily engaged in a crusade to induce Krishna Menon and Nehru to increase military spending and procure needed weapons. He had also concluded by the spring of 1962 that the Chinese were becoming more aggressive on the ground and that further small-scale confrontations would take place.[31] One of the major disagreements between Kaul and Krishna Menon was over the need to secure American weapons, and a meeting

between Kaul and Chester Bowles (special emissary of President
Kennedy in March 1962) was opposed by the defense minister.
Intelligence director Mullik suspected that Kaul had obtained from
Bowles some commitment of future American support, but evidence
from Kaul and Bowles refutes this idea.[32]

In September 1962 Kaul was away from Delhi when the decision
was made to try to push the Chinese out of the Dhola area. Upon his
return, during the first few days of October, his image of the situation
was that an operational plan had already been devised at lower
command levels in NEFA. All that was lacking was a forceful senior
commander to carry out the plan and get the NEFA officers to stop
dragging their feet. In his own view Kaul had shown himself
throughout his career to be an officer of dash, boldness, and personal
bravery. He had voluntarily gone to hazardous places in the past.
If a new commander was needed in NEFA, he was the obvious
candidate.

His political perceptions reinforced his determination. Personally
devoted to Nehru, Kaul thought the Nehru government needed a
savior of sorts. If no action were taken against the Chinese in NEFA,
the government might fall.[33] In addition, Kaul had the impression
that the government would fully support him in the field by allo-
cating scarce resources and making appropriate modifications of
policy.

In this optimistic frame of mind, he flew to NEFA and plunged into
frenzied activity. Only a Chinese attack on the Tseng Jong position
near Dhola (see Map 8 in Chapter 9), on 10 October, sobered him.
But on 11 October he could not bring himself to explain the full
dimensions of the NEFA problem to Nehru, Krishna Menon, and their
advisers. As a result, from 11 October until war broke out on 20
October, Kaul faced conflicting and unresolvable pressures—from
the government's demands, on the one side, and from his sense that
those demands were unrealistic, on the other. Depression produced by
that conflict was compounded by the onset of physical illness
(pulmonary edema acquired from overexertion at high altitudes).

While recovering from that illness, he lost contact with realities in
NEFA. On his sickbed in New Delhi, and again subject to the influence
of the political faction to which he belonged, he too thought that
withdrawals from the Dhola area were unnecessary and wrong. On 20
October he was just as surprised as any civilian when the Chinese
overwhelmed his troops.[34]

PERCEPTIONS OF THREAT, TIME LIMITATIONS, AND LIKELIHOOD OF HOSTILITIES

Initially, the Chinese crossed the Indian-defined NEFA border by climbing over Thagla Ridge and entering the Namkachu Valley on the southwestern side of the ridge (see Map 8). There they threatened the Dhola post, situated on the south bank of the river, a post manned by Assam Rifles constabulary.

If perceived in isolation, this particular Chinese action would have posed little threat. But it was perceived by Indian decision-makers as the start of Peking's effort to respond to the forward policy in the Western Sector by opening a new front in the Eastern Sector. So it was what one official has called "the next step in the game."[35] Unless some Indian show of determination was made at this time, future Chinese nibbling at NEFA could not be forestalled, since "[the] length of the eastern boundary and the already stretched resources of the Indian Army would make it impossible to prevent such piecemeal incursions once they began in earnest."[36]

Thus, the decision-makers' crucial perception was that they faced a "no alternative" situation.[37] Unless the Chinese were dealt a blow, the Ladakh situation would be replicated in NEFA. Such a blow should ideally be delivered while Chinese troop strength near Dhola was low, and before the onset of winter.

The Chinese would probably respond in Ladakh to an Indian military action in NEFA, although such a response was expected to be limited in nature. Some forward policy posts, probably including Galwan, were likely to be attacked. But the prevailing view, at least among the civilian decision-makers and their civilian consultants, was that the Chinese "would not launch any general attack."[38]

Of greater concern was danger from a different quarter—Pakistan. In June 1962 the IB had supplied some detailed information on Pakistan's intentions. That information described a recent talk given by the president of Pakistan, Ayub Khan, to his military chiefs. Ayub had reportedly outlined a strategy wherein Chinese guerrillas would keep Indian forces heavily engaged while Pakistan attacked from the west.

From then on, the possibility of "military collusion between Pakistan and China remained imprinted in the minds of our leaders."[39] Nehru, for example, in a private letter to the chief ministers of the Indian states (dated 3 September 1962), spoke of the

Pakistani threat in terms of "invasion" and discussed the Chinese threat only in terms of "tension" and "petty conflicts."[40]

Domestic politics also constituted a source of threat. For political reasons (i.e., so as not to forfeit public confidence and to retain diplomatic flexibility), Nehru felt that his government should have the army do its best to push the Chinese out of NEFA. Exactly what could or could not be done was for the army to decide. Even if the army's best effort did not evict the Chinese, India would at least have given "the appearance of taking strong action."[41]

Krishna Menon also believed that Indian public opinion would not forgive any surrendering of territory. Therefore, even if no military operation could be staged in NEFA during the remainder of 1962, the defense minister demanded that India's force at Dhola not be allowed to pull back into winter quarters, but remain in its established positions confronting the Chinese.[42]

The perception of a domestic political threat to the Nehru government was accurate. The Congress Parliamentary Party (i.e., the Congress Party contingent in parliament) was extremely sensitive to anything that smacked of appeasement and was suspicious of the assurances given by Nehru and Krishna Menon about the state of NEFA defenses. Its leaders assumed that those defenses were not good, because of Krishna Menon's softness on China.[43] Charged with gathering political intelligence within India as well as abroad, Intelligence director Mullik became alarmed. In an effort to stop the army chief, Thapar, from protesting to Nehru about the dangers of taking military action in NEFA, Mullik hinted (or even said) that the government might fall.[44]

Reinforcing that possibility was the publicity being given to the situation in NEFA. Journalists, politicians, and the newspaper-reading public had been made acutely aware of the Dhola confrontation. Among their sources of information had been press briefings provided by politicians and officials since early September. In some of the briefings, as London *Times* correspondent Maxwell recalls them, the blame for inaction was put on the NEFA commanders generally, and more specifically on Lieutenant General Umrao Singh, Commander of XXXIII Corps.[45]

Yet neither Nehru nor Krishna Menon ever thought that the NEFA and domestic political situations were so grave as to require curtailing their plans for travel abroad. Such confidence was possible because both men were convinced that once the decision to remove the Chinese from NEFA had been made, the initiative lay with India. On 18

September Krishna Menon departed for the annual United Nations General Assembly session in New York, saying publicly that there was no need for a feeling of crisis.[46] His private reasoning was that he would be back by the end of September, that no Indian military operations would take place before the first few days of October, and that if anything happened before then he could get back quickly.[47]

Nehru, who returned to New Delhi during the first week of October, changed his image of the situation only after learning the particulars of the sharp clash at Tseng Jong on 10 October. As he wrote privately on 12 October, the Tseng Jong incident and other facts had "brought to light that the Chinese had been strengthening their forces very considerably in this area." The situation along the northeast frontier, he continued, was definitely "a dangerous one, and it may lead to major conflicts ... conflicts on a bigger scale might take place there."[48] That same day, in a startling statement at the New Delhi airport, Nehru presented a less ominous public picture. He said that he had ordered the army to evict the Chinese from NEFA, but he implied that nothing would happen immediately.[49] He then proceeded with a three-day state visit to Ceylon.

Like Nehru, Krishna Menon changed his tone, to some degree, after the Tseng Jong fighting of 10 October. Trying to prepare public opinion for the knowledge that no Indian military action would be forthcoming soon, he gave a speech in Bangalore on 14 October, in which he reiterated India's determination to push the Chinese out of NEFA "whether it takes one day, a hundred days or a thousand days." If attacked in Ladakh, India would fight "to the last man, to the last gun." He saw no room for a feeling of crisis, he said, but an independent India could not forget its responsibilities.[50]

Despite their reluctance to use the term *crisis* in public, India's main decision-makers did perceive the situation as one of crisis. High threat to basic values was anticipated, since uncontested Chinese "nibbling" at NEFA would threaten Indian territorial integrity and the domestic standing of the Nehru government. Indian national security would be threatened if Pakistan and China were indeed prepared to act in collusion. Other dimensions of a "crisis" situation were noticeable as well. Hostilities were expected, even though they would supposedly be limited in nature. Time limitations existed because oncoming winter weather had become a factor in Indian calculations.

Thus, by early October the perceived situation was indeed a "crisis," according to the definition of that term being used in this study,[51] even if it was not yet considered a crisis of the gravest sort.

CHAPTER NINE

The Major Prewar Decisions, 8–22 September 1962

THE STRATEGIC DECISION: USE OF FORCE

ONLY ONE STRATEGIC decision was made during the prewar phase of the 1962 crisis: to evict the Chinese from the Dhola–Thagla Ridge area, using armed force if necessary. This decision was made on 10 or 11 September. The military operation it called for would be code-named Operation Leghorn. The tactical decisions initially designed to implement the strategy were made between 11 September and 17 September. Several other tactical decisions of considerable significance were made between 22 September and the outbreak of war on 20 October. These later decisions will be examined individually in the next chapter.

The Decision "Flow"

The decision to use force in NEFA was made via several small steps, as part of a decision "flow."[1]

The immediate Indian response to the Chinese crossing of Thagla Ridge on 8 September was to have the Dhola post contacted and reinforced. Primary responsibility for this task was given to an army battalion (9 Punjab), parts of which were already at the forward staging positions called Lumpu and Shakti (see Map 8). On 9 September the entire battalion (and not just detachments from it) was ordered to go to Dhola. More important, the entire brigade of which 9 Punjab was a part (7 Brigade) was told to move out within forty-eight hours, so as to concentrate in the Dhola area too.[2]

The orders for moving the entire brigade came officially from Eastern Command Headquarters at Lucknow.[3] The eastern theater commander, Lieutenant General L. P. Sen, had been in contact via the military telephone system with Army Chief Thapar in New Delhi and had acted together with him.[4] It is not clear whether the defense minister was involved in this decision. Nevertheless, he must at least have been informed.

Relief of certain forward posts (including Dhola), should they get into trouble, had been part of army contingency planning. But the order to dispatch all of 7 Brigade to the rescue of Dhola not only bore no relationship to the existing contingency plans; it also altered the entire Indian defensive disposition in NEFA. Tawang, the recently designated "vital ground" for 4 Division in NEFA, would be stripped of most of its garrison and would be covered only by makeshift reinforcement efforts in subsequent weeks. A modest defense plan for western NEFA, devised during the past few months by General Prasad of 4 Division, had thus come undone, as had all other defense plans before it.[5]

Only slightly less ominous was the confusion allowed to reign within the army chain of command. General Prasad at 4 Division Headquarters received a signal directly from Army Headquarters, calling for an attack on the Chinese after relief of the Dhola post. This was just one of many contradictory early missives that Prasad thought he could ignore, with the support of his immediate superior.[6] That superior officer was the commander of XXXIII Corps, Lieutenant General Umrao Singh, who considered deliberate caution to be the best way to contain what he saw as panic in Delhi. Reacting to another Army Headquarters order that there be no firing, he signaled for specific instructions on just how the intruding Chinese were to be handled.[7]

The authoritative decision to use force to remove the Chinese from the south and southwest slopes of Thagla Ridge came on 10 or 11 September. Whether it was partly a response to Umrao's signal or was made independently is not clear. This decision contained several elements. Chief among them were (1) Physical contact had to be maintained with the Dhola post even if that required the use of force. (2) The government would not accept any withdrawal from Dhola unless Indian troops were pushed out by superior Chinese forces. (3) The government was not prepared to accept intrusions of any kind into NEFA; therefore, if the Chinese came, they had to be thrown out by force.[8]

The decision was taken at a New Delhi meeting chaired by Krishna Menon. Among those present were Generals Thapar and Sen and

Foreign Secretary Desai. The immediate stimulus for the decision was the perception that Chinese strength near Dhola was at the battalion level, while the Indians now had a brigade moving up. If the brigade arrived on time, Chinese positions might not yet be well prepared and further reinforced.[9]

Army Headquarters still was asked to pass judgment (along with Sen) on the feasibility of the operation. General Thapar, Major General Dhillon (Kaul's deputy), and the Army Headquarters staff thought it was feasible, given the reasonable assumption that the brigade would take three days (closer to forty-eight hours) to arrive. The Chinese later covered that distance in reverse more quickly. Army Headquarters determined that sufficient supplies were available for maintaining a brigade via air supply. Dhillon's perception was that Army Headquarters did provide the necessary logistical air support at the time.[10]

The Gap between the Decision and Reality

If calculations in Delhi presented an optimistic picture, the view from NEFA was entirely different. General Sen, who bore the primary responsibility for getting the required speed out of the officers and troops in NEFA, had already found Umrao Singh uncooperative. Sen then encountered fierce resistance at a meeting in Tezpur on 12 September, when he read out the order for the oncoming military operation to the commanders of XXXIII Corps (Umrao), 4 Division (Prasad), and the Assam Rifles. Also present were the head of the Indian Air Force, Air Chief Marshal M. M. Engineer, and other necessary (subordinate) officers. The strongest objections came after the open session, during a private conference between Generals Sen and Umrao Singh.[11]

By this time Umrao had his own reasoned argument to offer. It was based on a preliminary assessment of the Dhola situation offered by the 7 Brigade commander, Dalvi, and on the conclusions drawn from a helicopter reconnaissance of Thagla Ridge by the division commander, Prasad.[12] But Sen had already cut short the comments of both Umrao and Prasad at the open meeting. In addition, the personal relationship between Sen and Umrao was one of "long-standing personal animosity."[13] Therefore, the private talk between Umrao and Sen was not reasoned but, instead, was conducted in an atmosphere of deep resentment.

Umrao handed a written version of his views to Sen several hours later, and then filed another copy with Eastern Command Headquarters.[14] The substance of Umrao's written statement has been accurately summarized as follows:

> He assured his superior officers that he was determined to take prompt action, but suggested that the nature of that action must be based on the capabilities of his forces. He pointed out that the Chinese, who could build up quickly to divisional strength north of Tawang, could steadily outbid any reinforcements that the Indians could put into the Thagla area. All Indian supply to troops around Dhola Post would have to be by air-drop, while the Chinese roadhead was only a few miles behind Thagla Ridge. His troops would be operating at altitudes of between 13,000 and 16,000 feet; winter was closing in, and therefore they would need heavy clothing and tents. In conclusion, Umrao Singh suggested that Dhola Post should simply be withdrawn to the map-marked boundary about three miles to the south . . . but if that were ruled out for political reasons, the Army's commitment should be limited to two battalions which should be deployed south of Dhola Post, and south of the map-marked McMahon Line to meet any further advance by the Chinese.[15]

Other points made by Umrao verbally or in his written statement (or both) were that sending 7 Brigade to the Namkachu area exposed Tawang, the protection of which remained the army's primary responsibility in NEFA; that XXXIII Corps' responsibility for Nagaland and Manipur would grow more onerous if Indian troops were drawn from there; and that Pakistan could take advantage of any Indian involvement in NEFA.[16] Another of Umrao's arguments was that he and his field commanders needed time to devise a longer, written "Appreciation" of the situation and conduct a proper logistical buildup. The normal process of preparing for a military operation could not be shortened.[17]

Sen, reflecting New Delhi's point of view, continued to insist that the NEFA operation had to be implemented. He demanded that Umrao and his subordinates produce a detailed plan. Thus, two entirely different definitions of the NEFA situation had come into being by 12 September, along with major command problems. Why were such contrasting perceptions adopted by the different Indian command levels?

The perceptions at Army Headquarters in New Delhi rested on what can be described as a textbook approach to the Dhola problem. Rapid movement by 7 Brigade could be expected only if one could assume conditions of access, mobility, and logistical support that were

simply nonexistent in NEFA at the time. No one at Army
Headquarters—except for the momentarily absent Director of Military Operations, Brigadier Palit—had direct experience of NEFA as
a theater of military operations.[18]

From the vantage point of Thapar and Dhillon at Army Headquarters, the Operation Leghorn decision was logistically practical because
of the availability of air support. They did not recognize that simply
rounding up enough aircraft would not solve all problems. As
Brigadier Dalvi of 7 Brigade was already realizing by 10 September,
weather conditions in NEFA were uncertain at best; dropping zones
were "indifferent"; and helicopters and other "carrying agencies" to
supplement the aircraft, or for getting supplies from the dropping
zones to the forward echelons, were in short supply. The most basic
fault was that no system had been developed in advance; "the Air
Force cannot control the weather, procure additional aircraft, train
pilots, or manufacture supply dropping equipment in a matter of a few
days."[19]

The differences in perception flowed as well from the fact that the
only NEFA defense plan in existence in September 1962 was that of 4
Division (as endorsed by XXXIII Corps). The vacuum in military
planning at higher levels encouraged ad hoc thinking and action. If
procedure, manpower, matériel, and finance had earlier been committed to NEFA on a sustained basis, the outlook of the defense minister,
Army Headquarters, and Eastern Command would have more closely
matched that of the NEFA theater commanders and their staffs.

Furthermore, the estimate of Chinese capabilities devised at the
NEFA levels of command was greatly different from that prevailing
in Delhi. The XXXIII Corps and 4 Division estimates were that the
Chinese had as much as one division and a half in the Dhola area.
Delhi (Mullik) was insisting that the Chinese had nothing like that
strength.[20]

On the Indian side, 7 Brigade on 12 September had just two
understrength battalions. Only one of them (9 Punjab) was available
for Dhola, since the other (1 Sikh) had to try to cover Tawang. A third
battalion (1/9 Gurkha) was on its way down to a rest assignment and
had to be recalled and sent on the forced march up to Tawang and
Dhola. For these Gurkhas the journey would be approximately 250
miles long. A fourth battalion (2 Rajput), recently withdrawn from
Walong in eastern NEFA, was subsequently added and sent up to
Dhola via the same route. A last addition to 7 Brigade (4 Grenadiers)

would not arrive at Dhola until just before the outbreak of war in October.

These troop dispositions would mean that the Indians would be outnumbered by the Chinese in the general Dhola-Thagla area at all times. Even if the four Indian battalions finally stationed along the Namkachu River near Dhola by late October had been at full strength, they would have fielded only 3,600 men. The strength of a Chinese division was estimated by the Indian Army to be approximately 17,000 men, but a more likely figure is 8,000 to 10,000 men.[21]

The trails from Tawang to Dhola had been reconnoitered by the commander of 9 Punjab, Lieutenant Colonel Misra,[22] but the prospective combat zone was largely unknown. The troops would have to rely on pouch ammunition. Porterage and mules for supplies never ceased to be a problem. Except for 9 Punjab, the Dhola battalions would arrive in poor physical condition. They did not have proper equipment or clothing and were exhausted, affected by the altitude, and hampered by high rates of illness.

These salient problems were never properly explained to Delhi by General Sen, whose responsibility it was to do so. It is doubtful whether he was even aware of them in early September. Nor did he ever comprehend their scope, since he had never been north of Tezpur in Assam. Instead, Sen quickly became convinced that his main problem was lower-level obstructionism. Sen later described his immediate subordinates—Umrao, Prasad, and Dalvi—as "ghastly failures."[23]

Sen's mind was also focused on strategic matters. Indeed, throughout September the usual roles of the chief of Eastern Command and the top-level decision-makers in New Delhi were in some ways reversed. While General Sen did tell the defense minister's group that an attack on Thagla Ridge would fail disastrously, he asserted himself mainly on the question of whether large-scale Chinese retaliation could be expected all along the NEFA border. He felt that the Chinese were sure to eliminate the NEFA forward-policy posts. He later recalled that he and Thapar were told by Krishna Menon that the matter of China's reaction to Operation Leghorn was political and lay outside their sphere. Sen replied with some heat that politics did come into his sphere as far as the NEFA operation was concerned.[24] But he allowed himself to be overruled.

Only to a limited degree was Sen prepared to be a buffer between Delhi and the NEFA field commanders, thereby mediating the opposed definitions of the military situation. Primarily because of the way he defined his role, the Delhi civilians and Army Headquarters remained isolated and the NEFA officers remained alienated.

Operation Leghorn Delayed

Detailed tactical ideas about small-unit placement and maneuver were being pressed upon both Sen and his subordinates, directly from New Delhi. On or about 15 September, the implementing orders to 7 Brigade from Army Headquarters were made quite specific: 9 Punjab battalion was to capture a Chinese post opposite Dhola, clear the Chinese from Thagla Ridge, and establish posts on the watershed heights west of Thagla Pass. The authoritative signal, signed by Thapar, identified the places to be occupied on the ridge. These were Yumtsola and Karpola II, both of them at approximately 16,000 feet.[25] (See Map 8.)

General Prasad in NEFA registered his objection with Umrao, with notices sent to Army Headquarters (and presumably to General Sen at Eastern Command Headquarters). The division commander's point was that Chinese strength south of Thagla Ridge had increased to two companies, or approximately 400 men. One Indian battalion (800 to 900 men, but only at full strength) was not enough to deal with them.[26]

Sen thought that the Chinese were on Thagla Ridge in battalion strength when he conferred with Thapar on 16 or 17 September. He did not think that posts could be established at Karpola II or Yumtsola, not only because of Chinese numbers but also because of the difficult terrain and his inability to support the posts logistically. But rather than question anything basic, he secured the army chief's support for a delay in the implementation of Operation Leghorn until all of 7 Brigade was in place.

By now Krishna Menon was holding a meeting each day with the appropriate officials and military officers, to deal with the NEFA operation. At the meeting held on 16 or 17 September, Sen reported that more time would be needed for the whole of 7 Brigade to concentrate in the Dhola area. He assured his listeners that the brigade would carry out its assigned mission, but he preferred to wait. According to Mullik, Sen seemed unsure of the numbers of Chinese in the Thagla Ridge area, particularly since they had larger forces north of the ridge line. Sen reportedly said that he did not want to "stick his head out too far till he was quite sure of his own position." He gave 2

October as the likely starting date of the offensive; 7 Brigade would have been situated properly by then.[27]

The following major decisions emerged from the deliberations at the meeting on 16 or 17 September: (1) 9 Punjab would wait until the entire brigade had arrived but would carry out a reconnaissance in force. (2) The reconnaissance would be directed toward establishing posts north and northwest of Dhola and on the Indian-claimed McMahon line. (3) The Chinese would be contained in their present positions south of Thagla Ridge.[28] If possible and as an additional step, an Indian post would be established at a position called Tsangle (see Map 8). Thapar reasoned that holding Tsangle would "deny the Chinese the opportunity to outflank our positions on the river and also to secure our back towards Bhutan."[29]

ADDITIONAL IMPLEMENTING DECISIONS

The meeting on 16 or 17 September also featured Mullik's daunting assessment of Chinese activities along the entire border. After Mullik's report Thapar asked "if there was danger of an all-out war breaking out all over the frontier if we took action at Dhola" (Mullik's words).[30] In NEFA Thapar had sufficient troops only for the Kameng region (he meant the Tawang, Khinzemane, Dhola sector). Foreign Secretary Desai replied that, since the Dhola operation would be a limited one, general Chinese escalation was unlikely, although Indian posts in one or two more places might be threatened. Chinese behavior along other parts of the frontier showed this pattern. As his statements and actions were to prove, Thapar was not reassured. But at this particular meeting he was still ready to initiate the offensive once the troops were in place.

Tactical planning for the offensive itself was supposedly being done at 4 Division Headquarters in Tezpur. General Sen had set up his own temporary headquarters nearby and was pressuring General Prasad. Prasad recommended that there be no frontal assault against the positions the Chinese had prepared on Thagla Ridge. Instead he favored a flanking movement from the west toward the east and northeast. Although Prasad later called this his "tongue-in-cheek" plan, concocted under intense pressure, the notion of flanking the Chinese from the west became the basis of all subsequent Indian tactical thinking.[31]

Prasad considered his plan a fantasy for all sorts of logistical reasons, but he did not explain them to General Sen. By naming airdrop zones, and by defining an Indian line of advance, the 4 Division commander reinforced Sen's conviction that all things were possible if enough pressure were applied to lower formations. Prasad made the attack contingent on stocking supplies for thirty days at the Lumpu rear staging area, and he called for fifteen days' supplies further forward at Tsangdhar. He apparently hoped that Sen would recognize the logistical impracticality of it all, but he was wrong.

Meanwhile, 9 Punjab battalion had reached the Namkachu River on 15 September, after an arduous but rapid traverse over the Hathungla Pass (approximately 13,400 feet). It was not the first column to contact the beleaguered Dhola post; an Assam Rifles detachment had done that a few days earlier. But finding a company of Chinese troops on both sides of the river, Lieutenant Colonel Misra of 9 Punjab bypassed the Chinese on the south bank by taking a company (approximately 120 men if this unit was close to full strength) upstream to the Dhola post. Most of his battalion was left to cover the southern ends of two log bridges (designated I and II by the Indians) over the presently unfordable stream. Dhola post lay near yet another bridge (III), which the Chinese had previously destroyed; and one other bridge (IV) lay a short distance upriver. A platoon (40 men at most) was placed on top of Tsangdhar, a knoll commanding bridges III and IV and vital to the entire Dhola position. (See Map 8.)

With his battalion under orders not to fire except in self-defense, and needing to block the Chinese from coming further into Indian-claimed territory, Misra had spread his force out along the south bank of the Namkachu. The drawbacks to this tactical situation were later summarized by Dalvi: "The Namka Chu from Bridges I to IV had become the *de-facto* military boundary. The Chinese had control of the whole of Thagla Ridge, which was ours. Unfortunately the Punjabis were pinned down over 7 to 9 miles in small localities, manning flag-posts to prevent minor incursions. Their localities had no mutual support, limited fields of fire and no room for manoeuvre. They had only pouch ammunition and two 3-inch mortars."[32]

A Chinese infantry company met by 9 Punjab near Dhola on 15 September called for a meeting with the appropriate local Indian civil officials to discuss the limits of each side's control in the area. An Indian political officer was sent forward to meet his Chinese counterpart, but his journey was halted by a high-level policy decision. According to one account, that decision was made by Nehru in

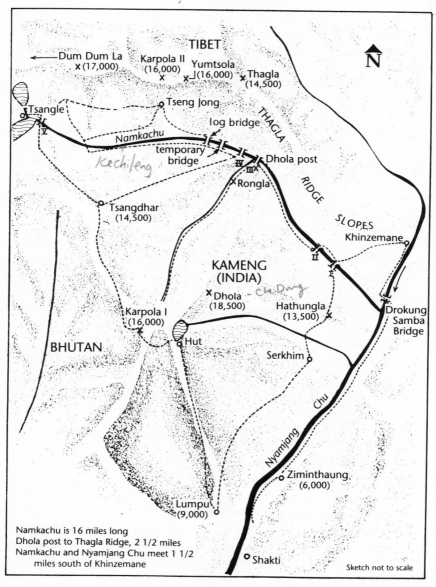

TIBET

← Dum Dum La ×(17,000)   Karpola II
(16,000)   Yumtsola
(16,000)   Thagla
(14,500)

Tsangle   Tseng Jong

log bridge

Namkachu   temporary
bridge   Dhola post

Kechileng   Rongla

Tsangdhar
(14,500)   RIDGE

SLOPES

Khinzemane

KAMENG
(INDIA)   *Chi Ding*

×Dhola
(18,500)   Hathungla
(13,500)   Drokung
Samba
Bridge

Karpola I
(16,000)   Hut

BHUTAN   Serkhim

Chu

Nyamjang

Ziminthaung
(6,000)

Lumpu
(9,000)

Namkachu is 16 miles long
Dhola post to Thagla Ridge, 2 1/2 miles
Namkachu and Nyamjang Chu meet 1 1/2
 miles south of Khinzemane   Shakti

Sketch not to scale

Map 8.   THAGLA RIDGE AREA AS OF 8 SEPTEMBER TO 20
OCTOBER 1962.

London; according to another, the matter was decided in New Delhi.[33] In either case the choice was entirely consistent with the Indian contention that Thagla Ridge was the border to be respected, as the Chinese had been told during the officials' talks of 1960.

On the strength of telephone conversations held by Thapar and Sen between 17 and 19 September, Thapar was told that the first of 7 Brigade's battalions had reached Dhola, the second would arrive on 24 September, and the third would arrive on 29 September.[34] Thapar thus gave Krishna Menon the impression that things were going well enough.

The defense minister's meeting held on or about 18 September focused on Ladakh. Lieutenant General Daulat Singh of Western Command was present in the room and Krishna Menon asked him to explain his plans. He said that the shortage of troops in Ladakh left him unable to defend any positions beyond the central valley near Leh, and he wanted to withdraw from his forward positions so as to concentrate around Leh itself. This remark came after Mullik had given an intelligence report; such summaries had become normal practice at these meetings, although Krishna Menon had especially wanted Daulat to hear this one. Daulat found the IB's details alarming, but others did not, and Thapar would not support Daulat. There was no consensus that the forward policy posts should be abandoned.

Daulat relented, particularly since reinforcements were promised. He had asked for an extra battalion plus artillery for the town of Chushul, and these requirements were eventually met (as were later requests). Air Chief Marshal Engineer, participating in the meeting and among those opposed to a Ladakh pullback, was ready to increase the Indian airlift to Ladakh.[35]

Once back in Western Command, Daulat Singh was prepared to act vigorously to buttress his positions in Ladakh and elsewhere, and to do so with or without Delhi's urging. Using his own available ground and air transport resources, as well as what had just been allotted to him by the air force, Daulat began transferring troops to Ladakh from the Kashmir sector of his command. This operation began in early October, some weeks prior to the outbreak of war, and continued during the war itself.[36] Many of the troops sent before the outbreak of war had already been earmarked to go to Leh and beyond, but they had been awaiting the completion of preparations for their maintenance. Now they were part of a forced effort to bring forward posts up to their full complements of men.[37]

There is some question whether New Delhi knew precisely what Daulat was doing and whether Daulat was doing more than Delhi had anticipated. But Army Headquarters most likely was aware and made no move to interfere. Daulat Singh himself was a cautious man, unlikely to act on his own, and great leeway was normally allowed the western commander, who controlled nearly half the combat strength of the Indian Army.[38]

The proper use of the Indian Air Force came under discussion at the same New Delhi meeting that Daulat had attended (on or about 18 September). Tactical bombing of Chinese fortifications and troop concentrations in western Tibet, bordering Ladakh, was considered. There was debate within the defense minister's group over whether the Chinese possessed advanced Soviet fighters (MiG-21s). Krishna Menon argued vehemently that the Soviets had supplied them to no other country but India. The decision was that, given the many imbalances between the Chinese and Indian air forces, air combat should be avoided; otherwise, civilian targets in India, such as Calcutta and Kanpur, might be endangered. No corresponding targets existed in Tibet, and worthwhile targets in China proper lay outside the capability of India bomber aircraft. The air force's role would thus remain limited to transport and supply.[39]

The first shooting incident on the Dhola front occurred on 20 September. Starting at some time after 9 P.M. and continuing intermittently throughout the night, the firing produced wounded on the Indian side and fatalities among the Chinese, or so the conflicting accounts indicate. The evidence suggests that the firefight was initiated by the Chinese.[40]

Literally overnight the character of the Dhola confrontation, for the Indian soldiers, became radically different. Previously, occupation and counteroccupation of positions had taken place with much communication between the two sides. Now the communication continued, but there was tense confrontation.

The 20 September incident did not change the thinking in New Delhi, where it was overshadowed by other concerns.

THE ROLE OF DIPLOMACY

Since the overall Indian response to the Dhola problem had been worked out by 18 September, Krishna Menon felt free to leave the country. Most likely he was still present, however, when the Indian government decided to agree to talks with the Chinese, beginning in

Peking on 15 October, as proposed in a Chinese diplomatic note dated 13 September. This decision was probably made by the Krishna Menon group in consultation with Nehru and reflected the confidence they now felt about India's abilities to cope with the NEFA situation.

The MEA communicated this decision to the Chinese in a note sent on 19 September, but it was made clear that China would first have to accept the Indian version of what the talks should cover. As defined by India, the discussions would focus only on "measures to restore the status quo in the Western Sector which has been altered by force in the last few years and to remove the current tensions in that area."[41] As had been the case since August, Chinese withdrawal from Ladakh was no longer defined as a precondition for talks, but the Indian approach was still quite different from that of the Chinese. The Chinese had again proposed a 20-kilometer withdrawal by both sides along the entire boundary and were prepared to discuss this proposal. They were also interested in moving on to discuss the Officials' Report, as the Indian side had wanted.[42] The Indian government still rejected the 20-kilometer proposal and would not agree to any substantive discussions until agreements about (mainly Chinese) withdrawals in Ladakh had first been reached and implemented.

CHAPTER TEN

Later Prewar Decisions, 22 September to 19 October 1962

THE FINAL TACTICAL decisions of the prewar phase of the crisis period, made in the month before the outbreak of war on 20 October, can be listed as follows: (1) to override the objections of Army Chief Thapar (decision made on 22 September); (2) to change the generals in NEFA (3 October); (3) to avoid use of force and attempt positional maneuver (7–8 October); (4) to postpone Operation Leghorn indefinitely (11 October); (5) to hold the Indian positions in the Dhola area for the winter (17 October). As will be noted below, some of these dates are approximate.

TO OVERRIDE THAPAR'S OBJECTIONS

A need for a confirming decision would arise in Krishna Menon's absence. At the defense meeting of 22 September, General Thapar predicted that the Chinese, in response to the NEFA operation, would most likely attack Indian posts in the Galwan Valley and elsewhere in Ladakh, in order to move up to their 1960 claim line. Thapar had spoken to Mullik a day or two earlier of his concern over India's suffering a reverse at Dhola and his being blamed, although (judging from the tenor of his reported remarks at the 22 September meeting) he was more certain about what would happen in the Western Sector. Accordingly, Thapar now wanted his orders in writing. The demand was partly a protest and partly an attempt to "fortify himself" so as to avoid blame.[1]

It is legitimate to ask why he did not take his stand earlier. One reason is that Thapar generally sought to stay out of Krishna Menon's way, to avoid the browbeating of subordinates in which the defense minister often indulged.[2] Thapar was an honest man but not an energetic one.[3] Nor was he politically adept or influential; his limited role had been well defined before the crisis began. Kaul was the strongman in the army, not Thapar. It took some deliberation and courage on Thapar's part to assert himself.

Thapar had his "moment of truth" on 22 September, when he received his written order, and perhaps he should have resigned at that time.[4] But such a step would not have achieved much. In 1959, when Thapar's predecessor, Thimayya, threatened to resign over another issue, Nehru made him look foolish. In the current public mood, Thapar would have looked like a coward or worse.

An Army Headquarters staffer close to Thapar has described some additional ambiguities that the army chief faced. It is true that a military commander in such circumstances does have a legitimate choice: "Either he resigns and the government must find someone else to carry out its order, or he implements the decision irrespective of the consequences."[5] At the same time, he realizes that armies are often committed to battle when necessity demands, even with little or no chance of victory. Judging from all descriptions of him, Thapar—having warned the government of the grave consequences likely to follow—would choose to follow orders and hope for the best.

It has been reported that Thapar received his written orders after Krishna Menon was telephoned in New York.[6] But an informant close to these events has disagreed. He has argued that a senior civil servant under the Indian governmental system can sign a statement of established policy without consulting higher authority.[7] In this case the decision was that the statement would be written and signed by H.C. Sarin, Krishna Menon's right-hand man in the defense ministry (although not formally the highest-ranking civil servant). In a few sentences addressed directly to Thapar, Sarin simply confirmed the instructions that had already been discussed and agreed upon. According to one well-placed source, no verbatim text of the order has been made public; the one published version of it is inaccurate.[8]

The decision to override Thapar and confirm the policy of using force in NEFA did not ease Thapar's concern for the Western Sector. On 22 September Army Headquarters warned Western Command that the NEFA operation might cause some forward posts in Ladakh to be attacked, and it ordered that the troops be alerted. The 22 September warning further required that (in the words of one source) "the post defenses [be] strengthened" if possible and that the posts should "fight it out" if they were attacked. However, one participant in these events claims that the message had a different meaning. According to Palit, a discussion at Army Headquarters resulted in Thapar's agreeing that these posts could not be asked to fight if no plan had been made to support them operationally. But Thapar knew that Daulat Singh wanted a general withdrawal, and for that step Western Command could not be given permission. So the army chief decided that the "penny packet" posts could be pulled back, but only after inflicting maximum casualties on the Chinese.[9]

The 22 September warning therefore said that Western Command should strengthen (i.e., consolidate) its *positions*. Whether the warning also spoke of strengthening individual *posts* is unclear, as is Daulat's interpretation of the warning. But independent accounts of the later fighting (see Chapter 12) show that posts were withdrawn on the orders of Western Command after fighting well, as Thapar had allegedly wanted.

TO CHANGE GENERALS IN NEFA

Lieutenant General Umrao Singh's resistance to Operation Leghorn had never relented after his contretemps with General Sen on 12 September, and he remained a formidable impediment. Umrao's could conceivably have been an influential voice once his friend Kaul returned to New Delhi. The XXXIII Corps commander was on excellent terms with Kaul. But he and General Sen were personal enemies.[10]

Umrao had been ordered by Sen to produce an operational plan, since Sen had not accepted the "tongue-in-cheek" plan devised by General Prasad. Umrao passed the new assignment along to Prasad, who in turn passed it to Brigadier Dalvi of 7 Brigade. On a typewriter in a tent at Lumpu, and in the presence of Prasad, Dalvi and his staff wrote a new Appreciation and plan. Following the tactic used earlier by Prasad, Dalvi attempted to show just how unrealistic Operation Leghorn was. The envisaged operation would require supplies and equipment set to specifications and amounts beyond what the airdrop system could deliver prior to the coming of winter. This last point was implied rather than stated outright.

The Dalvi plan held that at least ten days would be required for an approach march, and required stockpiling of supplies within two weeks. It is not clear whether any specific dates were mentioned, but it was clear that the two-week preparation period would last until

10–15 October. Since the Chinese could reinforce faster than the Indians, surprise was important (but would soon be lost when Tsangle, on the approach route, was reconnoitered and then occupied by Indian troops on orders from Delhi). The jumping-off point for the Indian flanking maneuver was a small knoll further forward, called Tseng Jong. Tseng Jong was situated across the Namkachu River from the Indian lines, next to Thagla Ridge, slightly to the northwest of the Chinese river positions (see Map 8). The Indian move would therefore come from the Indian left flank and the Chinese right. Tseng Jong (spelled Singjang in some accounts) could not be occupied prematurely or else the Chinese would know what was afoot; but in any case the Chinese could observe the move to Tseng Jong, and their reactions would determine any Indian steps thereafter.

Dalvi tried to show that open warfare with the Chinese might be avoided. The Chinese could be removed from the Namkachu bridges nonviolently, as Indian troops rolled down from Tseng Jong onto their river positions. In Dalvi's mind the plan was "not really a military one, as it did not cater for any Chinese retaliatory action." Instead, it was more "a police action to herd out intruders; and a probe in strength to gauge the Chinese reaction."[11] It was also obsolete in that it was designed to remove much of a Chinese battalion, this being the estimate of Chinese strength Dalvi was told to use. Dalvi and Prasad both knew that Chinese strength in the Thagla Ridge area (on the southeast side of the ridge itself and behind it on the Tibetan side) was much higher.

On 26 or 27 September Umrao Singh was in Lumpu and was shown the Dalvi draft. Umrao was not satisfied with the Dalvi Appreciation, thinking it still too optimistic. He recalled many years later that Dalvi had "tried to bite off more than he could chew."[12] Umrao wanted no doubt left about the impossibility of launching the operation, given the inadequate forces and logistical support available.

Asked by Umrao to add his own comments, Prasad provided them in writing on 29 September; his published memoirs describe the final product as his draft Appreciation, rather than Dalvi's. Judging from Prasad's recollection, he upgraded Dalvi's plan to allow "for a Chinese build-up of a regimental . . . group [equivalent to an Indian brigade] on Thag La." This matched his own current estimate, "confirmed by the local IB representative."[13]

Ultimately, the three NEFA commanders produced a plan requiring the strength of more than a fully armed and equipped Indian division.[14] The final document represented the degree of consensus that Umrao, Prasad, and Dalvi were able to achieve at Lumpu. The manpower and logistical requirements were raised, and the proximity of winter weather was emphasized. It was made clear that the operation could commence only if the buildup of supplies was completed by 15 October.[15] Winter shelters and resources for six months would have to be assured for those troops forward of Lumpu by the end of November.

At the end of this process of consultation, Umrao felt compelled to add his own written statement to the effect that the operation "was just not on."[16] He handed the plan and his addendum to Sen personally in Tezpur on 29 September and got an initial response. Sen remarked that everyone seemed to have gotten cold feet. He emphasized that the air force could be used to meet the supply problems.[17] Although he recognized that it was impossible to meet the logistical specifications named by the field commanders, he refused to believe that such stocking was truly necessary.

Overruled a second time, Umrao again lodged a written protest, submitting it to Sen several hours after they had met. He confirmed it as a formal (radio) signal to Army Headquarters, with copies sent to all appropriate echelons. He objected not just to Operation Leghorn but also to General Sen's entire handling of the situation.

Sen's interference was not a new issue for Umrao Singh. From the start of the 1962 crisis, he had tried to get Sen's headquarters to stop moving his troops. Nor was the 29 September protest the first time he had gone over Sen's head. On 28 September he had signaled Army Headquarters directly, in response to the order to dispatch a patrol of not less than one company to Tsangle near Dhola. The order, sent through Eastern Command by Thapar, covered other small-unit dispositions as well. The Umrao response was caustic, as was true of his signals generally. A copy went to Sen, although the message was primarily meant for Thapar.[18]

There could be little surprise in Delhi on 2 October, when General Sen blamed the NEFA delays and failures on Umrao. On the advice of Brigadier Palit, Sen took up the Umrao problem with the army chief.[19] Later that day, at the regular defense minister's meeting, he described his difficulties with Umrao. Krishna Menon was surely present, having returned to Delhi on 30 September.

Sen apparently accused Umrao of having an operational plan but refusing to implement it.[20] Because of Umrao Singh's failure to carry out orders, Sen said, the positioning of 7 Brigade's battalions near Dhola could not be completed on schedule. Thus, there was no prospect of military action in the next day or two. Unless a change in command was made immediately, the government might be let down at a critical moment.

Later that day Thapar and Sen met with the defense minister and asked for permission to remove Umrao from command of XXXIII Corps. Krishna Menon agreed, but he lost his temper when Sen asked for the appointment of Lieutenant General S. H. F. J. Manekshaw in Umrao's place.[21] Sen's suggestion was extraordinary, since Manekshaw was an outspoken combat soldier who had been persecuted for his criticism of Krishna Menon and Kaul. But Sen was probably looking for someone strong enough to manage the NEFA operation and act as a buffer between Sen himself and Army Headquarters. An irate Krishna Menon would not have it.

Another candidate was already at hand, seemingly able to serve the purposes of all concerned. Kaul had returned to Delhi on 1 October, but was officially still on a leave. On 2 October Thapar took the opportunity to recall him as the Chief of General Staff, and the next day Kaul returned to active service.[22]

Among Krishna Menon's group of consultants, a proposal to send Kaul to NEFA, in place of Umrao, met with opposition for several reasons. Mullik , Sarin, and Palit wanted Kaul to continue as Chief of General Staff. There was also a feeling within the Army Headquarters staff that Kaul needed to be protected from himself. Those loyal to him were mindful of his lack of combat experience and his tendency to overdo.[23] At least one senior staffer privately begged Kaul not to go.[24] But Kaul would not be dissuaded. In his own mind, and in the thinking of those who appointed him, Kaul was the "bulldozer" who would bring to NEFA the motivation and initiative needed to make Operation Leghorn succeed.[25]

On 3 October Krishna Menon, Thapar, and Kaul decided that Kaul would replace Umrao Singh. Thapar and Krishna Menon anticipated a short military operation, with Kaul returning to his regular post quickly. The decision was not described this way to the press and the public. Instead, it was announced that a new corps (IV Corps) would be created, with Kaul as commander. Left unknown to the public was the fact that no new troops were going to NEFA, except for Kaul and the staff for his new headquarters.[26]

Prior to his departure early in the morning of 4 October, Kaul may have leaked news of the command change to the press. Even if he did not, the public was told that a special "task force" had been created to accomplish the task of pushing the Chinese back beyond Thagla Ridge. Members of Kaul's new staff, who were with him on the flight to Tezpur, "later testified that while on the plane he had told them that the newspapers would headline his appointment next morning, and said that if he failed in his mission the Government might well fall."[27]

As Kaul was being sent to NEFA, the Indian government responded to the latest Chinese diplomatic initiative. The Chinese government had said, in a note dated 3 October, that China would not withdraw from "vast tracts of its own territory," despite India's setting this step as a precondition for serious talks about the boundary question. But the Chinese wanted talks to start anyway and proposed that each side discuss whatever aspect of the conflict the other wished to raise, including questions pertaining to the Eastern and Middle sectors.[28]

In its response, on 6 October, the Indian government demanded a Chinese pullback from the Dhola area as a precondition for talks. It also demanded a Chinese acknowledgment that for the immediate future such talks would cover tension-reducing measures (i.e., Chinese withdrawals) in the Western Sector. Implementation of such measures would be required prior to discussion of larger issues on the basis of the Officials' Report. Furthermore, India would no longer agree to the start of Sino-Indian talks in Peking on 15 October, or to any talks "under duress or continuing threat of force."[29]

TO AVOID FORCE AND ATTEMPT
POSITIONAL MANEUVERING

After Kaul arrived in Tezpur on 4 October to take up his NEFA command, he learned that two of 7 Brigade's battalions had gone no further than Lumpu. He helicoptered to Lumpu on 5 October. In the absence of Brigadier Dalvi (whom Prasad had hastily sent forward, toward Dhola), as well as Dalvi's battalion commanders and most of his officers, Kaul ordered the Lumpu troops to move out for the Tsangdhar drop zone. He did so over the protests of the brigade major whom Dalvi had left in charge. Kaul revealed his state of mind by bullying this junior officer and denouncing the performance of 7 Brigade to date.[30]

The two battalions (1/9 Gurkha Rifles and 2 Rajput), plus the 7

Brigade headquarters staff, did depart from Lumpu in the morning. To use Maxwell's succinct description, the troops "marched out— still in cotton uniforms, with one blanket per man; carrying fifty rounds per man and their light weapons, leaving other equipment at Lumpu or still further behind.... They were sent over the more difficult of the two routes to the Namka Chu, the 16,000 foot Karpo La I Pass, and then down to Tsangdhar at 14,500 feet, there to await further orders."[31] Deaths from illness occurred among these troops because of conditions on the march and because of their own weakened state.

When Kaul joined up with Prasad on 6 October, and proceeded with him by helicopter and on foot toward Dhola, Kaul revealed that in Delhi he had become convinced that a 4 Division plan existed, which he would implement. The plan in Kaul's mind covered everything that had been devised by Dalvi, Prasad, and Umrao between 25 and 29 September, as presented by Sen at Army Headquarters. No one had told Kaul how impractical it all was; only now could Prasad, another friend of Kaul's, explain to him how such planning had been done and how different the real situation now was. Although Kaul showed some flexibility, he was going to carry on with Operation Leghorn. He took seriously the latest in the series of dates specified by Sen for completing the operation—10 October.[32]

Kaul and Prasad reached Dhola late on 6 October. The last part of the journey, a climb over the Hathungla Ridge to reach the Namkachu Valley on the other side, was especially strenuous for Kaul, who was not acclimatized. Although he was carried by porters part of the way, he was risking serious illness. The region he had entered so abruptly was rugged. As described by Prasad, the topography in the northwestern corner of NEFA next to Bhutan

> is a mix of rugged mountains and valleys. The lower slopes, right down to the river line, are covered with large rhododendron bushes, in places as dense and extensive as a forest. Pines and firs grow on the high slopes and afford good cover. The tree line stops at about 15,000 feet on the southern slopes of mountains and at 13,000 feet on the northern slopes, which do not get as much of direct sunlight. Even at the height of summer the slopes and valleys in the shadows of northern sides of ridges can be covered with banks of snow and ice.[33]

There was no pause in Kaul's activity on 6, 7, and 8 October. He was shown around the Namkachu river line (at approximately 10,500– 12,500 feet in altitude), seeking observation points and making his own assessment. Prasad, Dalvi, and 7 Brigade's battalion commanders were hoping that Kaul would become aware of the tactical obstacles and dangers that they faced. Since his first talk with Prasad, Kaul had been drafting signals for Army Headquarters, outlining the difficulties but his messages were two-sided. Despite the problems, he was saying, every possible step was being taken and through his efforts he might still rescue the situation. Behind the signals was not only bravado but also a conviction that he still had to implement the plan. He did warn, however, that after any initial success the Chinese could dislodge his troops from the positions they had gained and could even overwhelm 7 Brigade.[34]

The heart of Kaul's updated plan, revealed to Prasad and Dalvi in discussions held on 7–9 October, was to place a battalion on Thagla Ridge itself, across the river. On 8 or 9 October he described to the brigade staff the mission that the designated battalion (2 Rajput) would undertake. The Rajputs, he said, would climb up the slopes of Thagla Ridge toward unoccupied Yumtsola Pass at the crest. He gave Dalvi the impression that the battalion would occupy Yumtsola itself, to the northwest of both the Chinese positions on Thagla Ridge and those down on the north bank of the Namkachu River, so as "to sit behind the Chinese."[35]

To another of his listeners, General Prasad, it was clear that Kaul did not mean for the Rajputs to go all the way up to the pass. Instead, the point was to establish an Indian foothold anywhere on Thagla Ridge. Kaul did not intend to launch an attack; making a token move would suffice.[36] This extension of the forward policy tactics developed in Ladakh would satisfy New Delhi, and Kaul hoped that the maneuver would not arouse the Chinese.

Kaul's plan came under challenge from Dalvi, who in turn was under pressure from his own officers. It was plain to him that the advancing battalion might become subject to artillery fire and to attack. He questioned Kaul about getting some artillery cover for his troops. His other questions reflected the horror in his mind over having a battalion sit in the snow on Yumtsola at 16,000 feet without proper clothing or means of supply. The Chinese could easily cut its line of communications by imposing a blocking force behind it. To all objections Kaul gave sweeping and unrealistic assurances, based on the assumption of Delhi's future logistical support for any gamble he might now take.

At the desperate urging of Dalvi (and in keeping with a suggestion by Prasad the night before) Kaul agreed to probe forward with just a patrol rather than commit a whole battalion. On 8 or 9 October one platoon was sent by 9 Punjab battalion across the river to climb toward the Tseng Jong knoll, which lay on Thagla Ridge but far below Yumtsola Pass (and nearby Karpola II Pass). The patrol reached Tseng Jong; the Chinese made no move to oppose it.[37]

Kaul thought his gambit was succeeding. During the evening of 9 October, he dictated an optimistic signal to Delhi. By "bold and speedy tactics," as well as surprise, his message said, he had begun the task of clearing the Chinese off Thagla Ridge. "He reported that his troops were in fact already in occupation of the crest."[38]

At approximate 10 P.M., however, consternation in the Indian lines south and southwest of the river was caused by an "awesome eerie sight."[39] A series of Chinese torchlight processions were moving across Thagla Ridge from east to west in the general direction of Tseng Jong. Shortly thereafter the Tseng Jong platoon reported that approximately one enemy battalion was massing against it. The officer commanding at Tseng Jong thought the Chinese would stage an attack at dawn. Kaul's mood turned gloomy.

At first light the next morning 10 October, things were still quiet, if ominously so. Nevertheless, by 6 A.M. the Rajput battalion was advancing, in small groups, along the river toward its crossing point to start its climb toward Tseng Jong, and perhaps Yumtsola.

TO POSTPONE OPERATION LEGHORN

Until 10 October Indian decision-makers had thought themselves in control of the escalation process and able to determine whether or not the line between positional chess playing and limited war would be crossed. That illusion ended on the morning of 10 October, when the Chinese threw an assault force of approximately 800 men, supported by mortar fire, against the Indian platoon (approximately 50 men) on and near Tseng Jong.

Prasad recalls that Kaul was "too stunned for an hour or so" to reason coherently. But Kaul was saying that Delhi would "have to do a complete rethink."[40] In response to a query from Dalvi, the movement of 2 Rajput along the river was stopped. During the entire 10 October affair, in fact, tactical direction on the Indian side fell to Dalvi. It was he who communicated with the beleaguered force at Tseng Jong and managed its withdrawal. The patrol reached the safety of the Indian lines. It had left behind six dead and five men missing and brought back eleven wounded (including the commanding officer).[41]

Even before the Tseng Jong patrol had returned, Dalvi and Prasad urged Kaul to abandon any thought of evicting the Chinese from Thagla Ridge. After days of argument Prasad believed that he had nearly convinced Kaul to order a pullback to Hathungla Ridge. But Kaul continued to shy away from such a step, claiming that he had no authority for it.[42] Instead, he set off, with a small accompanying party and General Prasad, to recross the Hathungla and fly to Delhi as soon as possible.

A signal sent before his departure sounded despairing and alarming when received at Army Headquarters around midnight.[43] Kaul claimed that a grave situation had arisen and that it was imperative for him to see the prime minister. He knew that Nehru was to leave shortly for Ceylon.[44] According to Mullik, Kaul also said that "he had himself seen the Chinese positions and their reactions. He felt that the Chinese were vastly superior to the Indians at this place. They were heavily equipped with artillery, mortars, and MMGs [machine guns]. They could overrun Indian positions easily and in that case Tawang and Bomdila and even the plains of Assam north of Brahmaputra would be threatened."[45]

When Kaul arrived in Delhi on 11 October, he was ill, although not yet noticeably so. Coming back over the Hathungla, he had collapsed with chest pain and breathing difficulties. He had contracted pulmonary edema, the altitude-induced form of pneumonia that had already killed a number of his men.[46] His determination to force a policy change at the highest level was weakened by his deteriorating physical condition and by his susceptibility to the group context to which he now returned.

From the many accounts of the meeting held at the prime minister's house that evening (11 October), certain key elements are discernible. "Nehru was in the chair." Krishna Menon, Thapar, Sen, Mullik, and other lesser figures were present. Kaul gave a careful and cogent lecture, complete with maps, sketches, and photographs. But it had the same psychological quality as his signals from NEFA. He described all the obstacles confronting him, including the estimate that 7 Brigade now faced an entire Chinese division. Yet he left the impression that things could still be done through heroic effort, which he was prepared to undertake.[47]

By his own account, Kaul offered three alternatives: (1) launch an attack despite Chinese superiority; (2) cancel any order to attack but hold on to present positions; (3) withdraw to more advantageous positions elsewhere. The prime minister's position, according to several accounts, was that he did not want Indian troops committing suicide. However, since the situation was a military one, he would leave the choice to the soldiers.[48]

General Sen, backed by Thapar, maintained that an Indian brigade should be able to defend its position against an enemy division. Sen thus urged that the brigade be kept in place even if no Indian attack were mounted soon. Kaul did not challenge this view and General Thapar concurred with it. According to Mullik, everyone then breathed a collective "sigh of relief," and Nehru simply confirmed what had apparently been agreed upon.[49]

The next day at Palam airport, before flying to Ceylon, Nehru publicly hinted at the postponement of Operation Leghorn. Asked by the press when he expected the Chinese to be removed from NEFA, he replied (according to one version): "Our instructions are to free our territory... I cannot fix a date, that is entirely for the Army."[50] The newspapers had been reporting versions of the Namkachu clashes, suggesting that they were Chinese inspired but were going in India's favor. Nehru now strengthened that impression by saying that casualties on the Chinese side in the latest incident (Tseng Jong) were heavier than India's. But he did caution that wintry conditions were setting in, that the Chinese had larger numbers of men, and that the Chinese were situated on higher ground and were near their main base (Le, on the other side of Thagla Ridge), which he did not mention by name.[51]

Given the context of what had transpired at the previous night's meeting, Nehru's remarks were intended to be cautionary. To a press and public that had come to expect immediate and successful military action, he was hinting that nothing could be done now. But that was not how his statements were interpreted by those not privy to the government's private deliberations. The key item, as far as the domestic and foreign press was concerned, was his confirmation of earlier unattributed reports about Indian military intentions. He was described as saying that the Indian Army had been instructed to "throw out" the Chinese from NEFA.[52]

Thus, Nehru's impromptu press conference, instead of having a calming effect, became a national and international event. Moreover, it committed him to taking India beyond the strategy that Kaul had tried to institute in NEFA. Kaul had reverted to positional maneuver, but India was now publicly committed to a limited war whenever the army chose to initiate it.

TO HOLD INDIAN POSITIONS FOR THE WINTER

General Kaul flew from New Delhi to Calcutta and onward to his new corps headquarters in Tezpur on 13 October. From this time forward he would experience severe depression for reasons separate from his advancing physical illness and fever. He thought himself trapped with no way out. He had seen the true situation on the NEFA front but could not get Delhi to relent. Kaul was now placed, as he said privately when Umrao Singh visited him at Tezpur, in the same untenable situation from which Umrao had been removed.[53]

When reacting to the Tseng Jong battle on 10 October, Kaul had intended to get 7 Brigade released from its commitment to remain along the river, but he had wanted no withdrawal made until he made his case in Delhi. To take personal responsibility for leaving the brigade so exposed, he had put his orders in writing.[54] These orders then became ironclad when Kaul sought to implement the consensus of the 11 October New Delhi meeting. On 13 October he signaled Dalvi and Prasad that

   a) The bridges along Namkachu [except for the bridge leading to Tsangle]... will be held at all costs.
   b) Line of communications via Lumpu will be protected.
   c) Hathung La... will be held.
   d) Positions at Tsangley [Tsangle] will be held at the discretion of GOC [General Officer Commanding], 4 Division [Prasad].[55]

General Prasad came to see Kaul on 15 October, because he wanted once again to insist on the withdrawal of his brigade. This time he used several new arguments: (1) Logistically, 7 Brigade could be maintained for only a few more days. (2) The buildup of supplies "just had not materialized, despite the Air Force's maximum efforts to drop supplies on Tsangdhar and Lumpu."[56] (3) 7 Brigade would be unable to stay on the Namkachu once snowfall prevented porters from crossing Hathungla. The entire position would have to be abandoned no matter what the Chinese did.

Kaul was impressed enough to promise another attempt to persuade Delhi if Prasad gave him written factual data on the logistical problems. By 16 October Kaul was also responding to urging from his own staff and from the inspector general of the Assam Rifles. Kaul's own handpicked staff brigadier, K. K. Singh, added to the case for withdrawal: "He urged that... the force on the Namka Chu should be thinned out to one battalion and concentrated in positions tactically supporting Dhola post. The other three battalions should be pulled back to winter and re-equip in Lumpu. This was almost exactly what General Umrao Singh had recommended six weeks before."[57] Kaul's personal feelings, and the growing effects of his illness, left him more susceptible to such persuasion than the prodding he was probably receiving from Army Headquarters. Even before Prasad's report came in on 16 October, Kaul dispatched another signal that some persons in New Delhi found upsetting.

Kaul's signal repeated the arguments he had used earlier to show that the Namkachu front was untenable. He wanted to withdraw his troops from the valley and "re-group along Tsangdhar, Karpo La and Hatung La," as well as pull back from the Indian post at Khinzemane.[58] But Kaul was still reluctant to oppose his New Delhi colleagues so directly. Therefore, his signal focused mainly on trying to reopen the question of keeping troops in one peripheral post, Tsangle.

Located some distance northwest of the area of confrontation, Tsangle was no longer considered a likely jump-off point for an Indian movement against the Chinese right flank. But, in Kaul's view, it was likely to come under attack because of its position on the north side of the Namkachu River. Kaul first pointed out to Delhi the logistical and other problems involved in maintaining Tsangle; he then added that the post might be liquidated by the Chinese, who were concentrating in its vicinity in battalion strength. So he recommended giving preference to "discretion over prestige" by having the occupying Punjabis fall back.[59] As he later hinted in an interview, he would not have used the "discretion" phrase if he were referring to Tsangle alone.[60]

Either in the same signal or by some other means, Kaul told Army Headquarters and Eastern Command of his overall supply problems. But he apparently wanted to express this news in a positive fashion. The main problem, or so he indicated, was that he did not have enough aircraft.[61] He suggested that additional Dakotas (DC-3s) and Caribou be given to the air force or that the civilian contractor previously responsible for air supply in NEFA be given additional government aircraft to do the job.

Kaul further blurred his meaning by again offering alternatives. His 16 October signal listed them as: (1) Reinforce Tsangle by up to a battalion. (2) Give preference to "discretion over prestige" and withdraw from Tsangle. (3) Let the Tsangle garrison fight it out. (4) Resist and then withdraw. He hinted at his preference for the second option by not urging options 3 and 4 and by pointing out that a reinforcing battalion (option 1) might get itself attacked and thus made useless to the force at Dhola, enabling the enemy to capture one of the bridges. If that happened, the valley position would be irretrievable.[62]

The significance of Kaul's communication was understood well enough by those who received it. Mullik recalls that the "depressing" 16 October signal was brought to his residence by Krishna Menon and Thapar late in the evening and that they all departed (along with Sarin of the defense ministry) for Tezpur by plane that very night. General Sen was picked up at Lucknow, and they all conferred with Kaul at IV Corps Headquarters the next morning (17 October 1962).[63]

The meeting began with a lengthy discussion in Kaul's map room. The main issue to be decided was whether to withdraw from the Namkachu and not just from Tsangle. At some point in the discussion, Kaul reviewed the situation, probably speaking of Indian deficiencies as well as Chinese buildups on Thagla Ridge and near Khinzemane. He no longer thought that the Namkachu line was tenable. Kaul was supported by his headquarters staff and by the Assam Rifles commander.

In Kaul's later account of this meeting, Krishna Menon contended that Tsangle was crucial, politically, given its location on the India-Bhutan-Tibet map trijunction. According to Mullik, Krishna Menon argued that Indian public opinion would not tolerate additional loss of territory. It was Thapar and Sen, says Mullik, who thought Tsangle important because it commanded the trijunction. They also argued that Tsangle covered three subsidiary passes, which the Chinese could use to avoid the Indian garrison near Dhola and come straight to Tsangdhar.

After several hours of discussion, the civilians removed themselves from the room to allow the generals to make a supposedly military decision. Thapar, Sen, and Kaul then decided that there would be no withdrawals. Both the Namkachu River line and the Tsangle sector would be held. Special efforts would be made to ease deficiencies in supply and equipment, and an Indian troop buildup would continue.

Another battalion would be dispatched to hold the route from Hathungla to Lumpu, while Tawang would continue to be built up to brigade strength.[64]

The 17 October decisions thus having been made, the VIPs departed. Several hours later Kaul collapsed from his neglected pulmonary illness. After various forms of medical consultation, he was flown to New Delhi on 18 October. Hospitalization was not necessary, and Kaul convalesced at his house without relinquishing authority over his command. He maintained contact with Tezpur by telephone and Army Headquarters signals. Apparently, Nehru and Krishna Menon did not question this new arrangement, nor did Thapar, although the normal procedure would have been for command authority to pass to the next-ranking officer in the theater of operations (General Prasad) until a replacement for Kaul could be found.[65]

Kaul's actions from his sickbed showed that he now accepted the belief (presented to him before the Tseng Jong battle by Prasad and Dalvi) that the Chinese regarded the Namkachu as the de facto boundary. Like Prasad and Dalvi, he expected the Chinese to try to eliminate Tsangle because it was north of the Namkachu, just as they had swept away Tseng Jong. But by 18 October Prasad and Dalvi were certain that the Chinese intended to stage a general attack on 7 Brigade. Kaul's staff in Tezpur probably told him of his field commanders' views, but he was not prepared to accept this information in New Delhi. Thus, his signals of 18 and 19 October dealt only with Tsangle and he demanded its reinforcement. Kaul knew that a shooting incident had just occurred at Tsangle, leaving one Chinese noncombatant (possibly an interpreter) dead and other Chinese personnel probably wounded.[66] He also knew that Prasad was opposed to reinforcing Tsangle.

To get his orders obeyed, Kaul threatened to remove any resisting officer. For various reasons he apparently was not obeyed, but the threat ensured that Prasad would not authorize any withdrawals from the Namkachu front.[67]

If Brigadier Dalvi could not pull his troops out of the Namkachu Valley, he wanted to concentrate and link together his positions on the valley floor. Kaul had brought all of Dalvi's battalions down into the valley and had ordered 7 Brigade to stay spread out along the river line with gaps between its positions. As a result, a skillful Chinese commander could destroy 7 Brigade by engaging just one-third of it, cutting off the rest. The Chinese, in large numbers, could penetrate or infiltrate through the gaps in the line. But Dalvi did not think he could change the positioning of his men, so explicit had Kaul's 10 October orders been. Nor could Prasad give him the permission he wanted.

Judging from his general conduct in September–October 1962, Dalvi has justly been called "an outstanding officer."[68] But surely he could now have claimed a signals breakdown or some such excuse for acting on his own. He might have relied on coming events to vindicate him after he and his troops on 18 October saw the Chinese preparing for a "night advance and a dawn attack" with "marking parties and guides moving to forming-up places."[69]

Unfortunately, Dalvi remained too focused on shaking up the thinking of higher echelons. His anger may also have blocked clear thinking. On the telephone with Prasad on 19 October, he threatened to resign his command and his commission. The thought of resignation had "oppressed" him "particularly from 10 October onwards." He could not have been serious, since such action would have meant abandoning his men on the eve of hostilities. Indeed, he decided to remain with his troops. But he felt free to denounce all the senior officers who, in his view, had agreed with his assessments, made promises which they had then dishonored, and had conspicuously absented themselves from the front since Tseng Jong.[70]

Having started to infiltrate in force between 7 Brigade's positions during the night of 19–20 October, the Chinese began their full onslaught at dawn.[71]

4

THE WAR, 20 OCTOBER TO 21 NOVEMBER 1962

CHAPTER ELEVEN

The Wartime Decision-Makers and Their Psychological Setting

On 20 OCTOBER, 7 Brigade was destroyed in and near the Namkachu Valley by a Chinese force later thought to contain three regiments (each equivalent to an Indian brigade). Brigadier Dalvi led a small isolated party of retreating Indian troops, among the groups trying to make their way back to Indian-held territory. He was taken prisoner on 22 October.

The Chinese attack in western NEFA came not only at Dhola but also along two other routes. One of them, lying to the east of the Dhola-Thagla area, was the main trade route from Tibet to Assam, passing through Khinzemane and Tawang. The other route entered NEFA even further eastward, through the pass called Bumla. The monastery town of Tawang emerged as the major objective of the Chinese general offensive.[1] (See Map 9, in Chapter 12.)

Near Dhola the Indian post at Tsangle was eliminated, giving the Chinese control of the western (i.e., Bhutan) end of NEFA.[2] Far away, close to the eastern (Burma) edge of NEFA, fighting commenced near the Indian strongpoint at Walong (see Map 7).

Also on 20 October the Chinese started an offensive against the Indian forward posts in the Western Sector (Ladakh). Over the next few weeks, the besieged Galwan post was taken, as were most of the early Chinese targets. Some Indian posts would fight to the death.

The Ladakh fighting showed a certain pattern dictated by the Chinese. Their object was to eliminate all Indian gains from the forward policy by removing the Indian presence beyond China's 1960 claim line. This they did systematically, concentrating first against the northern end of Ladakh between 20 and 22 October, then against the central section, and finally the southern section on 27–28 October.[3]

As information reached New Delhi, surprise was immense. Neither

163

the decision-makers nor those advising them had been really prepared for war.

THE DECISION-MAKERS

On or about 24 October, Prime Minister Nehru began to preside over the daily defense meetings initiated by Krishna Menon in September.[4] But these sessions were no longer the primary place where decisions were formulated. Instead, they were just one part of the process. Krishna Menon himself became a consultant to Nehru, until he relinquished his cabinet portfolio on 7 November.

The broad policy decisions concerning the war and its diplomatic repercussions came from consultations between Nehru and individuals or small groups in charge of particular jurisdictions. This was Nehru's customary style, and his use of it in matters concerning border developments had started to intensify as far back as August.[5] From the earliest days of the war until the arrival of Y. B. Chavan (Krishna Menon's replacement) in early November, Nehru dealt with Army Headquarters directly.

Someone on whom Nehru reportedly came to rely heavily during the war, in a consultative capacity, was a former finance minister and Nehru confidante, the businessman T. T. Krishnamachari. Appointed to the cabinet at first as "Minister Without Portfolio" and then as "Minister of Economic and Defense Coordination," he held "the Defense portfolio, pro tem" during the interregnum between Krishna Menon and Chavan.[6] Another person in close consultation with Nehru was Foreign Secretary M. J. Desai. As Krishna Menon's role declined, Desai asserted himself.[7]

There had been several emergency meetings of the cabinet between 8 September and 20 October, and the Foreign Affairs Subcommittee of the cabinet had started to function in a regular way. With the outbreak of war, the subcommittee was consulted seriously and met continuously, having been reconstituted into an Emergency Committee.[8] Most matters of diplomatic significance came under its purview. Besides the prime minister and defense minister, its members were Home Minister Lal Bahadur Shastri, Finance Minister Morarji Desai, Planning Minister G. L. Nanda, and Krishnamachari.[9]

With Kaul sick in bed and Nehru delegating all military authority to Army Headquarters, the normally retiring Thapar had to become the military decision-maker in New Delhi, although he depended heavily on his staff. In the last days of the war, Army Chief Thapar resigned and was replaced by Lieutenant General J. N. Chaudhuri. Because of the dire military conditions then prevailing, General Chaudhuri immediately became a very active decision-maker. Like Thapar before him, Chaudhuri attended Emergency Committee meetings, as did M. J. Desai.

Shifts in the command structure in NEFA early in the war meant that Kaul's IV Corps came temporarily under the control of Lieutenant General Harbakhsh Singh. But before Harbakhsh could do more than make his own NEFA assessment, he was pushed aside to allow the return of a partially recovered and still active decision-maker from New Delhi—Kaul himself. In the Western Sector Daulat Singh continued as the theater commander.

THE DECISION-MAKERS' ATTITUDINAL PRISM

One psychological element shared by Indian decision-makers at the onset of the 1962 war was an openness to perceptual change. This element was reflected in an often-quoted statement by Nehru: "we were getting out of touch with reality in the modern world and we were living in an artificial atmosphere of our own creation. We have been shocked out of it, all of us, whether it is the government or the people; some might have felt it less and some more."[10] Nehru was referring specifically to a basic belief that India had reached safety, after independence, and could concentrate on peaceful development. But the world was a cruel place; China and the world had betrayed India and had forced her to adopt the ways of war.[11]

Surely Nehru also must have meant that fundamental Indian assumptions about Chinese conflict management and Indian military capabilities had been stripped away. These assumptions were (1) that the Chinese would not respond in a large way to the forward policy and Operation Leghorn and (2) that the army could acquit itself well in NEFA if the Chinese mounted an attack there. Although the Tseng Jong incident earlier in October had raised doubts about the first of these assumptions, confirmation of those doubts had not been expected.

During the second stage of the 1962 war, the major offensives staged by the Chinese in November shattered the renewed Indian confidence that had emerged by the end of October. Such confidence can be called part of a "phony war" mentality, and it generated bravado among some politicians and the press. Yet it was reasonable enough, since it reflected the conclusion that the causes of the October defeats were correctable. From the government's point of view, the earlier setbacks had come about because India had been taken by surprise, Indian troops had been outnumbered, and 7 Brigade in NEFA had been in an untenable topographical position. Chinese advantages in preparation, logistics, equipment, and weapons had counted as well. The assumption was that, during any second round, an alert and better-prepared India could presumably meet the challenge and hold the Chinese at bay. Moreover, the army could now maneuver and fight from better positions.[12]

In October a major reappraisal of Indian priorities led to requests for foreign shipments of weapons and matériel. It had quickly become clear that the Western countries would be willing suppliers of military aid, but the Soviet Union was shifting from neutrality to a pro-Chinese stance. Evidently, the involvement of the Soviets in the Cuban missile crisis of October 1962 was requiring them to seek support throughout the rest the Communist world, including China.

The Soviet change of attitude caused a certain shock and dismay within the Nehru government. Only after the Cuban affair had ended did the Soviets revert to neutrality.[13] Thus, the Indian view of the world as multipolar rather than bipolar, and the Indian conception of the Communist bloc as polycentric, was not vindicated until the last moment.

The American diplomatic and military involvement with Pakistan—so alarming in the past because of the long-range military implications for India—now seemed to have some virtue, since the American connection could serve as a military restraint on Pakistan. In general, communications with the Pakistanis were channeled through the American ambassador to India, John Kenneth Galbraith.[14] But because of ham-handed American and British pressure on India over the Kashmir issue, the Indian perception of the America-Pakistan link soon returned to its old moorings.

The 1962 war also shook, at least temporarily, an important Indian assumption about nonalignment. Just as India was never supposed to be neutral in clear-cut cases of aggression, it was thought that other nonaligned nations would actively oppose aggression when they saw it. But now the nonaligned states did not rise to India's support, either verbally or materially. Instead, they made clear their intention to apply the concept of nonalignment to the India-China conflict too.

The most important "honourable exceptions" to this trend were Nasser's Egypt and Tito's Yugoslavia.[15]

The attitudes of Nehru and those around him during the 1962 war were influenced by strong emotions, including defiance, pride in the aroused patriotism and unity demonstrated by Indian public opinion, and determination to fight a long war if necessary. In addition, there was an absolute conviction of the righteousness of India's cause. The Nehru government was determined, too, that nonalignment would be preserved, whatever the temporary adjustments to India's foreign policy necessitated by the crisis.[16]

CHANGING IMAGES

Nehru

The major change in the prime minister's image of the Chinese, induced by the 20 October attack, was that he now regarded them as betrayers. That perception dominated his thinking, since it carried with it much emotional weight. Rarely did he show such emotion openly; that was not his way. "[He] was somewhat shy of being discovered in any sort of emotional state, a trait due perhaps to his old public school tradition. [But] those who saw him at close quarters in that week in October of 1962 saw him moved, as only a person like him could be moved, who had given his trust and stood by it, and who could not just accept the fact of betrayal as a part of a political game, of realpolitik."[17]

Nehru's sense of realpolitik had always had an element of Gandhianism in it. As such, it had always colored his image of the opponent. Thus, the forward policy had been carried on with the implicit assumption that certain rules of the game would be observed by an adversary who had at least some sense of appropriateness or propriety, not to speak of honor. That had been one of the nationalist movement's key assumptions about the British, and Gandhi had generalized it into a principle of conflict management: One does not regard the other side as an enemy or relegate its members to less than human status. Instead, the positive traits of the adversary's character are to be assumed, and even exploited, so that both sides come to recognize and respect tactical limits. Although never a person to accept Gandhi's religious ways of describing such an outlook, Nehru had absorbed it.[18]

Nehru's perception of China remained linked to his image of India. Naively perhaps, he had long regarded the Indian personality as fundamentally peaceful, despite occasional breakdowns of self-control. Now the Indian nation would have to adopt a war psychology or "war psychosis." To Nehru this meant that the Indian national character might have to suffer from militarization, brutalization, and misplaced priorities.[19]

Nehru's image of himself and his own role could hardly have been pleasing either. As a leader, he had been able to shape public opinion because he embodied much of the Indian national character; but he was not trained to be a war leader. With his diffident and questioning nature, Nehru did not have the self-confidence of a Winston Churchill. He was a rather different kind of person.

Nehru described some of his wartime images of India and the Indian Army during a meeting with the Army Headquarters staff on 3 November.[20] He thought the morale of the country amazing and wonderful. The response from the entire nation had demonstrated the fundamental soundness of the Indian people. The country's first priority was to defeat the Chinese, although India had to proceed by anticipating the worst that could happen—namely, a full-scale Chinese invasion. How to prepare for that contingency was for the military to decide.

Reviewing what had happened at Dhola, he said that in September the decision-makers had at first believed that the Chinese could be pushed back; but then "we" realized the massiveness of the Chinese preparation. Thereafter, he claimed, the question of where and what to defend had been left to the military chiefs. His policy now too was that military appraisal must be the task of commanders on the spot; "you" are the best judges of such things. While broad strategy had to be governed by political factors, and while it remained the policy of the Indian government to drive the Chinese out, strategy and tactics were subject to military considerations.

Probably influenced by the calculations of two of his consultants (the director of the MEA's China Division, N. B. Menon, and Brigadier Palit, working through M. J. Desai), Nehru predicted that the Chinese would face increased logistical problems as they moved further and further into Indian territory. He could not say how far the Chinese wanted to go, but it was a basic fact that ultimately supplies would have to be brought from China—something not easy to accomplish. It was also unclear how far the Chinese would come under winter conditions.

Indian troops had been abruptly sent into the mountains without adequate preparation, he said, alluding to their other difficulties as well. But it was presently necessary for Indian forces to adapt themselves to the frontiers, where a state of war could be expected to continue indefinitely.

Krishna Menon

One observer of the defense minister's immediate reaction to the onset of the 1962 war describes him as "entangled in his own temperament."[21] More likely, the Chinese attack had dashed all his expectations; and, having no immediate reference points available to him, he could at first imagine the Chinese doing almost anything. If they wanted to, they could even reach Calcutta, Madras, or some other part of interior India, and there might be a ten-year war.[22]

Although he was forced to recognize new political realities, Krishna Menon's image of his own role remained positive. He defended his right to remain in the defense ministry; and he made an effort to show that he could be a viable channel through which aid could be secured from the Americans.[23]

But he saw that he had become a political liability for Nehru. As a campaign for his removal from office mounted, he came to consider himself a minister who had lost the confidence of his party and country, and who therefore should leave the cabinet.[24] Had the prime minister unequivocally wanted him to remain, he would have done so.[25] Yet the time came when even Nehru's support wavered.

In Krishna Menon's view the war had given the government's political opponents an opportunity to attack nonalignment and had given Indian foreign policy a pro-Western slant.[26] In part the demands for his own resignation fell within that context. Having told the Chinese in 1960 that their behavior was helpful to all the reactionary elements in India, he was now convinced that such elements were benefiting greatly from the war.

The only possible strategy for defending India, Krishna Menon argued, was one designed to keep the Chinese out of as much territory as possible, for reasons of public opinion. In addition, in October–November 1962 he still regarded Pakistan as a serious threat.

The danger from Pakistan, in his view, militated against transferring Indian troops to other places where they were needed.[27]

Thapar and Army Headquarters

After the Namkachu disaster, Army Headquarters was engaged in trying to find and dispatch reinforcements to the NEFA front. Most of the staff work fell to the Acting Chief of General Staff, Dhillon, but the responsibility was Thapas's as Chief of Army Staff.

Army Headquarters agreed with Krishna Menon and the Intelligence Bureau that the danger from Pakistan precluded transfer of large formations from the western border. Although the best-armed and best-organized Indian divisions were located in the Punjab and Kashmir, only one division was sent to NEFA before the war ended. It was not actually moved until the second big Chinese push through NEFA began in late November.[28] "So when the COAS [Chief of Army Staff, Thapar] was raising new Divisions in NEFA he was really pulling out odd battalions from all over the rest of India, some with deficient equipment. He had no other alternative."[29] Some of Thapar's units came from Ranchi in Bihar.[30] The one larger formation he could use was the division stationed in Nagaland, and even that had to be broken up.

New brigades were being both inducted into NEFA and formed there, in the area between Tezpur and Tawang, still under the rubrics of 4 Division and IV Corps. A new division was being raised for Walong and eastern NEFA. New commanders were appointed to each of these units.[31] The 4 Division commander, Prasad, was himself replaced on 24 October. Furthermore, these units had never operated in tandem with one another; and the commanders of the major fighting formations were not accustomed to working together and were unfamiliar with the conditions to be faced in this particular theater of operations. In general, lack of confidence coupled with lack of experience would influence the morale and fighting spirit of Indian troops in the Eastern Sector.

A strategic plan for NEFA was being devised at Army Headquarters. Advocated by Palit and accepted by Thapar, it focused on the two great ridges, one some distance behind the other. (See Map 9.) Se La Pass was the key feature on the first ridge, while, to the southeast, Bomdila Pass dominated the second ridge. An Indian-built stretch of road, some 60 miles long, connected Bomdila and Se La. The plan envisaged the creation of a "box" at each pass. A "box" was a strong, self-contained position capable of holding out even if surrounded by the Chinese.[32]

Generals Harbakhsh Singh and Kaul

The box concept was also crucial to a plan developed by Kaul's temporary replacement in NEFA, Lieutenant General Harbakhsh Singh. The Harbakhsh strategy was either authored independently or built upon the prior thinking of Brigadier Palit. Se La was to be the "vital ground," backed up by another large garrison at Bomdila, 60 miles to the rear. After these strongpoints had been built up to the requisite strength, they could be further reinforced from the plains, if possible, but "the road between them was to be discarded before it became the target of Chinese infiltration tactics."[33]

Until the road was abandoned, it would be used (along with air supply) for stocking both Se La and Bomdila for a siege lasting fifteen to twenty days. Once the road was abandoned, air transport would take over and make use of the excellent drop zones within the Se La and Bomdila defense perimeters. Air supply would really serve a supplementary function once the fighting began; the major supply operation already would have been completed. Intermittent foul flying weather in NEFA therefore did not have to be a cause for concern.[34]

In his instructions to his officers, Harbakhsh described Dirang Dzong, the lowest point on the road between Se La and Bomdila, as the "well of death" to be avoided. Dirang Dzong was sure to be the first target of a Chinese pincer movement coming around both sides of Se La. Even if, for some reason, Dirang Dzong needed to be defended, a hill position just behind it could be fortified and made difficult for the Chinese to capture.

Capture of any main Indian position in western NEFA would presumably be difficult for Chinese troops, and they could not sustain a siege for long. Indeed, Palit at Army Headquarters thought the weather would allow Chinese operations for just a few weeks, when snow would close the Chinese supply routes. Harbakhsh thought the Chinese lacked artillery, were carrying only light weapons and mortars, and could carry supplies only for a few days. In contrast, Indian troops at the major strongpoints would have artillery and other heavy weapons at their disposal. The main approach to Se La, up from the Tawang Chu, Harbakhsh christened the "graveyard" of the Chinese army.[35]

Harbakhsh may not have been correct about the likely logistical capacity of the Chinese, since they soon built a road from Bumla to Tawang and extended in onward to Jang by improving the Indian road. The Chinese used artillery (or heavy mortars) along the approach from Jang to Se La in both October and November, and they could exploit that stretch of the Indian road once they captured it.[36] Properly defending Se La against a frontal attack would require hard and costly fighting.

Yet a box or "fortress defense" strategy seemed right for Harbakhsh, given not only his optimistic assessment of the NEFA situation but also his professional knowledge. The teaching of basic tactics at the Indian Military Academy, when Harbakhsh studied there, had drawn on the Indian Army's experience against Pathans on the northwest frontier. In that kind of mountain warfare, Indian units often held on to hill positions with no line of communications and learned to avoid sitting on low ground. Harbakhsh had also been trained in using boxes in Malaya during World War II.[37] Quite likely, Harbakhsh, Palit, and Thapar were all mindful of the success of boxes during the 1942–1945 Southeast Asian campaigns of the allied armies against the Japanese.

Both Harbakhsh and Kaul would reject still another possible strategy. General Sen and Kaul's staff brigadier, K. K. Singh, favored falling back to Bomdila.[38] The use of Bomdila as the defensive anchor of western NEFA had also been advocated in the Thorat-Sen defense plan several years earlier.

The idea had much to recommend it. Bomdila was readily supportable from the Assam plains to the south, if top priority were given to keeping the connecting road open. The Chinese, coming from the northwest, would stretch their supply lines over rugged terrain if they tried to attack Bomdila in force, or they would have to build up forward supply bases first.[39] But the Bomdila alternative obviously had a major political drawback. It would require handing over more NEFA territory to the Chinese.[40]

Both the Se La and Bomdila alternatives were the result of detailed tactical thinking about military operations in the NEFA terrain. When Kaul replaced Harbakhsh in NEFA in early November, his thinking was entirely different. Although he agreed with Harbakhsh and Palit about the defensive superiority of Se La over Bomdila, he was not content to focus only on the specific problem of NEFA's defense. Kaul conceived of his own role as that of super strategic planner for all of India.

Among the persons to whom he revealed his ideas was the American ambassador, who visited Kaul when he was convalescing at home from his illness, just before the start of the war. According to Galbraith, Kaul spoke of evicting the Chinese from Indian territory soon, but he said that Nehru, Krishna Menon, and the rest of the government did not appreciate all that was required. The task would be possible only with American help: "Accordingly, he told me, he had advised the Indian government to abandon its commitment to non-alignment and seek our assistance. He took for granted that such was our antipathy to Communism we only had to be asked."[41]

Galbraith was not encouraging, since he did not take the conversation seriously. But for Kaul this line of thought was a logical extension of his campaign for increased military spending, carried on during the previous spring. It also followed his earlier probe of American intentions, undertaken during the visit of Chester Bowles. Kaul was to develop his ideas further and to become (from his sickbed) a powerful lobbyist in their cause.

To Kaul the situation required a reorganization of the Indian Army's command and control system (so as to meet the threat from the Himalayas) and the raising of substantial new forces.[42] In a paper submitted at Krishna Menon's request, Kaul wrote that India must raise ten new divisions and train, equip, and deploy them—all within twelve months. Such great military changes, plus the tasks of redirecting the economy and its resources, would require the creation of a new army command. Its top officer would act as a higher or supreme commander, with headquarters at Delhi or perhaps Agra. In effect, a dictatorship would have to be instituted in India, presumably for the war emergency only. Kaul also discussed in his paper the possibility of inviting foreign armies to help the Indian Army mount an offensive over the Himalayas and of persuading Chiang Kai-shek and South Korea to invade the Chinese mainland, assisted by American forces in the Western Pacific.[43] He called for an American air umbrella over the vulnerable parts of northern India and for massive American air attacks on China, launched from Indian soil.[44]

The lack of proportion in Kaul's thinking was perhaps related to his emotional state. Some people who observed him personally at different times during October and November questioned not just his judgment but his emotional stability. From their descriptions and adjectives (e.g., "a bit unstrung," "manic," "off-colour"), one finds Kaul swinging between gloom and grand optimism.[45]

Kaul was a man being pushed (by himself and others) to a point beyond his perceptual and emotional limits, but it would be unfair to explain the entirety of his thinking in this fashion. His inability to match Harbakhsh's tactical grasp came largely from his lack of combat command experience, while his career as a military politician inclined him to make sweeping political recommendations. During the past year Kaul had also been frustrated in his efforts to persuade Nehru and Krishna Menon to enlarge the scale of their military planning. Before the war Kaul and his Army Headquarters staff had prepared expansion plans for the army but were uncertain that the government would approve these plans.[46] Now Kaul had the momentum of events on his side, and he wanted to take advantage of that fact.

After Kaul returned to NEFA and no longer had a direct influence on decision-making in New Delhi, he still attempted to change the parameters of the strategic game. He demanded that the government abandon its earlier decision not to use the Indian Air Force for direct combat support.[47] After hearing an alarming intelligence report from Mullik, Kaul insisted that a proper defense of NEFA would be impossible unless he was sent no less than two additional infantry divisions.[48]

THREAT AND OTHER CRISIS PERCEPTIONS

The Chinese October offensives in both NEFA and Ladakh left no doubt in New Delhi that India was at war and that both territory and security were now subject to the most intense threat. Adding to the sense of threat, to use the terms of the Brecher-ICB model, was a "perceived deterioration in the state's...military capability vis-a-vis the enemy."[49] Indian military and civilian decision-makers first perceived such "deterioration" when they became certain that 7 Brigade was lost and that the Chinese would take Tawang and its immediate environs in NEFA. They knew, too, that the Chinese would quickly eliminate most of India's forward policy posts in Ladakh. But far worse was their sense of deterioration in India's military capacity when the Indian Army lost its major military strongholds in NEFA: Se La and Bomdila.

Lack of direct experience with war on a large scale helped exaggerate the capabilities of the enemy in the minds of the Indian leaders.[50] Consequently, when Se La was abandoned during the night of 17–18 November, and when Bomdila fell on 19 November, the

and distance, a fighting retreat from Se La would not be possible without detailed prior planning. Se La should instead be made into a "box," able to hold out while still blocking the main Chinese invasion route. Bomdila would be behind it as another strong position.

He may or may not have said so, but the brigadier was certain that supplies sufficient for a "box" strategy could be provided. Enough could be stored at Se La to cover any interruptions in air supply. Eventually, seven days' regular rations (i.e., fifteen days' holding-out rations) were included in the plans for stocking Se La, along with equivalent stores of other matériel. With winter snow expected to close the routes into NEFA from Tibet quite soon, the Chinese would encounter supply problems of their own, sufficient to limit them to a short military campaign. India would then have another six months to prepare for the next round. Moreover, he was sure that only small parties of Chinese troops could infiltrate past Se La and Bomdila, and they could (and should) be interdicted by small Indian units sent out from the main positions.[7]

Even before Palit had completed his presentation, Nehru responded that the army should do whatever it thought best. He was confident that whatever territory was lost, "you" will get it back eventually. Almost immediately, Palit ran back to Army Headquarters to get the Se La order issued.[8] Thus, when he met with Prasad in Tezpur in the evening of 24 October, he could tell (the already dismissed) Prasad that Army Headquarters firmly intended to hold Se La as the divisional defense position.[9]

While Army Headquarters was watching NEFA closely and making detailed decisions concerning the area, a looser method of supervision was being applied to Ladakh. Either before or just after the start of the war, Western Command, not New Delhi, had determined what would constitute vital ground in Ladakh. That ground was the village of Chushul, lying in the Spanggur gap, on what would be the most obvious Chinese route to Leh (see Map 6). Western Command had been reinforcing Chushul, having completed the road from Leh by the first week of October. Chushul became a brigade position by the middle of November. Holding Chushul required defending hills to the east of the town and planting outposts (some more than 16,000 feet high) in frozen ground. While Leh, Chushul, and the Chushul airstrip lay on the Indian side of the Chinese (1960) claim line, the Chushul outposts were on the Chinese side.[10]

In keeping with the spirit of the orders sent to Western Command

by Army Headquarters on 22 September, certain small garrisons—
including Daulat Beg Oldi—were allowed to fall back during the
October and November portions of the war. The Daulat Beg Oldi post
itself was never occupied by the Chinese, since it was over their claim
line.[11]

When the posts just forward of Chushul were attacked in over-
whelming force by the Chinese on 18 November, those that were not
overrun were evacuated as the Indians regrouped on high ground
around the brigade headquarters in the valley. The Chinese did not
invade the Chushul Valley, because they were deterred by Indian
military strength and because Chushul also was beyond their claim
line.[12]

The Indian command and reinforcement system for Ladakh operated with much autonomy, as Lieutenant General Daulat Singh
brought troops up from Kashmir at a steady and rapid pace.[13] That
practice, as well as higher morale and better terrain, enabled the
Indian brigades in Ladakh to perform better than their counterparts in
NEFA. None disintegrated or were destroyed, although some posts
fought to the last man. India's troops in the Western Sector forced the
Chinese to pay dearly for the territory they won.[14]

TO REMOVE TROOPS FROM THE PUNJAB

In a meeting held at the defense minister's house on the evening of
26 October, an ad hoc group considered the question of how the China
war would influence India's defensive posture on the border with
West Pakistan. Krishna Menon and Thapar were present, as was M. J.
Desai, Mullik, and Sarin. A decision on this question was essential, not
only because further Chinese advances in NEFA seemed imminent
but, more important, because Chinese troops were concentrating on
the Sikkim border and thereby placing all of eastern India in danger.
The forces being collected by Thapar from Nagaland and other
nearby places were needed to stop the Chinese in NEFA, so how could
he protect Sikkim? This was Thapar's quandary, and it was the
immediate cause of the 26 October meeting.

According to Mullik's testimony, Thapar said that Sikkim and
north Bengal could not be protected unless he could transfer troops
from the west. The opposing voice was Mullik's, protesting that
"Ayub was on the prowl and, if our Punjab defenses were weakened,

he would certainly try to carry out his grand strategy of which we [the IB] had given a detailed report a few months earlier."[15]

The nub of the discussion was whether to seek protection from an "imminent" threat or guard against a "possible" one from another direction. The group chose the former option, and Krishna Menon then walked over to the prime minister's house to get ratification. Within a half hour the defense minister was back with Nehru's agreement that there was no alternative. The prime minister had also wanted to initiate a diplomatic effort to contain Pakistan. That work was entrusted by Krishna Menon to M. J. Desai.[16] In carrying it out, the Indian foreign secretary would in coming days rely heavily on the Americans.

In the meantime, the Indian Air Force moved swiftly to airlift troops from Chandigarh in the Punjab, and from Palam airport outside New Delhi, to Siliguri[17] —the main Indian jump-off point for Sikkim. Three divisions were eventually withdrawn from the Pakistan border, with one sent to Sikkim and the other two destined for NEFA.[18] But the first of the divisions earmarked for NEFA (5 Division) would not actually be moved until orders for its dispatch were given by Thapar from Tezpur on 17 November. At that moment Se La seemed in danger, and the Chinese had also moved to cut the road between Se La and Bomdila. Because the Chinese advance through NEFA was so swift, this division would not arrive in time to take part in the NEFA fighting.[19]

TO REINSTATE GENERAL KAUL AS NEFA COMMANDER

When the war started on 20 October, Kaul had been persuaded to hang up the telephones linking his bedroom with NEFA and to relinquish command of his corps.[20] On 24 October, after some further persuasion by Krishna Menon and Mullik, Kaul was officially replaced by Harbakhsh Singh. Kaul's condition for allowing the substitution was a pledge that he would be reinstated as IV Corps commander once he had been declared medically fit.[21]

Visits from Nehru, Krishna Menon, Mullik, Cabinet Secretary Khera, and Galbraith, as well as repeated visits by Thapar, were not able to compensate Kaul for what he regarded as the loss of his combat command. Thapar urged him to come back to Army Headquarters to resume his role as Chief of General Staff, but Kaul felt that such a move would leave him in disgrace, since it would "smack of either a punishment or evasive action on my part."[22]

Kaul was desperately concerned by what he regarded as a virulent propaganda campaign being waged against him publicly and privately within India. He told Mullik that "unless he went back to the front, he would not be able to rehabilitate himself either in the army circles or in the public eye."[23] He also felt that he could still make a contribution in a situation where "the country's fate hung in the balance."[24]

Some of the people professionally and personally closest to Kaul were opposed to his returning to NEFA. They begged him to reconsider. Among the arguments used were the state of his health (not yet fully restored) and the possible danger to his life of returning to activity at high altitudes.[25]

Ultimately, Kaul's ability to influence the prime minister allowed him to prevail.[26] The decision-makers therefore were Kaul and Nehru, and the decision to have him return to NEFA was probably made between 26 October (when Kaul got medical permission) and noon on 28 October, when Ambassador Galbraith saw him "on his way back to Tezpur."[27] The full particulars of the decision were that Kaul would return to IV Corps and Harbakhsh would be transferred to XXXIII Corps, while Umrao Singh would be "kicked upstairs" from XXXIII Corps to a staff post in Delhi.[28]

At least one part of the Indian government apparatus noticed that Kaul's reappearance in NEFA on 29 October had a detrimental effect on morale among his junior officers and other ranks. The intelligence Bureau, which either directly examined letters sent home from the front or had access to the impressions of those entrusted with the task, became aware of the objections those letters expressed.[29]

The appearance of a morale problem was understandable. General Prasad's regrouping of units around Se La, and his preparations to defend that position, had established a certain momentum. That momentum continued with the arrival of Harbakhsh as the new corps commander on 24 October. Harbakhsh was driven up to Se La Pass in the company of his new 4 Division chief, General Anant Pathania. Brigadier Palit, who knew the ground, showed them around it.[30] Harbakhsh personally went all over NEFA by aircraft. He covered Bomdila and Walong and briefed the IV Corps Headquarters staff at Tezpur. General Thapar pronounced himself pleased with the improvement in morale when he saw Harbakhsh on 28 October.[31] That same evening the abrupt announcement of Harbakhsh's dismissal broke the momentum. Kaul would not be able to restore it. His reputation had suffered after the Tseng Jong battle. Even worse, Kaul refused to be put in the tactical picture when Harbakhsh offered to brief him on 29 October.[32]

TO COUNTERATTACK AT WALONG

Shortly after his return to command of IV Corps, Kaul visited Se La, against medical advice. But he also took time to go to Walong, at the far eastern end of NEFA. During the ensuing battle at Walong, Kaul showed a pattern of behavior that he would repeat during the later battles for the main Indian NEFA positions. Thus, it is important to outline the Walong action.

When the Chinese had attacked near Walong as part of their general October offensive in NEFA, they were held off for a short time at a forward position called Kibithoo.[33] The Chinese subsequently kept probing the Walong defenses, despite the overall NEFA lull that followed the fall of Tawang. (See Map 7, in Chapter 7.)

The Indian Army's (never implemented) defense line plan had called for the main Indian positions in this defensive sector (i.e., the far eastern corner of NEFA) to be at Hayuliang in the foothills and Teju in the Brahmaputra-Lohit Valley.[34] Harbakhsh Singh, during his short tenure as IV Corps commander, believed that the Walong position was undefendable, because of the existence of a route bypassing it, and that wind conditions at the Walong airstrip would not allow any substantial Indian troop buildup. He wanted to have covering troops in Walong, who would also watch the bypass track, while Hayuliang, further back, would be the main Indian position.[35]

The decision to stage an Indian counterattack in the Walong sector was taken by the commander of newly formed 2 Division, Major General M. S. Pathania (the other Pathania's cousin), and seconded by Kaul shortly before 11 November.[36] Kaul does not seem to have been aware of the tactical thinking done by Harbakhsh (or the earlier Thorat thinking). Thus, operating in a vacuum, he was prepared to follow the initiative of a subordinate. He was probably also acting on two assumptions: that Walong was a key position for political reasons and that the Nehru government could use a victory.[37]

Pathania's premise was that if one more battalion were added to the brigade already stationed at Walong, the Chinese could be pushed back to the McMahon line. Kaul's staff at IV Corps Headquarters disagreed with that premise, having estimated that a full Chinese division was being inducted into the Rima-Walong area.[38] But Kaul had been persuaded, and the operation was planned for 13 November.

The Indian reinforcements began arriving in airlift relays on 13 November, but the Indian counterattack began on 14 November, even before the reinforcements were in place.[39] Several explanations have been given for the haste. The most plausible is the threat posed after the Chinese occupied two hills, the "Yellow Pimple" and the "Green Pimple," which dominated the Indian positions in the hills around Walong.[40] From there the Chinese began to direct their artillery fire more accurately and better position themselves for an offensive. Tactical problems shaped Indian timing thereafter.

On 14 November an attack was staged on the Yellow Pimple by an Indian battalion (made up of Kumaoni hillmen, accustomed to the altitude), but it could not be taken. The battalion's retreat either triggered or coincided with the next Chinese general offensive in the Walong sector, which started on 15 November.[41]

Kaul, who had visited Walong on 12 and 13 November, returned again on 16 November when the situation worsened.[42] Several times earlier in his career, he had assumed that physical exertion on his part was necessary for the success of an army endeavor, and now he had to be personally present at the battle site even if he could not take full tactical command. He also felt that his presence would inspire confidence in his men. During the course of the fighting, he would be unable to remain just an observer but would become involved in specific tactical decisions.

From his own account Kaul was called on by the brigade commander at Walong, Brigadier N. C. Rawlly, for instructions; and he issued these instructions, thereby bypassing the division commander, General Pathania, who was present.[43] Brigadier Rawlly asked what should be done now that his forward localities were being overrun and the main brigade positions were becoming untenable. Rawlly also asked Kaul to determine the priorities to be set in extricating the brigade's weapons and personnel. Kaul gave permission for the brigade to withdraw but couched his order to Rawlly in the following fashion:

   (a) He was told to hold on to his present position to the best of his ability.
   (b) If the position became untenable, he was to take up an alternative position and hold it to the best of his ability.

(c) In the event of the alternative position also being untenable, he was to continue holding [a] series of such positions and keep delaying the enemy as much as he could.[44]

In other words, he gave the appearance of making a firm decision, but—by issuing a doubled-edged order—he really placed the responsibility for deciding whether to stay or withdraw on the subordinate officer. Although Kaul's order resembled the one given by Army Headquarters to Western Command on 22 September to cover the forward policy posts, that earlier directive had represented a compromise reached by a three-person committee (Thapar, Palit, and Dhillon). But here at Walong Kaul was temporizing, all by himself. To his credit, he apparently placed the highest priority on saving the men, rather than saving the heavy equipment (including artillery and mortars) recently sent forward with great effort.

General Kaul left Walong on the next to last aircraft. Although he had specified that troops should withdraw first to an alternative position and then to successive defensive positions, a major tactical disaster occurred at Walong—the breakup of a fighting unit. The retreating brigade disintegrated and made its way downward, toward the Brahmaputra-Lohit Valley, in useless pieces.

Kaul's next action was a curious one for a high-level commander to undertake personally. It typified his inability to delegate and his penchant for seeking situations of personal risk, although it also showed his continuing concern for the condition of his men. On the morning of 17 November he got an air force helicopter to fly him (and some companions, presumably from his staff) as close to Walong as possible, so that he could locate the remnants of the Walong brigade. He did so despite the danger of coming under enemy small-arms fire. Upon spotting Brigadier Rawlly and a small party, Kaul landed the helicopter and offered various kinds of assistance. Out of touch with his own corps headquarters at Tezpur, he missed the start of Chinese pressure on Se La. Only after he learned that Generals Sen and Thapar would shortly arrive in Tezpur did he leave the Walong sector to join them.

TO RETREAT FROM SE LA DURING CHINA'S NOVEMBER OFFENSIVE

The main military action of the 1962 war was the Chinese offensive through both Se La and Bomdila passes (see Map 9, below). Chinese forces completed their advance in four days, destroying 4 Division. One key Indian decision made such a disaster possible. It came on the night of 17–18 November, when the brigade guarding Se La Pass was permitted to start withdrawing even before heavy Chinese pressure was exerted against the Se La defense perimeter itself. The decision was made by the division commander, Major General A. S. Pathania, but Kaul did not forbid it—again preferring to follow the lead of a subordinate. Nor was Kaul able to regain control of the situation afterward, so that Indian units and positions were lost serially to the Chinese invading force.

Kaul had considerable resources available to him during the Se La–Bomdila campaign, although Thapar's reinforcement effort was not yet complete. By 17 November the Se La–Bomdila axis had come under the protection of a reconstituted 4 Division. The division now had ten battalions backed by artillery and other heavy weapons. This was still not a division at full strength, since a number of support and maintenance personnel had to be left behind while the combat troops were rushed up to NEFA. But it contained 10,000–12,000 men[45] and had some paramilitary troops (Assam Rifles) to draw on as well.

Se La itself, under 62 Brigade, was manned by five battalions. Sixty miles down the road, Bomdila was held by 48 Brigade, with three battalions. In between was the division headquarters located near the former Tibetan administrative center at Dirang Dzong, protected by 65 Brigade, with two battalions.

Not all of 4 Division's troops were in the main positions. Some (along with Assam Rifles units) were acting as screening forces, guarding infiltration routes and drop zones and reconnoitering; and two additional battalions were just arriving. But during the Chinese offensive of 16–19 November, Indian forces in western NEFA should have been sufficient to counter the Chinese thrust, using the box strategy, until the Chinese offensive stalled because of the winter. The Chinese reportedly used two divisions in western NEFA, "one normal and one light" (i.e., a total force of 18,000–20,000 men), although only a small fraction of these troops took part in the fighting.[46]

Equipment that had been lacking earlier was now available to the Indian force—for instance, field artillery, light tanks, heavy mortars, and (as yet undistributed) American automatic rifles. Indian equipment was of World War II vintage or even earlier (the .303 Lee-Enfield rifle used by Indian troops was of World War I vintage), while Chinese equipment was more modern.[47] But the Indian Army's equipment problems and shortages were not really a cause of the Indian defeat.

One important cause was Kaul's decision to deviate from the Harbakhsh-Palit plan by allowing Pathania to place his divisional headquarters back at Dirang Dzong, rather than at Se La itself. Since Pathania required a brigade to protect Dirang Dzong, only one brigade was left to defend Se La, instead of the two (i.e., a division less a brigade group) that Harbakhsh had wanted. Similarly, the hill behind Dirang Dzong had not been made into another fortified strongpoint, again contrary to the Harbakhsh plan.[48] Another change in plan made by Kaul was to give Pathania the option of retreating from Se La to Bomdila if the Chinese attacked Se La before 4 Division had built up sufficient strength to hold it. Kaul had been imprecise about what sort of situation would either justify or obviate this move.[49]

Thus, again lacking any real understanding of prior planning, Kaul had combined the Se La buildup with the idea (perhaps pressed on him by his staff) of making Bomdila a key Indian defensive positon, while also agreeing to Pathania's request to have his headquarters at Dirang Dzong. One serious problem with this compromise strategy (or nonstrategy) was that Pathania could not easily comprehend the situation ahead of him at Se La, and he could not readily travel up to Se La by road—a one-and-a-half to two-hour drive. Nor could Kaul at IV Corps Headquarters, located back in Tezpur (in the Brahmaputra Valley), readily coordinate the actions of his NEFA garrisons.

The most problematical elements, however, were these: (1) The Se La, Dirang Dzong, and Bomdila garrisons could now not readily hold out independently of support by road (i.e., as boxes), although this tactic still could be tried at Se La and Bomdila if necessary. (2) Too much now depended on keeping open a single 60-mile-long road (winding northwest from Bomdila to Dirang Dzong and then to Se La), which was soon to be the objective of infiltrating Chinese troops. (3) Kaul took too seriously the idea of interdicting such infiltrating forces. (4) Kaul's major troop concentrations were too far apart and could not readily provide one another with mutual support.

On the evening of 17 November, General Pathania, at 4 Division headquarters at Dirang Dzong, began repeatedly telephoning corps headquarters at Tezpur. He was disturbed by the tactical situation which had developed that day. For Pathania the situation contained the following key elements: (1) The Chinese were staging probing attacks on the northwest and northeast approaches to Se La. (2) The Indian battalion and other covering units just forward of Se La had sustained several Chinese attacks. (3) Despite their stout resistance, these forward troops were being pulled back into the Se La perimeter. Yet another crucial concern of Pathania's was that the Chinese had sent a force down the long, difficult infiltration route from Poshing La, thereby bypassing the Se La position from the east. The Indian battalion covering that route had come under heavy attack and was overwhelmed at a place called Thembang (see Map 9). The road between Bomdila and Dirang Dzong had thereafter been cut, near Bomdila.[50]

Pathania first spoke to Thapar and Sen, who (along with Palit) had reached IV Corps Headquarters before Kaul's return from Walong. He told them that he wanted to bring 62 Brigade down from Se La to Dirang Dzong. But Thapar and Sen wanted to wait for Kaul. They also resisted fervent pleas from Palit that Indian forces under pressure at both Se La and Thembang be ordered to hold their prepared positions, and that no Se La withdrawal be contemplated.

For some reason a signal was then sent out from corps headquarters giving Pathania the permission he was seeking. Although Palit got it canceled, after securing the support of Thapar, Pathania at 4 Division Headquarters may have been informed of it. If so, Pathania would have concluded that corps headquarters was seriously considering such a retreat, even if no order to undertake it was now being issued.[51]

When Pathania finally got through by telephone to Kaul himself (at about 7:45 P.M. on 17 November), the two men discussed the news that the Chinese had not only blocked the road near Bomdila but might soon cut it again, just behind Se La at a place called Senge. If so, 62 Brigade on Se La would be hemmed in from behind. Pathania pointed out that if the Se La brigade did not fall back immediately, withdrawal might prove impossible. Although Kaul did not agree, he did not "refuse the permission definitely."[52] In yet another telephone conversation, held at some time between 9 and 10 P.M., Kaul told Pathania that 62 Brigade should stay on Se La until they (Kaul and Pathania) could talk again in the morning. Then Kaul would issue final orders.[53]

General Kaul had been consulting closely with Thapar, Sen, and Palit. One version of events is that when Thapar and Palit finally left Kaul's headquarters for their billets, they were under the impression that Kaul's final order to Pathania had been to hold Se La for the night.

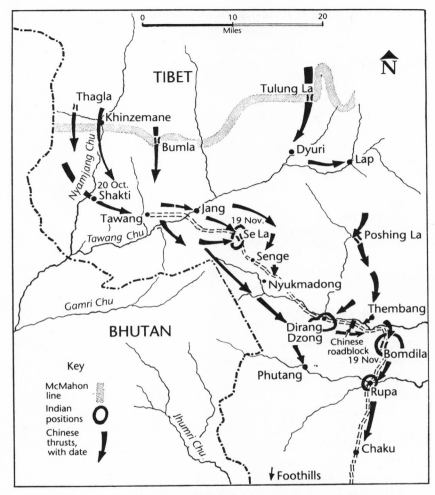

Map 9. CHINESE CAMPAIGNS IN NEFA, OCTOBER–
NOVEMBER 1962.

Yet, within minutes of their departure, a formal order was sent by IV Corps Headquarters to Pathania in Kaul's name. Another version (Kaul's) is that the signal was sent by Kaul, with the agreement of Thapar and Sen.[54] In any event, the order was ambiguous:

> (a) You will hold on to your present position to the best of your ability.
> (b) When any position becomes untenable, I delegate the authority to you to withdraw to any alternative position you can hold.
> (c) Approximately 400 enemy have cut the road Bomdi La–Dirang Dzong.
> (d) I have ordered commander 48 Brigade at Bomdi La ... to attack the enemy force tonight speedily and resolutely and keep this road clear at all costs.
> (e) You may be cut off by the enemy at Senge.
> (f) Your only course is to fight it out as best you can.
> (g) Reinforcements of two battalions will reach Bomdi La by 18th morning.
> (h) Use your tanks and other supporting arms to the fullest extent to clear your lines of communication.[55]

From the resemblance between this order and the one Kaul had issued at Walong, one may conclude that the thinking conveyed here was Kaul's. He was again passing the responsibility over to a subordinate, while covering himself by giving the appearance of steadfastness. Originally, his signal may have been designed simply to confirm and embellish what he had just told Pathania on the phone,[56] but other meanings were conveyed.

Before the Kaul order reached him, Pathania telephoned Se La before midnight.[57] Apparently, he was under the impression that in their last conversation Kaul had agreed to the start of preparations for a withdrawal, with final orders to come in the morning.

A battalion was then pulled back from a key prepared position on the Se La perimeter and told to occupy a point just behind and below Se La Pass, presumably to protect the retreat route. This was normal army procedure when starting a retreat.[58] Brigadier Hoshiar Singh, the commander at Se La, may have ordered this move on his own; but that is unlikely, since his personal inclination was to hold the Se La position.[59] The battalion's passage rearward through the Se La perimeter probably proved disturbing to the men of 62 Brigade, since it came late at night. Also disturbing was the continuing return of Indian screening troops from in front of Se La. The morale of 62 Brigade was already low for a variety of reasons, including the destruction of a 200-man patrol by a Chinese attack on 16 November.

Conditions were still unsettled when the Chinese moved into some of the places just vacated by the withdrawing battalion, and opened fire. Fighting became heavy; there was some hand-to-hand combat.[60] The brigade began to dissolve, although Hoshiar still controlled most of his troops. It is not certain whether Hoshiar Singh then ordered a general withdrawal from Se La or whether he was already engaged in one. But when dawn broke, his troops were coming down the road toward Senge and Dirang Dzong, having abandoned their heavier equipment and supplies. Some were under fire from the Chinese, who were still taking over deserted Indian positions around Se La Pass.[61]

At 5:30 in the morning of 18 November, Pathania reported to Kaul that 62 Brigade had begun retreating from Se La. It was only then that he finally got Kaul's official permission for that action.[62] The next question should have been whether to attempt some defense of Dirang Dzong or to have all of 4 Division withdraw to Bomdila. No orders were issued by Kaul on this subject; he left the matter to Pathania's discretion.

Pathania opted for something else entirely. 65 Brigade at Dirang Dzong was ordered to head not for Bomdila but for the Assam plains far to the south. With his headquarters now under fire from infiltrating Chinese, Pathania departed at approximately 7:30 A.M., with only a few accompanying officers and troops, leaving no one in command. He subsequently claimed that he had been moving toward Bomdila by a circuitous route and had headed for the plains only after he learned that Bomdila had fallen.[63] No formal notice of Pathania's action was provided to corps headquarters, although a brief radio message was received by 48 Brigade at Bomdila. Thus, Kaul in Tezpur could not be certain on 18 November of what had happened at Dirang Dzong.[64]

Pathania's decision was influenced by the main elements he had probably perceived in the 18 November situation. He knew that the Se La garrison was retreating to Dirang Dzong, but he thought that the Chinese force near Senge might block the retreat.[65] He was aware, too, that a company sent to cover one of the Chinese infiltration routes to Dirang Dzong had come under heavy attack. The Chinese had also "opened light small arms fire on divisional HQ from a range of about a thousand yards."[66] Finally, Pathania was aware that the Chinese had placed themselves between Dirang Dzong and Bomdila, after forcing the Poshing La route.

But Pathania was only vaguely aware of the fuller picture. That is, besides attacking frontally, Chinese forces were advancing down both sides of 4 Division, stretched as it was from Se La to Bomdila, and were engaged in a large-scale enveloping or encircling movement (see Map 9). They were deployed in many columns, so that Se La was being attacked from the northeast and northwest; but another Chinese thrust further to the west, and several others further to the east, bypassed Se La entirely. Most of the bypassing units would come through the mountainous and forested terrain of NEFA to reach the Indian road from one side or the other at various places, including places further south than Bomdila. Among the bypassing forces, one to the east of Se La reached the Indian road near Senge (a major airdrop zone), behind Se La. Still further to the east, other Chinese troops had come down the Poshing La route, moving south toward the road and Bomdila. Some of them veered westward, toward the Dirang Chu River and Dirang Dzong. Dirang Dzong came under pressure from Chinese troops on its own side (western side) of the Dirang Chu as well.[67]

Yet, by 18 November, only small parties of Chinese had reached the vicinity of Dirang Dzong. Using the approximately 3,000 Indian troops under his command[68] (combatants and noncombatants from 65 Brigade and other smaller units), Pathania could have put up a stiff fight if he had chosen to do so.

Before his departure Pathania had given hurried orders to the crews of his few tanks. They were told to head for Bomdila and to abandon their vehicles if a breakthrough proved impossible. Several junior officers, acting independently, combined these tanks with some infantry and support troops and formed an organized column. The column disintegrated after encountering Chinese resistance along the road. One battalion remained intact and reached the plains, but most of the other troops formed small parties to escape as best they could. Casualties among them were subsequently caused by Chinese ambushes, as well as the terrain and the weather.[69]

Sixty-two Brigade, descending from Se La, also crumbled when it came under heavy fire from a Chinese roadblock near Senge. Since the roadblock could be neither reduced nor bypassed by the brigade's main column, small groups broke away to make for the plains. Brigadier Hoshiar Singh himself was subsequently killed when his party was ambushed several days after the Chinese-declared cease-fire of 22 November.

TO WEAKEN THE BOMDILA DEFENSES

The last remaining Indian stronghold in NEFA was Bomdila, held by 48 Brigade and commanded by Brigadier Gurbax Singh. This brigade should have been able to put up stiff resistance to the Chinese advance; but its chances of doing so were reduced by the earlier dispatch of companies and platoons for tasks elsewhere, on the orders of Pathania and Kaul. These extra missions had included efforts to block the Chinese infiltration routes; such efforts had begun prior to the start of the Chinese November offensive.

On 18 November 48 Brigade at Bomdila was down to six companies in a perimeter designed to hold twice that number.[70] Gurbax had made this fact clear to Kaul in a telephone conversation held on the night of 17 November, when Kaul had wanted a force sent out from Bomdila to clear the road to Dirang Dzong. The brigadier had protested any further thinning out of his troops and recommended aggressive patrolling instead.[71] But Kaul was convinced that 48 Brigade could spare men for road-clearing operations. He believed that two extra battalions to reinforce Bomdila would arrive soon.

Mid-morning on 18 November, 48 Brigade was waiting for the Chinese in prepared positions. The troops were backed by field guns, heavy mortars, "and the guns of four light tanks."[72] At approximately 11 A.M. Kaul telephoned Gurbax and again ordered a column sent toward Dirang Dzong. According to one account, Gurbax "protested again: his position had not changed, no reinforcements except fifty men of the advance party had arrived, to pull troops out of his defenses would be to open Bomdi La to the Chinese. Kaul angrily and categorically ordered him to get the mobile column on the road within half an hour, whatever the consequences to Bomdi La."[73] This account is credible since it is generally supported by a second source.[74] Clearly, Kaul's concern was still with Dirang Dzong.

At the time of the morning conversation between Kaul and Gurbax, Gurbax already knew that Pathania had left Dirang Dzong, and therefore Kaul did too.[75] It is difficult to discern why Kaul still wanted a strong force sent up the road. He may have wanted to send only a small probing patrol to contact the Chinese and find out whether Dirang Dzong was really lost.[76]

The impression at Bomdila, however, was that a strong force had to be sent out. Two infantry companies, two of the brigade's four tanks, and two mountain guns were all collected into a column on the road by 11:15 A.M., and were ready to move.[77] It was then that some Chinese were seen emerging from hidden positions on wooded slopes nearby. Some of these Chinese troops advanced toward bunkers just vacated by one of the companies in the Indian column. By noon more such bunkers were in Chinese hands, as the Indian column moved north.[78]

It went only a short distance before being stopped by fire from a Chinese ambush. The troops from the column dispersed and tried to return to their original positions, now held by the Chinese. By one account a Chinese assault against the main Bomdila perimeter was already in progress, hitting a makeshift section of the Indian line manned by sappers, clerks, and cooks.[79] Another version has Chinese fire against the perimeter mounting steadily but being answered by effective Indian "gun and mortar fire from close range."[80]

After several hours of fighting, the Chinese had captured Indian bunkers in both the forward and rear areas of the perimeter and were pressuring one flank. There was still no sign of effective Indian reinforcement coming up the road from the south. Under these circumstances, Gurbax Singh at about 4 P.M. decided to order a withdrawal from Bomdila.[81] He expected to regroup and fight again at Rupa, some eight miles to the south, thinking that the reinforcing battalions sent by Kaul would already be there.[82]

The withdrawal of 48 Brigade was slow; its battalions were retreating by two different routes; and stragglers were left behind. Such confusion occurred either because of poor communications or because Gurbax had not made his intentions clear.[83] After Gurbax's own departure a reinforcing battalion finally reached Bomdila at approximately 6:30 P.M. It had never been told to go elsewhere. That battalion and the Bomdila stragglers (some from Thembang) constituted a force that held a portion of the Bomdila position left vacant by the Chinese but under fire.

According to one account, the question of defending Bomdila came up again when Gurbax Singh returned to Bomdila with that idea in mind. An officers' conference was held, at which serious consideration was given to counterattacking and recapturing lost positions. The decision not to do so was based on the conviction that, by the time success was achieved, other Chinese infiltrating parties would have cut the new Bomdila garrison's line of supply and communication. That second decision for withdrawal from Bomdila was reached just before 3 A.M. on 19 November.[84]

Later in the morning Gurbax issued orders to defend Rupa. Sources differ on how and why that decision was aborted.[85] But the brigade was breaking up, and problems were being caused by the fact that General Kaul and his own headquarters had issued contradictory instructions. Kaul again had gone forward and was out of touch with his staff.[86]

The last remnant of 48 Brigade finally dissolved under Chinese fire at Chaku, a position further down the road beyond Rupa, at approximately 3 A.M. on 20 November. These troops also would reach the plains in small groups.[87] All resistance by 4 Division had ended.

CHAPTER THIRTEEN

Three Decisions of War, Diplomacy, and Politics

DURING THE 1962 war three additional major decisions were made in New Delhi. The first was made during the early days of the war, the second during the lull between the two Chinese military offensives, and the third as a result of the fall of Se La and Bomdila. These were decisions of diplomacy and politics, rather than strictly military decisions.

TO ASK THE UNITED STATES FOR MILITARY EQUIPMENT

On 21 October 1962, the day after the start of the border war, the U.S. State Department issued a declaration condemning the Chinese attack. Any Indian request for military assistance, it said, would receive sympathetic consideration.[1] An American official expressed sympathy again on 22 October, although the United States government was already being distracted by the emerging Cuban missile crisis.[2] India's foreign secretary, M. J. Desai, thus knew of the likely reaction when on the afternoon of 23 October he met with the U.S. ambassador, John Kenneth Galbraith. Desai first reminded Galbraith that the Soviet Union had adopted a more pro-Chinese line since the war began; consequently, he said, India now had little hope that the Soviets would restrain the Chinese. Desai then raised the matter of American aid.

India would have to turn to the United States for substantial assistance, he said, within the next few days. He hoped that America would not force India into an alliance or denigrate Indian sovereignty by imposing unacceptable inspection procedures governing the use of American arms. While Galbraith promptly reassured the foreign secretary on both points, he mentioned two minor problems. Krishna Menon had alienated American opinion during the preceding year, and India's arms procurement system was in a bad state. The latter point involved Krishna Menon also, since weapons acquisition was the defense minister's responsibility.[3]

Beyond this preliminary approach to the United States, the Indian government was casting its nets as widely as possible. On 24 October Nehru responded appreciatively to a sympathetic message from Britain's prime minister, who was already sending aid. India and Britain discussed aid cautiously, probably because of the sensitivity in India to anything British. The Indian government, especially Krishna Menon, sought to avoid publicity and denied reports about specific Indian aid requests. But by 27 October British supplies were already on their way,[4] and Britain would become India's second-largest foreign supplier of arms and equipment during and immediately after the 1962 crisis.

France, Belgium, and Canada were approached, with positive results; and on 27 October Nehru issued a general letter appealing to all friendly nations. Negotiations with Israel were ended without results because of the objections of Egypt's president, Gamal Nasser.[5]

Krishna Menon seemed resistant to the notion of making a formal request to the Americans, specifying what was needed.[6] Possibly to help overcome that resistance, Nehru wrote a note to the defense minister. In the note Nehru said that he did not know how he would explain the entire military equipment problem to parliament. "The fact remains that we have been found lacking and there is an impression that we have approached these things in a somewhat amateurish way."[7] But Nehru too had his own doubts about an action that would constitute a reversal of policy. That there were conflicting impulses in Nehru's mind over seeking assistance from Western countries had been shown as early as 22 October, when he said in a BBC television interview that India would not ask for military aid from the West but would buy Western military supplies and equipment instead.[8]

At the back of the prime minister's mind was a diplomatic strategy he did not want to compromise. He would avoid alienating the Soviet Union, to allow for the possibility that the Soviets would revert to their original diplomatic position (vis-à-vis India and China) once the Cuban missile crisis had passed.[9] He seems to have reasoned that such a reversion, plus Western aid and world opinion favorable to India, would prove a deterrent to the Chinese. If the Soviets were to move closer to India, the Chinese might not want to continue their war.

Yet both the prime minister and the defense minister were under pressure from General Kaul, whose opinion was still valued. During a visit to his house by Nehru and Krishna Menon on or about 23 October, Kaul vigorously urged that military aid be secured from "some foreign power or powers."[10] Krishna Menon came to see Kaul again a few days later. The defense minister was "in an agitated state of mind."[11] and asked that Kaul reduce his ideas to writing. After consultations with experts, Kaul dictated a paper from his sickbed. This was the same paper that called for a temporary military dictatorship in India. In it he also developed his conception of possible American intervention to grandiose proportions. Kaul produced the paper during a visit by Cabinet Secretary Khera, on or about 26 October. Knowing that Khera had come at the behest of Krishna Menon, Kaul

> produced from under his pillow a paper he had prepared, with an earnest plea that the action he recommended should be considered most urgently. . . . Fortunately, he had not signed his name to it.
> The paper urged that India should seek the aid of some major foreign military power or powers. . . . India might have to persuade Chiang Kai-shek and also South Korean forces, assisted by the United States' potential in the West Pacific seaboard, to invade the Chinese mainland; at the same time, India should invite some foreign armies to come and assist the Indian army to mount a major offensive over the Himalayas.[12]

Kaul also proposed that the United States Air Force should provide an air umbrella for the vulnerable cities (and other likely targets) of north India. He also wanted the USAF to "launch massive attacks on China from bases in India."[13]

Krishna Menon telephoned Galbraith on the morning of 29 October. The call made the ambassador think that the Indian government had finally decided to make a formal request of the Americans. The defense minister wanted a meeting immediately; he was prepared to come over to the embassy if necessary. But Galbraith had just received a personal letter for Prime Minister Nehru from President Kennedy. It was a reply to Nehru's general appeal for international support, sent to foreign heads of government on 27 October. The ambassador was convinced that (for reasons having to do with American public opinion) any official Indian request for arms should come directly from Nehru rather than Krishna Menon. He was therefore determined that the prime minister be handed the Kennedy letter first, before any talk with the defense minister took place. He had already made an appointment to see Nehru for that purpose, and despite a series of phone conversations, Krishna Menon could not persuade Galbraith to change his mind.[14]

Nehru's statement to Galbraith was categorical, if still reserved: "The Prime Minister said they did indeed have to have aid and it would have to come from the United States. He went on to say they wanted to avoid irritating the Soviets as much as possible. The Soviets had indicated that they realized that assistance from us was inevitable, but hoped that this would not mean a military alliance between the United States and India."[15] Galbraith emphasized that the American administration would not call for a military alliance.

Galbraith's impression was that the Indian initiative had been Krishna Menon's (these two men met later that day), undertaken to show that he was persona grata with the Americans. But Galbraith also saw that, by this time, the need for United States aid was so urgent that no one could resist it. Having recognized this fact, Krishna Menon was trying to gain from it.[16]

M. J. Desai, Morarji Desai, and Kaul had communicated with Galbraith about United States aid during the week or so before Krishna Menon did, which suggests that foreign military assistance was a subject being discussed by Nehru with each of these men, and probably with the newly formed Emergency Committee of the cabinet. The American aid decision was quickly approved by the full cabinet on 29 October, and was thus made final.[17] The decision represented a broad consensus.

There were a number of additional facets to the Indian decision, and to the emerging Indo-American relationship. Starting on 27 October the U.S. armed forces attachés at the American embassy were brought into the Indian military picture in an intimate way. Subsequently, embassy personnel would work closely with the Indian defense ministry to devise figures on Indian military needs, since the Americans (and British) thought that the original estimates were not fully accurate.[18] Liaison work would be done in Washington as well, and the American military staff in Delhi would undergo needed expansion.

The first American weapons started arriving on 3 November, and the initial American airlift of mobile weapons and equipment for NEFA was completed by 12 November. But compared to what was to come, this was a token consignment. The operational side of the Indo-American military relationship would not really commence until late November.[19]

Despite Galbraith's earlier assurances that India would not be unduly restricted in using American equipment, India was ultimately asked to promise that the supplies would be used only against China.[20] The Americans were obviously worried about Pakistan.

TO DISMISS KRISHNA MENON

The Indian decision-maker for whom the onset of the border war would immediately bring the most serious career consequences was Krishna Menon. During the first several days after 20 October, he had been quite visible, giving public speeches. On 26 October he (along with Nehru) described the NEFA terrain and situation to the top policy committee of the ruling Congress Party (the Congress Working Committee), without hearing any criticism of himself.[21] But agitation against him had already begun within the party's ranks. The initiators were some thirty Congress members of parliament. This group had met informally in New Delhi on 23 October to discuss the NEFA fighting and related matters. Led by such figures as H. K. Mahatab, the deputy leader of the Congress Parliamentary Party (CPP), they expressed concern about the NEFA defeats.

Their prime concern was that Nehru and parliament had allegedly been misled about security arrangements on the northeast frontier. Repeatedly they had been told of the vulnerability of Ladakh to a Chinese advance, but the position in NEFA had been described in confident terms. They wanted to urge that the persons responsible for this description be properly held to account, and they decided to convey that opinion to the prime minister at a forthcoming joint session of the Executive Committee and the External Affairs Committee of the Congress Parliamentary Party.[22] While this was the sense of the meeting, presumably reported to Nehru and Indira Gandhi by Mahatab when he saw them that evening on other business, there had been other points of view. Some members had felt that the entire government and ruling party, more than the defense minister, were responsible for the failure to read the Chinese mind. The intelligence services had come in for criticism as well. The members wanted to urge Nehru to get those services upgraded, or to supplement them by establishing links with the intelligence agencies of other countries.[23]

On 29 October the press reported that several senior ministers had told Nehru during the past few days that a change at the defense ministry had become a political and psychological necessity. The line of argument being used within "high Congress circles" was that Krishna Menon had lost the confidence of the country because his defense policy had failed.[24] A symbolic change was needed, and for effective inspirational leadership to be provided in the current emergency, a less controversial figure would have to be installed in Krishna Menon's place. The Soviet policy shift in China's direction had also invalidated Krishna Menon's entire approach to Indian defense requirements against China.

The convergence of members of parliament in Delhi for meetings of the committees of the CPP, and for the early convening of the parliament, allowed further momentum to gather against the defense minister. At a session of the Parliamentary Executive (i.e., Executive Committee of the CPP) on 29 October, some members became extremely critical of the supply and equipment deficiencies hampering the troops in NEFA. Despite Krishna Menon's presence at the meeting, a few persons at the meeting suggested that the prime minister himself take over the defense portfolio. Nehru, who had recently advised elsewhere against postmortems and recriminations, reportedly listened to the criticism "patiently and silently."[25]

Clearly, the affair would not end here. Many senior party figures had reportedly written letters to the prime minister, urging the withdrawal of the defense portfolio from Krishna Menon. Some members of the Parliamentary Executive had agreed among themselves to impress on the prime minister, in a concerted fashion, what they saw as the Parliamentary Party's general dissatisfaction with Krishna Menon's past performance.[26]

The first decision to downgrade Krishna Menon's role came on or about 31 October. A few days earlier Krishna Menon had told Mullik after a defense meeting that he could face the wrath of the opposition parties but not the sentiment in the Congress. Although he retained the prime minister's confidence, he no longer commanded the confidence of his own party and therefore had decided to resign.[27] A day later Krishna Menon submitted his resignation to the prime minister and was certain that Nehru would accept it.

On 31 October it was announced publicly that Nehru himself was taking over the defense portfolio, while Krishna Menon would head a new ministry and retain his cabinet rank. He would be "Minister of Defense Production," in control of such things as technical directorates, ordnance factories, and defense research and development. But he would no longer have any administrative control over the army, navy, and air force; and he would not be involved with the purchase of foreign (and especially American) military equipment.[28] Instead, as was revealed the next day, a Ministry of Supplies would coordinate Indian domestic weapons production with procurement of arms from abroad. This ministry was soon placed in the hands of T. T. Krishnamachari.

The cabinet secretariat had been expected to issue (as of 1 November) what one newspaper called "a detailed business allocation order specifying the responsibilities of the new Ministries of Defense and Defense Production."[29] But the list could not be issued because Krishna Menon had just left for Tezpur to pay his last visit there as defense minister. The major complication, however, was surely Krishnamachari's misgivings about the overlap between the two new military supply ministries. His uneasiness, as well as his personal suspicion of Krishna Menon, was communicated to the press and erupted into an incident in which Krishnamachari accused the former defense minister of having enlisted the IB to spy on him.[30]

The situation was not improved when the press reported a statement that Krishna Menon allegedly had made in Tezpur. Because he was still in the cabinet and still sitting in the defense ministry, he said, "Nothing is changed."[31] A defense ministry spokesman made it appear as if no new ministry was going to be created after all. Instead, the defense ministry would be kept whole, with Nehru in overall charge of it, while Krishna Menon took responsibility only for defense production within the ministry. The impression from this and other published information was that Krishna Menon remained firmly entrenched in the Ministry of Defense.

Efforts in the Congress to dislodge him now accelerated. Those members of the Parliamentary Executive who had wanted Krishna Menon's removal had not been satisfied with his demotion. They were now incensed. Larger issues were involved as well. The leadership of the Congress parliamentary delegation believed basically in party guidance of a prime minister. This was an issue in party-government relations which Nehru had seemingly settled in his own favor some time earlier, but now it emerged again. Krishna Menon's critics in the Congress parliamentary leadership also felt that the whole thrust of China policy needed change. The socialist affinity felt by Krishna Menon for China could no longer be tolerated, nor could Nehru's naïveté about India-China friendship.[32]

On 6 November it was reported in the press that three senior members of the Congress Parliamentary Party had decided to approach Krishna Menon to resign a second time. They were the CPP secretary, Raghunath Singh; Mahavir Tyagi, a former Minister of State in the Ministry of Defense; and a leading Maharashtra politician, R. K. Khadilkar. In consultation with other CPP members they had concluded that inducing Krishna Menon to act would be the only way to save Nehru embarrassment. The argument they would presumably use was that Krishna Menon's presence was diverting energy toward controversy and that the former defense minister should devote his abundant energies toward meeting the emergency in a nonofficial capacity.[33]

It was further reported that several members of the CPP had given notice of resolutions to be introduced at meetings to be held on 7 November, in preparation for the opening day of parliament on 8 November. Some resolutions would come to the scheduled session of the Parliamentary Executive; others would be brought later that day, at the full formal gathering of the CPP. One such resolution would say that, since the country had accepted a policy of arms purchase from Western countries, only those persons who had faith in the policy should be in charge of defense.[34]

The decisive action came at a private meeting held at the house of H. K. Mahatab on the evening of 6 November. There, a majority of the members of the Parliamentary Executive composed a letter to Nehru, listing their objections to Krishna Menon's continuing in office. They decided that they would act jointly to secure his removal and agreed on tactics to be used at the Parliamentary Executive meeting the next day.[35] Such tactical planning by informal gathering was usual whenever the executive (and particularly its leadership) wanted to assert itself. But the members had never met informally beforehand to determine how to ask the prime minister to drop a member of his cabinet.[36]

The tactical planning was detailed. The normal practice was that the group supporting the leaders of the Parliamentary Party would sit at executive meetings in such a way that opponents could not cluster together. But this time the members of the group also planned to remain silent, sad, and morose throughout the session, with eyes cast down, not meeting Nehru's eyes. Heads were to be shaken in disagreement any time a favorable reference was made to Krishna Menon. But Mahavir Tyagi was to be allowed to shout.[37]

The group's letter was delivered to the party secretary's office, since it was thought to be a party matter rather than a governmental one. Nehru brought it with him to the meeting of the executive on 7 November and opened the discussion by saying that the letter's signers had acted unfairly in conspiring against Krishna Menon. In an unplanned retort, a Karnataka member (Mr. Hanumathiya) claimed that there had been no conspiracy but merely joint action on the part of those who were of the same point of view. He went on to say that the prime minister had not acted properly in showing the letter to Krishna Menon or in bringing him to the meeting, as had been done.

Contrary to custom, the members of the executive had not risen when Nehru came into the room. Added to the planned atmosphere of the meeting was a sense of strain as the dialogue grew heated. Mahavir Tyagi appeared to grow quite excited, and it was made to appear as if several persons in the room were trying to restrain him.[38] Other members of the executive spoke very critically of Krishna Menon.[39]

Finally, Nehru (in the context of a heated discussion) said that he would resign if he could not have the ministers he wanted. Tyagi then told Jawaharlal Nehru that he should be ashamed to call himself the son of Motilal Nehru. It was improper for the prime minister to threaten this way during an hour of crisis. The prime minister is the servant of the parliament, he said, and not the other way around. Tyagi had been a friend of Nehru's father and was therefore in a position to make such a personal remark.[40]

Tyagi had also touched on a theme of great importance to Jawaharlal Nehru—the independent functioning of parliament and the need for its institutionalization.

Tyagi's comment had implied that Nehru might have to resign, too, if he would not abandon Krishna Menon and his policies. Mr. Hanumathiya was more explicit about this point, heatedly telling Nehru that it did not matter if he resigned.[41] No one said so, but the possibility of a Nehru resignation had been considered by the leadership group, which had thought of Rajendra Prasad, the retired president of India, as the most suitable replacement. But the group's estimate had been that Nehru would yield to the executive on the Krishna Menon matter, just as he had done on past occasions when he knew the true feelings of the party.[42] That estimate was correct. Apparently taken aback by the Tyagi outburst, Nehru said that the prime minister of India was indeed the servant of the parliament. He would not want anyone to assume that he thought otherwise.[43]

The meeting ended inconclusively with the prime minister leaving. During the hours between the meeting of the executive and the session of the full parliamentary party, Khadilkar took it upon himself to see Nehru. Known for his skill at negotiation (and nicknamed "Peshwa" by his colleagues, after the politicians—*Peshwas*—who had administered the Maratha empire), Khadilkar communicated the determination of the Executive Committee. He stated outright that Krishna Menon should be made the scapegoat and dropped. Otherwise, the party's anger might turn toward the prime minister himself. Nehru responded with silence.[44]

Even more dire warnings were being pressed upon the prime minister, either at this time (7 November) or during the previous few days. While many cabinet members wanted Krishna Menon removed and yet did not want to confront Nehru out of love or fear of him, the blunt Morarji Desai was not reticent. He went so far as to say that he "would not be surprised" if failure to act on the Krishna Menon matter led to "violent actions. Some people were even talking of committing murder."[45] He was referring to the possibility of assassination or liquidation of government leaders.[46] Much the same point of view was held by Home Minister Shastri, although he may not have been so open to Nehru about it.[47] It was Morarji's impression that the president of India, Sarvepalli Radhakrishnan, and other cabinet colleagues had pressed Nehru as well. There could be little doubt on the prime minister's part about how isolated he had become.

Nehru announced his decision during the full CPP session that evening (7 November). Krishna Menon's offer of full resignation, made in a letter submitted by him on 30 October, would be accepted with great regret. Nehru also said that he was convinced of Menon's worthy record of performance but was aware that the controversy surrounding the former defense minister was unlikely to cease and would inevitably impede the defense effort. The prime minister reportedly went on to say (in the words of a newspaper summary), "Any minister who had lost the confidence of the party or the public would have to go and this principle applied to him [Nehru] as well."[48]

The text of Krishna Menon's letter, which had been read at the morning executive session, was also read out at the larger forum.

Despite the fulsome praise that Nehru heaped on the former defense minister (who was present), there was no further criticism from those assembled in the room. But Nehru's original announcement had brought cheering. The party revolt had succeeded.

TO REQUEST AMERICAN AIR COVER

On 17 November official New Delhi reacted to word of the Walong disaster. Accompanying the news had been a message from Kaul, saying, in effect, that the "threat from the Chinese was now so great and their overall strength so superior that foreign troops should be asked to come to India's aid."[49] The result was another request to the Americans—this time for transport aircraft to fly in troops from the Punjab. The planes would be manned by American pilots and crews.[50]

The day before (16 November), T. T. Krishnamachari had seen the American ambassador to discuss the possibility of obtaining interceptor aircraft to guard Calcutta. He also raised the question of an additional American loan to India, of the magnitude of a half-billion dollars.[51] That discussion had been informal, and no specific proposal was made by the Indian government at this stage. But on 19 November a far-reaching proposal was put forward. In two letters written to President Kennedy on that date, Prime Minister Nehru asked for U.S. aircraft and pilots to cover Indian cities, while the IAF took on a combat role along the India-China frontier.[52]

Clearly prompting that final move was the fall of Bomdila on 18–19 November, preceded by the loss of Se La. The Chinese were also shelling Chushul airfield in Ladakh and seemed likely to move against Leh. The loss of still other parts of India, and the crossing of other parts of the frontier by Chinese forces, seemed imminent to Nehru and to those in close consultation with him.[53]

Nehru transmitted his letters to the American government through the Indian embassy in Washington. Galbraith in New Delhi was notified only after the second letter had already been decided upon, but he was able to alert Washington that both letters were coming.[54] Nehru considered this second "midnight" letter so sensitive that the sole Indian copy was kept in the files in his office and was never given to the Ministry of External Affairs.[55]

Specifically, Nehru proposed the immediate delivery of a minimum of twelve squadrons of American fighter aircraft. These all-weather interceptors would not attack Chinese targets but would protect the cities of northern India and thereby free Indian warplanes for use in the war. India would strike at Chinese communications lines, so as to stem or slow down the Chinese advance.[56] As Kaul had been demanding, the government would now reverse its 18 September decision not to use Indian aircraft against Chinese targets in Tibet, Ladakh, and NEFA.

In his letters Nehru made clear that radar stations should accompany the American aircraft so as to make up an integrated air defense system. United States personnel would fly the American fighter planes and operate the radar installations. Indians would take over from Americans both in the air and on the ground as soon as they could be trained to do so.

The prime minister further requested two squadrons of American B-47 bombers. They would supposedly "enable India to strike at Chinese bases and air fields; but to learn to fly these planes Indian pilots and technicians would be sent immediately for training in the United States." Assurance was given that all "such assistance and equipment would be utilized solely against the Chinese."

In all, Nehru's thinking was that American personnel would be used only for the defense of the heartland of India and only for the short term. But if the Chinese reacted quickly to the tactical use of the Indian Air Force, and IAF interceptors were unable to cope with them, Americans might have to fight in the airspace over India's frontier battle zones. This possibility was raised by a passage contained in one of Nehru's letters. It said that, in addition to the fighter squadrons already requested, the United States should, if possible, send planes flown by American personnel "to assist the Indian Air Force in any battles with the Chinese in Indian air space; but aerial action by India elsewhere would be the responsibility of the Indian Air Force" (this is a paraphrase).[57]

The persons whom Nehru had reportedly consulted on this decision were T. T. Krishnamachari, Home Minister Shastri, Finance Minister Morarji Desai, and probably both IB director Mullik, and Foreign Secretary M. J. Desai. Most, if not all, of these men had conducted informal discussions among themselves instead of convening the Emergency Committee of the cabinet or the cabinet as a whole. But no one besides Nehru (and most likely M. J. Desai) had a hand in drafting the letters to Washington.[58] As one outside observer later pointed out, such secretiveness was "most unusual behavior on Nehru's part, indicating an awareness that his decision of 19 November undermined, or could be interpreted as a grave violation of, the hallowed principle of nonalignment."[59]

Implementation depended on an American government whose ambassador to India disagreed with the whole plan. Rather than lobby Washington for its acceptance, Galbraith spent hours at India's Ministries of External Affairs and Defense urging that the Indian Air Force not join in the fighting. On 20 November he informed the State Department that he did not expect the Chinese to invade India all along the frontier, contrary to Indian thinking. The Chinese were not magicians and could not maintain a supply line over the whole Himalayan mountain spine.[60] Galbraith was also influenced by his own crisis management axiom: that air war so greatly accelerates the pace of combat as to preclude diplomatic possibilities, whereas in ground war diplomacy is possible because escalation is slowed by the obstacles to rapid advance by the forces of either side.[61]

Ambassador Galbraith told his own staff, and presumably Washington as well, that the Indian air arm was not highly effective and could not retaliate against China proper; at the same time, the cities of the Ganges plain were vulnerable from Tibet. He also said that, from the technical standpoint, the United States could not immediately supply the protection Nehru wanted. Nor did he share the Indian hope that the IAF could halt the Chinese drive. The Chinese were moving through woods and at night, and the American experience in Korea had taught that, even with complete control of the requisite airspace, air power could not prevent the Chinese from supplying their troops or continuing an offensive push.[62]

What Galbraith did recommend, and urgently requested from Washington on 20 November, was that units of the American Seventh Fleet come into the Bay of Bengal.[63] He announced to his staff, and presumably proposed to Washington, that some "American-piloted air transport" be brought in right away and that the American airlift of supplies to India be intensified and put on a regular schedule, especially in view of the Indian loss of matériel.[64] The United States did send C-130 transports "to ferry replacement troops from the Punjab and to fly supplies to Ladakh."[65] This last step was Galbraith's response to the earlier (17 November) Indian request for help in transporting troops. The ambassador viewed all these measures as "morale-stabilizing."[66]

Washington's response to Nehru's requests and Galbraith's comments was swift. The secretary of state, Dean Rusk, raised political questions about Pakistan and other issues in a cable to Galbraith.[67] More important was a cable to the U.S. ambassador from President Kennedy. In it Kennedy offered to send a high-level mission immediately to assess India's needs. He also promised an airlift, proposed air delivery of urgently needed spare parts for the American-made transport planes already being used by the IAF, and spoke of dispatching three additional American teams of experts to work with India in prosecuting the war.[68] These were just interim ideas, although some would be implemented immediately after the war ended.

The United States government was in the process of drafting a favorable reply to Nehru's air cover proposal (Galbraith's countervailing efforts notwithstanding) when the Chinese announced their cease-fire on 21 November. But, prior to 19 November and independently of Galbraith's request for Seventh Fleet vessels, Washington had decided to send an aircraft carrier to the Bay of Bengal, notice of which was sent to New Delhi and, indirectly, to Peking.[69] Sending a carrier force would supplement other forms of American aid and would signal China that "the United States was prepared to intervene with air power to protect India's cities, if the Chinese continued their advance on the plains."[70]

Thus, as of 21 November, the United States had already intervened with air power—not by using the U.S. Air Force but by using the threat of naval air strength to deter the Chinese from advancing further into India. At the time of the Chinese cease-fire announcement, which followed the receipt of Nehru's second letter in Washington by only ten hours,[71] the American aircraft carrier task force was not yet on station. But the Chinese knew it was coming.

The carrier and its escorts stayed several days near Calcutta before Ambassador Galbraith succeeded in having them leave. By then he had concluded that his request for naval units was a mistake, caused by the tension of the moment.[72] The carrier force withdrew from the Bay of Bengal only when the American government was persuaded that the Chinese cease-fire was genuine and that no new round of warfare was likely.[73]

Although Washington had supported Galbraith's effort to keep IAF fighters and bombers on the ground during the war,[74] the Americans did intend to have the USAF support Indian air operations eventually, once proper preparations had been made. The holding of joint IAF exercises with American and Commonwealth air force squadrons, during the fall of 1963, showed a continuing commitment by the United States to providing the kind of air support Nehru had requested.

CONCLUSION

The Chinese probably ended the 1962 war because they had achieved their immediate military and political objectives, via a "giant punitive expedition," and not because of overconcern about American intervention.[75] Furthermore, the stability of the India-China cease-fire after 1962, and India's increasing reliance on the Soviet Union in place of an increasingly unreliable America, eventually prevented the establishment of any permanent military link between India and the United States. For these reasons India's 1962 decisions involving the United States were not as important as they seemed at the time. Instead, the crucial decisions, from which the Indian government is still obliged to learn lessons, were those that led to India's military failures.

The various explanations given for those failures have ranged from well-considered criticism of the military wisdom of the Se La strategy, and its implementation by Kaul and A. S. Pathania,[76] to a conspiracy theory suggesting that Western intelligence agencies had plotted with the Chinese to destroy India's nonalignment. Supposedly, the plot had employed Western-oriented Indian army officers interested in settling scores with the Kaul faction in the army.[77]

The main causes, however, were clearly (1) military leadership (Kaul's and Pathania's generalship) and (2) personnel management (that is, Nehru never should have allowed Kaul to return to NEFA). Still another major cause was the earlier unwillingness of Nehru and Krishna Menon to finance the army's expansion plans, for which Kaul had fought hard. The simple availability of more troops and equipment would have permitted implementation of defense plans for NEFA before the 1962 war broke out, thereby eliminating India's later need to form new plans on short notice and to seek massive military help from abroad.

5

THE POST-CRISIS PERIOD, 22 NOVEMBER 1962 TO 28 FEBRUARY 1963

CHAPTER FOURTEEN

The Post-crisis Decision-Makers and Their Psychological Setting

THE OFFICIAL STATEMENT announcing the Chinese cease-fire was dated 21 November 1962. In it the Chinese pledged to end hostilities at 00:00 hours on 22 November and begin withdrawing on 1 December "to positions 20 kilometers behind the line of actual control which existed between China and India on November 7, 1959." For the Eastern Sector that "control" line would correspond to "the illegal McMahon Line."[1] In the Western and Middle Sectors they would withdraw behind the line that they had allegedly established by 7 November 1959 (see Map 6). Their 20-kilometer pullback would include the Middle Sector, although no fighting had occurred there.

THE DECISION-MAKERS

Despite some slippage in his authority, Prime Minister Nehru remained in command of the Indian political system and the national decision-making process throughout the immediate postwar period. In 1963 he was noticeably losing the zest and verbal vigor with which he had dominated the houses of parliament; yet he still set the nation's agenda. As always during the time of his prime ministership, he remained a legitimizing symbol and, to many, the embodiment of his nation. The war with China had curtailed his role as an international statesman and champion of peace, but he had become instead the focal point of national and international sympathy.

Decisions on China-related matters remained in Nehru's hands, and he worked in his customary style with officials, cabinet members, and military personnel. But an important change in the structure of the consultation process took place during the post-crisis period, with the enhancement of the role of the cabinet. On foreign policy and security matters, the Emergency Committee of the cabinet, formed soon after the Chinese attack, became the key consultative body. Its members were those people who had served on it during the war, although Y. B. Chavan had replaced Krishna Menon.[2] Thus, it consisted of Nehru, T. T. Krishnamachari (Economic and Defense Coordination), Morarji Desai (Finance), Lal Bahadur Shastri (Home), G. L. Nanda (Planning), and Y. B. Chavan (Defense). The Ministries of Defense and Finance now cooperated with each other in supplying information and implementing policy, as they had not done in Krishna Menon's time. But well into 1963 there was still some confusion over the jurisdictions of the various ministries in charge of rebuilding India's defenses. Among other problems the functions of Chavan's Ministry of Defense partially overlapped with those of Krishnamachari's Ministry for Economic and Defense Coordination.[3]

Besides Nehru there were just two other true decision-makers between 22 November 1962 and 28 February 1963: Chavan and the new Chief of Army Staff, General J. N. Chaudhuri. Chavan was a burly, vigorous career politician who had been dominating the Congress Party in the state of Maharashtra. Until called to join the cabinet in New Delhi, he had been the Chief Minister of his state (which includes the populous city of Bombay). General Chaudhuri had been made Chief of Army Staff on 20 November, after the resignation of Thapar, even though he had previously earned the enmity of the Kaul faction in the army and had faced some opposition in the defense ministry.

Like Kaul, Chaudhuri had ambition, an outgoing personality, sharp political instincts, and a controversial political record. But he was far more the professional soldier than Kaul, since he had extensive combat experience. Because Nehru needed a professional such as Chaudhuri for military reasons and domestic political appearances, Chaudhuri wielded more authority than Thapar (or even Kaul) had, although he worked closely with Chavan. To improve communications between the military and the cabinet, all three armed service chiefs were invited to meetings of the Emergency Committee on an ad hoc basis.[4]

Among the members of the old Nehru "faction," B. N. Mullik remained chief of the IB, a valued consultant to Nehru, and a policy initiator and implementer. But he was starting to come under fire from the army and other critics. Therefore he was losing some of the clout he had enjoyed earlier, although he managed to maintain good relations with Home Minister Shastri and Defense Minister Chavan.[5]

In the Ministry of External Affairs, M. J. Desai continued during the post-crisis period as foreign secretary, and then in late 1963 he took over the post of secretary-general from R. K. Nehru. In that capacity he remained the prime minister's chief consultant within the MEA, although Nehru regularly saw other MEA officials as well.[6]

THE ATTITUDINAL PRISM OF THE DECISION-MAKERS

Fundamental to the worldview of Indian decision-makers and consultants just after the 1962 war were beliefs already present before the war. The war confirmed these beliefs and made them into a coherent and long-lasting belief system. Confirmation also came from the polemical battle that China began conducting against the Soviet Union when the Sino-Soviet rift became openly acknowledged by the two Communist countries in the spring and summer of 1963.[7]

The most important of the now-confirmed Indian beliefs was that China, long hostile to India for ideological and national character reasons, wanted to hold the premier position in Asia. The Chinese had a preferred structure for relations among Asian countries, one that required at least senior-partner status for China. A fully self-directed India did not fit into that structure; therefore, India would have to be reduced to a position of subordination or subservience. Furthermore, the Chinese could gain an edge in an Asian power rivalry by demonstrating India's military weakness. They had therefore acted in 1962 to eclipse India in international standing and prestige.[8]

China's effort to enhance its influence in Asia, in the Indian view, was directed against the Soviet Union as well as India. By showing that newly independent non-Communist countries such as India could not play a progressive role in history, China would gain an advantage in the ideological argument that had already started to divide the Communist world. The Soviets believed in peaceful coexistence between the Communist and non-Communist worlds, whereas the Chinese regarded war as inevitable. The Chinese were seeking to prove that Soviet aid and other support for developing countries would strengthen bourgeois governments and rightist-reactionary social elements. To demonstrate to the Soviet Union and other Communist states how mistaken such an approach was, China felt obliged to push the Indian government away from nonalignment and thereby reveal India's true nature as an Asian outpost of the Western powers.

Seemingly, the Chinese thought that if the Soviets could be pressured into taking the same hard-line position on nonalignment already adopted by China, China would be left to control the Communist bloc's relations with the non-Communist Asian states. In effect, the Chinese would have established their own sphere of influence. The Soviets opposed such a design because the Soviet Union was partly an Asian power and still wanted India to serve as an Asian counterweight to China.

That the Chinese expected the 1962 war to deal a serious blow to the Indian economy was another basic Indian belief, inferred from reading Chinese published statements. India needed peace for economic growth, but the Chinese were determined to force India to divert its resources to military expenditure. Moreover, there was the suspicion that the Chinese were striking politically at the Nehru government, hoping for its downfall and replacement by something more malleable. Indeed, it seemed to be China's intention to cast doubt on the whole Indian democratic-socialist experiment.

A China pursuing such objectives would remain dangerous for some time to come. But if India cultivated positive relationships with both the Soviet Union and the United States, the Chinese would be deterred from attacking again. An opportunity for the Chinese had been provided by Soviet and American preoccupation with the Cuban missile crisis of October 1962; the Chinese may even have had advance warning of it. But with successful resolution of that crisis, both of the superpowers were free to share a common interest in an independent and nonaligned India.

Nonalignment thus remained vital to Indian security in the long term, despite the anxieties and problems that a lack of formal allies had caused during the war. While the war lasted and in the months that followed, India's nonalignment posture had enabled it to receive various forms of aid from countries as diverse as West Germany, Yugoslavia, the Soviet Union, Turkey, Canada, New Zealand, Rhodesia, Italy, France, and Australia, not to speak of Britain and the United States.[9] Ongoing military relationships between India and Western countries now existed, but the Soviet Union would still supply equipment (including helicopters and transport planes) on a purchase basis.

Nevertheless, India's nonalignment would never be the same again. The "missionary" zeal, previously shown in mediating Cold War tensions and leading the nonaligned world, had now passed.[10]

Nonalignment would subsequently be interpreted in a more passive sense—that is, as "almost a withdrawal from conflicts external to India's narrowly-conceived national interests."[11] This change was prompted in part by India's profound disappointment with the behavior of the nonaligned nations. A number of those states were adopting an "even-handed" position between a leader of the nonaligned world (India) and a great Communist power. Among them were the so-called Colombo states (see Chapter 15). Despite public comments by Nehru defending the Colombo group's diplomatic stance as being essential to the assumption of a mediator's role, there was dismay at the behavior of these countries. That dismay persisted until India and China's diplomatic maneuvering over the "Colombo proposals" was seemingly resolved in India's favor in early 1963.[12]

Just after the 1962 war, another cause for Indian resentment was the pressure exerted by the United States and Britain. They wanted the Nehru government to make concessions in Kashmir to a Pakistan that seemed to be determined to take advantage of India's China disaster. They tied the Kashmir issue to the question of continued military assistance to India.[13] The abrasive British cabinet member sent on special missions to India, Commonwealth secretary Duncan Sandys, caused particular discomfort, more so than his more tactful American counterpart, Averell Harriman.[14] But the Indian government did ultimately agree to have talks with Pakistan. Six rounds of them were held during the winter of 1962–63 and the spring of 1963, with no positive results.

CHANGING IMAGES

Nehru

Prime Minister Nehru believed strongly that the Chinese were seeking primacy in Asia—not so much by achieving physical domination as by forcing "a mental surrender."[15] He thought too that China had sought to exert pressure on many countries in Asia and Africa and had tried to mold them ideologically. The Colombo powers, especially, were being much influenced by China, not so much because of ideology but more because of their fear of a great neighbor whom they must not oppose. The case of India had shown the trouble such opposition might bring.

Sino-Soviet issues also influenced China's confrontation with India. Just as China and India were two large countries facing each other, so China and the Soviet Union—two huge land powers—were bound to come into conflict. China was claiming that it was the leader of a continuing revolution, which would liberate mankind from imperialism and colonialism; at the same time, China accused the Soviets of having lost their claim to leadership by compromising with the imperialists. The unrestrained verbal attacks that China was directing at the Soviets were largely caused by Moscow's refusal to favor China in the Sino-Indian conflict. Nehru was also inclined to believe that the Soviet Union, by not supporting Chinese aggression, and via action of some kind, had exercised some pressure on China to stop the war and withdraw. If India now made the mistake of aligning with the West, the Soviet Union and China would come closer together.[16]

Nehru recognized that some sort of military relationship with the West would be necessary if the challenge from China were to be met. But he believed that India's nonalignment had remained untarnished even though India had accepted military assistance from the West. Since India had joined no power bloc and still remained responsible for its own defense, nothing fundamental had been changed.[17] What was new, he said, was India's attitude toward the United States and the United Kingdom. India now had a friendly feeling for the United States, and to a lesser extent for Britain, because these nations had come to India's aid so rapidly. The speed of the American response, he thought, along with such other factors as the unexpected anger and unity of an aroused Indian people, had contributed to the Chinese offer of a cease-fire.[18]

Given these attitudes, Nehru saw nothing wrong with still asking for military help from the United States and Britain. According to Galbraith, on 1 December 1962 M. J. Desai raised the question of a "tacit air defense pact" between India and the United States: "The Indians would prepare the airstrips and radar; if the Chinese came back they [the Indians] would commit their tactical aircraft and we [the United States] would undertake defense of their cities."[19]

Thus, immediately after the war India was still prepared to pursue the arrangement requested in Nehru's letters to Kennedy of 19 November. But the American State Department and the Kennedy administration now preferred to defer to Great Britain and the Commonwealth. After the Nassau meetings between Kennedy and Macmillan in December 1962, the idea was left in limbo. Although the Kennedy administration remained interested, the enthusiasm of the Nehru government declined during 1963. The IAF did engage in joint training exercises with American and Commonwealth aircraft over northern Indian in November 1963, some months after the post-crisis period had ended, but the opportunity for America to forge a long-term military tie with India had been lost. Moreover, because of the United States State and Defense Departments' concern for Pakistan, India had received much less military aid than it had requested.

In addition to its new attitude toward the United States and Great Britain, Nehru noted two other basic changes in his country's outlook as a result of the Chinese invasion. One was a new anger at China's betrayal of Indian friendship. The other was a new determination not to submit under military pressure to any dishonorable settlement of the border dispute.[20]

Nehru was personally determined that Indians should perceive the Chinese invasion as an education, and as a blessing in disguise. The new mood of the country could and should be used to promote industrial development to undergird military readiness. If India was now engaged in a marathon race with China, India's fundamental socialist commitments would impart the strength and vision necessary for that race. Revitalizing the country required continued use of science and technology, as well as growing character and a will to end social injustice and poverty.[21]

The prime minister still sounded reluctant to shift resources to the military. But he could now justify such a step to himself and others by claiming that Indian military spending did not detract from economic development and was in fact compatible with it. Agriculture, transport, electric power, public health, and primary and technical education were sources of military strength, as well as basic economic necessities. As he told a meeting of the National Development Council (a consultative planning body), 85 percent of India's development plans were essentially part of defense, and the remaining 15 percent were indirectly connected with it or with part of it.[22]

In the wake of the military disaster in NEFA, Nehru spoke of basic flaws in the army's preparedness and performance, but he did not criticize the generalship involved. He could say in anguish to Mullik that "the army did not fight in Sela."[23] But he thought that basic causes—rather than the shortcomings of individuals—explained such failure. In an unpublished letter sent to the chief ministers of India's states in December 1962, his description of those basic causes was detailed.[24] The Chinese had enjoyed two main advantages, he said: choice of terrain and acclimatization. He mentioned other causes, but to his mind they were secondary.

The problem of terrain had been the lack of "easy access" to it by road or other means of communications. The Chinese had a road system going right to the border, whereas the Indians "had...to send everything by dropping from the air." Although "from a purely military point of view, we should have selected a much more effective line of defense which was connected by road at least to our main supply centers," to have done so would have meant retiring on Indian territory and allowing "the Chinese to march along it without major fighting."

The prime minister placed great store in acclimatization. Indian troops needed time to adjust to the altitude, but the Chinese were already used to it. The Indian army's better military performance in Ladakh, compared to that in NEFA, was due primarily to this factor. In general, a sudden altitude change, he said, produces headaches, sleeplessness, and general devitalization. It was not feasible for the Indian side to station large numbers of troops at higher altitudes before the crisis began, because of an incomplete road system and the difficulties with airdrops. Chinese troops stationed in Tibet were already living at high altitudes.

The Chinese, he said, were experts at mountain fighting, after many years of war, and were especially trained for this purpose. Their methods of fighting were a mixture of regular orthodox warfare and guerrilla warfare. They had shown what they could do in Korea, and since then had obtained better weapons and perfected their mountain methods. They had long been preparing for some such invasion in Tibet at high altitudes and had accumulated large amounts of supplies in Tibet. But it was another matter "for them to have to face this question of supplies continuously. This was perhaps one other reason why they had their cease-fire and withdrawal."

The prime minister did address the question of leadership within the Indian Army by referring to the resignations of Thapar and Kaul. Unkind things had been said about them, "without much justification." As honorable men they had offered their resignations, but the fault was hardly theirs. The "faults" that had occurred were those of "commanders of Brigades and the like who had to decide on the spur of the moment what they should do when they were being overwhelmed by large numbers of the enemy."

Plainly, there was in Nehru's images much denial of reality. Indeed, in creating many of his images, the prime minister was dealing with reality very selectively. India shared no responsibility for the war, he thought; the Chinese had acted entirely on the basis of calculations ranging beyond the border conflict itself. A fundamentally hostile China had caused a war for reasons related to international politics generally, and to the Asian region specifically. The action-reaction dynamics between India and China on the frontier, including the forward policy, should not figure in explanations of the Chinese attack. Nor should the defeat be blamed on India's failure to spend and plan adequately for defense against China, or on the poor performance of certain army generals, or on the fact that a prime minister's judgment of their capabilities had been flawed.

The large-mindedness for which Nehru had justly been famous, however, revealed itself in his images in several ways. He had a revised image of the West and now recognized the need for major increases in defense spending. Moreover, despite his own sense of personal grievance, he still believed that there should be no legacy of Indian hostility toward China and no permanent embittering of India-China relations, although real peace could not come until China's attitudes toward herself, India, and the world underwent basic change [25]

Chaudhuri and Chavan

The point of view of the army and its new ally, the defense ministry, during the post-crisis period was quite different from Nehru's. Chaudhuri strongly believed that Kaul had to retire, since a great many army personnel thought that they had suffered from his incompetence in NEFA.[26] In general, Chaudhuri's view was that the army had now come into the hands of the military professionals, who viewed the Kaul-Thapar era as a disaster. A similar change had occurred in the defense ministry.

The broader images being formed by Chaudhuri and Chavan were reflected in an investigative report on the 1962 war. This report, produced primarily on Chaudhuri's initiative, was compiled by an army investigating team led by Major General Henderson Brooks and Brigadier P. S. Bhagat. It was written mainly by Bhagat, who had once been Director of Military Intelligence.[27] So strong were some of the allegations in the Henderson Brooks report, and so unpalatable was much of what it implied, that it was never made public despite pressure from parliament on several occasions. But the report was summarized in a very general way when the lessons to be learned from it were discussed by Defense Minister Chavan before the Lok Sabha in September 1963.

More attention would have to be paid, he said, to the work and procedures of the General Staff at the different levels of military command: Army Headquarters in New Delhi, the headquarters of the regional commands, and other commands further down the hierarchy. The focus would be on coordination between the command levels and operational planning, including logistics. Preparedness depended on the quality of General Staff work and the depth of prior and timely planning.[28] Essential preparedness required, too, that training be oriented toward the particular terrain in which troops would have to live and fight. Moreover, the government's political directives must be reasonably related to the size and equipment of the Indian Army. No more was made of this point by Chavan, but it is known that the report questioned the "higher direction of war" and the failure of the Kaul-Thapar team to oppose wrongheaded civilian policies imposed on the military.[29] Chavan also noted that the collection of military intelligence had not been satisfactory. But he avoided direct criticism of the IB and alluded to the need to strengthen the army's military intelligence directorate, presumably so that it could function independently of the IB.[30]

On the basis of the Henderson Brooks report and other sources, Army Headquarters concluded in 1963 that, while planning for army expansion had gone quite far before the war, now was the time for a major buildup. The armed services could get all they wanted from the government in the way of financial and political backing. Imaginative projects devised by Krishna Menon, such as the production of the indigenously designed Ishapore automatic rifle, could go ahead, as could commitments made only after his departure.[31] Two foreign countries, the United States and Britain, seemed willing in late 1962 and early 1963 to assist in the reequipping of India's army and the raising of new divisions, although this perception soon began giving way to disillusionment.[32]

THREAT AND OTHER POST-CRISIS PERCEPTIONS

During the months immediately following the Chinese cease-fire, the Indian perception of threat declined sharply,[33] despite an initial fear that the cease-fire might be tenuous. But the intensity of Indian threat perception never did fall to the level of the pre-crisis period, when war with China had been considered highly unlikely. Ever since 1962 Indian defense planning has had to take into consideration the definite possibility of a war with China, as well as the risk of a two-front war with China and Pakistan. Indian strategic doctrine (perhaps justified by the 1965 and 1971 wars) has been predicated on fighting a full-scale war with Pakistan ("ground, sea, and air") and a limited ground war with China, on the pattern of the 1962 conflict. India's defense planners must also grapple with an unsettling strategic reality: China has acquired a nuclear weapons capability.[34]

Between 22 November 1962 and 28 February 1963, there was no perception of finite time for most decisions, although a strong sense of urgency existed. Nehru gave five years as the time that the current emergency was likely to last. He did not mean that the country would be continually at war with the Chinese during that time, but he wanted to warn that the danger from China would last at least that long.[35]

The Indian government therefore had entered into a post-crisis phase of decision-making. Such a phase is defined by "an observable decline in intensity" of one or more of three perceptions: threat, time pressure, and war probability.[36] There had been declines in all three.

The decision to double the Indian defense budget, taken in mid-February 1963 and presented to parliament on 28 February, marked the end of the immediate post-crisis stage of Indian thinking. This was the point at which short-term threat perception created by crisis and war was replaced by an effort to cope with ongoing threat in a permanent fashion.

CHAPTER FIFTEEN

The Post-crisis Decisions, 22 November 1962 to 28 February 1963

DURING THE POST-crisis period the Nehru government made three strategic decisions pertaining to China: (1) to accept the Chinese cease-fire in a de facto fashion but not de jure (decision made on 22–24 November 1962); (2) to accept the Colombo proposals (12–13 January 1963); (3) to double Indian military spending (mid-January to 28 February 1963).

TO ACCEPT THE CHINESE CEASE-FIRE DE FACTO

Instead of openly accepting or rejecting the Chinese cease-fire declaration outright, Nehru told the Lok Sabha on 21 November that he was withholding comment until an official version was received from Peking. In the chamber there was much objection to the cease-fire, with speakers from the opposition parties demanding rejection and the Congress benches quietly holding the same opinion. But the government took no further action.

Contributing to this initial policy of caution was private lobbying (on 22 November) by Galbraith and the British ambassador, Paul Gore-Booth. In the current atmosphere of high excitement, in which the Indian government could be forced into further military adventures, Galbraith wanted it made known that America and Britain were not joining together with the hawks in Indian politics, who wanted a march on Peking.[1]

It soon became apparent that the Indian government would not agree openly to China's proposal for a 20-kilometer withdrawal, by both sides, from what the Chinese were calling the "line of actual control." According to the proposal, the Chinese would maintain administrative control of the 20-kilometer zone on their side of the

224

frontier, despite the lack of military control.[2] In other words, areas lying within the Chinese zone would remain under Chinese civil jurisdiction, with posts manned by police. China's government would notify India's government, through diplomatic channels, about the location of those posts.

These conditions presented certain problems for India. Foremost among them was that, even if the Chinese moved back from their line by 20 kilometers, disputed frontier points and zones, such as Thagla Ridge, would remain under Chinese police control. India's gains from the forward policy would be eliminated. Furthermore, the Chinese claim line differed greatly from any line held by them on 7 November 1959 and reflected their efforts to establish claims to Indian territory by force, both before and after their massive attack on Indian outposts and forces on 20 October 1962. In some places the line still went beyond the territory that the invading Chinese army had reached.[3] For these reasons India could not accept an argument put forward by the Chinese in their immediate post-war communications; namely, that their proposals would secure more for India than would the Indian demand for a return to the status quo as of 8 September.[4] Far from giving up their war gains, the Chinese would be much better off than before the war.

The Indian decision not to acquiesce to the Chinese demands, but not to formally reject them either, evolved in late November and early December 1962. Hesitation became a strategy of masterly inactivity by 23 November, when Foreign Secretary M. J. Desai called in the Chinese chargé d'affaires and "put to him several points in the Chinese cease-fire proposals" that supposedly "required clarification."[5] The Nehru government was determined not just to play for time; it also wanted to make a point. If the Chinese cease-fire plan required tacit agreement by India to abandon portions of Ladakh in return for China's withdrawal from NEFA, then the Indian government would have no part of it.[6]

In a memorandum dated 8 December 1962, the Chinese said that India could establish civil posts in the 20-kilometer zone on the Indian side of the control line.[7] But the Chinese were fearful that India would try to resume the forward policy, as they showed by adding an objection to Indian questions about possible posts "on" the actual control line. They also objected to India's refusal to accept that line as China had described it. In their diplomatic notes the Chinese reserved for themselves the right to take military action if India attacked any

Chinese troops or attempted any forward movement on the ground.

India tacitly accepted these stipulations, but the issues surrounding the Chinese cease-fire proposals were never resolved. To China there was little cost arising from India's refusal to give de jure acceptance to the cease-fire. In effect, China had achieved its main aim of securing control over the Aksai Chin and related areas, in return for allowing the Indians to retain control of NEFA. India's refusal to grant legitimacy to China's "line of control" would not change the fact that India was now forced to tolerate it.

Although India has continued to press its objections during talks conducted with China since 1981, that de facto toleration has continued (for the most part) since 1962.

TO ACCEPT THE COLOMBO PROPOSALS

Representatives of six Asian and African states (Ceylon, Burma, Cambodia, Indonesia, Egypt, Ghana) met in Colombo, the capital of Ceylon, on 10–12 December 1962 to discuss the India-China situation. The Colombo conference produced a document containing suggestions but no offer of sustained mediation or arbitration. Foremost among the Colombo proposals was to have China fulfill its pledge to withdraw 20 kilometers from the cease-fire line, but only in the Western Sector. India would not have to withdraw anywhere. If the Chinese did pull back in the Ladakh-Sinkiang-Tibet area, a demilitarized zone would come into existence in the Western Sector, "to be administered by civilian posts of both sides to be agreed upon, without prejudice to the rights of the previous presence of both India and China in that area."[8]

As for the Eastern Sector, the "line of actual control" as agreed upon by the two sides could serve to separate their forces, without the need of a demilitarized zone. The places in this sector which (like Thagla Ridge) were still subject to political dispute would presumably be left alone for the time being.

Vague as they were, the Colombo proposals still represented a gain for India. The Indians not only could have posts right on the cease-fire line in Ladakh but could even go beyond it; and Indian forces would not have to stay away from what both sides considered the line of control in NEFA (the McMahon line), except in places such as Dhola and Walong. Thus, there was reason to suspect that India had profited from advocacy of its views by the United Arab Republic (Egypt) at Colombo and elsewhere, and from Indian diplomatic efforts to convince the skeptical among the Colombo governments.[9]

Nevertheless, Indian decision-makers were faced with the task of reconciling these proposals with the bedrock Indian attitude on Chinese withdrawals: that the Chinese must return to their 8 September positions on the ground—that is, not just their prewar positions but those held prior to the Dhola incursion. This was India's precondition for any talks.

ie w'd l'am Thogla?

The ambiguity found in the language of the Colombo document allowed the Indians to get substantive changes made, under the guise of semantic alterations, when the Ceylonese prime minister, Sirimavo Bandaranaike, led a mission to New Delhi on 10 January. Publicly, the impression given was that specific "clarifications" of the proposals had been provided to India by the Bandaranaike delegation. But the private reality was that the revised wording had been drafted by the Indian government.

Whereas the original Colombo plan had implied that Chinese and Indian civilian posts could exist in the Western Sector demilitarized zone if both New Delhi and Peking agreed to the idea, the new version indicated that such posts would be created in any event.[10] Another change concerned NEFA. Indian military (and not just civilian) personnel could move up to the McMahon line, and the Chinese could do the same from their side of the frontier. Restrictions applied only to two disputed places, which were now openly identified—Dhola and Longju. As long as the Indian and Chinese governments did not agree about the actual location of the McMahon line, neither side was to hold Dhola and Longju.

The adoption of this version of the proposals by the Bandaranaike delegation seemingly brought the Colombo states and the Nehru government into agreement, after two days of discussion (12–13 January 1963). Approval by the Indian parliament came on 25 January.

The Chinese, for their part, had already accepted the original Colombo plan in principle. But they had added two "points of interpretation," which proved to be serious reservations about both the original and the revised versions. The main idea of one of them was China's refusal to accept Indian civilian posts in a 20-kilometer demilitarized zone behind the Chinese control line in the Western Sector. To accept such posts would be tantamount to legitimizing India's earlier forward policy. The Chinese preferred to withdraw their own posts from the area, so that neither side would have them. The other Chinese point was that Indian military forces in the Eastern

Sector, the Middle Sector, and the Western Sector should stay where they were and not come closer to the Chinese-claimed border.[11]

After the conclusion of the Colombo episode, the Chinese would say that neither India nor China should require acceptance of a particular interpretation of the Colombo proposals as a precondition for negotiations. The Colombo states, or so Peking meant, had offered their proposals in the spirit of mediation, rather than arbitration, so that full adherence to them was not necessary. Differences in interpretation could be settled at the conference table along with other matters.[12] In contrast, the Nehru government believed that it had agreed to the only correct version of the Colombo plan and that, by failing to agree to the plan without reservations (i.e., "in toto"), the Chinese had in fact rejected it.[13]

This claim was unfair, but the truth was that China had refused to grant a debating point made by India to the Colombo states and (in the Indian perception) accepted by them. The point made by India concerned China's "line of control" in the Western Sector. That line of control, in India's view, represented neither a traditional customary boundary nor the administrative reality prevailing before the 1962 war. It was only the line that the Chinese had reached by the use of military force. The actual prewar limit of Chinese control had been the criss-cross zone of Indian and Chinese posts created during the spring and summer of 1962. By suggesting (in their original proposals) that new Indian and Chinese civilian posts be placed in the same area where the earlier criss-cross had been, and then subsequently agreeing that India should have such posts by right rather than by Chinese permission, the Colombo states seemed to have come down on the Indian side of the argument.

It was from this perspective that, as late as 1983, the Indian government was still pressing the Chinese to accept the ("clarified") Colombo proposals and tacitly admit that the "line of control" concept was nonsense.[14] From the Indian perspective, no proposal or formula can be allowed to legitimize what the 1962 war accomplished for the Chinese.

TO DOUBLE INDIAN MILITARY SPENDING

During the 1962 war or immediately thereafter, the raising of six additional army divisions—all of which were to be mountain divisions—was sanctioned. Army Headquarters (under Kaul and Palit) had drawn up plans for the new divisions before the war, as part of a master plan for the modernization of the army. But the government might not have approved the plan if the border war had not erupted. The immediate postwar thinking at Army Headquarters was that India's army should contain ten mountain divisions within a decade.[15] This goal was pursued vigorously. A new three-year defense plan was hastily devised, to be followed by a five-year plan later in the 1960s. Apparently, the mountain divisions were raised within seven years.[16]

To achieve this and other military objectives, a major reallocation of financial resources was necessary. The crucial first step in the reallocation process was a December request by the Ministry of Defense to the Ministry of Finance for extra expenditure of about one hundred crores of rupees (i.e., one billion rupees) over the amount already allocated in March 1962. These funds would be added to the 1962–63 budget and would bring the expected spending for that fiscal year up to 451.81 crores of rupees.[17] The request came in response to pressure in parliament to do something drastic about defense. It also arose from uncertainty about the amount of equipment forthcoming from Western sources. Such uncertainty was to influence Indian defense planning generally,[18] until the Soviet Union became India's major source of foreign arms after 1965.

In accordance with normal procedures, the defense ministry's (Chavan's) regular budget request probably went to the finance ministry (Morarji Desai) in mid-January, although some indication would already have been received by finance ministry officials at the end of December. The finance minister and his subordinates had to place these requests within the context of the overall governmental budget and work out the final figures, along with an appropriate tax program. Thus, the ultimate responsibility for doubling the defense allocation over what had been spent during the previous fiscal year was Desai's, although the finance minister would have kept the prime minister informed.[19]

The appropriate cabinet-level venue for consideration of the new budget estimates in 1963 was the Emergency Committee, but discussion may have taken place in the full cabinet as well. Both the final decision by Desai and official cabinet approval of it came between mid-January and the end of February 1963. The amount allocated for defense was to be Rs. 867 crores, nearly double the amount spent the year before.[20] According to Morarji's own recollection, it was he who convinced Nehru not to create a supplementary budget for 1962–63 but, instead, to make permanent changes in taxation and expenditure, beginning with the 1963–64 budget.[21]

One important dimension of the overall budget decision was the government's determination not to forgo expenditure on basic economic development. Development expenditure would have to proceed in tandem with expenditure on defense. The budget deficit would therefore have to be increased, and new funds would have to be raised.[22] Domestic sources would supply most of those funds; heavy reliance on foreign aid and on India's foreign exchange reserves would be avoided.[23]

The rise in defense expenditure had a considerable impact on the government's overall budget. Although the gross increase in India's budget was not much greater than that of the year before (a 34 percent rise for 1963–64 as compared to 29 percent for 1962–63), the proportion of the national budget devoted to defense in 1963 was 28 percent, as opposed to the usual 15–17 percent of previous years. A heavy defense burden now affected "all classes and sectors of the economy," and large expenditures on defense would be a permanent feature of subsequent Indian budgets.[24]

The new budget implied a long-term commitment to expansion and modernization of the army. The most important task was to recruit and train personnel for the mountain divisions. But the main items of additional expenditure would be (1) paying for officers and men, (2) improving border communications, (3) adding more transport and supplies, and (4) producing automatic rifles, ammunition, and light mountain artillery.[25]

Indian military development thus was given a certain momentum in late 1962 and early 1963, and that momentum was to continue long past the end of the post-crisis period. The process by which India would become the dominant military power in the South Asian region had begun.[26]

EPILOGUE

The new border situation, established during the post-crisis period that followed the 1962 war, remained generally stable for nearly a quarter of a century, despite episodes such as the India-China clash at Nathula Pass in 1967. India's growing military strength, and the many other preoccupations of India and China, surely contributed to that stability.

In 1986–87 various events worsened the situation on the frontier. Among them were the amending of the Indian constitution by India's parliament on 10 December 1986 to make NEFA (called Arunachal Pradesh since 1972) a full-fledged state in the Indian union. The very next day the Chinese protested strongly, and on 17 December Beijing issued another statement in which territorial concessions were demanded in Arunachal Pradesh. Indian and Chinese military buildups on the frontier followed during the winter and spring of 1986–87. Each country reportedly placed approximately 200,000 troops along its own side of the border by May 1987.[27] The Chinese accused India of strengthening its border forces, as well as other provocations, and issued warnings about the consequences. A "top ministerial source" in the Chinese government said that China did not want anything "unpleasant" to happen on the border, but if something unpleasant did happen, "it is not China that would have provoked it."[28]

After May 1987 the tension eased after spokespersons in New Delhi and Beijing vigorously denied that the troop buildups had occurred to the extent reported by the Western press. Both public and private assurances of nonhostile intent were exchanged. Also involved in the tension reduction were diplomatic approaches by the United States, expressing concern and urging restraint on both the Indian and Chinese governments.[29]

The most immediate cause of the 1986–87 tension was a spiral of action and reaction resembling what had happened between 1959 and 1962. According to a respected Indian journalist, Inder Malhotra of the *Times of India*, in 1985 an IB post was set up in the valley of the Sumdorong Chu (not far from the Namkachu) and left there until withdrawn at the start of winter. Instead of protesting, the Chinese responded in kind and established a permanent (although small) military presence in the Sumdorong area before the Indians could return in 1986. Worried about Chinese intentions, the Indians reinforced their troops and engaged in preemptive movement into zones (the "grey areas") that China insists are north of the correctly drawn McMahon line. The Chinese then brought in more reinforcements of their own.[30]

Certain new elements in the India-China conflict during 1986–87 should be emphasized: (1) the sensitivity the Chinese began to show about Arunachal Pradesh during the early 1980s; (2) the 1986 Chinese demand for additional territory there, presumably in the "grey areas"; (3) China's construction of a helipad at Wangdung in the Sumdorong

Valley in the spring and summer of 1986; and (4) China's reluctance to resume border talks with India in 1986–87, having held seven rounds since 1981.[31] These trends and occurrences surely figured in the escalatory spiral. So did "Operation Chequer Board," a largely unpublicized Indian military exercise conducted by the Indian Army's Eastern Command during the spring of 1987. It followed the heavily publicized "Operation Brasstacks" exercise, which produced alarm and countermeasures in Pakistan. Chinese comments showed that they were much concerned about "Chequer Board."[32]

Several similarities between the 1959–1962 and the 1986–87 situations are worth noting. In 1987 Chinese and other diplomatic sources (including senior American diplomats) gave the Indian press the impression that China perhaps wanted to "teach India a lesson," so as to get a satisfactory border settlement with India and raise the overall status of China in Asia.[33] No real invasion was expected, but it was feared in New Delhi that China might stage "pinprick" incidents and try to move further into certain disputed valleys.[34] Such journalistic speculation probably reflected opinion within the Indian government.

As in 1962, threatening statements from China were tempered by assurances that China did not want war. As in 1962 (when the Soviet Union needed China's support during the Cuban missile crisis), the Chinese seemed to be taking advantage of an improvement in their relations with the Soviet Union (under Mikhail Gorbachev) to push India toward settling the border dispute via the barter or "package deal" China has favored since 1960. China may also have directed such pressure at New Delhi when a series of domestic political crises had weakened the Rajiv Gandhi government.[35]

Just as significant, however, were the differences between 1962 and 1987. Prime Minister Rajiv Gandhi (Jawaharlal Nehru's grandson) had hinted at some flexibility with regard to the "grey areas" along the McMahon line. Most dealings and communications between India and China were friendly in 1987, rather than hostile. India's defense minister, K. C. Pant (Pandit Pant's son), was in China briefly during April; and the foreign minister, N. D. Tiwari, was expected to be in Beijing in June. The Indian Army, under General K. Sundarji, was not obliged to defend every foot of terrain in Arunachal Pradesh and was poised to defend the area as a whole with a preplanned strategy. According to independent observers, the forces of India and China were evenly matched in 1987.[36]

In view of Gorbachev's overture to China, the Soviet Union was likely to want any Sino-Indian hostilities prevented. But in a new Sino-Indian war, Soviet support was likely to go to India, since the Soviet Union had a friendship treaty with India and a border dispute of its own with China. The Americans also wanted to forestall a Sino-Indian war, given their good relations with both India and China. But the United States has shown a "tilt" toward China and Pakistan since the early 1970s and would probably not come to India's aid again.[37]

Still another important difference was that the Indian Army and the Gandhi government were not prepared to cross the line between military maneuver and military action. General Sundarji publicly conceded in the spring of 1987 that China's perception of the line of control along the frontier may be different from India's, and in stationing Indian troops he was giving the Chinese "the benefit of doubt."[38] In October 1986 a planned attack by an army brigade against the Chinese in the Sumdorong Valley was reportedly delayed several times and then canceled. Apparently, an army survey team later concluded that the Chinese might still be on their own side of the border.[39]

There was no new war in 1986 or 1987, but the events of those years did not demonstrate that another Himalayan war is impossible. They suggested instead that basic Indian and Chinese attitudes, images, and reactions to perceived threat—all of which had created the border dispute and the 1962 war—were still potent as recently as 1987.

6

INDIAN DECISION-MAKING ANALYZED: 1959–1963

CHAPTER SIXTEEN

Indian Decision-Making Mechanisms

IN THIS CHAPTER the discussion focuses on answering the research questions raised in Chapter 1 about India's decision-making during the pre-crisis, crisis, and post-crisis periods. Chapter 17 then deals with answers to the theoretical questions listed in Chapter 1. As noted earlier, the ICB model of foreign policy decision-making regards information processing, the interactions among decision-makers and their consultants, decisional forums, and methods of making choices as the "coping mechanisms" of decision-makers.[1] The research questions that this study has raised reflect this view of the decision-making process.

INFORMATION PROCESSING

The research question posed on information processing in Chapter 1 was: Why did India's government, and its intelligence community, fail to absorb information showing that China would attack Indian frontier forces in 1962? Before and during the 1962 border crisis, why did the Nehru government fail to deal adequately with information about Chinese intentions and capabilities?

The Pre-crisis Period

A certain mental rigidity, along with difficulty in learning from negative results of past decisions, gradually appeared among Indian decision-makers and their consultants during the pre-crisis years. After the Kongka Pass incident of October 1959, a set of interrelated beliefs and images (i.e., a belief system) coalesced and became accepted. The elements in the Indian belief system have been described at length; together, some of them constituted an overall image of

China. This China was supposedly a hostile adversary that did not intend to engage in general war with India but was developing its own strategy of infiltrating into Indian territory, placing posts, and staging incidents. Such a strategy was ultimately aimed at forcing India to barter away territory in Ladakh in return for being allowed to keep territory in NEFA.

India's decision-makers and their consultants relied far too heavily on such an image. Information that should have forced a reconsideration did not do so. Included in that information were Chinese warnings—most notably, a warning that appeared in response to the forward policy. The newspaper *People's Daily* said on 9 July 1962 that the Indian government should "rein in on the brink of the precipice" and that "conflicts causing bloodshed on the Sino-Indian border areas may happen any time."[2] Another such warning (dated 10 October) addressed the Dhola confrontation:

> The fact that the Indian Government sent its aggressive troops across the upper reach of the Kechileng [Namkachu] river to launch new attacks on the Chinese frontier guards and spread the war flame over the Che Dong [Dhola] area...shows that it is determined to realize by armed attack its ambition of continuously biting off Chinese territory and fully reveals the real policy of the Indian Government invasion under the cover of a false willingness to negotiate and provocation under the false desire to ease tension. The Chinese Government warns...if the Indian side does not immediately stop its armed attacks and withdraw from the Che Dong area...the Chinese side will surely act resolutely in self-defense and the Indian government must bear full responsibility for all the consequences.[3]

While the more ominous Chinese pre-crisis statements, like this one, implied war, they did not explicitly threaten war as opposed to more border clashes and infiltration. Nehru himself told Foreign Secretary Desai in the summer of 1962 that it was difficult to decide whether China's verbal warfare indicated that military action would occur in the next few months. In public the prime minister described Chinese notes as having a "characteristic ambivalence," breathing fire and urging negotiations, but he thought that no major clash would occur.[4]

Further disguising the meaning of China's warnings was countervailing "noise" (i.e., statements and actions from the external environment that are either meaningless or misleading). A prime source of noise was the series of meetings between Krishna Menon and Chinese

Foreign Minister Chen Yi when both men were attending the Geneva conference in Laos in July of 1962. From those discussions Krishna Menon derived the impression that the Chinese were willing to continue constructive talks, and he returned home convinced that the Chinese were not an immediate danger to India. Much communication between the Indian and Chinese governments over the possibility of talks was taking place both publicly and privately at this time and during the ensuing weeks.[5] Clearly, the Indian side placed too much stock in such activity (perhaps because of wishful thinking).

The information presented by the Intelligence Bureau during the spring and summer of 1962 did not contradict what the top-level decision-makers wanted to believe. The problem was not that too little intelligence information was available but that it was assessed inappropriately. Small pieces of information, meaningless in themselves, were gathered in great abundance; incorrect inferences then were drawn from them, or no conclusions were reached at all.[6]

According to IB director Mullik's memoir,[7] a review of the frontier security situation, compiled by the IB in May 1962, emphasized Chinese forward patrolling and the intent of the Chinese to move up to their 1960 claim line. But no contrary conclusion was drawn from the fact that the review also reported that Chinese troop strength along the Indian and Nepalese borders had recently increased by nearly two divisions, bringing the total to nearly seven.

At roughly the same time, the IB received important information from a source in the Communist Party of India.[8] The Chinese consulate in Calcutta was letting it be known that China considered military action essential to remove the Indian intrusion in Ladakh. The Chinese were saying much the same thing in the *People's Daily*, although more elliptically.[9] There was IB reportage as well of possible military collusion between China and Pakistan against India. This information figured heavily in the later reluctance of Krishna Menon and Thapar to withdraw troops from the Punjab to use against the Chinese.

The IB also discovered, in June and July of 1962, the presence of senior Chinese army officers on the NEFA frontier, inquiring about routes and suitable places for opening new posts. The IB's inference was that these officers were really deciding on tactics, in the event that war with India became inevitable. New Chinese troop movement was also reported opposite NEFA. But the IB thought that the Chinese possibly were planning to intrude into unguarded parts of the NEFA frontier "and then force the Government of India to vacate the areas in Ladakh in return for the Chinese quitting NEFA."[10]

Still another IB security review was made on 31 August 1962. Increased Chinese activity in the Western Sector and just across the NEFA border in Tibet included post building, road construction, pressure on Indian posts, and the wooing of the NEFA tribal population. The IB concluded again that a big Chinese push was coming in both Ladakh and NEFA but Mullik's language in his memoir indicates that he thought it would take the form of infiltration and localized clashes rather than open warfare. The IB's recommended response was for India to accelerate the filling of gaps with Indian posts and troops.

Finally, on 7 September the IB's last precrisis assessment of Chinese dispositions across the northern frontier reportedly produced the conclusion that the Chinese were apparently well prepared for an offensive at this time in Ladakh, Sikkim, and in NEFA.[11] Mullik's own assertions notwithstanding,[12] there is no evidence that the IB clearly warned Nehru, Krishna Menon, or Army Headquarters that such an offensive would be of an entirely different character than past Chinese forward movement. To the contrary, the prime minister was allowed to leave for a trip abroad on 8 September. The Chinese move against Dhola, that same day, was interpreted by Mullik as the start of the expected infiltration campaign into NEFA.[13]

As a hedge, Mullik probably did mention the possibility of larger military conflict. But his practice, as was true of all members of the Nehru faction by this time, was to look for areas of agreement with the prime minister, while treading lightly on those matters likely to annoy him. For Mullik this practice required presenting facts, both palatable and unpalatable, in a complete and professional manner, and making some sort of assessment. But he would not put the facts together in a confrontational way or contradict policies that he himself favored.[14]

After the war Mullik argued publicly that the specialized task of assessing raw intelligence information for military meaning had in 1962 belonged not to the IB but to Army Headquarters and to the army's Directorate of Military Intelligence (DMI).[15] Mullik further claimed that an interagency committee should have arrived at the final assessments, this being the practice in other countries where the army leadership is reluctant to accept intelligence reports unsuited to its preconceived ideas. Thus, in India the Joint Intelligence Committee (JIC) should have had the final say, but the JIC was at that time subordinate to Army Headquarters. The IB experienced difficulty in getting reports accepted with which the DMI (representing the army chief) disagreed. Therefore the IB did make its own assessments and gave them to both Army HQ and the government as an informal duty only.

The army's counterargument was that, from the early 1950s onward, the IB had come to be the Nehru government's premier intelligence gathering and assessment agency, possessing most of the available resources and wielding most of the influence. The DMI had been neglected and staffed by what one informant has called "birds of passage" seeking other assignments.[16] As for the Joint Intelligence Committee, it was moribund. It hardly ever met,[17] and when it did the meetings were dominated by the IB representative, who supplied most of the available information.[18]

Judging from the role Mullik played in Indian decision-making between 1959 and 1962, the army's argument was the more correct one. Mullik's role gave the IB de facto (and final) responsibility for warning of military disaster, whatever the formal jurisdictional considerations might have been. Yet part of the problem did lie with the army. Until 1962 the army's intelligence operation had not really tackled the problem of dealing with the security concerns of an independent country. Under the British Empire, with its global intelligence orientation, the most important information had come from London.[19] This was no longer the case by 1962, but India's Directorate of Military Intelligence was still not accustomed to collecting information on its own, accumulating it, and organizing it for the most effective army and governmental use.

Governmental reliance on the IB's assessments in 1962 was reinforced by a psychological practice shared by India's decision-makers and their consultants. It can be called "conceptual failure"—that is, a failure to creatively anticipate some unorthodox alternative or possibility that the situation might permit.[20] From 1959 onward thought had been given to the possibility of invasion or, alternatively, to the likely continuation of small-scale Chinese "pinpricks."[21] But there was no expectation that the Chinese might try a mid-range alternative, such as a large frontier raid or punitive expedition of short duration.

One of the reasons for this failure of imagination has been mentioned earlier: the prime minister's lack of military experience. Defense Minister Krishna Menon, General Kaul, and Mullik (who had formerly had a police career) also lacked such experience. But just

as important was the key decision-maker's image of the global system
of international politics. When contemplating a Sino-Indian war,
Nehru could think only of a big war between the major states of Asia,
likely to produce a great-power reaction. Perhaps the ultimate source
of this outlook was his version of Indian nationalism combined with
pan-Asianism. A newly independent India and a newly resurgent
China were great states, which could do things only on a grand scale.

The Prewar Phase of the Crisis

With the onset of the crisis period on 8 September 1962, Defense
Minister Krishna Menon and the consultants with whom he met daily
needed information and made continual requests for it from Mullik,
Army Headquarters, and General Sen. Through extraordinary and
improvised channels of communication, information was transmitted
with unusual speed to the top of the organizational pyramid. But until
the war started, there was no increased openness or receptivity to the
larger implications of that information. Instead, Krishna Menon,
M. J. Desai, and General Kaul showed an even more pronounced
propensity (in view of the questions being raised by the western
commander, Daulat Singh; the eastern commander, Sen; and the
NEFA generals) to rely on past experience rather than accept what the
current information might imply.

An effective method of avoiding recognition of discordance between incoming information and long-held beliefs is to avoid drawing
conclusions from that information. Its prime practitioner was Mullik,
who continued to report most of his information throughout the
prewar phase of the crisis period in "bits and pieces."[22] This practice permitted him to focus on threats to particular posts, which
were his primary concern, without raising questions about the larger
picture. Army intelligence did not challenge the practice; most of the
information sent by Army Headquarters to Kaul and other leaders
came in the same undigested form that it probably had when it was
originally received from the IB. The army's Directorate of Military
Intelligence must share the responsibility for this lapse.[23]

Between 8 September and 4 October, General Sen was largely
responsible for distorting the military information flowing from the
NEFA commanders to Krishna Menon and other important civilian
officials. Sen communicated New Delhi's demands downward to
Umrao, Prasad, and Dalvi in NEFA, but their objections and problems
were not accurately conveyed upward.

The roles played by Mullik and Sen thus insulated the Krishna Menon group (and ultimately Nehru) from the negative information (feedback) being produced by the efforts to implement Operation Leghorn. Only when Kaul reported on the Tseng Jong incident at the prime minister's meeting of 11 October was a true picture of Chinese reactive behavior finally provided. But even then the full meaning of Kaul's report was blurred by the ambiguities he included in it. Right up to the time when the Chinese were preparing to attack, neither Kaul nor the government faced the fact that 7 Brigade in NEFA was in imminent danger. Especially important in disguising reality during the final days before the war were Kaul's attempts to command from his sickbed in Delhi and his reconversion to the Nehru faction's group-think about Chinese actions and intentions.

Another dimension of the problem was what can be called information overload. From 8 September onward the persons present at meetings in New Delhi sought detailed military information that would allow them to dictate orders to field commanders even at the brigade and battalion levels. The New Delhi decision-makers and their consultants were so heavily exposed to such information that there was little time or energy to spare for questioning the entire pattern of shared assumptions. Another form of information overload served to limit the usefulness of an agency that should have been a prime source of information. The China Division of the MEA was overburdened because of the need to react to fast-breaking events. Starting with the Chip Chap and Galwan affairs of May–July 1962, and continuing until November, there were constant statements and communications from the Chinese (many issued at odd hours of the night), as well as constant calls for information from ministers, parliament, and the press. The China Division then had to respond quickly.[24]

Such distraction helps to explain why the MEA did not regard most of the warning signals from the Chinese side as particularly threatening.[25] Also, the China Division's new director, N. B. Menon, had taken office at the time of the Chip Chap affair, when Chinese language had already become intense. Subsequent variations in Chinese phraseology, or in the volume of China's communications to India, did not seem particularly significant to him.[26]

The China Division also did not attach significance to certain changes in Chinese behavior after 22 August: (1) a strengthening of Chinese frontier forces—in logistics, combat readiness and actual troop strength—during August and early September; and (2) a more pronounced reaction to Ladakh and NEFA incidents, whereby each was now played up in protest notes, in contrast to recent restraint. Chinese press (public) arousal over the Dhola confrontation increased markedly from 21 to 30 September and again after 10 October.[27]

The China Division was aware that the language of the Chinese had become more shrill after 22 August, but that was all. Their tone still seemed in keeping with their modes of expression at earlier moments in the border conflict, such as the affair of the 1959 Pan Tzu-li note. The Chinese practice of recording and playing up each incident was not new either, and India had been doing the same.[28]

As for the Chinese troop buildup, the China Division thought that the IB and the army, rather than the MEA, should evaluate this matter. Because the China Division was not closely informed of Indian military plans after 8 September,[29] it could not readily see how the Chinese were reacting to Indian actions or to events along the Namkachu in NEFA. No China expert focused on Dhola itself in the defense minister's daily meetings or any other consultative forum.

Moreover, on the basis of an alternative source of information, the director of the China Division did not think the Chinese had the logistical capacity or the intent to invade India. Either during the prewar phase of the crisis or just before it began, he and the army's Director of Military Operations, Palit, tried to gauge the adversary's logistical capacity, basing their estimates on the Chinese frontier road system. That system was thought incapable of supporting an invasion far into Indian territory. Chinese development of north-south roads in Tibet had not progressed enough yet, nor were there adequate lateral roads. The barriers posed by the Himalayas and bad weather were overestimated, especially since the heavy snowfall needed to block the passes came unusually late in 1962.[30]

To be fair to all of India's China watchers during the prewar phase of the 1962 crisis (8 September to 19 October), noise and ambiguity remained problems until the outbreak of war. China's interest in initiating formal talks was seemingly conveyed with all seriousness through the diplomatic correspondence being received by the MEA, although (unknown to New Delhi) Chinese preparations for a massive military offensive had surely commenced. The Chinese, in their statements, were making vague but ominous military threats but were portraying these threats as reactions to what Indian military forces had allegedly done and might still do.[31] No single interpretation of these signals could be definitive, and the Chinese may well have been practicing strategic deception by this time.

The War

The Indian set of beliefs became more open to incoming information with the onset of the war and its attendant stress. Nehru specifically rejected past experience, the lessons of which he now considered largely illusory. A whole new defense for NEFA had to be improvised, so Nehru and Army Headquarters were seeking new information and were receptive to it. There was greatly increased communication between the Indian government and major world leaders, and United States ambassador Galbraith became an important figure in securing American military assistance.

But India's decision-makers still had not learned enough from negative feedback, as shown by the decision to send General Kaul back to NEFA. And—largely because of its overreliance on Kaul—New Delhi was not really able to gauge the military situation in NEFA any better than before the war. Two of Kaul's chief wartime problems, collection of random information and information overload, would not have plagued him if he had adopted a strategic plan rather than a hodgepodge. A workable plan would have provided him with a set of mental categories into which information could have been placed and properly classified.

The Post-crisis Period

As the stress felt by Indian decision-makers declined rapidly in the weeks and months after the war, their receptivity to information did not increase significantly, contrary to what one might expect. During the war Nehru had agreed to let Thapar and Krishna Menon resign, and he accepted Kaul's resignation after the war; but in his postwar explanations of military defeat he could not include any recognition of military leadership failures. Nor did he question his own personnel decisions and managerial skills. In addition, Nehru had understood in August 1962 (just before the war) that a spiral of conflict and escalation was taking place between India and China, but he could not include that fact in his postwar explanations of Chinese behavior.

India's post-crisis information processing was therefore more open in only two spheres: (1) military planning and expenditure and (2) relations with the West.

CONSULTATION

The research question posed in Chapter 1 on consultation was: Prior to the attack, and during the war, how well were Prime Minister Jawaharlal Nehru and other Indian decision-makers served by their regular consultants—that is, the officials and military officers who provided them with information and advice?

The Pre-crisis and Prewar Phases

The information-processing problems just discussed were related more closely to the Nehru government's style of using (or misusing) consultants than to the failings of particular individuals. During the years immediately preceding the 1962 war, Nehru usually consulted persons whom he respected and trusted more for his personal relationships with them than for the formal posts they held. Such consultation was one-sided in that he could shape their belief systems but they could not shape his, beyond supplying information and reinforcement.

Mullik's overall role between 1959 and 1962 is perhaps best explained in these terms. He has been charged with structuring information according to what Nehru and his colleagues wanted to hear.[32] But it is more accurate to say that Mullik himself accepted Nehru's worldview almost worshipfully, as did most of Nehru's officials, and he was particularly in need of Nehru's guidance because he regarded his own intellectual background as limited.[33] Thus, he could not readily see how any small piece of new information, or even an accretion of them, might prove Nehru wrong in a major way. Although Mullik did not just provide Nehru and others with raw information—he made some assessments—he seems to have relied on Nehru to integrate it all.[34]

Mullik was also strongly and personally committed to certain policies that his IB could implement either independently or in tandem with the army. Therefore, he wanted the information he supplied to Nehru and Krishna Menon to be congruent with these policies.[35] Moreover, while generating, advocating, and implementing his preferred policies, Mullik allowed an element of one-upmanship with the army to influence his thinking.[36]

Like many other persons immediately around Nehru, Mullik wanted to avoid Nehru's displeasure and to maintain access to him.[37] Mullik's behavior was thus part of the factional style of consultation that had become established by 1962; that is, consultation took place

positions in NEFA had grown much firmer after Kaul was appointed to implement Operation Leghorn. A week later, on 12 October, the consensus was greatly reinforced by the press treatment given to Nehru's public statements at the New Delhi airport.

Thus, in the prewar phase of Indian crisis decision-making, the longer the amount of decision time, the greater was the consensus on a final (erroneous) choice.

Upon the outbreak of war, however, the Indian leadership style became more appropriate to the real needs of the situation. Nehru was in charge politically but wanted military decisions left to the army. Initiative could thus pass to a relatively junior officer at Army Headquarters, Brigadier Palit, who seemed to know what he was doing. An experienced professional soldier, Harbakhsh Singh, was posted to NEFA, and Kaul was made to stand aside. On the ground in NEFA, leadership was assumed temporarily by a division commander, Prasad, who pushed aside a nonfunctioning theater commander, Sen, despite the disparity between them in formal rank and authority.

But as the crisis dragged on, during the lull between China's October and November offensives, and as Indian threat perception and feelings of time urgency (i.e., time limitation) declined, inappropriate changes in leadership were made. No real need existed for another change of corps commanders in NEFA, but Kaul badly wanted to return to IV Corps for personal and career reasons, and his personal relationship with Nehru allowed him to prevail.

In addition, the longer decision time did not reinforce the Indian consensus (achieved early in the war) on defending western NEFA primarily from Se La. Instead, that consensus was weakened fatally when Kaul allowed another plan to evolve, one that was to prove unworkable.

In general, too much Indian leadership activity was ad hoc in 1962, for reasons of insufficient institutionalization of the decision-making process and insufficient commitment to military planning. Ad hoc decision-making forums such as the defense minister's September–October meetings are normally created by governments during crisis situations. But it was not normal to appoint an ad hoc military commander, Kaul, to an ad hoc military formation, IV Corps, that had been created just for one military operation. Ad hoc groups were then convened (on 11 October in New Delhi and 17 October in Tezpur) to consider whether or not to withdraw from the Namkachu. During the 1962 war an ad hoc group decided to withdraw Indian troops from the

Punjab; another decided to place the main NEFA defensive position at Se La. Kaul and Pathania constituted another such group when withdrawal from Se La was being considered. The decision to abandon Se La was actually made (in a confused fashion) by a subordinate decision-making forum consisting of two battlefield commanders, Pathania and Hoshiar Singh, acting without clear direction from Kaul.

Ad hoc-ism was accompanied by mistimed and misplaced centralization and decentralization. While Operation Leghorn was being devised and debated, decision-making was at first centralized around Krishna Menon, when more authority should have been given to the military commanders in NEFA. During the war there was an appropriate degree of decentralization when Nehru delegated authority to Army Headquarters, but then Nehru intervened again to have IV Corps returned to Kaul. He, in turn, passed too much authority to lower-ranking but seemingly more experienced officers, such as Pathania.

The willingness of Krishna Menon, Kaul, and other members of the Nehru faction to go beyond procedure and outside regular chains of command was considered a commendable trait in this group's subculture. Thus, the group had no hesitation about forcing Operation Leghorn on NEFA commanders who considered it a violation of both bureaucratic and military norms. The person who protested most strongly, with bureaucratic arguments, was Lieutenant General Umrao Singh of XXXIII Corps in NEFA, and for his resistance he was punished. The longer the crisis continued, and the more intense it grew, the more unorthodox the NEFA military procedures were. The climax perhaps came during November, when General Kaul relied not on a plan drawn from the professional experience of someone like Harbakhsh Singh but on reactive improvisation.

ALTERNATIVES AND CHOICE

The research question posed in Chapter 1 on the Nehru government's handling of alternative strategies was: Did these decision-makers and their consultants escalate the conflict with China to the level of armed confrontation and ultimately war, instead of seeking alternatives such as meaningful negotiations? How open was the Nehru government to considering constructive alternatives in its dealings with China?

Between 1959 and 1962 India's decision-makers, in formulating alternatives and choosing among them, generally adhered to a certain style or pattern. The general practice was to formulate and adopt a series of "satisficing" alternatives—that is, alternatives that addressed some but not all of the ends the decision-makers had in mind. These options constituted partial and short-term solutions to problems, and after implementation they could still be modified in whatever way the situation seemed to require. They could also resolve (at least temporarily) disagreements over goals, strategies, and tactics among such people as Nehru, Krishna Menon, and Pant, even if these options or alternatives were heavily influenced by Nehru's wishes.

Thus, India's pre-crisis alternatives were formulated incrementally. The Nehru government did not usually respond to situations by jointly and explicitly formulating multiple alternatives. Although individuals did propose various options to the prime minister, he put aside some options and combined others into one policy or strategy, which was then implemented, only to be serially followed by others. Each strategy was an outgrowth of the previous one, and as such each was thought likely to ameliorate present problems without creating unforeseen difficulties. Each also allowed the Indian government to draw on past experience and make use of available resources, rather than alter long-established priorities in resource allocation. Finally, each policy or strategy was guided by an emerging Indian "operational code," in which historical models, recent experience, and ideological principles all had their place.

Since this style is often used by large organizations facing situations of uncertainty, there is no need to be critical of its use by the Nehru government.[38] Certainly, its use did not necessarily reflect an Indian interest in avoiding negotiation and resolving the Sino-Indian conflict by use of force. In fact, the question of force arose only after other options had been tried. But a close observer might suggest that had Prime Minister Nehru been more sophisticated as an administrator or manager, he might have put in place a formal mechanism whereby individual options received more searching evaluations than they did. As it was, debate over alternatives was sorely needed in the early autumn of 1962, when the Dhola problem had to be dealt with. But such debate was not required by the structure of the decision-making process.

The Pre-crisis Period

If the Indian decision-making style between 1959 and 1962 was not to consider multiple alternatives, there was a time during the fall and winter of 1959–60 when several alternatives were being discussed. This was a time of rising stress, especially after the Kongka Pass incident.

The discussion focused on the prime minister, although it was not confined to any one institutional forum. A number of people were involved, including Prime Minister Nehru, Home Minister Pant, Defense Minister Krishna Menon, other cabinet members, and several MEA officials. Their deliberations were still continuing as late as the time of the Chou En-lai visit to New Delhi in April 1960.

The main purpose of these deliberations was to reach an accommodation—that is, to find an honorable way out of the oncoming conflict with China without having to cede territory in any formal fashion.[39] That purpose was pursued privately; publicly, Nehru was making statements about the negative long-term consequences of having China as an enemy along an immense border, and the desirability of avoiding this eventuality. He did so partly to dampen public and parliamentary emotionalism, evident since the Tibetan rebellion. However, as someone who could not refrain from revealing his personal thoughts in public speeches, he was expressing a primary personal motivation.

One idea being considered was to lease the Aksai Chin to the Chinese, as long as Indian sovereignty was acknowledged.[40] Krishna Menon was particularly interested in trading the Aksai Chin for Chinese concessions, such as giving India the Chumbi Valley. But whatever the specifics involved, Krishna Menon's main point was that a truly "political" solution to the Sino-Indian conflict, rather than one based on historical documentation, had to be worked out.

Krishna Menon's perception was that—at least in April 1960, when Premier Chou En-lai was either in New Delhi or expected soon— Nehru also preferred a political approach. Years later Krishna Menon said that such an approach could not be taken because "other people, some of them senior men, although they did not veto it, said 'Why all this now, we will see when it comes.'"[41] One of those "senior men" was Pandit Pant. Of him Krishna Menon said that "the Home Minister, who had by that time acquired a powerful influence over the Prime Minister, was not in favor of negotiation."[42]

Krishna Menon may not have understood or accepted a certain portion of Nehru's thinking. The director of the MEA's Historical Division, Gopal, during discussions with Nehru in the fall and winter of 1959–60, found the prime minister much concerned with scholarly

why reject Swaraj

integrity. If the historical evidence showed the Chinese to have a reasonable claim to the Aksai Chin, Nehru seemed open to letting them have it. However, once Nehru had gone over the evidence thoroughly with Gopal, his sense that India's was the valid claim was reaffirmed. Thus, there was no need to reopen a matter that had been settled in 1954. The Officials' Report of early 1961 convinced him even more completely.[43]

But Krishna Menon was justified in complaining, as he sometimes did, that Nehru's thinking and the political atmosphere of the country had been greatly affected by "China's own mistakes."[44] By "mistakes" he meant episodes such as Kongka Pass.

It certainly is fair to say that part of Nehru's problem was that he allowed public and parliamentary reactions to box him in during the fall of 1959. Care in the weighing of alternatives, which was possible as long as the prime minister resisted such reactions, was ultimately rendered less necessary after the Kongka Pass affair by his sense that he neither could nor should go against the popular mood and that a hostile China now threatened India. Moreover, the Indian nationalist in Nehru made him share the public emotionalism to some degree.

If the Chinese government had approached Nehru when he was still not convinced of the historical basis for India's Aksai Chin claim, and if the Chinese had not allowed the Kongka Pass affair to happen (despite IB director Mullik's activities), the results might have been positive. Thus, the Kongka Pass incident and the Chinese effort to create military realities on the ground (which lay behind that incident) were part of a mistimed and inappropriate method of managing the emerging border conflict. So was the attempt to secure diplomatic ratification of those realities in April 1960, when Chou En-lai came to New Delhi.

Chinese misrule

The entire Chinese strategy was made even more inappropriate by their arguing that no "historical" border could provide a sound basis for boundary delimitation. India needed the "historical" border concept for national identity purposes, just as much as China needed strategic boundaries for security purposes.

In the summer of 1962, however, Nehru showed a renewed interest in seeking alternatives. Given the apparent success of the forward policy, and Krishna Menon's talks with Chen Yi, Nehru now wanted to discuss with China some ways to alter the drift toward greater escalation of the conflict. The Chinese also seemed interested in such discussions. At that time India's government was formally demanding that China make withdrawals in the Western Sector, and discuss the Officials' Report, so as to provide a basis for any settlement. Had the Chinese been willing to comply, Indian consideration of alternative ways to achieve some sort of settlement with honor (i.e., informal Indian territorial concessions but no formal Indian alienation of territory from India) could well have revived in the autumn of 1962. But such demands were too much for the Chinese to accept, and the Indians were not willing to be more creative.

The Prewar Phase of the Crisis

During the crisis period itself, Krishna Menon's September–October decision-making group did not make a careful search for strategic alternatives, although the group examined tactical alternatives in detail. The group assumed (erroneously) that only one strategy was possible: to take military action against the Chinese near Dhola.

Clearly, there was premature closure during the weeks immediately before the war; that is, there was an inadequate assessment of the situation before a strategic choice was made. Contributing to this behavior were a concern with the immediate rather than the long-run future and an inadequate assessment of consequences—these being frequent human responses to stress. Management of an impossible military operation in one small river valley received minutely detailed attention, whereas only minimal consideration was given to the overall military situation in NEFA. Thus, a stressful situation also helped produce a narrowing of the decision-makers' attention span (i.e., "tunnel vision").[45]

The tactical alternatives pertaining to the Namkachu Valley were not considered with any great degree of realism either. As time pressure increased, because of the concern that winter was coming in NEFA, the Prasad-Dalvi fantasy plan was accepted in New Delhi and passed along to Kaul. Only the defeat at Tseng Jong on 10 October brought about some realistic thinking by one top decision-maker, General Kaul.

Nehru and Krishna Menon must share with Kaul, however, the responsibility for failing to evaluate alternatives properly, especially at the New Delhi meeting of 11 October. Of the three alternatives Kaul described (continue Operation Leghorn; postpone it but keep 7 Brigade along the Namkachu; or withdraw the brigade to more tenable positions), the one chosen seemingly represented the middle and most sensible course. But Kaul himself, who initially favored withdrawal and was unable to say so, had misrepresented the seriousness of the military situation by delineating it in this (three-alternative) fashion. Neither the prime minister nor the defense minister nor the IB director would question Kaul on this score, because Kaul's depiction allowed each man to find a solution that suited his own goals. Ultimately, the consensus that was reached served several people's goals and avoided certain short-run costs, but it bore little relationship to reality.

The War

Immediately after 20 October 1962, Indian decision-makers were genuinely searching for military strategic alternatives, and they made a careful assessment of these alternatives, despite the intense stress of the moment. For a short time the choice among alternative strategies for NEFA's defense was handled by people who actually knew the NEFA terrain. The decision on whether troops could be pulled out of the Punjab was reached with some care, as was the political decision to accept Krishna Menon's resignation. But during the Chinese November offensive, when stress was at its height, less care was exercised, primarily because the focus was so strongly on the immediate future rather than the long run. Kaul made shortsighted choices, because of Pathania's demands for immediate permission to withdraw and because Kaul had no real long-term strategy. Weapons had to be secured from the United States speedily, and air cover for northern India had to be requested, whatever the eventual implications for maintaining Indian nonalignment.

Yet the main factor determining whether the most important choices were made sagaciously during the war was neither the level of threat nor the pressure of time. It was the person or persons making the choices, and characteristic personal failings that stress only aggravated.

Thus, Prime Minister Nehru, who had shown poor judgment earlier in his career when evaluating the competence or integrity of individuals loyal to him,[46] allowed Kaul to displace Harbakhsh Singh in NEFA. And Kaul, with his characteristic bravado and lack of combat experience, proved susceptible to tunnel vision after refusing to absorb Harbakhsh's strategic grasp of the NEFA defense problem. His narrowed span of attention was especially evident at the highest moments of stress. Another of Kaul's problems was his inability to make clear choices, rather than hedged or ambiguous ones, whenever pressured by seemingly more experienced subordinates. Moreover, some of Kaul's choices were impulsive and did not take into account results that a careful assessment of information might have revealed. He always remained too ready to "overdo."

It was not General Kaul, however, but General Pathania (Kaul's main source of information about the fighting around Se La) who demanded that choices be made before adequate information had been processed. Why a military commander with a distinguished record of earlier combat achievement should have acted in this fashion in November 1962 is still unclear.[47]

The Post-crisis Period

Immediately after the cease-fire, and under conditions of declining stress, the search for alternatives became careful. Ways of avoiding outright acceptance of the Chinese terms were sought, along with ways to modify the Colombo proposals to India's advantage. New policies were being generated in the military sphere, with the decision to increase expenditure and expand the army.

Paradoxically, such care was exercised despite the leading decision-maker's retention of much of the prewar belief system. But no large policy changes were needed in the diplomatic sphere, where Nehru's beliefs and values had undergone little change; therefore, attention could be given to subtle and semantic changes. Care was possible, too, in the military and expenditure spheres, where the prime minister's beliefs had changed somewhat. More important, the responsibility for carefully reviewing proposed military and financial plans now lay with people justly valued for their professional competence: Defense Minister Chavan, Army Chief Chaudhuri, and Finance Minister Morarji Desai. Quite properly, Nehru allowed these men the maximum possible autonomy.

CHAPTER SEVENTEEN

Normality and Uniqueness in Indian Decision-Making

As INDICATED IN Chapter 1, the concepts used in this study are parts of a specific theoretical model,[1] which should be described fully before the theoretical questions raised in Chapter 1 are discussed. A diagram of this model is shown as Figure 1.

THE MODEL

The term *crisis* has many meanings in common parlance and in political science. Drawing on research and experience to refine further a definition originally put forward by Charles F. Hermann,[2] the ICB model defines a foreign policy crisis (i.e., a crisis for a single nation-state) as a "situational change in the external or internal environment" of the nation-state "that creates in the minds of the incumbent decision-makers...a perceived threat from the external environment to basic values to which a responsive decision is deemed necessary."[3] To elaborate further, a crisis is a perceived situation containing three necessary and sufficient conditions.

The first such condition is perceived threat to one or more basic values—that is, "core values" and "high-priority values." Core values are few in number and vary little over time because they are fundamental to the decision-makers' worldview. Safeguarding national security and preserving national independence are among them. High-priority values are core or other values made salient at any given moment by a particular situation or context. Their source is the relevant decision-makers' shared ideological and material perspective concerning the situation. In a crisis situation the high-priority values considered threatened will include one or more core values, and not just lesser values alone.

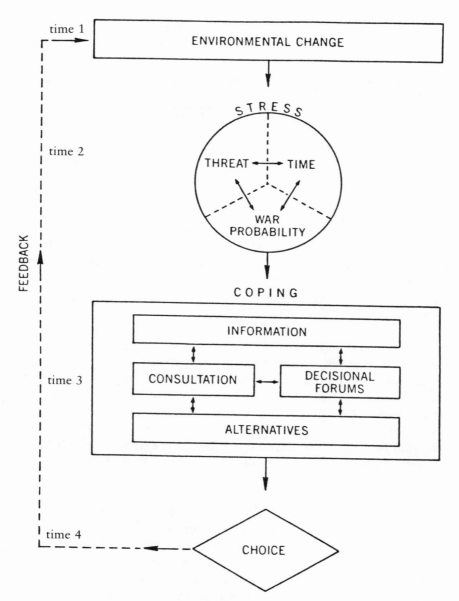

Figure 1.   DIAGRAM OF THE INTERNATIONAL CRISIS
BEHAVIOR (ICB) MODEL.

Associated with threat perception is the simultaneous or subsequent perception that there is a "finite" time for response to the threat—not necessarily a specific deadline but some sense that a decision will be required within a certain time span. Even if that span is not short, and is vaguely defined, there is an awareness that it is limited.

The last condition integral to this definition of crisis is the perception that the nation-state is highly likely (or much more likely than before) to become involved in military hostilities. Likelihood of hostilities is perhaps the most crucial condition of a foreign policy crisis. Many foreign policy situations involve perceived threat and a sense of finite time, but a feeling of crisis generally appears only when these variables are accompanied by a high estimate of the likelihood of armed action, or a marked rise in that estimate.

The three crisis perceptions are closely interactive. When a perceived threat is linked to the likelihood of military hostilities, its level will be greatly increased; indeed, the entire character of the threat will be changed. Similarly, the sense that decision time is finite will be heightened when it is linked to a sense that military hostilities are likely. Once warfare becomes a certainty, however, there may be a lowered perception of threat if, for instance, the decision to initiate hostilities is made while the military capacity of one's own nation-state is clearly superior to that of the adversary.

In the ICB model the three crisis perceptions taken together are said to constitute "stress." The intensity of the three perceptions defines the level of stress being experienced by the decision-makers at a specific time. The authors of the ICB model intend their stress concept to be merely a summarizing or composite concept, which combines the three perceptions, rather than an effect or result that the perceptions produce. But they recognize that stress is not just a perceptual matter but an emotional one as well, having overtones of anxiety, fear, and other related human feelings.

The model postulates that one of the initial responses to stress is to seek information about the environmental source of the threat. *Information search* is one of the coping methods or mechanisms that form the decision-making process. *Consultation* is another. A third is the establishment of *decisional forums* (i.e., defining those who will make the decision). A fourth is *evaluation of alternatives*. These methods also constitute distinct steps in the decision-making process, although they overlap and are closely interrelated.

Each coping method is conceptually different from the others.

Information search refers to the process of securing and disseminating relevant information among decision-makers and their consultants, and showing greater or lesser degrees of receptivity to that information. *Consultation* refers to the formation and functioning of groups of persons who communicate steadily with one another about the threat and responses to it. A consulting group will include not only high-level decision-makers but also those persons who advise them and shape the flow of information to them. Career officials, military officers, personal friends, opposition party leaders, and leaders of nonpolitical elites are among the persons who can take part in the consultative subprocess.

But the establishment of a decisional forum requires identification of those who will evaluate and make the authoritative choice among alternatives. While previously defined roles and other situational factors may do much to determine the composition of a decisional forum, its final type, size, structure, and degree of authority will be influenced as well by the intensity of stress. Indeed, all the coping mechanisms are constantly subject to the influence of stress.

Evaluation (or analysis) of alternatives requires a determination of the extent to which different actions and strategies are appropriate to the threatening situation and to the decision-makers' goals and values. It is not merely a question of adjusting tactics and strategies to fixed threat, time, and likelihood-of-war perceptions. These perceptions, too, are revised as different options are considered. Priorities among values are revised as well.

The end product of the entire coping process is a decision resulting from choice. That decision may consist of a single action or a strategy containing a number of mutually consistent actions. But the overall decision-making process is still not complete. Perception of how well a decision works (i.e., feedback) leads to modification by those implementing it. If a required modification is serious enough to bring about involvement by the highest-level decision-makers, the entire coping process will again be called into play, and a new decision may result. The decision-making process thus becomes circular and self-correcting (i.e., "cybernetic").[4]

The context for the entire process of decision-making is provided by the "psychological environment" of the members of the decisional forum (and their consultants). The psychological environment has two parts: (1) the "attitudinal prism" shared by the decision-makers and (2) the "elite images" held by each individual decision-maker.

The attitudinal prism contains basic beliefs, orientations, preferences, and other psychological predispositions. Taken together, these predispositions constitute a screen or filter through which information must pass and be structured or shaped. Its origin lies not in the immediate situation but in "societal factors, such as ideology and tradition, which derive from the cumulative historical legacy; and...personality factors—the idiosyncratic qualities of decision-makers...which are not generated by their role occupancy."[5]

Images are more subject to change, because they are previously established or currently forming perceptions of particular objects. The objects of images may include international actors, such as other states, one's own state, international organizations, and multinational corporations. Still other objects may be the domestic political system and actors within it. The roles played by external and domestic actors also can be the objects of images, as can specific issues of a military-security, political-diplomatic, economic-developmental, or cultural-educational-scientific nature.[6]

Certain flexible dimensions built into the ICB model make it particularly suitable for a study of India's China conflict between 1959 and 1963. One is the way in which the periods immediately preceding and following a crisis are identified. During a "pre-crisis" period there is a perception of environmental change and a conspicuous increase in perceived threat to some values.[7] But the other two necessary conditions of a crisis (time pressure and war likelihood) are missing. Pre-crisis periods thus can vary in length from case to case, since decision time is not considered finite (although a sense of urgency may be experienced at times). This provision permits even a time span as long as 15 March 1959 to 7 September 1962, in the Indian case, to be treated as a pre-crisis period.

The ICB model shows further flexibility in allowing for decisions to be either strategic or tactical.[8] Recognition is thus given to the possibility that—during certain phases within the pre-crisis, crisis, or post-crisis periods—formulation of broad strategies, rather than small-scale actions, may be the focus of the decision-making process. Where one or more of the decision-makers are particularly prone to think mainly about their nation-state's role in the international political system, and in various regional or ideological subsystems, the adoption of a strategic posture (or series of them) is normal behavior. No decision-making study of the Nehru era in Indian foreign policy can overlook that point.

One other feature that makes the ICB model appropriate for the Indian case is its treatment of the relationship between crisis and military hostilities. The model allows for a number of possible combinations. The start of hostilities may mark the end of a crisis if the military capability of the nation-state under scrutiny is superior to that of the other side. But if the outbreak of hostilities causes a crisis, the ICB model replaces "probability of war" as a defining crisis condition with another condition—namely, "perceived decline in military capability vis-à-vis the enemy."[9]

In the 1962 case a war began while a crisis was already in progress, and the fighting soon brought about an accurate Indian perception of the inadequacy of India's military preparations to cope with the Chinese. The ICB model nicely covers this situation too. Rather than marking the beginning of a crisis, a "perceived decline in...military capacity" adds greatly to the intensity of perceived threat in the midst of a crisis.[10]

The ICB model prompts the analyst of foreign policy crises, such as the 1962 crisis, to answer some crucial questions. The broadest of these questions is "What is the impact of changing stress" on "(a) the processes and mechanisms through which decision-makers cope with crisis; and (b) their choices?"[11]

From this general question flow a number of more specific ones. These were described in Chapter 1 of this study and can be summarized in the following fashion: How does rising stress (among other factors) affect (a) the information-processing capabilities of decision-makers and the consultants who serve them; (b) the ways in which decision-makers consult with advisers and with one another; (c) decision-making forums (i.e., units); and (d) the performance of decision-makers and their consultants in perceiving alternative strategies and actions, and in choosing among them?[12]

HYPOTHESES AND FINDINGS

Certain testable hypotheses, derived from past political science research and used in earlier ICB studies of crisis decision-making, can be associated with each of these questions.[13] Several such hypotheses, seemingly confirmed by the material presented in Chapter 16, will now be discussed.

This discussion is undertaken not only so that this case study might provide empirical support for these hypotheses but also to show how

Indian decision-making in many ways followed what might be called "normal" practices, found in governments elsewhere. The fact is that these hypotheses represent the generalizations which political scientists are prepared to make (even if only tentatively) about what is normal in foreign policy decision-making behavior. Although opinion in India sometimes assumes that the 1962 affair was unique, India's 1962 tragedy came about not just from practices that are peculiar to India but also from behaviors that may be quite usual in international affairs.

Information Processing

One hypothesis that describes behavior to which Indian decision-making conformed states: "The greater the crisis, the greater the propensity for decision-makers to supplement information about the objective state of affairs with information drawn from their own past experience."[14] Certainly, such a description matches Indian behavior well, especially when the Dhola intrusion was first being assessed for its meaning and when General Kaul sought to use forward policy tactics against the Chinese on Thagla Ridge.

Another hypothesis about information processing, confirmed by the Indian case, is: "The higher the stress in a crisis situation, the greater the tendency to rely upon extraordinary and improvised channels of communication [and information]."[15] This hypothesis holds true for the prewar phase of the crisis, when much information was being personally brought by consultants to meetings chaired by Krishna Menon or Nehru, and less reliance was placed on ordinary bureaucratic channels. But it was not true of the war (i.e., the peak stress period).

Still other hypotheses to which Indian decision-making conformed, in a broad sense, were the following: (1) "The more intense the crisis, the less the sensitivity to, and learning from, negative feedback." (2) "The more intense the crisis, the greater the tendency to an overabundance of new information (information overload) and a paucity of usable data on decision-making levels." (3) "The more intense the crisis, the greater the tendency of decision-makers to perceive that everything in the external environment is related to everything else."[16] The first and second of these propositions apply better to the pre-crisis period of rising stress, and to the prewar weeks of the crisis, than to the war itself. The third hypothesis, however, is persuasively illustrated by India's intense effort to seek international support during the war, and by Nehru's wartime determination to induce both of the great powers to deter China. He did so even though the Soviet Union was at that time unwilling to support India and even though India's policy of nonalignment could have been damaged if India had received direct and massive military assistance from the United States. The hypothesis is supported most strongly by Nehru's use of beliefs about the interrelatedness of international issues, as stress rose during the pre-crisis and prewar years and months, to convince himself and others that the Chinese would not attack India.

One further hypothesis about information processing is confirmed by Indian decision-making during the post-crisis period: "As crisis-induced stress declines, receptivity becomes permeated by more bias."[17] Some decline in receptivity was to be expected in the Indian case, as the prime minister's worldview reemerged after the war and as some realities were screened out by denial.

A plausible but probably simplistic hypothesis can be only partly confirmed by the Indian case: "The greater the stress, the greater the conceptual rigidity of an individual, and the more closed to new information the individual becomes."[18] This hypothesis may help to explain General Kaul's behavior, but because cognitive rigidity was already pronounced among other Indian decision-makers (Nehru and Krishna Menon) before the 1962 crisis began, the onset of crisis made little difference. Thereafter, Nehru showed considerable flexibility during the war (and peak stress) phase.

No hypotheses yet used in ICB studies adequately cover such features of Indian information processing as "noise," "conceptual failure," failure to put informational "bits and pieces" together, distraction by alternative interpretations of incoming information, misjudgment of the capability of the enemy, and possible victimization by strategic deception. Clearly, they are needed, since these forms of behavior are documented (with the possible exception of "bits and pieces" reporting) in the political science literature and other writings on decision-making.[19]

Consultation

Two hypotheses on consultation are broadly confirmed by what happened in the 1962 Indian case: (1) "The longer the decision time...the greater the consultation with persons outside the core decisional unit." (2) "The greater the crisis, the greater the felt-need for face to face proximity among decision-makers." Another hypothesis to which Indian decision-making conformed, especially in terms of the wider circle of people consulted about a wider variety of topics (i.e., "scope" of consultation), is: (3) "As crisis-induced stress increases, the scope and frequency of consultation by senior decision-makers also increase."[20]

A remaining hypothesis about the style of consultation is confirmed by the Indian case: (4) "As crisis-induced stress increases, decision-makers increasingly use ad hoc forms of consultation." So is another, because the Nehru government's newly formed cabinet-level Emergency Committee was still functioning as an ad hoc consultational body during the weeks immediately following the 1962 war: (5) "As crisis-induced stress declines, consultation relies heavily on ad hoc settings as high-level consultation reaches its peak."[21]

However, the ICB hypotheses on consultation do not summarize some key aspects of the Indian case. The factional or groupthink style of consultation is not addressed, nor is the fact that changes in consultational style are not necessarily correlated with greater or lesser openness to incoming information. Yet groupthink is surely a normal feature of decision-making in large organizations elsewhere in the world; and one suspects that the gap between consultational style and receptivity to information is not peculiar to the Indian case either. One thing that is unique about this particular case—an intelligence chief who apparently relied heavily on the leading decision-maker's worldview to correlate intelligence "bits and pieces" for him—may also appear in other cases in different guises.

Decisional Forums

A hypothesis confirmed by the Indian use of decisional forums in 1962 is the following: "The longer the crisis, the greater the felt-need for effective leadership within decisional units." This hypothesis, however, does not address a point suggested by the Indian case: that such a search for leadership may substitute for careful thinking about the problem that leadership is expected to resolve.

One other confirmed proposition is: "The longer the decision time, the greater the conflict within decisional units."[22] A third hypothesis about decisional forums describes Indian behavior as well, but it applies mainly to the pre-war phase of the crisis: "The longer the amount of time available in which to make a decision, the greater will be the consensus on the final choice."[23] The same is true of another hypothesis (which applies mainly to Kaul): "The more intense the crisis, the greater the tendency of decision-makers to conform to group goals and norms, and the less the dissent within the group."[24]

The ad hoc nature of most Indian decisional forums during the 1962 crisis confirms the following hypothesis: "The more intense the crisis, the less the influence of 'standard operating procedures.'" Another hypothesis is confirmed by the role of General Kaul (a "political" soldier rather than a strictly "professional" one) in Operation Leghorn and in the November NEFA defeats: "The more intense the crisis, the greater the role in decision-making of officials with a general rather than 'parochial' perspective."[25] But, since Nehru ordinarily included such persons in decisional forums, the intensification of crisis was not the main causative variable.

Finally, the Nehru government's extreme ad hoc-ism during the 1962 crisis confirms the following hypothesis: "The more intense the crisis, the less the influence of vested interests in the bureaucracy."[26] The Indian case, however, stands in stark contrast to other cases where the bypassing of bureaucratic interests and procedures, during a crisis, produced beneficial results.[27] In India in 1962 the results were not beneficial, and those persons who argued for the use of proper military-bureaucratic procedure should have been allowed to prevail. Moreover, the bypassing of bureaucratic vested interests was part of a practice that has been called (in this study) "misplaced centralization and decentralization." Such a practice may be worthy of a descriptive hypothesis of its own.

Alternatives and Choice

The general pre-crisis style of decision-making in the Nehru government featured: (1) consultation by the leading decision-maker with individuals and groups, rather than problem solving mainly by groups; and (2) formulation of single serially developed strategies, rather than consideration of multiple alternatives. Such activity constitutes reverse evidence in support of the following hypothesis: "The greater the reliance on group problem-solving processes, the greater the consideration of alternatives."[28]

Indian consideration of alternatives during the prewar phase of the crisis, and General Kaul's handling of alternatives during the crisis, match several hypotheses: (1) "As crisis-induced stress increases, the evaluation of alternatives becomes less careful." (2) "As stress increases, decision-makers become more concerned with the immediate than long-run future." (3) "The more intense the crisis, the greater the tendency of decision-makers to narrow their span of attention to a few aspects of the decision-making task ('tunnel vision')." One hypothesis in this area must be rejected: "Despite the rise in stress, choices among alternatives are not, for the most part, made before adequate information is processed; that is, there is not a tendency to premature closure."[29] In the Indian case there was premature closure.

During the war, however, when the Indian strategy based on Se La was being formulated, a level of stress far higher than that prevailing earlier first led to more careful choice among alternatives, rather than less. Carelessness set in again later, during the lull between the two Chinese offensives. Therefore, the Indian case cannot confirm the following ICB hypothesis: "The relationship between stress and group performance in the consideration of alternatives is curvilinear (an inverted U)—more careful as stress rises to a moderate level, less careful as stress becomes intense."[30] But it does support another hypothesis: "As crisis-induced stress increases, the search for options tends to increase."[31]

All during the 1962 crisis, one cardinal difference between the capacity for choice shown by Nehru and Krishna Menon, on the one hand, and Kaul, on the other, is outlined by the following hypothesis: "The more intense the crisis, the more likely that decision-makers will be forced to make a clear choice rather than postponing choices or drifting into policy."[32] The prime minister and the defense minister were prepared to make clear choices under stress, even though some of those choices proved to be erroneous. But Kaul was not—a finding that points to the importance of personality as an intervening variable.

One last hypothesis summarizes well the Nehru government's treatment of alternatives in the post-crisis period: "As crisis-induced stress declines, the evaluation of alternatives reaches its maximum care, more so when time salience is low."[33] Indian decision-makers were still conscious of time pressures after the war, knowing that India remained in long-term danger because of Chinese hostility and inadequate Indian defenses. But the awareness (i.e., salience) of time was declining as the sense of immediate threat declined. It was during the post-crisis period that long-accepted financial and military priorities (i.e., alternatives) were reconsidered, and careful planning for a new armed posture was undertaken.

Several important dimensions of the Indian process of considering alternatives are not covered by the ICB hypotheses: (1) the relationship between an image of the adversary as "hostile" and the consideration of alternatives; (2) the influence of domestic political pressures on the decision-makers' consideration of alternatives; (3) the influence of injury perception on the consideration of alternatives. Still another practice, exhibited by Indian decision-makers on at least one occasion, is not covered by the hypotheses; that is the practice of depicting alternatives, and choosing among them, in a fashion that serves the differing—and sometimes mutually incompatible—goals of several people. Eventually, these practices (each of which is hardly unusual in cases of decision-making outside of India) should be the subject of hypothesis formulation.[34]

In all, the normal dimensions of India's decision-making about its relations with China between 1959 and 1963 were quite numerous, even if they are only partly described by the current list of ICB hypotheses. A study of India's role in the India-China conflict helps us become mindful of how easily normal behavior by a nation's decision-makers can lead to tragedy. Acquisition of greater knowledge of China's role by independent scholars, if ever truly permitted by China's government, might serve the same worthwhile purpose.

Notes

AUTHOR'S NOTE

MANY OF THE informants in interviews between 1966 and 1970, relatively soon after the 1962 war, did not want their comments openly attributed to them. Between 1983 and 1988 those persons interviewed again were asked to allow their earlier comments to go on public record. Most agreed, but preferred that the material be attributed to their 1983–1988 interviews. Material obtained from interviews in 1966–1970 is dated as such when the informant granted permission or where the informant is now deceased and the material is unlikely to be politically sensitive.

As a fledgling researcher on this subject from March 1966 to June 1970, I recorded interviews by year only. Therefore, in the footnotes that follow, these early interviews are designated by year, although the appropriate month has been added whenever possible. Citations of the interviews conducted between 1983 and 1988 include exact dates.

CHAPTER ONE

1. Early but sound scholarly works leaning toward the Indian side include Margaret W. Fisher, Leo E. Rose, and Robert A. Huttenback, *Himalayan Battleground: Sino-Indian Rivalry in Ladakh* (New York: Praeger, 1963); Dorothy Woodman, *Himalayan Frontiers: A Political Review of British, Chinese, Indian, and Russian Rivalries* (New York: Praeger, 1969); P. C. Chakravarti, *India's China Policy* (Bloomington: Indiana University Press, 1962); W. F. Van Eekelen, *India's Foreign Policy and the Border Dispute with China* (The Hague: Martinus Nijhoff, 1964).

2. Among Alastair Lamb's major books on the border dispute are *The China-India Border: The Origins of the Disputed Boundaries* (London: Oxford University Press, 1964) and *The Sino-Indian Border in Ladakh* (Columbia: University of South Carolina Press, 1975).

3. The citations from the Maxwell book used here come from the paperback edition: *India's China War* (New York: Doubleday, 1972).

4. Sarvepalli Gopal, *Jawaharlal Nehru: A Biography*, 3 vols. (Cambridge, Mass.: Harvard University Press, 1976–1984).

5. This point has been raised by many authors, including Maxwell, *India's China War*, 179–303 passim; and Yaakov Vertzberger, *Misperceptions in Foreign Policymaking: The Sino-Indian Conflict, 1959–1962* (Boulder, Colo.: Westview Press, 1984), xv–xvi, 1–62, 75–297 passim. The mystery is not resolved by the memoir of Nehru's intelligence chief, B. N. Mullik, called *The Chinese Betrayal* (New Delhi: Allied Publishers, 1971).

6. Another much-discussed issue by authors such as Vertzberger, *Misperceptions*, 257–85; Karunakar Gupta, *The Hidden History of the Sino-Indian Frontier* (Calcutta: Minerva Associates, 1974), 26–35; and Gopal, *Nehru*, 3: 220.

7. For a succinct and scholarly criticism of India on this score, see Neville Maxwell, "China and India: The Un-negotiated Dispute," *China Quarterly* 43 (July–Sept. 1970): 47–80; and *India's China War*, 175–268, 309–385. For an Indian view see Gopal, *Nehru*, 3: 32–221 passim.

8. This question and the others that follow are versions of those found in Michael Brecher, with Benjamin Geist, *Decisions in Crisis: Israel, 1967 and 1973* (Berkeley and Los Angeles: University of California Press, 1980), 27.

9. Explained in Brecher, with Geist, *Decisions in Crisis*, 1–32.

10. Ibid., 23–26.

CHAPTER TWO

1. Gupta, *Hidden History*, 22–23.

2. Ibid., 23. The Trelawney Saunders line is mentioned in Lamb, *China-Indian Border*, 86; the Ardagh-Johnson line is discussed in Maxwell, *India's China War*, 14–21. The names now used for the several proposed borders of British days were coined by Alastair Lamb in his *China-India Border* book. Prior to that, it seems that the only Kashmir boundary given an official name was the Durand line (letter from Alastair Lamb, 7 May 1984).

3. G. Narayana Rao, *The India-China Border: A Reappraisal* (New York: Asia Publishing House, 1968), 59–60. Rao uses another name for this boundary.

4. Interview with Alastair Lamb, 12 Jan. 1989; letter from Lamb, 11 Apr. 1989.

5. My conclusion based on Gupta, *Hidden History*, 23; and letter from Lamb, 11 Apr. 1989.

6. Karunakar Gupta, "A Note on Source Material on the Sino-Indian Border Dispute— Western Sector," *China Report* 17 (May–June 1981): 51–55; Lamb, *China-India Border*, 100–104.

7. Interview with Alastair Lamb, 21 May 1983. See also Lamb, "Studying the Frontiers of the British Indian Empire," *Royal Central Asian Journal* 53 (Oct. 1966): 247.

8. Subimal Dutt, *With Nehru in the Foreign Office* (Calcutta: Minerva Associates, 1977), 20–22; Jeffery Benner, *India's Foreign Policy Bureaucracy* (Boulder Colo.: Westview Press, 1985), 34–35. From August 1947 to early 1949, the name was Ministry of External Affairs and Commonwealth Relations.

9. Lamb, "Studying Frontiers," 246.

10. Interview with Alastair Lamb, 21 May 1983.

11. The text of Elgin's official reaction appears in Woodman, *Himalayan Frontiers*, 364–65.

12. Lamb, *Ladakh*, 12. This conclusion is contrary to the impression of Leo Rose, another student of the same period, as indicated in an interview on 24 July 1984.

13. Rao, *India-China Border*, 59.

14. Much of Hardinge's text can be found in Woodman, *Himalayan Frontiers*, 79–82. For a complete text of the Ardagh memorandum, see Woodman, Appendix 5.

15. Lamb, *Ladakh*, 11–12, 66–68.

16. Gupta, "A Note on Source Material," 54. Gupta's own interpretation of the Indian Army information is that there had been no Government of India acceptance of a definite

boundary for the Western and Middle sectors of the India-China frontier before India's independence in 1947.

17. Lamb, *China-India Border*, 122–27; Parshotam Mehra, *The McMahon Line and After* (New Delhi: Macmillan, 1974), 1–15; Rao, *India-China Border*, 73–82.

18. Letter from Alastair Lamb, 11 Apr. 1989; see also Alastair Lamb, *The McMahon Line*, 2 vols. (London: Routledge and Kegan Paul, 1966), 2: 292–305; for the official Indian view of the Assam-Tawang-Tibet relationship, see Rao, *India-China Border*, 63–70.

19. Lamb, *China-India Border*, 134–37; Gupta, *Hidden History*, 11; Woodman, *Himalayan Frontiers*, 121; Rao, *India-China Border*, 83–84.

20. Rao, *India-China Border*, 83–84; Lamb, *China-India Border*, 138–39.

21. Lamb, *China-India Border*, 141–47; Gupta, *Hidden History*, 67–68. On the 1913–1914 talks see also the use of documents from Government of India archives in H. K. Barpujari, *Problem of the Hill Tribes: North-East Frontier* (Gauhati: Spectrum Publications, 1981), 3: 191–208. The actual Simla negotiation with the Tibetan delegate was conducted by MacMahon's deputy, Charles Bell (see Lamb, 156).

22. Gupta, *Hidden History*, 67–68; Maxwell, *India's China War*, 42–44; Parshotam Mehra, *The North-Eastern Frontier: A Documentary Study of the Internecine Rivalry between India, Tibet and China*, 2 vols. (New Delhi: Oxford University Press, 1979–80), 1: xxxviii–xliii. See also Mehra, "India-China Border: A Review and Critique," *Economic and Political Weekly*, 15 May 1982, 835–36; and Mehra, *McMahon Line*, 247–410, 413–20.

23. Gupta, *Hidden History*, 68–77; Barpujari, *Hill Tribes*, 236–38; Mehra, "India-China Border," 836. On the Caroe episode see also Woodman, *Himalayan Frontiers*, 196–205.

24. On the Aitchison episode see Gupta, *Hidden History*, 73–74, 82–84. For the view that this matter was not especially irregular, and not especially significant, see Mehra, "India-China Border," 836–37. The Aitchison volume is: C. U. Aitchison, *Collection of Engagements, Treaties, Sanads* (Calcutta: Government of India), vol. 14 of 1929 ed.

25. Gupta, *Hidden History*, 84–85.

26. Lamb, *China-India Border*, 159–65; Gupta, *Hidden History*, 31, 79–82, 85–92; Woodman, *Himalayan Frontiers*, 201–9; Barpujari, *Hill Tribes*, 246–83.

27. Barpujari, *Hill Tribes*, 280–83; Woodman, *Himalayan Frontiers*, 213–14.

28. Lamb, *China-India Border*, 165–66.

29. Interview with Sarvepalli Gopal, 23 May 1983; see also Badruddin Tyabji, *Indian Policies and Practice* (New Delhi: Oriental Publishers, 1972), 7–8.

30. Interviews with N. R. Pillai, 16 May 1983, and J. S. Mehta, 6–7 Jan. 1986.

31. Interview with S. Gopal, 23 May 1983.

32. This point of view is Alastair Lamb's, much more fully elaborated in his review of the Maxwell book for *Modern Asian Studies* 5, no. 4 (1971): 392–97. Parts of this summary were taken from an interview with Alastair Lamb, 21 May 1983, and from letters from Lamb dated 7 and 17 May 1984.

33. On the failure of Nehru to secure such a border, see Gopal, *Nehru*, 2: 176–81. For a more definite (but not yet substantiated) claim that the Himmatsinghji committee advised the Nehru government to claim the Aksai Chin, see Karunakar Gupta, "Sino-Indian Relations: Getting the Facts Straight," *The Statesman* (Calcutta), 11 May 1981.

34. Gopal, *Nehru*, 2: 176.

35. B. N. Mullik, *My Years with Nehru, 1948–1964* (New Delhi: Allied Publishers, 1972), 78–80.

36. Gupta, *Hidden History*, 30–31; Maxwell, *India's China War*, 66–67.

37. Interview with S. Gopal, 23 May 1983.

38. A new edition of Nehru's *The Discovery of India* states that the book was first published by Signet Press in Calcutta in 1946. On Nehru's view of the historic non-British India, see this edition of *The Discovery of India* (New Delhi: Oxford University Press, 1981), 49–84. For a classic statement of the countervailing British view, see the statement by John Strachey, quoted in

Ainslie Embree, *India's Search for National Identity* (New Delhi: Chanakya Publications, 1980), 17.

39. From Rao, *India-China Border*, 30; also from S. Gopal's review of the Maxwell book in *The Round Table* 245 (Jan. 1972): 117 (issued by Institute of Commonwealth Studies, Oxford University), and from interviews with Gopal, 24 Mar. 1983, 10 Jan. 1986, and with a source who wishes to remain anonymous, Mar. 1983.

40. Lamb, *China-India Border*, 67–68.

41. Maxwell, *India's China War*, 7. The comparison to the European "march" land is taken from an interview with Alastair Lamb, 21 May 1983.

42. Based on informal personal and telephone conversations with J. S. Mehta, Apr.–May 1984, and confirming letter from J. S. Mehta, 22 May 1984.

43. Gopal, *Nehru*, 3: 303. Details of the Indian Aksai Chin evidence are given in the Indian portion of the "Officials' Report" compiled by Indian and Chinese teams in 1960 and 1961. See Ministry of External Affairs, Government of India, *Report of the Officials of the Governments of India and the People's Republic of China on the Boundary Question* (New Delhi: Ministry of External Affairs, 1961), 41–70, 137–64. See also Fisher, Rose, and Huttenback, *Himalayan Battleground*, 118–19.

44. From interviews with Indian sources who wish to remain anonymous, Mar.–July 1966, and with Gopal, 24 Mar. 1983; and from the *Report of the Officials*, 124–25. See also Rao, *India-China Border*, 61–73, 87–88, 93–94, and Gopal, *Nehru*, 3: 305–6.

45. Gopal, *Nehru*, 3: 306. These remarks were directed primarily against Lamb and Maxwell.

46. The interested reader should consult the volumes by Lamb; Maxwell; Rao; Gupta; Woodman; Fisher, Rose, and Huttenback; and the *Report of the Officials* (all cited above). See also Steven A. Hoffmann, "Ambiguity and India's Claims to the Aksai Chin," *Central Asian Survey* 6, no. 3 (1987): 37–60.

47. Gupta felt that Nehru was deceived; see his "Getting the Facts Straight," *The Statesman* (Calcutta), 11 May 1981. That Nehru practiced deception himself was a view expressed by Neville Maxwell in interviews on 17 May and 18 May 1983.

48. Some of Nehru's private comments were mentioned by K. Gopalachari in New Delhi interviews in Mar.–Aug. 1966 and Aug.–Sept. 1967. He had been a research officer in the MEA Historical Division since 1949 and was acting director in 1958–1959. In interviews in Mar.–May 1983, Dr. Gopal also described his interactions with Nehru. Neither Gopal nor Gopalachari, however, felt that any deciphering of ambiguity was involved. In their view, Nehru was simply being told the factual truth.

49. The term *attitudinal prism* is taken from Brecher, with Geist, *Decisions in Crisis*, 37n.

50. My summary of part of the Chinese outlook, as expressed during the border conflict, was influenced by the articles in John K. Fairbank, ed., *The Chinese World Order: Traditional China's Foreign Relations* (Cambridge, Mass.: Harvard University Press, 1968), 2–3, 5–12, 19, 180–97, 206–24; Alan Whiting, *The Chinese Calculus of Deterrence* (Ann Arbor: University of Michigan Press, 1975), 3–41; Maxwell, *India's China War*, 7, 16–18, 36–39, 99–103, 271–303; Vertzberger, *Misperceptions*, 63–73, 75–102, 151–76; and Morris Rossabi, *China and Inner Asia* (New York: Universe Books, Pica Press, 1975), 9–22, 218–87.

CHAPTER THREE

1. On the creation and composition of the committee, see Mullik, *Chinese Betrayal*, 115–27, and Gupta, *Hidden History*, 9–10.

2. Lorne Kavic, *India's Quest for Security: Defense Policies, 1947–1965* (Berkeley and Los Angeles: University of California Press, 1967), 46–51; Mullik, *Chinese Betrayal*, 125–27. Other measures are described by these sources as well.

3. Mullik, *Chinese Betrayal*, 126, 127.

4. Gopal, *Nehru*, 2: 181.

5. See Mullik, *Chinese Betrayal*, 180–83.

6. Nehru's attitude is described in Mullik, *Chinese Betrayal*, 182–84. On the CIA's role the literature includes David Wise, *The Politics of Lying* (New York: Random House, 1973), 163–78. Another source, citing recently declassified U.S. government documents, reports that, as late as 1958, the Americans did not expect much from the Tibetan resistance either (John Prados, *Presidents' Secret Wars* [New York: Morrow, 1986], 161).

7. J. P. Dalvi, *Himalayan Blunder* (New Delhi: Thacker, 1969), 22. General Kulwant Singh had also been a member of the Himmatsinghji committee.

8. Gopal, *Nehru*, 2: 177–79.

9. Ibid., 177–81. See also K. M. Panikkar, *In Two Chinas: Memoirs of a Diplomat* (London: Allen and Unwin, 1955), passim.

10. On Panikkar's role and style, see Michael Brecher, *Nehru: A Political Biography* (London: Oxford University Press, 1959), 572; and K. M. Panikkar, *Asia and Western Dominance* (New York: John Day, 1954).

11. Maxwell, *India's China War*, 69–70.

12. Paraphrase of original document by the Indian journalist D. R. Mankekar, quoted in Maxwell, *India's China War*, 74.

13. Gopal, *Nehru*, 2: 180–81.

14. For the text of the agreement, see Ministry of External Affairs, Government of India, *Notes, Memoranda and Letters Exchanged between the Governments of India and China: White Papers*, 8 vols. (New Delhi: Ministry of External Affairs, 1959–1966), 1: 98–101. (Hereafter cited as *White Papers*.)

15. An account of this incident from the Tibetan perspective is found in John F. Avedon, *In Exile from the Land of the Snows* (New York: Knopf, 1984), 46–47. For the Indian view see Gopal, *Nehru*, 3: 36.

16. Gopal, *Nehru*, 3: 89.

17. Letter from J. S. Mehta, dated 5 Dec. 1984, and interviews with J. S. Mehta, 6–7 Jan. 1986. See also Dutt, *Foreign Office*, 116–17.

18. Interviews with K. Gopalachari, Mar.–Aug. 1966, Aug.–Sept. 1967.

19. See Dutt, *Foreign Office*, 116–17.

20. Interview with a source who wishes to remain anonymous, Apr. 1983.

21. These conclusions are based on Mullik, *Chinese Betrayal*, 196–201, 205–6; Geoffrey Hudson, "The Aksai Chin," *St. Anthony's Papers* 14 (1963): 20–22; and S. S. Khera, *India's Defence Problem* (New Delhi: Orient-Longmans, 1968), 157–59.

22. Dutt, *Foreign Office*, 117–19; *White Papers*, 1: 22–32, 46–47.

23. Ibid., 113–15.

24. Interview with a source who wishes to remain anonymous, Apr. 1983.

25. *White Papers*, 1: 48–51.

26. Dutt, *Foreign Office*, 143–45; Gopal, *Nehru*, 3: 78–83.

27. Information in this paragraph is taken from Gopal, *Nehru*, 3: 78–82; Gupta, *Hidden History*, vi–viii; and Avedon, *Exile*, 114, 117. Avedon's Tibetan sources report that by 1961 the IB was effectively hampering the travel of Tibetans inside India, allegedly because it was looking for Chinese spies, and was blocking the crossing of Tibetan guerrilla recruits into East Pakistan, on the way to training in the United States.

28. Letter to the author, 2 Dec. 1988. A hostile view of the CIA's role is presented in Gupta, *Hidden History*, vi–viii. For a Tibetan view see Avedon, *Exile*, 47, 114–25. An American version is found in Prados, *Presidents' Secret Wars*, 149–170.

29. The full text of the Chou note appears in *White Papers*, 1: 52–54.

30. Inferred from an interview with a source who prefers to remain anonymous, Aug. 1967, and a letter from J. S. Mehta, 11 Dec. 1984.

31. Material on the MEA's Historical Division was obtained from interviews with S. Gopal, 1 Apr. and 23 May 1983. Information on MEA note-drafting procedure was obtained from interviews with J. S. Mehta, 10 Apr. 1983, 6 Jan. 1986, and from an interview with a source who wishes to remain anonymous, Apr. 1983.

32. The full text of Nehru's letter appears in *White Papers*, 1: 55–57.

33. Mullik, *Chinese Betrayal*, 203–6.

CHAPTER FOUR

1. For a full treatment of Nehru's many roles, see Brecher, *Nehru*, 426–640.

2. Michael Brecher, *Succession in India: A Study in Decision-Making* (London: Oxford University Press, 1966), 94–102, 124–37; Shashi Tharoor, *Reasons of State* (New Delhi: Vikas, 1982), 23–24.

3. Interview with N. R. Pillai, 4 July 1985.

4. Ibid.

5. This conclusion is drawn from an interview with a source who wishes to remain anonymous, 1966; an interview with N. R. Pillai, 4 July 1985; and the *Times of India*, 4 Sept. 1962.

6. Tharoor, *Reasons of State*, 23; see also J. Bandhyopadyaya, *The Making of India's Foreign Policy* (Calcutta: Allied Publishers, 1970), 6.

7. On the early bureaucratization of the MEA, see Benner, *Foreign Policy Bureaucracy*, 43–66, and Dutt, *Foreign Office*, 20–34.

8. The view of MEA veteran Badruddin Tyabji, cited in Tharoor, *Reasons of State*, 31.

9. Brecher, *Nehru*, 573.

10. See Gopal, *Nehru*, 2: 140.

11. Brecher, *Nehru*, 573–75.

12. Frank Moraes, *Jawaharlal Nehru: A Biography* (New York: Macmillan, 1956), 331.

13. A. M. Rosenthal, "Krishna Menon: A Clue to Nehru," *New York Times Magazine*, 7 Apr. 1957, 11, 68–71.

14. Brecher, *Nehru*, 573.

15. See Gopal, *Nehru*, 2: 140–44, 3: 129–30; Maxwell, *India's China War*, 111.

16. Dutt, *Foreign Office*, 29–30, 280–81; see also Gopal, *Nehru*, 2: 224–25, 310, and M. O. Mathai, *Reminiscences of the Nehru Age* (New Delhi: Vikas, 1978), 170–71.

17. Interview with a source who wishes to remain anonymous, Apr. 1983.

18. This description of Krishna Menon is taken from Gopal, *Nehru*, 3: 129–32; Mathai, *Reminiscences*, 180–82; B. M. Kaul, *The Untold Story* (New Delhi: Allied Publishers, 1967), 203, 206–15; Dutt, *Foreign Office*, 30, 101–2, 163, 180–83; interviews with sources who wish to remain anonymous, Mar.–May 1983 (exact dates withheld to preserve confidentiality); interview with N. R. Pillai, 4 July 1985; and personal experience, Mar.–Aug. 1966.

19. Interview with J. S. Mehta, 10 Apr. 1983.

20. Interviews with sources who wish to remain anonymous, Aug. 1967, Apr. 1983, May 1983, June 1985 (exact dates withheld to preserve confidentiality).

21. Mullik, *Years with Nehru*, 124.

22. On Pant's nationalist career and association with Nehru, see Jawaharlal Nehru, *Toward Freedom: The Autobiography of Jawaharlal Nehru* (New York: John Day, 1941), 3, 6, 134, 137; Vijayalakshmi Pandit, *The Scope of Happiness* (New York: Crown Publishers, 1979), 91, 133.

23. See Paul Brass, *Factional Politics in an Indian State* (Berkeley and Los Angeles: University of California Press, 1965), 45, 46.

24. Morarji Desai, *The Story of My Life*, 2 vols. (New Delhi: Macmillan, 1974), 2: 50–51, 164; Brass, *Factional Politics*, 51–52; Mullik, *Years with Nehru*, 351–65; Gopal, *Nehru*, 3: 54–65.

25. See Vertzberger, *Misperceptions*, 143, 149.

26. See Krishna Menon's comments in Michael Brecher, *India and World Politics: Krishna Menon's View of the World* (London: Oxford University Press, 1968), 149, 212, 214, and Desai, *My Life*, 2: 50–51, 146. Morarji reports that Pant felt that he could not influence Nehru, but all the available evidence shows that he could.

27. Interviews with his son, K. C. Pant, May–June 1966. See also M. Chalapathi Rau, *Govind Ballabh Pant: His Life and Times* (New Delhi: Allied Publishers, 1981), 368.

28. Mathai, *Reminiscences*, 183.

29. Brecher, with Geist, *Decisions in Crisis*, 37n.

30. The text is in Jawaharlal Nehru, *Independence and After: A Collection of Speeches, 1946–1949* (New York: John Day, 1950), 3.

31. Ibid., 219.

32. Ibid., 248.

33. Mullik, *Years with Nehru*, 75. Information on Nehru's views was obtained from an interview with M. J. Desai, Feb. 1966; Mullik, *Years with Nehru*, 73–75; and Brecher, *Nehru*, 555–94. For a general review of Nehru's views, see Ministry of Information and Broadcasting, Government of India, *Jawaharlal Nehru's Speeches*, vol. 4 (New Delhi: Ministry of Information and Broadcasting, 1964), passim.

34. Quoted in M. N. Das, *The Political Philosophy of Jawaharlal Nehru* (New York: John Day, 1961), 234.

35. A. D. Gorwala, quoted in Adda Bozeman, "India's Foreign Policy Today: Reflections upon Its Sources," *World Politics* 10 (Jan. 1958): 259–60.

36. See their interpretations of China's ideological statements, below.

37. Gopal, *Nehru*, 3: 80; interviews with MEA sources who wish to remain anonymous, Mar.–Aug. 1966, Mar.–Apr. 1983, confirmed by N. B. Menon, 20 Apr. 1983.

38. See Gopal, *Nehru*, 2: 72, 221–22, 252–55, and 3: 50, 60–61.

39. Michael Edwards, *Nehru: A Political Biography* (New York: Praeger, 1971), 267; see also 272–74.

40. Ibid., 272–74. See also Gopal, *Nehru*, 2: 186–90, 254, and 3: 42, 43–46, 50, 87–88, 104; Brecher, *Nehru*, 581–88; and comments by the veteran Indian diplomat T. N. Kaul, in his *Reminiscences, Discreet and Indiscreet* (New Delhi: Lancers, 1982), 156–58.

41. On the Commonwealth tie see Michael Brecher, "India's Decision to Remain in the Commonwealth," *Journal of Commonwealth and Comparative Politics* 13 (Mar. 1974): 62–90.

42. See Nehru's speeches on the Commonwealth in India's Constituent Assembly, found in *Independence and After*, 265–91.

43. See the comment by his sister in Pandit, *Scope of Happiness*, 252–53.

44. See Ministry of External Affairs, Government of India, *Prime Minister on Sino-Indian Relations: Parliament*, 2 vols. (New Delhi: Government of India Press, 1961–1962), 1: 130–31. (Hereafter cited as *PMSIR: Parliament*.)

45. Vertzberger, *Misperceptions*, 158–59.

46. Source who wishes to remain anonymous, Apr. 1983.

47. Gopal, *Nehru*, 2: 108. See also Mullik, *Years with Nehru*, 81–82.

48. Mullik, *Years with Nehru*, 78–79.

49. Ibid., 78–80.

50. Gopal, *Nehru*, 2: 190.

51. Ibid., 195.

52. From the official notes of that meeting, made public in Gopal, *Nehru*, 3: 90.

53. Ibid., 36, 82.

54. Vertzberger, *Misperceptions*, 159.

55. Interview with M. J. Desai, Feb. 1966; interview with T. S. Murty, 12 June 1983.

56. See *PMSIR: Parliament*, 1: 130–31, 147, 150, 153, 188, 209–10, 213–15; *Times of India*, 22 Oct., 2 Nov. 1959; *The Hindu*, 21 Dec. 1959; Maxwell, *India's China War*, 132.

57. This and subsequent material in the section, except where indicated, comes from Brecher, *Krishna Menon's View of the World*, 300–320 (quotations on p. 301). Brecher's source was a set of in-depth interviews with V. K. Krishna Menon conducted in 1964 and 1965.

58. Ibid., 318; see also Khera, *India's Defence Problem*, 200.

59. Brecher, *Krishna Menon's View of the World*, 321.

60. *Times of India*, 11 Sept. 1959.

61. *The Hindu*, 19 Oct. 1959.

62. *Times of India*, 10 Jan. 1960.

63. *Times of India*, 4 Apr. 1960.

64. Interview with K. Krishna Rao, Aug. 1967; for a time Dr. Rao worked closely with Krishna Menon. On the Chinese encirclement theme, see also *The Hindu*, 19 Oct. 1959.

65. Brecher, *Krishna Menon's View of the World*, 152.

66. Maxwell, *India's China War*, 117–18, 510n. Extended to cover more than the Nehru cabinet by interviews with sources who wish to remain anonymous, Mar.–Aug. 1966, Aug.–Sept. 1967, Mar.–May 1983. This description of Krishna Menon's general outlook was confirmed in an interview with J. S. Mehta, 26 Mar. 1983.

67. The reference to Krishna Menon's belief in India's "progressive" stance was made by J. S. Mehta in an interview on 26 Mar. 1983. Other points in this paragraph and the next are taken from Brecher, *Krishna Menon's View of the World*, 323 (quotation), 142, 165, 148, 151, and from an interview with a source who wishes to remain anonymous, Apr. 1983.

68. Interview with J. S. Mehta, 6 Jan. 1986.

69. Interviews with J. S. Mehta, 26 Mar. 1983, 10 Apr. 1983, 6 Jan. 1986.

70. See Pant's statements in the *Hindustan Times*, 12 and 23 Nov. 1959 and 11 Mar. 1960.

71. Interview with J. S. Mehta, 6 Jan. 1986.

72. Interview with a source who wishes to remain anonymous, 11 Apr. 1983; interview with K. D. Malaviya, former minister in Nehru cabinet (and Krishna Menon supporter), 1966.

73. Taken from Brecher's ICB model; see Alan Dowty, *Middle East Crisis: U.S. Decision-Making in 1958, 1970, and 1973*. (Berkeley and Los Angeles: University of California Press, 1984), 8.

74. Maxwell, *India's China War*, 120.

75. Interviews with J. S. Mehta, 26 Mar. 1983, and S. Gopal, 1 Apr. 1983.

76. *Peking Review* 2 (12 May 1959): 14.

77. Interview with N. R. Pillai, 16 May 1983. He was referring to himself and to Foreign Secretary Dutt.

78. *White Papers*, 1: 73–76.

79. Dutt, *Foreign Office*, 155, and interview with a source who wishes to remain anonymous, Apr. 1983.

80. Interviews with J. S. Mehta, 10 Apr. 1983; S. Gopal, 1 Apr. 1983; and a source who wishes to remain anonymous, Apr. 1983.

81. Interview with J. S. Mehta, 10 Apr. 1983.

82. See his parliamentary statements in *PMSIR: Parliament*, 1: 19–27, 42–44, 129–42 (quotation is on p. 44).

83. Ibid., 131.

84. On the role of a "concept" in this context, see Robert Jervis, "Hypotheses on Misperception," *World Politics* 20 (1968): 454–79.

85. See his variations on this theme in *PMSIR: Parliament*, 1: 150; also 1: 147.

86. See, for example, one of his (unpublished) "Fortnightly Letters" to the chief ministers of the Indian states, 1 Oct. 1959; and see *PMSIR: Parliament*, 1: 153.

87. See the reference he made to a change in his thinking in the *Times of India*, 2 Nov. 1959. See also Ministry of External Affairs, Government of India, *Prime Minister on Sino-Indian Relations: Press Conferences*, 2 vols. (New Delhi: Government of India Press, 1961–1962), 1: 64. (Hereafter cited as *Press Conferences*.) In this particular press conference (5 Nov. 1959), Nehru

was responding to a question about a statement he had made on 21 Oct. (before news of the Kongka Pass incident reached him), in which he intimated that he was not sure of China's deeper motives. Although he was not now questioned further about what he had said on 21 Oct., on that occasion he was still inclined to explain China's border incursions mainly by linking them to the Tibetan revolt and its aftermath. (See *Times of India*, 22 Oct. 1959.)

88. See *The Hindu*, 21 Dec. 1959.

CHAPTER FIVE

1. See Gopal, *Nehru*, 3: 88–89, on Indian government policy.

2. This sentence is a summary from an interview with J. S. Mehta, 10 Apr. 1983.

3. Gopal, *Nehru*, 3: 89–90. The expression "a free government" is from the official record of the Nehru–Dalai Lama meeting.

4. Interviews with J. S. Mehta, 10 Apr. 1983, 6 Jan. 1986.

5. *PMSIR: Parliament*, 1: 35.

6. Interviews with J. S. Mehta, 26 Mar., 10 Apr. 1983.

7. *White Papers*, 1: 75, 74.

8. Interview with J. S. Mehta, 10 Apr. 1983.

9. Dutt, *Foreign Office*, 155.

10. *White Papers*, 1: 77–78.

11. See *White Papers*, 1: 84–95, 2: 70–92; and *PMSIR: Parliament*, 1: 60–64.

12. Whiting, *Chinese Calculus of Deterrence*, 17. On the overflights see Whiting, 12–19; *White Papers*, 4: 34–35, 39; Avedon, *Exile*, 114–30; Victor Marchetti and John Marks, *The CIA and the Cult of Intelligence* (New York: Dell, 1974), 128–31, 157. The extent of Indian knowledge (at any government level) of 1950s and 1960–1962 CIA assistance to the Tibetans, involving Indian soil or airspace, is unclear, although Nehru probably did not know of the major CIA-Tibetan operation as late as John Kenneth Galbraith's 1961–1963 ambassadorship to India (from Galbraith's letter to the author, 8 Dec. 1988). The small bits of published evidence available do not clarify the matter, but see (for example) Prados, *Presidents' Secret Wars*, 158, 169, and Marchetti and Marks, *CIA and the Cult of Intelligence*, 157. On the CIA-Tibetan operation itself, run for a time from the U.S. embassy in New Delhi, see Prados, 149–70, and John K. Galbraith, *A Life in Our Times: Memories* (New York: Ballantine, 1981), 394–97.

13. Dutt, *Foreign Office*, 156–57. The Nehru government had to resist some domestic pressure; in the autumn of 1959, India's parliament considered a motion urging the government to take the Tibetan issue to the United Nations.

14. *The Hindu*, 14 Aug. 1959.

15. *PMSIR: Parliament*, 1: 74; see also 93–96. The prime minister of Bhutan disagreed with Nehru's version of the Indian-Bhutanese relationship (see Maxwell, *India's China War*, 113).

16. *PMSIR: Parliament*, 1:65–67. See also 1: 56; Chakravarti, *India's China Policy*, 66–68, 167; and *PMSIR: Press Conferences*, 1: 35–36.

17. Interview with J. S. Mehta, 6 Jan. 1986.

18. *PMSIR: Parliament*, 1: 92.

19. For another version of the white paper decision, see Gopal, *Nehru*, 3: 95–96.

20. *White Papers*, 1: 34; see also 44–45.

21. *White Papers*, 1: 41; *PMSIR: Parliament*, 1: 86–92, 102–3.

22. D. K. Palit, chapter on 7 Brigade (from unpublished memoir, 1985), 1. I am grateful to General Palit for allowing me to see two chapters of his manuscript.

23. See Maxwell, *India's China War*, 103–6.

24. Interview with K. Gopalachari, Mar.–Aug. 1966; interview with a source who wishes to remain anonymous, Apr. 1983.

25. Interview with T. S. Murty, 11 June 1983.

26. *PMSIR: Parliament*, 1: 90–91.

27. Interviews with sources who wish to remain anonymous, Mar.–Aug. 1966, Aug.–Sept. 1967; see also *White Papers*, 1: 44.

28. *PMSIR: Parliament*, 1: 81, 104, 116–17. Nehru was still troubled, too, by the treatment of Indian nationals in Tibet.

29. *White Papers*, 1: 44–45; the "strange silence" remark is from *PMSIR: Press Conferences*, 1: 35.

30. *White Papers*, 2: 34.

31. *PMSIR: Parliament*, 1: 129.

32. Ibid., 152; see also 155–56.

33. *White Papers*, 2: 43.

34. *PMSIR: Parliament*, 1: 138–39.

35. *White Papers*, 1: 44.

36. Gopal, *Nehru*, 3: 98.

37. Ibid. For the text of much of this memo, see Maxwell, *India's China War*, 129.

38. Nehru letter to U Nu, 29 Sept. 1959; made public in Gopal, *Nehru*, 3: 98.

39. *PMSIR: Press Conferences*, 1: 45–46.

40. The Chinese letter is quoted in Chakravarti, *India's China Policy*, 108–9; the Indian reply appears in *PMSIR: Press Conferences*, 1: 47.

41. Mullik, *Chinese Betrayal*, 237; Maxwell, *India's China War*, 107, 144; *Times of India*, 21 Oct. 1959. The Indian government later doubted that the Chinese actually did withdraw. See Nehru's letter of 16 Nov. 1959 in *White Papers*, 3: 48.

42. *White Papers*, 2: 58–124. See also *Hindustan Times*, 30 Oct. 1959.

43. *White Papers*, 2: 45.

44. *PMSIR: Parliament*, 1: 119.

45. Interviews with K. Gopalachari, Mar.–Aug. 1966, Aug.–Sept. 1967; see also *PMSIR: Parliament*, 1: 134–35, 99, 101, 105–6.

46. *PMSIR: Parliament*, 1: 149, 148.

47. Ibid., 83, 98–101, 104–5, 119–20, 134–35, 148–51; *Press Conferences*, 1: 49–50.

48. That Nehru's comments on the Aksai Chin were just ruminations is an implication from an interview with K. Gopalachari, Aug.–Sept. 1967.

49. See the further discussion of Nehru's attitude toward the Aksai Chin in the next chapter.

CHAPTER SIX

1. Indian perceptions are derived from the *The Hindu*, 26, 28, and 31 Oct. 1959 and 2 Nov. 1959. Information on what the Indians thought was China's specific purpose in instigating violence at Kongka Pass is derived from interviews with J. S. Mehta, 25 Mar. 1983, and with a source who wishes to remain anonymous, Mar. 1983.

2. Mullik, *Chinese Betrayal*, 203–4.

3. Ibid., 202–4, 240–43.

4. *White Papers*, 2: 16; interview with a source who wishes to remain anonymous, Mar. 1983.

5. *Times of India*, 30 Oct. 1959.

6. *Times of India*, 30 Oct. 1959; *The Hindu*, 31 Oct. 1959; Maxwell, *India's China War*, 132.

7. Conclusion drawn from interview with J. S. Mehta, 10 Apr. 1983.

8. Gopal, *Nehru*, 3: 100. Accounts differ, but these figures are from a recent source. Any figures should include two Indians taken prisoner on 20 Oct., the day before the clash.

9. *White Papers*, 3: 4–5, 8–9, 47; *PMSIR: Parliament*, 1: 194; see also *PMSIR: Parliament*, 1: 255, 260–61.

10. Mullik, *Chinese Betrayal*, 243–44; see also 245. A misprint in the Mullik book dates this meeting "23 Sept."

11. See *PMSIR: Parliament*, 1: 229–31, 242–44; *PMSIR: Press Conferences*, 1: 54, 57–59; Karunakar Gupta, *India in World Politics* (Calcutta: Scientific Book Agency, 1969), 167.

12. Dalvi, *Himalayan Blunder*, 56; see also 55–58. This description of haste and unpreparedness is confirmed by D. K. Palit in his chapter on 7 Brigade, 1–3.

13. Mullik, *Chinese Betrayal*, 243–44.

14. Ibid., 245–46; Maxwell, *India's China War*, 206–7, 211.

15. *White Papers*, 3: 44.

16. Ibid., 44–45.

17. Mullik, *Chinese Betrayal*, 251–52; *Times of India*, 10 Nov. 1959.

18. Statements about India's reaction to the Chou proposal are derived from interviews with S. Gopal, 24 Mar. 1983, and J. S. Mehta, 10 Apr. 1983; *Times of India*, 10, 11 Nov. 1959; *White Papers*, 3: 47–48; *Hindustan Times*, 10, 11 Nov. 1959. The general problem of movement in NEFA valleys was described by Niranjan Prasad in an interview on 23 Mar. 1983.

19. Interview with S. Gopal, 24 Mar. 1983.

20. See Gopal, *Nehru*, 3: 103, although Gopal's view of Nehru's motive for making the offer differs from that presented here.

21. *White Papers*, 3: 49.

22. Ibid., 47–48.

23. *White Papers*, 2: 20–22.

24. See *White Papers*, 1: 42.

25. Interviews with S. Gopal, 24 Mar., 1 and 8 Apr. 1983.

26. Ibid. For Nehru's "foolproof" statement, see *PMSIR: Parliament*, 1: 383.

27. For a full account of the debates in parliament, see Nancy Jetly, *India-China Relations, 1947–1977* (Atlantic Highlands, N.J.: Humanities Press, 1979), 126–27 and passim.

28. See *PMSIR: Parliament*, 1: 214–15.

29. Gopal, *Nehru*, 3: 133.

30. Gupta, *India in World Politics*, 165–66, 174; Gopal, *Nehru*, 3: 103–5.

31. *White Papers*, 3: 55.

32. See *White Papers*, 2: 20–24, 3: 48–50.

33. The quotations are from Gopal, *Nehru*, 3: 128. That India was pressuring China is my interpretation, not Gopal's. China's activities, of course, constituted pressure on India.

34. Maxwell, *India's China War*, 206; *The Hindu*, 26 Oct. 1959.

35. From Nehru's explanation in parliament (*PMSIR: Parliament*, 1: 303, 307–12). On p. 303 he suggests 31 Jan. as the approximate date of the decision.

36. Inference drawn from Gopal's description in *Nehru*, 3: 133. One informant (J. S. Mehta, in a 10 Apr. 1983 interview) stressed that respecting the Soviet interest was just one reason for this decision.

37. Dutt, *Foreign Office*, 137; Gopal, *Nehru*, 3: 133.

38. Nehru's hope about Chou was mentioned by J. S. Mehta in a June 1970 interview; the "gambler" quote is taken from an interview with Lakshmi Menon, Mar.–Aug. 1966.

39. Maxwell, *India's China War*, 149–50.

40. *PMSIR: Press Conferences*, 1: 78–79, 101–2.

41. Gopal, *Nehru*, 3: 133–34; for the probable Chinese view, see Maxwell, *India's China War*, 161–62, 218–26. It was also noticed in India that the Chinese had agreed to recognize as the traditional boundary the stretch of the McMahon line that covers part of the Burma-China border (interview with J. S. Mehta, 6 Jan. 1986; see also Gopal, *Nehru*, 3: 134).

42. Interview with J. S. Mehta, June 1970.

43. Interviews with sources who wish to remain anonymous, Mar.–Aug. 1966, Aug.–Sept. 1967.

44. Quoted in Maxwell, *India's China War*, 164.

45. Interview with N. R. Pillai, 4 July 1985.

46. That Chou, at most, only *hinted* at this offer is the point made in Gopal, *Nehru*, 3: 136, citing an internal Government of India record of the talks.

47. Interviews with S. Gopal, 24 Mar. and 1 Apr. 1983.

48. *Times of India*, 18 April 1960.

49. Interview with J. S. Mehta, 6 Jan. 1986.

50. Maxwell, *India's China War*, 169; *PMSIR: Parliament*, 1: 383; see also 1: 333–34.

51. *PMSIR: Parliament*, 1: 333–34.

52. Desai, *My Life*, 2: 186–87; *Hindustan Times*, 20–23 Apr. 1960; *Times of India*, 20–24 Apr. 1960.

53. The point about Krishna Menon was made in an interview with a source who wishes to remain anonymous, Apr. 1983; see also Krishna Menon's comments in Brecher, *India and World Politics*, 149, 151–52.

54. Gopal, *Nehru*, 3: 136 (citing a Government of India record of the talks).

55. See *Report of the Officials*, 1. The report also indicates that K. Gopalachari advised the Indian delegation when the officials' meetings were held in Delhi. Biographical material is based on interviews with sources who wish to remain anonymous, Mar.–Aug. 1966.

56. Interview with T. S. Murty, 11 June 1983.

57. Interviews with J. S. Mehta, 10 Apr. 1983, 6 Jan. 1986.

58. On China's "traditional customary line," see *Report of the Officials*, Chinese section, 1–6, 33–52. This version of the origin of the 1960 Chinese line in the Western Sector is mine, inferred from the Kongka Pass affair and my interview with Alastair Lamb, 21 May 1983.

59. Interview with J. S. Mehta, 10 Apr. 1983.

60. Indian officials who wished to remain anonymous in interviews conducted by Michael Brecher, 1964–1966.

61. See Gopal, *Nehru*, 3: 206.

62. *PMSIR: Parliament*, 1: 394.

63. Interviews with R. K. Nehru, Apr.–Aug. 1966.

64. Ibid. See also *PMSIR: Parliament*, 2: 1–2, 7–8, and *White Papers*, 5: 158.

65. Gopal, *Nehru*, 3: 207.

66. See *PMSIR: Parliament*, 2: 2.

CHAPTER SEVEN

1. Maxwell, *India's China War*, 74.

2. Ibid., 206–7.

3. Ibid., 208–9.

4. D. K. Palit, "Director of Military Operations," chapter from unpublished and untitled memoir, 1986 (hereafter cited as DMO chapter), 28–29; Maxwell, *India's China War*, 208. I am grateful to General Palit for showing me two chapters of his memoir.

5. Mullik, *Chinese Betrayal*, 306. Information in this paragraph and the next one is taken from Mullik, 306–9.

6. From an interview with a source who wishes to remain anonymous, Apr. 1983.

7. Mullik, *Chinese Betrayal*, 309–11.

8. Ibid., 310.

9. Palit, DMO chapter, 33; Mullik, *Chinese Betrayal*, 312; and interview with a source who wishes to remain anonymous (date withheld to preserve confidentiality).

10. D. K. Palit, "Intelligence: Crucial Mistakes," *Hindustan Times Weekly Review*, 11 Apr. 1971; Palit, DMO chapter, 33. One wonders whether a similar thought was floating around the Chinese government just before the Kongka Pass incident of 1959.

11. Palit, DMO chapter, 35. On this episode see also B. M. Kaul, *Confrontation with Pakistan* (New York: Barnes and Noble, 1972), 292.

12. Palit, DMO chapter, 35. The quotation from the IB assessment appears in Palit, "Crucial Mistakes."

13. Palit, DMO chapter, 36. See also Kaul, *Confrontation*, 292; Maxwell, *India's China War*, 230–31.

14. Mullik, *Chinese Betrayal*, 311–12; Maxwell, *India's China War*, 230.

15. Palit, DMO chapter, 44.

16. Mullik, *Chinese Betrayal*, 314.

17. The wording of the 2 Nov. minutes is from Maxwell, *India's China War*, 231, and is confirmed by Palit, DMO chapter, 46–47.

18. Interview with a source who wishes to remain anonymous (date withheld to preserve confidentiality).

19. Kaul, *Untold Story*, 280.

20. Palit, DMO chapter, 45–46.

21. See Thapar's account in *The Statesman*, 9 Jan. 1971.

22. Palit, DMO chapter, 46–48 (quotation is on p. 48).

23. Palit, DMO chapter, 46. The point about the road link appears on p. 48. Information was also obtained from an interview with Palit, 17 Jan. 1986.

24. Palit, DMO chapter, 48–49.

25. Maxwell, *India's China War*, 242–43.

26. Palit, DMO chapter, 49.

27. Interview with a source who wishes to remain anonymous; Kaul, *Untold Story*, 318; Maxwell, *India's China War*, 242; Mullik, *Chinese Betrayal*, 325–28.

28. Maxwell, *India's China War*, 310.

29. Interview with Umrao Singh, 18 Mar. 1983. The April starting date is given in Dalvi, *Himalayan Blunder*, 109.

30. See Dalvi, *Himalayan Blunder*, 86–87; the prime minister's statements to parliament in *PMSIR: Parliament*, 1: 156 and 2: 111, 123; and Indian press reports found in *The Hindu*, 13 July 1962, and in G.S. Bhargava, *The Battle for NEFA* (New Delhi: Allied Publishers, 1964), 80–82.

31. Information on Thorat-Sen planning is taken from interviews with a source who wishes to remain anonymous; from Maxwell, *India's China War*, 417–18; and from Palit, 7 Brigade chapter, 5. See also Kavic, *India's Quest for Security*, 88–89.

32. Maxwell, *India's China War*, 313, 418; Palit, DMO chapter, 16; and interview with a source who wishes to remain anonymous.

33. From interviews with a source who wishes to remain anonymous; also from Palit, 7 Brigade chapter, 1–5.

34. The following material on nonimplementation of plans is derived from an interview with B. M. Kaul, Sept. 1967; interviews with a source who wishes to remain anonymous; interviews with D. K. Palit, 29 June 1985, 17 Jan. 1986; Palit, DMO chapter, 12–15, 16–19, 22–24, 25–27; and Kavic, *India's Quest for Security*, 89.

35. Khera, *India's Defence Problem*, 201; Kaul, *Untold Story*, 330–36.

36. For Nehru's 1962 parliamentary statement describing his general outlook on this subject, see *PMSIR: Parliament*, 2: 180–84; see also Kaul, *Untold Story*, 330–34, 335, 337–38.

37. The accusation about misleading the cabinet was made in an interview with a well-placed source who wishes to remain anonymous, 1966. A gentle version of this kind of accusation can be found in Desai, *My Life*, 187. General Kaul's impression was that Krishna Menon's view and Nehru's view were really indistinguishable (see *Untold Story*, 320–21, 337–40).

38. Kaul, *Untold Story*, 336–40; Palit, DMO chapter, 25–27.

39. Dalvi, *Himalayan Blunder*, 78–86, 107–14.

40. Maxwell, *India's China War*, 206–7, 211–13 (quotation is on p. 212).

41. The Chinese 30 Apr. note appears in *White Papers*, 6: 37–39; for the Indian reply see *White Papers*, 6: 41–43 (quotation is on p. 42).

42. Maxwell, *India's China War*, 242–43, 245–47. Information on the early shooting clashes is taken from Mullik, *Chinese Betrayal*, 328.

43. Interview with source who wishes to remain anonymous; Maxwell, *India's China War*, 247.

44. Mullik, *Chinese Betrayal*, 328.

45. The blocking of the Chinese Galwan Valley post was inadvertent, according to an interview with D. K. Palit, 12 Apr. 1983. But the Indians had themselves originally wanted to dominate the main Galwan Chinese position at Samzungling (Maxwell, *India's China War*, 248–49). The date of the Chinese pullback appears in *The Hindu*, 15 July 1962.

46. *The Hindu*, 13, 15 July 1962.

47. Press reaction is described in Maxwell, *India's China War*, 249–50, and *The Hindu*, 15 July 1962.

48. Gopal, *Nehru*, 3: 211.

49. Maxwell, *India's China War*, 250, 265, and interview with a source who wishes to remain anonymous. According to the Maxwell account, these orders were implemented in early Sept., when an Indian garrison opened fire "at point blank range" (p. 265) at Chinese troops who had come too near, killing several of them. No publicity was given to this incident by either the Chinese or Indian governments (although some foreign newspapers and the *Hindustan Times* picked it up).

50. *The Hindu*, 13 July 1962.

51. *PMSIR: Parliament*, 2: 116.

52. Ibid., 94.

53. *White Papers*, 6: 56–57.

54. Ibid., 7: 4.

55. Ibid., 36–37; *PMSIR: Parliament*, 2: 121.

56. The Geneva episode is described in Arthur Lall, *The Emergence of Modern India* (New York: Columbia University Press, 1981), 155–57; broadly confirmed in Neville Maxwell's interview with Chou En-lai, *Sunday Times* (London), 19 Dec. 1971.

57. *PMSIR: Parliament*, 2: 121.

58. Dalvi, *Himalayan Blunder*, 109; Niranjan Prasad, *The Fall of Towang*, (New Delhi: Palit and Palit, 1981), 16; Maxwell, *India's China War*, 310.

59. Maxwell, *India's China War*, 314.

60. Prasad, *Fall of Towang*, 22–23.

61. Ibid., 24–25.

62. Interview with Umrao Singh, 18 Mar. 1983; Prasad, *Fall of Towang*, 23–25.

63. Interview with D. K. Palit, 12 Apr. 1983; Prasad, *Fall of Towang*, 23–24. Prasad (ibid., 16–17, 23) says that the army map showed the line as drawn by Sir Henry McMahon in 1914. But more likely the army map was based on the map devised by the surveyor-general of India, at Olaf Caroe's instruction, in 1937.

64. Interview with S. Gopal, 1 Apr. 1983.

65. Interview with D. K. Palit, 12 Apr. 1983.

66. Michael Brecher, *The Foreign Policy System of Israel: Setting, Images, Process* (New Haven, Conn.: Yale University Press, 1972), 14.

67. On the circular "feedback" facet of decision-making, as used in the International Crisis Behavior project (ICB), see Michael Brecher, "A Theoretical Approach to International Behavior," in Michael Brecher, ed., *Studies in Crisis Behavior* (New Brunswick, N. J.: Transaction Books, 1978), 17.

68. For this view of "tactical" decisions, see Brecher, *Foreign Policy System*, 14.

69. See Maxwell, "Un-negotiated Dispute," especially pp. 60–66.

CHAPTER EIGHT

1. On the Nehru-Kaul and Menon-Kaul relationships, see Kaul, *Untold Story*, especially 206–15; Mullik, *Chinese Betrayal*, 338; and Kaul, *Confrontation with Pakistan*, 289–90. See also Maxwell, *India's China War*, 191–206, Welles Hangen, *After Nehru Who?* (London: Hart-Davis, 1963), 242–72; Khera, *India's Defence Problem*, 220–25; Palit, DMO chapter, 5, 7–8, 10–11.

2. For more on the typical Indian faction structure, see Steven A. Hoffmann, "Faction Behavior and Cultural Codes," *Journal of Asian Studies* 40 (1981): 231–54.

3. My conclusions on the structure of these personal relationships are based on an interview with M. J. Desai, Feb. 1966; interviews with a source who wishes to remain anonymous, Mar.–Apr. 1983; an interview with N. B. Menon, 15 Jan. 1986; Kaul, *Untold Story*, 313; Mullik, *Years with Nehru*, 58–67; Khera, *India's Defence Problem*, 221–22; Rosenthal, "Clue to Nehru," 11, 68–71; Brecher, *Krishna Menon's View of the World*, 188–89, and see 16–17. On Nehru's generous treatment of subordinates generally, see Dutt, *Foreign Office*, 28–29, 278–303 passim; and Y. D. Gundevia, *Outside the Archives* (London: Sangam Books, 1984), passim.

4. Palit, DMO chapter, 10. Impressions of Kaul and his support group are drawn from an interview with Umrao Singh, 19 Mar. 1983; interviews with a source who wishes to remain anonymous (some sources preferred all or some of their material to be undated to preserve confidentiality); an interview with another source who wishes to remain anonymous, Apr.–May 1983; interviews with D. K. Palit, 25 June and 31 Dec. 1985; and Palit, DMO chapter, 8, 10.

5. Kaul, *Untold Story*, 205, 208–9; Hangen, *After Nehru*, 99; interview with K. D. Malaviya, 1966; interviews with two sources who wish to remain anonymous, Mar.–Apr. 1983.

6. The MEA and M. J. Desai are described in an interview with a source who wishes to remain anonymous, Apr. 1983, and in an interview with N. B. Menon, 15 Jan. 1986. Mullik's disciple relationship with Nehru and Mullik's role in developing the IB are described in his *Years with Nehru*, 20–25, 58–62, 64–67, 214.

7. Kavic, *India's Quest for Security*, 156–68; Hangen, *After Nehru*, 61; Palit, DMO chapter, 5–8. M. J. Desai's role was described by a source who wishes to remain anonymous; see also Vertzberger, *Misperceptions*, 267, 279–84.

8. For a detailed, if somewhat extreme, interpretation of what might be called a "groupthink" proclivity on the part of the Nehru group, see Vertzberger, *Misperceptions*, 257–85. The "groupthink" concept itself comes from I. L. Janis, *Victims of Groupthink* (Boston: Houghton Mifflin, 1972).

9. Interview with N. B. Menon, 22 Apr. 1983. On Nehru's illness see Gopal, *Nehru*, 3: 266.

10. The expressions "areas of agreement" and "on thin ice" are taken from an interview with N. B. Menon, 21 Apr. 1983. The roles of Krishna Menon and M. J. Desai were described by N. B. Menon, in the 21 Apr. 1983 interview, and by N. R. Pillai, in an interview on 4 July 1985. On Nehru's temper, silences, the reactions they produced, and his vigor during the 1962 war, see Gundevia, *Outside the Archives*, 199–202, 234–37, and Dutt, *Years with Nehru*, 283–84.

11. Gopal, *Nehru*, 3: 133–34; interviews with J. S. Mehta, 3 May 1983, 6 Jan. 1986.

12. Interview with T. S. Murty, 12 June 1983.

13. Vertzberger, *Misperceptions*, 125; see also 124–27. The Indian denigration of Chinese troops is referred to in Dalvi, *Himalayan Blunder*, 405–6.

14. Source who wishes to remain anonymous, Apr. 1983; see also Nehru in parliament, *PMSIR: Parliament*, 2: 122–23.

15. "[General] impression among key civilians" is derived from interviews with a source who wishes to remain anonymous, Apr. 1983; with S. Gopal, 1 Apr. 1983; and with N. B. Menon, 20–21 Apr. 1983. See also Gundevia, *Outside the Archives*, 213. The army point of view and the instruction to 4 Division were described by J. S. Dhillon in interviews on 5 and 13 Apr. 1983.

16. *PMSIR: Parliament*, 2: 94, 115–16, 130–31. The statement that India's forward policy was aimed at talks is derived from an interview with S. Gopal, 24 Mar. 1983, and an interview with a source who wishes to remain anonymous, Apr. 1983; see also Gopal, *Nehru*, 3: 209.

17. *PMSIR: Press Conferences*, 2: 11.

18. Gopal, *Nehru*, 3: 188. This summary of relations between India and the United States is based on Gopal, *Nehru*, 3: 187–89, 197–203, 214–18; and on Vertzberger, *Misperceptions*, 94–95.

19. See Selig Harrison, "South Asia and U.S. Policy," *New Republic*, 11 Dec. 1961, 16.

20. Kavic, *India's Quest for Security*, 105, 106–8, 134–35.

21. For the "[Local] wars do not take place" quotation, see *PMSIR: Parliament*, 1: 279. For the statement that a China-India war would be protracted, see *PMSIR: Parliament*, 2: 93. The likely Soviet role was discussed by S. Gopal in an interview on 24 Mar. 1983.

22. *PMSIR: Parliament*, 2: 94–95.

23. My interpretation of Nehru's thinking, inferred from *PMSIR: Press Conferences*, 2: 26, and from Maxwell, "Un-negotiated Dispute," 73.

24. N. B. Menon, "The Integrity of Frontiers as a Function of State Power," *The State against People* (Bangalore: Ecumenical Christian Centre Publications, 1982), 50. Broadly confirmed in an interview with K. Krishna Rao, Aug.–Sept. 1967.

25. Khera, *India's Defence Problem*, 200; interview with N. R. Pillai, 16 May 1983.

26. Interview with N. B. Menon, 15 Jan. 1986.

27. Quoted in Brecher, *India and World Politics*, 151.

28. Interviews with T. S. Murty, 11–12 June 1983.

29. Brecher, *India and World Politics*, 153–55, 172–74.

30. Interviews with D. K. Palit, 12 Apr., 4 May 1983.

31. Kaul, *Untold Story*, 341; interviews with B. M. Kaul, Mar.–Aug. 1966, Aug.–Sept. 1967.

32. See Kaul, *Untold Story*, 340–42; Mullik, *Chinese Betrayal*, 338; Chester Bowles, *Promises to Keep* (New York: Harper and Row, 1971), 474.

33. Maxwell, *India's China War*, 347. Kaul's source for this belief apparently was General Thapar, who repeated (with some skepticism) what IB director Mullik told him or hinted to him. See Kaul, *Confrontation with Pakistan*, 284; and D. K. Palit, in *Hindustan Times Weekly Review*, 11 Apr. 1971.

34. This view of Kaul after 8 Sept. is derived from his memoir, *Untold Story*, 253–63, 353–99; and from Dalvi, *Himalayan Blunder*, 255–303; interview with Umrao Singh, 19 Mar. 1983; Prasad, *Fall of Towang*, 43–98; Maxwell, *India's China War*, 348–64, 378–80; and Mullik, *Chinese Betrayal*, 356–57.

35. Several interviews with a source who wishes to remain anonymous, Mar.–Aug. 1966, Mar. 1983.

36. Maxwell, *India's China War*, 319.

37. "No alternative" is a quotation from Krishna Menon in Brecher, *India and World Politics*, 172. A similar term was used by a former minister in Nehru's cabinet, in an interview in Sept. 1967, and by an MEA source who wishes to remain anonymous, in an interview in Apr. 1983.

38. Maxwell, *India's China War*, 333–34 (quotation is on p. 333).

39. Mullik, *Chinese Betrayal*, 333; see also 332–34, 351–52.

40. Cited in Vertzberger, *Misperceptions*, 113.

41. Gopal's words and analysis, in *Nehru*, 3: 219–20; Gopal's account is based on Kaul's report of his 3 Oct. conversation with Nehru, in *Untold Story*, 367–68.

42. See Mullik, *Chinese Betrayal*, 368–71.

43. Interview with H. K. Mahatab, 25 Apr. 1983. Mahatab, a minister in the Nehru cabinet, was a leader of the Congress Party delegation in parliament.

44. D. K. Palit article in *Hindustan Times Weekly Review*, 11 Apr. 1971; Kaul, *Confrontation with Pakistan*, 284.

45. Maxwell, *India's China War*, 342.
46. *Times of India*, 19 Sept. 1962.
47. Mullik, *Chinese Betrayal*, 351–52.
48. "Fortnightly Letters" 12 Oct. 1962.
49. *Times of India*, 13 Oct. 1962.
50. *Times of India*, 15 Oct. 1962.
51. See Brecher, with Geist, *Decisions in Crisis*, 1–8.

CHAPTER NINE

1. For the concept of decision flow, see Brecher, with Geist, *Decisions in Crisis*, 29.
2. From Prasad, *Fall of Towang*, 25–28; Dalvi, *Himalayan Blunder*, 169–70, 177–78; Maxwell, *India's China War*, 323.
3. Dalvi, *Himalayan Blunder*, 178; Prasad, *Fall of Towang*, 27.
4. Interview with a source who wishes to remain anonymous (some sources preferred all or some of their material to be undated to preserve confidentiality).
5. The information on contingency planning is derived from interviews with J. S. Dhillon, 5 and 13 Apr. 1983. Major General Dhillon was the officiating CGS in the absence of Kaul. Prasad's defense plan for western NEFA is described in *Fall of Towang*, 21–22. The term *vital ground* is from an interview with Niranjan Prasad, 23 Mar. 1983.
6. Prasad, *Fall of Towang*, 27.
7. Interview with Umrao Singh, 19 Mar. 1983.
8. Summary of information from an interview with a source who wishes to remain anonymous; an interview with B. M. Kaul by Michael Brecher, May 1965; and interviews with J. S. Dhillon, 5 and 13 Apr. 1983.
9. Interview with J. S. Dhillon, 13 Apr. 1983; Kaul, *Untold Story*, 355–56; and interview with a source who wishes to remain anonymous.
10. Interview with J. S. Dhillon, 13 Apr. 1983.
11. Interviews with Umrao Singh, 18 Mar., 18 Apr. 1983; the list of persons present at the 12 Sept. meeting is taken from Prasad, *Fall of Towang*, 32.
12. Dalvi and Prasad's assessments and communications with Umrao are described in Dalvi, *Himalayan Blunder*, 171–78, and Prasad, *Fall of Towang*, 28–32.
13. The quotation is from Maxwell, *India's China War*, 324. Sen's actions are described in Prasad, *Fall of Towang*, 32.
14. Interview with Umrao Singh, 18 Apr. 1983.
15. Maxwell, *India's China War*, 324–25, from unpublished documents.
16. Prasad, *Fall of Towang*, 33.
17. Interviews with Umrao Singh, 18 Mar., 18 Apr. 1983.
18. Interview with D. K. Palit, 12 Apr. 1983.
19. Dalvi, *Himalayan Blunder*, 178–79.
20. Interview with Umrao Singh, 18 Mar. 1983; Prasad, *Fall of Towang*, 29–30, 36.
21. The 17,000 estimate was the Indian figure in use in the early 1960s, as reported in an interview with a source who wishes to remain anonymous. But a reputable published source reports that, while 1955 People's Liberation Army specifications called for an infantry division of 17,600, "the established strength of the 1965 infantry division" was "about 10,000." The "mountain divisions," which were supposedly used by the Chinese against India in 1962, were manned at a level of 8,000–10,000 men. (See Samuel B. Griffith III, *The Chinese People's Liberation Army* [New York: McGraw-Hill, 1967], 219–20.) The Indian battalions were at approximately 60 percent strength. This estimate also was provided in an interview with D. K. Palit, 2 Sept. 1988.
22. Interview with Niranjan Prasad, 23 Mar. 1983.

23. The statement that Sen had never been north of Tezpur appears in Prasad, *Fall of Towang*, 45; confirmed in interview with Umrao Singh, 18 Mar. 1983. On Sen's point of view, see Maxwell, *India's China War*, 324; Mullik, *Chinese Betrayal*, 355–56. The quotation is from an interview with L. P. Sen, Sept. 1967.

24. Sen's recollections of what he was "told by Krishna Menon" were provided in an interview in Sept. 1967. The rest of paragraph is from an interview with a source who wishes to remain anonymous.

25. Kaul, *Untold Story*, 358–59; Dalvi, *Himalayan Blunder*, 211; and interview with a source who wishes to remain anonymous.

26. Kaul, *Untold Story*, 359; interview with a source who wishes to remain anonymous.

27. Interview with a source who wishes to remain anonymous; Kaul, *Untold Story*, 359–60. The quotation is from Mullik, *Chinese Betrayal*, 346; see also 345–46.

28. Interview with a source who wishes to remain anonymous. For a more aggressive version of these orders, see Kaul, *Untold Story*, 359.

29. Mullik, *Chinese Betrayal*, 346.

30. Ibid., 343–45 (quotation is on p. 345).

31. Prasad, *Fall of Towang*, 33–38.

32. Dalvi, *Himalayan Blunder*, 208–9 (quotation is on p. 209).

33. Maxwell, *India's China War*, 318, 328; Gopal, *Nehru*, 3: 219n.

34. The telephone conversations between Sen and Thapar were mentioned in an interview with B. M. Kaul by Michael Brecher, May 1965. Sen used either the same or similar sets of dates in the defense minister's meetings held 17 and 20 Sept. (see Kaul, *Untold Story*, 360; Mullik, *Chinese Betrayal*, 346). Mullik (p. 347) reports the 19 Sept. meeting being told that the second battalion had already arrived by that date.

35. Mullik, *Chinese Betrayal*, 341, 348–50.

36. From an interview with a source who wishes to remain anonymous; see also Maxwell, *India's China War*, 395–96, 423. Eventually, Daulat Singh inducted two new brigades into Ladakh.

37. Interview with Harbakhsh Singh, 30 Dec. 1985. Harbakhsh was Daulat's headquarters chief at this point.

38. Mullik, *Chinese Betrayal*, 525; interview with a source who prefers to remain anonymous; interviews with D.K. Palit, 25 Mar. 1983, 2 Sept. 1988. For the view that Daulat acted on his own, see Maxwell, *India's China War*, 423.

39. Mullik, *Chinese Betrayal*, 350–351.

40. Whiting, *Chinese Calculus of Deterrence*, 100–102.

41. *White Papers*, 7: 77–78.

42. Ibid., 17–18, 71–73.

CHAPTER TEN

1. Mullik, *Chinese Betrayal*, 353–54 (quotation is on p. 354); Maxwell, *India's China War*, 333–34; interview with a source who wishes to remain anonymous.

2. Khera, *India's Defence Problem*, 204; interview with a source who wishes to remain anonymous.

3. Interview with D. K. Palit, 12 Apr. 1983.

4. Maxwell, *India's China War*, 336.

5. Interview with J. S. Dhillon, 13 Apr. 1983.

6. See Maxwell, *India's China War*, 335–36.

7. This point and the rest of this paragraph are derived from an interview with a source who wishes to remain anonymous, Apr. 1983.

8. For the published version see Maxwell, *India's China War*, 335–36.

9. Ibid., 337; interviews with D. K. Palit, 12 Apr. 1983, 17 Jan. 1986, 2–3 Sept. 1988.

10. Prasad, *Fall of Towang*, 34; interviews with Umrao Singh, 18 Mar., 18 Apr. 1983.

11. Dalvi, *Himalayan Blunder*, 240, 236. For Dalvi's description of this episode, see 231–40; see also Prasad, *Fall of Towang*, 36.

12. Interview with Umrao Singh, 18 Mar. 1983.

13. Prasad, *Fall of Towang*, 40.

14. Interview with Niranjan Prasad, 23 Mar. 1983; Dalvi, *Himalayan Blunder*, 241.

15. Prasad, *Fall of Towang*, 40; interview with Niranjan Prasad, 23 Mar. 1983; interviews with Umrao Singh, 18 Mar. and 18 Apr. 1983.

16. Prasad, *Fall of Towang*, 40.

17. Interview with Umrao Singh, 18 Mar. 1983.

18. Ibid.

19. Interviews with D. K. Palit, 12 Apr. 1983, 25 June 1985.

20. Mullik, *Chinese Betrayal*, 355–56. Mullik says that Sen was not shown the "plan" because Umrao had not disclosed it. In the context of what had been said and shown to Sen in NEFA, this sounds unlikely. The dates that Mullik gives for events are sometimes questionable, and the narrative must be adjusted accordingly. The date of this meeting is mentioned by Kaul, *Untold Story*, 364–65.

21. Sen's testimony to Maxwell, *India's China War*, 343.

22. Ibid., 345; Mullik, *Chinese Betrayal*, 357; Kaul, *Untold Story*, 365.

23. Mullik, *Chinese Betrayal*, 356; interviews with a source who wishes to remain anonymous, Apr., May 1983; interviews with D. K. Palit, 4 May 1983, 25 June 1985.

24. Interview with a source who prefers to remain anonymous, May 1983.

25. Interview with B. M. Kaul, 1966.

26. Kaul, *Untold Story*, 365–66; Maxwell, *India's China War*, 345; Mullik, *Chinese Betrayal*, 356; interview with D. K. Palit, 25 June 1985.

27. Maxwell, *India's China War*, 350, 347. The statement that Kaul himself may have leaked the news was made by D. K. Palit in interviews on 12 Apr. 1983 and 17 Jan. 1986. A government communique, issued quickly, sought to correct the "task force" impression, but could not have had as much impact as the original announcement.

28. *White Papers*, 7: 96–98 (quotation is on p. 97).

29. Ibid., 7: 100–102 (quotation is on p. 101).

30. Dalvi, *Himalayan Blunder*, 262–66; Kaul, *Untold Story*, 370; Prasad, *Fall of Towang*, 47–50.

31. Maxwell, *India's China War*, 354.

32. Prasad, *Fall of Towang*, 47–49.

33. Ibid., 50.

34. Maxwell, *India's China War*, 357–58; Prasad, *Fall of Towang*, 49, 54–57. Altitude figures are from Dalvi, *Himalayan Blunder*, 293; Kaul, *Untold Story*, 375, 377.

35. Dalvi, *Himalayan Blunder*, 285–86 (quotation is on p. 286); see also Kaul, *Untold Story*, 377–80.

36. Interview with Niranjan Prasad, 23 Mar. 1983.

37. Dalvi, *Himalayan Blunder*, 288–93; Prasad, *Fall of Towang*, 56–59; see also Kaul, *Untold Story*, 375–84.

38. Maxwell, *India's China War*, 360 (quoting from unpublished documents). Kaul may have meant that Tseng Jong itself helped make up the slope of the ridge (inference from interview with Niranjan Prasad, 23 Mar. 1983) or that a section of the Indian platoon at Tseng Jong had been sent further forward onto the main slope, so as to provide Tseng Jong with some covering fire (Maxwell, *India's China War*, 360; see also Kaul, *Untold Story*, 381). In either case Kaul was exaggerating.

39. Prasad, *Fall of Towang*, 60.

40. Ibid., 64.

41. Kaul, *Untold Story*, 381–83; Dalvi, *Himalayan Blunder*, 292–301; Prasad, *Fall of Towang*, 61–64.

42. Prasad, *Fall of Towang*, 64–67; Dalvi, *Himalayan Blunder*, 293–95.

43. Mullik, *Chinese Betrayal*, 361.

44. Maxwell, *India's China War*, 362 (from unpublished documents).

45. Mullik, *Chinese Betrayal*, 361.

46. The name of Kaul's illness was mentioned by Umrao Singh in an interview on 19 Mar. 1983.

47. The quotation is from Maxwell, *India's China War*, 363. The rest of the information is from Kaul, *Untold Story*, 385–86; Mullik, *Chinese Betrayal*, 361–64; interview with J. S. Dhillon, 5 Apr. 1983; Maxwell, *India's China War*, 363–64; Khera, *India's Defence Problem*, 225.

48. The three alternatives are presented in Kaul, *Untold Story*, 386; confirmed by interview with D. K. Palit, 12 Apr. 1983. The "not...commit suicide" phrase is from Mullik, *Chinese Betrayal*, 363; confirmed by interview with J. S. Dhillon, 5 Apr. 1983.

49. Mullik, *Chinese Betrayal*, 363–64; Kaul, *Untold Story*, 386; interview with D. K. Palit, 12 Apr. 1983; interview with L. P. Sen, Sept. 1967.

50. *The Statesman*, 13 Oct. 1962.

51. *Times of India*, 13 Oct. 1962.

52. See headline of *Times of India*, 13 Oct. 1962.

53. Interview with Umrao Singh, 19 Mar. 1983; see also Mullik, *Chinese Betrayal*, 367.

54. Prasad, *Fall of Towang*, 65; for more details on the orders, see Dalvi, *Himalayan Blunder*, 296–97. Dalvi says that the orders were verbal and were confirmed by a later signal; so does Kaul, *Untold Story*, 388.

55. Kaul, *Untold Story*, 388.

56. Prasad, *Fall of Towang*, 74.

57. Maxwell, *India's China War*, 377. Information about the urging of Kaul by his staff and the Assam Rifles chief is from Mullik, *Chinese Betrayal*, 368.

58. Mullik, *Chinese Betrayal*, 368.

59. Source who wishes to remain anonymous; Kaul, *Untold Story*, 388.

60. Interview with B. M. Kaul, 1967.

61. Kaul, *Untold Story*, 388.

62. From a source who wishes to remain anonymous.

63. Mullik, *Chinese Betrayal*, 368–69.

64. Information on the 17 October meeting is taken from Mullik, *Chinese Betrayal*, 369–72; and Kaul, *Untold Story*, 388–89. Kaul's likely description of Chinese buildups on Thagla Ridge and near Khinzemane, as well as Indian deficiencies, is taken from Prasad, *Fall of Towang*, 78–83.

65. Maxwell, *India's China War*, 379; Kaul, *Untold Story*, 389–91; Mullik, *Chinese Betrayal*, 372–73; Dalvi, *Himalayan Blunder*, 343; Prasad, *Fall of Towang*, 86–87.

66. Interview with a source who prefers to remain anonymous; Maxwell, *India's China War*, 379–80; Prasad, *Fall of Towang*, 76–77, 79, 91–92. According to Prasad (p. 83), he was certain that some sort of Chinese offensive was coming, and he told Kaul about it on 16 October. See also Dalvi, *Himalayan Blunder*, 333.

67. Prasad, *Fall of Towang*, 92–94.

68. See Maxwell, *India's China War*, 457–58.

69. Dalvi, *Himalayan Blunder*, 333.

70. Ibid., 336–43; 357–59 (quotation is on p. 357).

71. Maxwell, *India's China War*, 381; Dalvi, *Himalayan Blunder*, 364.

CHAPTER ELEVEN

1. Maxwell, *India's China War*, 382, 393; interviews with D. K. Palit, 26 Aug. 1986, 2 Sept. 1988; Prasad, *Fall of Towang*, 113.

2. Mullik, *Chinese Betrayal*, 374. Maxwell (*India's China War*, 382) claims that the Chinese ignored Tsangle, since their maps, "like India's, probably showed it in Bhutan."

3. Mullik, *Chinese Betrayal*, 377.

4. Ibid., 400.

5. Interview with M. J. Desai, Feb. 1966.

6. Gundevia, *Outside the Archives*, 247; see also Michael Brecher, *Succession in India*, 100–102; and Hangen, *After Nehru*, 46.

7. Interview with N. B. Menon, 21 Apr. 1983.

8. Interview with M. J. Desai, Feb. 1966.

9. *Times of India*, 27 Oct. 1962; interview with M. J. Desai, Feb. 1966.

10. Speech made at the conference of information ministers of the states, 25 Oct.; quoted in Gopal, *Nehru*, 3: 223.

11. From the same speech; paraphrased in Gopal, *Nehru*, 3: 223.

12. The "phony war" phrase and a description of participation in this mentality by politicians and the press appear in Maxwell, *India's China War*, 405–14. The public comments by Nehru and other government spokespersons are reported in Maxwell (ibid.) and in a newspaper like the *Times of India*, 23–31 Oct. 1962. On the army's fighting from better positions, see Nehru's comment quoted in Gopal, *Nehru*, 3: 228. The expectations of Nehru, Palit, and Thapar for holding Se La, Bomdila, and the rest of NEFA are discussed in Mullik, *Chinese Betrayal*, 400–402, 411. For Nehru's view of the advantages to the enemy of surprise, numbers, and terrain, see *PMSIR: Parliament*, 2: 155, 164.

13. On Soviet movement toward China because of the Cuban crisis, and Indian awareness of it, see *Times of India*, 26 Oct. 1962; *The Hindu*, 27, 29 Oct. 1962; and *Pravda* editorials of 25 Oct. and 5 Nov. 1962 and the *Izvestia* editorial of 26 Oct. 1962, in *Current Digest of the Soviet Press* 14, no. 43 (1962): 17–19. See also the citations from Nehru-Khrushchev correspondence, published for the first time, in Gopal, *Nehru*, 3: 221–23.

14. This aspect of Indian decision-making is discussed in chapter 13.

15. Gopal, *Nehru*, 3: 223.

16. See Nehru's speech in parliament on 8 Nov. 1962, *PMSIR: Parliament*, 2: 138–53; and Michael Brecher, "Nonalignment under Stress: The West and the India-China Border War," *Pacific Affairs* 52, no. 4 (1979–80); Gopal, *Nehru*, 3: 226.

17. Khera, *India's Defence Problem*, 199.

18. For some of Nehru's references to Gandhianism in the context of China policy, see *PMSIR: Parliament*, 1: 131–32, 144–46; 2: 167–68. On Gandhi's principle of treating opponents as human beings, see Louis Fischer, *The Life of Mahatma Gandhi* (New York: Harper and Row, 1983), 195.

19. For Nehru's perception of Indian personality, see Maxwell, *India's China War*, 407–8. The term *war psychosis* (used often in 1959) can be found in *PMSIR: Press Conferences*, 1: 46. For Nehru's view of militarization, brutalization, and misplaced priorities, see *PMSIR: Parliament*, 2: 154–55, 162, 167–68, and Gopal, *Nehru*, 3: 226.

20. Nehru's remarks on this occasion were summarized by D. K. Palit in an interview on 4 May 1983.

21. Gopal, *Nehru*, 3: 224.

22. Ibid., 225n.

23. John K. Galbraith, *Ambassador's Journal* (Boston: Houghton Mifflin, 1969), 444.

24. Mullik, *Chinese Betrayal*, 382–83.

25. See Krishna Menon's comment in Brecher, *Krishna Menon's View of the World*, 160.

26. Ibid., 160–62.

27. Ibid., 170–72; see also Gundevia, *Outside the Archives*, 215–16.

28. Mullik, *Chinese Betrayal*, 410–11. The information that only one division was "earmarked" for withdrawal was provided by D. K. Palit, in an interview on 17 Jan. 1986 (see Punjab troop transfer decision, below).

29. Mullik, *Chinese Betrayal*, 411.

30. Interview with D. K. Palit, 17 Jan. 1986.

31. Interview with D. K. Palit, 2 Sept. 1988; Maxwell *India's China War*, 396; 419–20.

32. Interviews with D. K. Palit, 25 June 1985, 17 Jan. 1986, 20 Aug. 1986; Mullik, *Chinese Betrayal*, 400–401.

33. Harbakhsh Singh, "NEFA 1962: How a Foolproof Defense Plan Collapsed," *Indian Express*, 25 Apr. 1979.

34. Harbakhsh Singh, "Defense Plan," and interview with Harbakhsh Singh, 30 Dec. 1985.

35. "Well of death" and "graveyard" are from Harbakhsh Singh, "Defense Plan." Information on Palit's perspective was obtained from an interview with him on 2 Sept. 1988. The additional Harbakhsh information is from the 30 Dec. 1985 interview.

36. Mullik, *Chinese Betrayal*, 399; S. R. Johri, *Chinese Invasion of NEFA* (Lucknow: Himalaya Publishers, 1968), 108, 110, 117, 119; Maxwell, *India's China War*, 415. The statements about the possible Chinese use of mortars instead of artillery and the possibility of heavy fighting in front of Se La were made by D. K. Palit, in an interview on 2 Sept. 1988.

37. Interview with Harbakhsh Singh, 30 Dec. 1985.

38. The views of Sen and K. K. Singh are derived from interviews with D. K. Palit, 25 June 1985, 17 Jan. 1986.

39. For a critique of the Se La strategy, and a defense of the Bomdila idea, see Maxwell, *India's China War*, 393–94, 417.

40. Mullik's account indicates some civilian concern that even Bomdila might be abandoned. In that event, the entire Buddhist portion of the western NEFA population would come under Chinese control and might prove susceptible to Chinese influence. Civilian officials like himself much preferred the Se La plan, since it would presumably save most of the Kameng division of NEFA, southeast of Tawang (Mullik, *Chinese Betrayal*, 400–401).

41. Galbraith, *A Life in Our Times*, 429.

42. Kaul, *Untold Story*, 396.

43. Khera, *India's Defence Problem*, 230–31. The statement that Krishna Menon requested the paper from him is from Kaul, *Untold Story*, 397.

44. Mullik, *Chinese Betrayal*, 403–4.

45. The first of the quoted adjectives is from Galbraith, *A Life in Our Times*, 429; the second is from an interview with a source who wishes to remain anonymous, Apr. 1983; the third is from Mullik, *Chinese Betrayal*, 409.

46. The statement about uncertainty of approval of expansion plans before the war was obtained from an interview with K. Subrahmanyam, 29 Dec. 1985.

47. Interview with a source who wishes to remain anonymous, Apr. 1983.

48. Mullik, *Chinese Betrayal*, 409.

49. Brecher, with Geist, *Decisions in Crisis*, 7.

50. Interview with John Kenneth Galbraith, 7 Jan. 1985.

51. All foregoing quotes and information are taken from Gopal, *Nehru*, 3: 228.

52. Mullik, *Chinese Betrayal*, 438–39.

CHAPTER TWELVE

1. Prasad, *Fall of Towang*, 111–12, 122. Maxwell briefly indicates that he was given Sen's account of these events, which naturally differs (*India's China War*, 392).

2. Prasad, *Fall of Towang*, 111–31.

3. Maxwell, *India's China War*, 393–94. K. K. Singh's being overruled by Sen is confirmed by Kaul, *Untold Story*, 410–11.

4. Interviews with D. K. Palit, 12 Apr. and 4 May 1983, 26 Aug. 1986.

5. Interview with D. K. Palit, 4 May 1983; Mullik, *Chinese Betrayal*, 400–401. For the best description of the Poshing La route, see Maxwell, *India's China War*, 425–26.

6. Mullik, *Chinese Betrayal*, 400–401.

7. Interviews with D. K. Palit, 17 Jan. 1986, 2 Sept. 1988. On Se La supplies see also J. R. Saigal, *The Unfought War of 1962* (New Delhi: Allied Publishers, 1979), 69.

8. Interview with D. K. Palit, 12 Apr. 1983.

9. Prasad, *Fall of Towang*, 141.

10. Maxwell, *India's China War*, 423–24.

11. Information about army policy on withdrawals was obtained from interviews with D. K. Palit, 12 Apr. 1983, 17 Jan. 1986, 2 Sept. 1988. For withdrawals of posts themselves, see Maxwell, *India's China War*, 395, 423–24.

12. See S. R. Johri, *Chinese Invasion of Ladakh* (Lucknow: Himalaya Publishers, 1969), 183–84. Johri claims that the Chinese did not attack further because they were deterred by the available Indian military strength. It is Maxwell (*India's China War*, 424) who says that they did not cross their claim line.

13. Maxwell, *India's China War*, 395–96, 423–24.

14. Johri, *Chinese Invasion of Ladakh*, passim.

15. Mullik, *Chinese Betrayal*, 381.

16. The account of this decision and all quotations are Mullik's (see *Chinese Betrayal*, 381–82).

17. Ibid., 382.

18. Maxwell, *India's China War*, 414.

19. Interview with D. K. Palit, 17 Jan. 1986.

20. Maxwell, *India's China War*, 393.

21. Ibid., 393, 396; Mullik, *Chinese Betrayal*, 380–81.

22. See Kaul, *Untold Story*, 397–98 (quotation is on p. 398); Galbraith, *A Life in Our Times*, 429.

23. Mullik, *Chinese Betrayal*, 380.

24. Kaul, *Untold Story*, 398.

25. Interviews with sources who wish to remain anonymous, Apr.–May 1983.

26. Harbakhsh Singh recalled Thapar's telling him on 28 Oct. that Kaul was "pressuring Panditji" to be allowed to return (interview, 30 Dec. 1985).

27. Galbraith, *Ambassador's Journal*, 442; Kaul, *Untold Story*, 398.

28. Maxwell, *India's China War*, 415–17 (quotation is on p. 417).

29. See Mullik, *Chinese Betrayal*, 403.

30. Interviews with D. K. Palit, 25 Mar. 1983, 25 June 1985; Prasad, *Fall of Towang*, 142–43.

31. Interview with Harbakhsh Singh, 30 Dec. 1985.

32. The statement about Kaul's refusing to be put in the picture is from Harbakhsh Singh (the 30 Dec. 1985 interview).

33. Johri, *Chinese Invasion of NEFA*, 209; Mullik, *Chinese Betrayal*, 391–92.

34. Maxwell, *India's China War*, 418–19.

35. Interview with Harbakhsh Singh, 30 Dec. 1985.

36. Maxwell, *India's China War*, 420.

37. Inferred from Mullik, *Chinese Betrayal*, 401–2; and from Maxwell, *India's China War*, 420.

38. Maxwell, *India's China War*, 420; Kaul, *Untold Story*, 401.

39. Maxwell, *India's China War*, 420.

40. Johri, *Chinese Invasion of NEFA*, 215; Mullik, *Chinese Betrayal*, 412. For another explanation for the haste of the attack, see Maxwell, *India's China War*, 420–21.

41. Johri, *Chinese Invasion of NEFA*, 218-34. Maxwell, in *India's China War*, gives 16 Nov. as the starting date of the Chinese offensive.

42. Kaul, *Untold Story*, 405-6.

43. Ibid., 407.

44. Ibid.

45. The estimate of Indian troop strength is from an interview with D. K. Palit, 2 Sept. 1988. Other information on Indian dispositions is taken from Maxwell, *India's China War*, 424, and from Johri, *Chinese Invasion of NEFA*, 126-27. As indicated by D. K. Palit, in an interview on 2 Sept. 1988, a full-strength Indian battalion had approximately 900 men; a brigade, approximately 3,200 (three battalions plus support troops etc.); and a division, 14,000-16,000 (three brigades plus support troops etc.).

46. The information on the Chinese use of two divisions, as well as the quotation, is taken from Maxwell, *India's China War*, 455. The estimate of Chinese manpower is deduced from Griffith, *People's Liberation Army*, 219-20. Griffith rates a normal (1965) Chinese division as having 10,000 men, and a mountain division as having 8,000 to 10,000 men. It seems prudent to use the 8,000 figure to correspond to what Maxwell calls a "light" division. But, as Griffith (p. 219) points out, estimating the overall size of the Chinese armed forces in the 1960s, and the size of Chinese specialized (e.g., mountain) divisions in particular, places the observer in the "cloudy realm of uncertainty and speculation."

47. Maxwell, *India's China War*, 246, 424; Saigal, *Unfought War*, 54-55, 67. On Indian Army equipment shortages and problems, see Dalvi, *Himalayan Blunder*, 97-101; Kaul, *Untold Story*, 331-34.

48. This analysis is based on an interview with Harbakhsh Singh, 30 Dec. 1985; on Harbakhsh's article in the *Indian Express*, 25 Apr. 1979; and on an interview with D. K. Palit, 12 Apr. 1983.

49. Maxwell, *India's China War*, 426.

50. Interviews with D. K. Palit, 17 Jan. and 26 Aug. 1986; Johri, *Chinese Invasion of NEFA*, 129-33; Kaul, *Untold Story*, 412-13; Maxwell, *India's China War*, 427-29. According to Maxwell's sources, Pathania was also concerned that Se La would now depend entirely on air supply and could last for only a week until supplies ran out. It is not clear whether Pathania's estimate was correct. If Se La had seven days' full rations, these could be stretched to cover more days; moreover, Se La had a good drop zone (Senge), which should have been properly defended.

51. Interviews with D. K. Palit, 25 June 1985, 17 Jan. 1986, 26 Aug. 1986. Maxwell's view is that Kaul had already returned by this time and that he shares responsibility for this signal, (*India's China War*, 430-31).

52. The quotation is from Johri, *Chinese Invasion of NEFA*, 133; and the time of Kaul's return is from Kaul, *Untold Story*, 412.

53. This composite version of the Kaul-Pathania conversations is drawn from Kaul, *Untold Story*, 413, and from an interview with D. K. Palit, 17 Jan. 1986.

54. The controversy over whether Kaul took this step by himself is discussed and analyzed in Maxwell, *India's China War* (postscript of 1972 ed.), 483-85, where he cites the claim made by D. K. Palit (in the *Hindustan Times* [Overseas Edition], 21 Nov. 1970) and P. N. Thapar (in *The Statesman*, 9 Jan. 1971) that Thapar and Sen had already left for their billets. Kaul's version appears in *Untold Story*, 413-14.

55. Kaul, *Untold Story*, 413-14. A slightly different version of the Kaul signal appears in Kaul, *Confrontation with Pakistan*, 279-80; and in Maxwell, *India's China War*, 431.

56. Interview with D. K. Palit, 17 Jan. 1986.

57. See Maxwell, *India's China War*, 432.

58. The battalion withdrawal is described in Maxwell, *India's China War*, 432. D. K. Palit, in an interview on 20 Aug. 1986, indicated that this was normal retreat procedure.

59. Maxwell, *India's China War*, 429-30, 432. Maxwell bases this conclusion on "reports of

the surviving headquarters officers and battalion commanders of 62 Brigade" (p. 429). Kaul also believed that Hoshiar wanted to hold Se La (see *Untold Story*, 414, 416).

60. Maxwell, *India's China War*, 432–33; Johri, *Chinese Invasion of NEFA*, 135. This point, like several others in this section, represents an effort to reconcile the somewhat different accounts in several sources.

61. For interpretations of Hoshiar's role, see Maxwell, *India's China War*, 432–33; Kaul, *Untold Story*, 414–15; Johri, *Chinese Invasion of NEFA*, 134–39.

62. Kaul, *Untold Story*, 415–16.

63. Maxwell, *India's China War*, 434–35; Johri, *Chinese Invasion of NEFA*, 184.

64. Johri, *Chinese Invasion of NEFA*, 184; interview with D. K. Palit, 20 Aug. 1986.

65. Maxwell, *India's China War*, 434; for an account of Chinese movements, see Johri, *Chinese Invasion of NEFA*, 148–49.

66. Maxwell, *India's China War*, 434.

67. Johri, *Chinese Invasion of NEFA*, 108–96; Maxwell, *India's China War*, 308, 424–37. That the Chinese bypassed Se La from the west as well as the east was confirmed by D. K. Palit, in an interview on 2 Sept. 1988.

68. Johri, *Chinese Invasion of NEFA*, 156.

69. Maxwell, *India's China War*, 434; Johri, *Chinese Invasion of NEFA*, 156–59.

70. Maxwell, *India's China War*, 435. Johri (*Chinese Invasion of NEFA*, 183) reports that four more battalions were supposed to be in reserve, bringing the total needed for the Bomdila defense plan to sixteen. Kaul (*Untold Story*, 418) uses the same figure.

71. Kaul, *Untold Story*, 418.

72. Maxwell, *India's China War*, 435.

73. Ibid.

74. Johri, *Chinese Invasion of NEFA*, 182–84.

75. Ibid., 184.

76. Interview with D. K. Palit, 20 Aug. 1986.

77. Maxwell, *India's China War*, 435; Johri, *Chinese Invasion of NEFA*, 184–85.

78. Johri, *Chinese Invasion of NEFA*, 184–85; generally confirmed by Kaul, *Untold Story*, 418–19.

79. Maxwell, *India's China War*, 435–36; see also Johri, *Chinese Invasion of NEFA*, 185.

80. Johri, *Chinese Invasion of NEFA*, 184–85.

81. Ibid., 185.

82. Ibid. See also Maxwell, *India's China War*, 436.

83. Johri, *Chinese Invasion of NEFA*, 185–86.

84. Ibid., 186–87.

85. Ibid., 188–89. See also Maxwell, *India's China War*, 436.

86. Maxwell, *India's China War*, 436 (based on unpublished documents). Johri's version attaches no blame to Kaul (*Chinese Invasion of NEFA*, 188).

87. Ibid., 436–37. See a somewhat different description in Johri, *Chinese Invasion of NEFA*, 188–89.

CHAPTER THIRTEEN

1. Brecher, "Nonalignment under Stress," 613.

2. *Hindustan Times*, 23 Oct. 1962. Kennedy's "quarantine" speech was given on the evening of 22 Oct. Another newspaper explained that the United States was seemingly reticent about providing aid because it did not want to drive the Soviets to support the Chinese against India (*The Hindu*, 23 Oct. 1962).

3. Galbraith, *Ambassador's Journal*, 431.

4. Harold Macmillan, *The End of the Day*, 1961–1963 (London: Macmillan, 1973), 227–29;

Paul Gore-Booth, *With Great Truth and Respect* (London: Constable, 1984), 294–95; *The Hindu*, 26 Oct. 1962.

5. Gopal, *Nehru*, 3: 224; Galbraith, *Ambassador's Journal*, 435; Macmillan, *End of Day*, 228.

6. Galbraith's impression (see *Ambassador's Journal*, 435); see also Gopal, *Nehru*, 3: 224.

7. Gopal, *Nehru*, 3: 224.

8. *Times of India*, 23 Oct. 1962.

9. Gopal, *Nehru*, 3: 225–27, 230.

10. Kaul, *Untold Story*, 396.

11. Ibid., 397.

12. Khera, *India's Defence Problem*, 230–31. Khera writes as if he did not know about the paper beforehand and was not sent by Krishna Menon to collect it. See also Kaul, *Untold Story*, 397.

13. Mullik, *Chinese Betrayal*, 403.

14. Galbraith, *Ambassador's Journal*, 444–45; Brecher, "Nonalignment under Stress," 614. The American ambassador had been told by Kennedy to do business with Krishna Menon, but Ambassador Galbraith knew of the defense minister's political difficulties and was not about to rescue him. Galbraith did not want Krishna Menon to seem to be the initiator of the India–United States arms agreement. From an interview with J. K. Galbraith, Cambridge, Mass., 7 Jan. 1985.

15. Galbraith, *Ambassador's Journal*, 445.

16. Interview with J. K. Galbraith, 7 Jan. 1985.

17. Brecher, "Nonalignment under Stress," 613–14; Galbraith, *Ambassador's Journal*, 431, 435, 441, 443.

18. Galbraith, *Ambassador's Journal*, 440, 443, 446.

19. Brecher, "Nonalignment under Stress," 616–17.

20. Ibid., 616n.

21. *Times of India*, 27 Oct. 1962.

22. *The Statesman*, 24 Oct. 1962.

23. *The Statesman*, 25 Oct. 1962.

24. See *Times of India*, 29 Oct. 1962.

25. *Times of India*, 31 Oct. 1962.

26. Ibid.

27. Mullik, *Chinese Betrayal*, 382–83.

28. *Times of India*, 1 Nov. 1962.

29. Ibid.

30. See Mullik, *Chinese Betrayal*, 384–87. My inference that the person described by Mullik was Krishnamachari is drawn from a short notice in the *Times of India*, 3 Nov. 1962, stating that "TTK" had complained to Nehru on 1 Nov. that his telephone had been tapped. On Krishnamachari's uneasiness generally, see *Times of India*, 2 Nov. 1962.

31. *Times of India*, 3 Nov. 1962.

32. Interview with H. K. Mahatab, 25 Apr. 1983.

33. *The Statesman*, 6 Nov. 1962.

34. Ibid.

35. Interviews with Mahavir Tyagi, 1966, and H. K. Mahatab, 25 Apr. 1983. An account in the *Times of India*, 7 Nov. 1962, indicates that this group did not yet constitute a majority of the Parliamentary Executive.

36. Interview with H. K. Mahatab, 25 Apr. 1983.

37. Interview with M. Tyagi, 1966; confirmed in an interview with H. K. Mahatab, 25 Apr. 1983.

38. Interviews with M. Tyagi, 1966, and H. K. Mahatab, 25 Apr. 1983.

39. *Times of India*, 8 Nov. 1962.

40. Interviews with M. Tyagi, 1966, and H. K. Mahatab, 25 Apr. 1983.

41. Interview with H. K. Mahatab, 12 Jan. 1986.

42. Interview with H. K. Mahatab, 25 Apr. 1983.

43. Interview with M. Tyagi, 1966.

44. Interview with H. K. Mahatab, 25 Apr. 1983.

45. Desai, *My Life*, 2: 189. The point that cabinet colleagues did not wish to confront Nehru out of love or fear of him was made by H. K. Mahatab, in an interview on 25 Apr. 1983.

46. Inference from interview with Morarji Desai, 10 May 1983.

47. See Mullik, *Chinese Betrayal*, 383.

48. *Times of India*, 8 Nov. 1962.

49. Gopal, *Nehru*, 3: 228.

50. Galbraith, *Ambassador's Journal*, 481. This request had been based on an earlier suggestion by Galbraith, although the decision to transfer troops had been made earlier (see Chapter 12). Apparently, that decision was confirmed by the cabinet on 17 Nov. (see Brecher, "Nonalignment under Stress," 617).

51. Galbraith, *Ambassador's Journal*, 479.

52. See Gopal, *Nehru*, 3: 228–29.

53. Ibid., 228.

54. Galbraith, *Ambassador's Journal*, 486; interview with J. K. Galbraith, 7 Jan. 1985.

55. Brecher, "Nonalignment under Stress," 617. The allusion to a "midnight" letter appears in Galbraith, *Ambassador's Journal*, 489.

56. Gopal, *Nehru*, 3: 228–29; Brecher, "Nonalignment under Stress," 617–20; see also Bowles, *Promises to Keep*, 474.

57. Gopal, *Nehru*, 3: 229. The quotations from Nehru in this paragraph are Gopal's paraphrases.

58. Brecher, "Nonalignment under Stress," 617–18, 620. M. J. Desai would have been involved in this fashion, since by this time he was regularly drafting Nehru's letters.

59. Brecher, "Nonalignment under Stress," 617–18.

60. Galbraith, *Ambassador's Journal*, 487–90; interview with J. K. Galbraith, 7 Jan. 1985.

61. Interview with J. K. Galbraith, 7 Jan. 1985; Galbraith, *A Life in Our Times*, 438.

62. Galbraith, *Ambassador's Journal*, 487–88.

63. Galbraith, *A Life in Our Times*, 439; interview with J. K. Galbraith, 7 Jan. 1985; *Ambassador's Journal*, 487–88.

64. Galbraith, *Ambassador's Journal*, 487.

65. Galbraith, *A Life in Our Times*, 438.

66. Galbraith, *Ambassador's Journal*, 481, 487.

67. Ibid., 489.

68. Ibid., 488–89.

69. Brecher, "Nonalignment under Stress," 620–21.

70. Ibid., 621.

71. Ibid., 618, 620.

72. Interview with J. K. Galbraith, 7 Jan. 1985; letter from J. K. Galbraith, 2 Dec. 1988.

73. Brecher, "Nonalignment under Stress," 621.

74. Inferred from Brecher, op. cit., 621.

75. Quotation is from Maxwell, *India's China War*, 444. For a prominent American sinologist's view of the probable reasons for the Chinese cease-fire and withdrawal, see Whiting, *Chinese Calculus of Deterrence*, 147–69.

76. Maxwell, *India's China War*, 394–95, 424–37.

77. See Saigal, *Unfought War*, 119–20, 125–26, 153–60.

CHAPTER FOURTEEN

1. *White Papers*, 8: 19. An Indian interpretation of the announcement is found in Mullik, *Chinese Betrayal*, 452–53. On the mechanics of the Chinese announcement, see Maxwell, *India's China War*, 447–48; 7 Nov. 1959 was the date of the Chou En-lai note that first proposed the 20-kilometer withdrawal idea to India.

2. S. Gopal, in an interview on 10 Jan. 1986, and N. B. Menon, in an interview on 15 Jan. 1986, expressed the view that Nehru kept to his customary decision-making style, and that the Emergency Committee continued to be only a consultative body. (Menon emphasized that this was only his "impression" as an observer from the level of an official.) The statement about the increased importance of the Emergency Committee is derived from Brecher, *Succession in India*, 100–103.

3. See T. V. Kunhi Krishnan, *Chavan and the Troubled Decade* (Bombay: Somaiya Publications, 1971), 95–97; and Raju G. C. Thomas, *The Defence of India* (New Delhi: Macmillan, 1978), 83–84. On interministerial cooperation see J. N. Chaudhuri, with B. K. Narayan, *General J. N. Chaudhuri: An Autobiography* (New Delhi: Vikas, 1978), 184–85.

4. The important events in Chaudhuri's professional background are described in his *Autobiography*, 118–75; on his role as army chief, see Sukhwant Singh, *Defence of the Western Border* (New Delhi: Vikas, 1981), 260–76, and Maxwell, *India's China War*, 443, 450, 472–73. See also Kaul's comments on Chaudhuri in *Untold Story*, 132–33, 175, 177–78, 422–23, 475–79. On armed service chiefs and the Emergency Committee, see Thomas, *The Defence of India*, 87.

5. Mullik, *Chinese Betrayal*, 526–34, 432–47, 490–94; Brecher, *Succession in India*, 87; Thomas, *Defence of India*, 75.

6. This conclusion is drawn from interviews with M. J. Desai, Feb. 1966; N. R. Pillai, 16 May 1983, 4 July 1985; and S. Gopal, 10 Jan. 1986.

7. Material in this section is drawn from interviews with serving or retired MEA officials who wish to remain anonymous, Mar.–Aug. 1966, Aug.–Sept. 1967, and with M. J. Desai, Feb. 1966. Material also is drawn from interviews with S. Gopal, N. B. Menon, and sources who wish to remain anonymous, Mar.–May 1983 and 15 Jan. 1986 (Menon). See also Nehru's article "Changing India," in *Foreign Affairs* 41 (Apr. 1963): 453–65.

8. The "senior partner" concept is N. B. Menon's, from an interview on 20 Apr. 1983; on this subject see also Mullik on Nehru, in *Chinese Betrayal*, 454–55, and *Years with Nehru*, 217–20.

9. See Chavan's statement in the Rajya Sabha, *The Statesman*, 17 Aug. 1963.

10. Interview with a source who wishes to remain anonymous, 1966.

11. Brecher, "Nonalignment under Stress," 629.

12. Disappointment in nonaligned countries was expressed by Indian officials to Michael Brecher in 1964, 1965, and at various times between 1971 and 1974; see Brecher, "Nonalignment under Stress," 629n (quotation is from p. 629). Satisfaction with the outcome of the Colombo episode is shown in Mullik, *Chinese Betrayal*, 469–70. One Indian official believes that some of his colleagues were incorrect in their upbeat assessment of the Colombo results (interview with N. B. Menon, 15 Jan. 1986).

13. See Gundevia, *Outside the Archives*, 255–81, 350–51; Gopal, *Nehru*, 3: 256–57.

14. Galbraith, *Ambassador's Journal*, 502, 508.

15. Nehru, "Fortnightly Letters," 22 Dec. 1962.

16. This paragraph and the preceding paragraph are drawn from Mullik, *Years with Nehru*, 217–20; Mullik, *Chinese Betrayal*, 458–59; "Fortnightly Letters," 22 Dec. 1962; and *Times of India*, 1 Jan. 1963. In the "Fortnightly Letter" cited, Nehru claimed that much of his analysis of Chinese motivation was suggested to him by a Yugoslav vice president (Edward Kardelj) and an Arab leader (probably Nasser, whom Nehru had seen in September). But most of these themes had been in Indian thinking earlier.

17. See Brecher, "Nonalignment under Stress," 628; *The Statesman*, 28 July and 20 Aug. 1963; Mullik, *Years with Nehru*, 220.

18. *Times of India*, 19 Jan. 1963; Galbraith, *Ambassador's Journal*, 490–91; Mullik, *Chinese Betrayal*, 456–60. Among the other factors mentioned by Nehru was China's recognition that, in a prolonged war, China could be attacked by air (he may have meant by land also) from India and Taiwan and from United States bases in the Pacific. He expressed this view in a briefing to the IB in early 1963 (Mullik, *Chinese Betrayal*, 459–60). The Kaul influence on him was still apparent.

19. Galbraith, *Ambassador's Journal*, 504. The rest of the information on this episode is taken from Gopal, *Nehru*, 3: 251–54; Macmillan, *End of the Day*, 231–35; and *The Statesman*, 17 and 23 July 1963.

20. *Times of India*, 19 Jan. 1963.

21. Gopal, *Nehru*, 3: 239–44.

22. *Times of India*, 19 Jan. 1963.

23. Mullik, *Chinese Betrayal*, 474.

24. "Fortnightly Letters," 22 Dec. 1962.

25. Gopal, *Nehru*, 3: 237.

26. See Chaudhuri, *Autobiography*, 174. For Kaul's version see *Untold Story*, 448–51.

27. The information that the report was produced mainly on Chaudhuri's initiative and was written mainly by Bhagat was provided by D. K. Palit, in interviews on 25 Mar. and 12 Apr. 1983 and on 29 June 1985. Palit served as Chaudhuri's DMO during the post-crisis period.

28. Khera, *India's Defence Problem*, 216. These statements constituted implicit criticism of the practices of Army Headquarters and Eastern Command, before and during the war, and of Kaul's IV Corps.

29. Mullik, *Chinese Betrayal*, 477. The quotation on "higher direction of war" is taken from Maxwell, *India's China War*, 470.

30. Kunhi Krishnan, *Chavan*, 103; Mullik, *Chinese Betrayal*, 474, 476.

31. On Krishna Menon's projects see Khera, *India's Defence Problem*, 254, and Thomas, *Defence of India*, 155–62.

32. From Thomas, *Defence of India*, 157–58; interview with Nehru, reported in *Times of India*, 19 Jan. 1963; *Times of India*, 5 Dec. 1962; interview with K. Subrahmanyam, 29 Dec. 1985; and Sukhwant Singh, *Western Border*, 261.

33. Interview with D. K. Palit, 31 Dec. 1985.

34. Stephen P. Cohen and Richard D. Park, *India: An Emergent Power?* (New York: Crane, Russak, 1978), 38; Raju G. C. Thomas, *Indian Security Policy* (Princeton, N. J.: Princeton University Press, 1986), 19, 26–27. Thomas questions whether the facet of Indian strategic doctrine that projects only a replay of the 1962 war is really warranted (p. 27).

35. *Times of India*, 1 Jan. 1963.

36. Brecher, with Geist, *Decisions in Crisis*, 23.

CHAPTER FIFTEEN

1. The preceding paragraphs are drawn from an interview with J. K. Galbraith, 7. Jan. 1985; Galbraith, *Ambassador's Journal*, 490–91; Maxwell, *India's China War*, 450–51; *Times of India*, 22–24 Nov. 1962.

2. *White Papers*, 8: 19–20.

3. *Times of India*, 27, 28 Nov. 1962; and statement by Indian law minister Asoke Sen, *Times of India*, 28 Nov. 1962.

4. See an MEA official's analysis of the Chinese plan in *Times of India*, 27 Nov. 1962.

5. *Times of India*, 25 Nov. 1962. Clarifications had also been sought from a Chinese embassy representative two days earlier (Maxwell, *India's China War*, 451).

6. *Times of India*, 25 Nov. 1962.

7. *White Papers*, 8: 33.

8. Government of the People's Republic of China, *The Sino-Indian Boundary Question* (Peking: Foreign Languages Press, 1965), 41.

9. See Maxwell, *India's China War*, 460–61. Both India and China lobbied the Colombo governments (see *Times of India*, 1, 3 Dec. 1962).

10. *Sino-Indian Boundary Question*, 43.

11. Maxwell, *India's China War*, 461–62; and see Chen Yi statement in *Sino-Indian Boundary Question*, 8–9. See also *White Papers*, 9: 15, and Maxwell, *India's China War*, 461–62.

12. See Chou En-lai letter to Nehru, 20 Apr. 1963, in *White Papers*, 9: 10–11. In this letter Chou also rejected a recent Nehru offer to submit the China-India boundary dispute to a body like the International Court of Justice at The Hague, for arbitration, at some suitable time. Chou pointed out, as Nehru had done on earlier occasions, that international arbitration was not a suitable method for settling complicated matters of sovereignty over the large amount of territory in dispute between India and China (9: 11–12). But Nehru argued that the factual and historical aspects of the dispute were justiciable (i.e., capable of judicial interpretation). He felt that, if direct negotiations were not possible, international adjudication was preferable to another war (9: 18).

13. Nehru letter to Chou En-lai, 1 May 1963, in *White Papers*, 9: 14–20.

14. This and the preceding paragraph are drawn from an interview with an Indian source who wishes to remain anonymous, Mar. 1983.

15. Thomas, *Defence of India*, 157–58.

16. Kavic, *India's Quest for Security*, 192; Thomas, *India's Security Policy*, 27.

17. The actual 1962–63 increase (voted by parliament) was 95 crores of rupees, and the total extra expenditure was expected to come to 108 crores. See finance minister's budget speech of 28 Feb. 1963, in Government of India, Ministry of Finance, *Budget for 1963–64* (New Delhi: Ministry of Finance), 140. One crore is ten million rupees.

18. Interview with K. Subrahmanyam, 29 Dec. 1985. Mr. Subrahmanyam in 1962–63 was deputy secretary for the budget, in the defense ministry.

19. Interview with K. Subrahmanyam, 29 Dec. 1985.

20. Ibid. Figures are taken from finance minister's speech, *Budget for 1963–64*, 140–42. The amount actually spent in 1963–64 was 816 crores. (Maxwell, *India's China War*, 471).

21. Desai, *My Life*, 2: 190.

22. Financial column in *Times of India*, 1 Jan. 1963, and finance minister's speech, *Budget for 1963–64*, 141–57.

23. Thomas, *Defence of India*, 105–6.

24. Ibid., 106–8 (quotation is on p. 107).

25. Ibid., 106.

26. On India's emergence as a regional power, see Cohen and Park, *India: Emergent Power?* 9–53, 71–74; and Baldev Raj Nayar, "Regional Power in a Multipolar World," in John W. Mellor, ed., *India: A Rising Middle Power* (Boulder, Colo.: Westview Press, 1979), 147–88.

27. *Far Eastern Economic Review*, 1 Jan. 1987, 22–23, and 7 May 1987, 33–35; *Times of India*, 16 Apr. 1987; *New York Times*, 8 May and 2 June 1987.

28. Quotations are taken from an interview by Kuldip Nayar in Inder Malhotra's column in *Times of India*, 28 May 1987. Other information is drawn from *Far Eastern Economic Review*, 7 May 1987, 33; and 21 May 1987, 40.

29. *Times of India*, 23 May 1987; *The Statesman*, 28 May 1987; and *Far Eastern Economic Review*, 21 May 1987.

30. *Times of India*, 28 May 1987. The term *grey areas* is Malhotra's.

31. *Far Eastern Economic Review*, 1 Jan. 1987, 22–23; 7 May 1987, 33–34; and 21 May 1987, 40.

32. The statement about lack of publicity for Chequer Board is taken from *Times of India*, 16 Apr. 1987. The statement about Chinese concern over the operation is taken from *Far Eastern Economic Review*, 7 May 1987, 33, and from *The Statesman*, 7 May 1987.

33. The expression "teach India a lesson" is taken from *India Today*, 15 May 1987, 52. The phrase has been used frequently in Indian publications. It echoes a phrase used by the Chinese at the time of their 1979 incursion into Vietnam. The statement that the Chinese wanted to raise China's status in Asia is taken from Inder Malhotra's column in *Times of India*, 28 May 1987.

34. *Times of India*, 16 Apr. 1987.

35. The expression "package deal" appears in Malhotra's column in *Times of India*, 28 May 1987. Possible Chinese reasons for pressuring the Gandhi government are given in *India Today*, 15 May 1987, 52–53, and in *Far Eastern Economic Review*, 1 Jan. 1987, 22–23.

36. Rajiv Gandhi's flexibility is noted in *Times of India*, 28 May 1987, and in *Far Eastern Economic Review*, 7 May 1987. The army's orientation is inferred from *Times of India*, 16 Apr., 31 May 1987. The statement about the even balance of the two sides is taken from *New York Times*, 8 May 1987. Tiwari's visit and the friendly context of India-China relations are mentioned in Malhotra's column, *Times of India*, 28 May 1987. Stopover in China by Pant is noted in *India Today*, 15 May 1987, and in *Far Eastern Economic Review*, 7 May 1987, 34.

37. Information on Gorbachev's overture is taken from *Far Eastern Economic Review*, 1 Jan. 1987, 23 (it started with a Gorbachev speech on 28 July 1986). In 1987 the United States was seen in India as playing a role that aided the Chinese game (see *India Today*, 15 May 1987).

38. Sundarji's commitment is taken from *Times of India*, 31 May 1987.

39. India's decision not to attack in Sumdorong was noted by the military writer Ravi Rikhye, in *Times of India*, 16 Apr. 1987.

CHAPTER SIXTEEN

1. For the application of this concept in two crisis case studies that have used the ICB model, see Karen Dawisha, *The Kremlin and the Prague Spring: Decisions in Crisis* (Berkeley and Los Angeles: University of California Press, 1984), 310–16; and Avi Shlaim, *The United States and the Berlin Blockade, 1948–1949: A Study in Crisis Decision-Making* (Berkeley and Los Angeles: University of California Press, 1983), 393–401, 410–23.

2. Quoted in Sudhakar Bhat, *India and China* (New Delhi: Popular Book Services, 1967), 139.

3. Chinese note of 10 October 1962, in *White Papers*, 7: 105.

4. Gopal, *Nehru*, 3: 213.

5. Ibid., 213–14; Arthur Lall, *The Emergence of Modern India* (New York: Columbia University Press, 1981), 155–58; and Menon, "Integrity of Frontiers," 50.

6. See Roberta Wohlstetter's classic application of this concept to the Pearl Harbor case, in her *Pearl Harbor: Warning and Decision* (Stanford, Calif.: Stanford University Press, 1962), 1–4, 70–169, 382–401.

7. Mullik, *Chinese Betrayal*, 324–37.

8. Interview with K. Subrahmanyam, 29 Sept. 1983.

9. Mullik, *Chinese Betrayal*, 329–31.

10. Ibid., 334.

11. Ibid., 334–37.

12. Ibid., 330–31, 333, 337–39.

13. This conclusion is drawn from Mullik's comments in *Chinese Betrayal*, 339.

14. This information on Mullik is taken from interviews with N. B. Menon, 20–21 Apr. 1983, 31 Aug. 1986.

15. Mullik, *Chinese Betrayal*, 500–504.

16. From interview with a source who wishes to remain anonymous. The "bird of passage" phrase seems to have first been used by the Indian journalist D. R. Mankekar, in his book *The Guilty Men of 1962*, cited in Mullik, *Chinese Betrayal*, 512.

17. Interview with K. Subrahmanyam, 29 Sept. 1983.

18. Major General D. K. Palit (ret.), "Intelligence: Crucial Mistakes," *Hindustan Times Weekly Review*, 11 Apr. 1971. This article is one of the better public statements of the army's point of view.

19. Interview with K. Subrahmanyam, 29 Sept. 1983.

20. Joseph de Rivera, *The Psychological Dimension of Foreign Policy* (Columbus, Ohio: Merrill, 1968), 66–70.

21. The term *pinpricks* was used by a source who prefers to remain anonymous, in a 1966 interview.

22. Source who wishes to remain anonymous; confirmed for both pre-crisis and crisis periods by interview with N. B. Menon, 20 Apr. 1983.

23. See K. Subrahmanyam, "Intelligence: The Failure Continues," in *Hindustan Times Weekly Review*, 14 Mar. 1971; and Maxwell, *India's China War*, 330.

24. Interviews with N. B. Menon, 20–21 Apr. 1983, 15 Jan. 1986, 31 Aug. 1986.

25. Interview with M.J. Desai, Feb. 1966, and with N.B. Menon, 15 Jan. 1986.

26. Interviews with N. B. Menon, 15 Jan. 1986, 31 Aug. 1986.

27. Information in this paragraph is drawn from Mullik, *Chinese Betrayal*, 334–37, and from Whiting, *Chinese Calculus of Deterrence*, 91–106.

28. Interview with N. B. Menon, 15 Jan. 1986.

29. Interviews with N. B. Menon, 15 Jan. 1986, 31 Aug. 1986.

30. Interviews with N. B. Menon, 20–21 Apr. 1983, 15 Jan. 1986, 31 Aug. 1986. In an interview on 4 May 1983, Palit confirmed that he had consulted with Menon, but he recalled that the calculations about Chinese road capacity had taken place after the Chinese attacked (i.e., after 20 Oct.).

31. See *White Papers*, 7: 96, 103, 105, 112.

32. Maxwell, *India's China War*, 331.

33. See Mullik, *Years with Nehru*, 64–82.

34. That Mullik might have relied on Nehru for integration of material was a suggestion made by N. B. Menon, in an interview on 31 Aug. 1986. For some confirmation see Mullik, *Years with Nehru*, 64–65.

35. Interview with D. K. Palit, 25 Mar. 1983.

36. The term *one-upmanship* is taken from an interview with N. B. Menon, 20 Apr. 1983.

37. See Maxwell, *India's China War*, 330.

38. A substantial theoretical literature has been developed on the subject of incremental decision-making, "satisficing" alternatives, etc. See David Baybrooke and Charles E. Lindblom, *A Strategy of Decision: Policy Evaluation as a Social Process* (New York: Free Press, 1963); James G. March and Herbert A. Simon, *Organizations* (New York: Wiley, 1968), 169–71; Ole Holsti and Alexander George, "The Effects of Stress on the Performance of Foreign Policy Makers," *Political Science Annual* 6 (1975): 255–319. The term *operational code* is taken from Alexander George, "The 'Operational Code': A Neglected Approach to the Study of Political Leaders and Decision-Making," *International Studies Quarterly*, 13 (June 1969): 191.

39. This description of the nature of these discussions is taken from an interview with N. R. Pillai, 4 July 1985. The list of participants mentioned above represents my deduction from many interviews and the public statements made by Krishna Menon (see below), and should not be attributed to Mr. Pillai.

40. Interviews with a source who wishes to remain anonymous, Mar.–Apr. 1983.

41. Brecher, *Krishna Menon's View of the World*, 152.

42. Ibid., 149.

43. Interviews with S. Gopal, 24 Mar., 1, 8 Apr. 1983, 10 Jan. 1986.

44. Brecher, *Krishna Menon's View of the World*, 324; see also 152, 148.

45. These behaviors, associated with high stress, are widely known among analysts of decision-making who take a psychological perspective. See Dowty, *Middle East Crisis*, 15–17, as well as his sources: Brecher, with Geist, *Decisions in Crisis*, 377–78; Charles Hermann, "Threat,

Time and Surprise: A Simulation of International Crisis," in Charles Hermann, ed., *International Crises: Insights from Behavioral Research* (New York: Free Press, 1972), 210; Ole Holsti, "The 1914 Case," *American Political Science Review* 59 (June 1965): 365; Ole Holsti, *Crisis, Escalation, War* (Montreal: McGill-Queen's University Press, 1972), 14–17, 121, 200; G. T. Allison and M. H. Halperin, "Bureaucratic Politics: A Paradigm and Some Policy Implications," in R. Tanter and R. H. Ullman, eds., *Theory and Practice in International Relations* (Princeton, N. J.: Princeton University Press, 1973), 50; Dean G. Pruitt, "Definition of the Situation as a Determinant of International Action," in H. C. Kelman, ed., *International Behavior* (New York: Holt, Rinehart and Winston, 1966), 411; and Holsti and George, "Effects of Stress," 278–79.

46. See Gopal, *Nehru*, 3: 121–26.

47. A military source who wishes to remain anonymous (interviewed in 1983) has testified to Pathania's distinguished earlier record as a young officer, but mentioned that he may have been disoriented in 1962 after serving some years in administrative positions. Maxwell refers to this point as well (*India's China War*, 396).

CHAPTER SEVENTEEN

1. The entire ICB model is outlined in Michael Brecher, "Toward a Theory of International Crisis Behavior," *International Studies Quarterly* 21 (Mar. 1977): 39–74.

2. Charles F. Hermann, *Crises in Foreign Policy: A Simulation Analysis* (Indianapolis: Bobbs-Merrill, 1969).

3. Brecher, "Theoretical Approach to International Behavior," 6.

4. This point is an elaboration of Brecher, "Theoretical Approach to International Behavior," 17.

5. Brecher, *Foreign Policy System*, 11.

6. Ibid., 12–14.

7. Brecher, "Theoretical Approach to International Behavior," 21.

8. Brecher, *Foreign Policy System*, 14.

9. Brecher, with Geist, *Decisions in Crisis*, 23.

10. Ibid.

11. Ibid., 27.

12. These research questions are derived from Brecher, with Geist, *Decisions in Crisis*, 23–27.

13. These hypotheses were tested previously, by Brecher and Alan Dowty, on other cases of crisis decision-making. See Brecher, with Geist, *Decisions in Crisis*, 341–405, and Dowty, *Middle East Crisis*, 303–79.

14. As worded by Dowty, *Middle East Crisis*, 12 (based on Brecher's work), and ultimately derived from Glenn Paige, *The Korean Decision* (New York: Free Press, 1968), 295; T. W. Milburn, "The Management of Crisis," in Charles Hermann, ed., *International Crises: Insights from Behavioral Research* (New York: Free Press, 1972), 274; and findings presented in Holsti and George, "Effects of Stress," 281.

15. As worded by Dowty, *Middle East Crisis*, 12 (based on Brecher's work), and ultimately derived from Glenn Paige, *The Korean Decision* (New York: Free Press, 1968), 295; T. W. Missile Crises," in Hermann, *International Crises*, 75.

16. As worded by Dowty, *Middle East Crisis*, 13. Hypothesis 1 is derived from Holsti and George, "Effects of Stress," 282–83. Hypothesis 2 is from Holsti, *Crisis, Escalation, War*, 104–17, and Holsti and George, "Effects of Stress," 298. Hypothesis 3 is from Holsti and George, "Effects of Stress," 280, based on Milburn, "Management of Crisis," 275.

17. Dowty, *Middle East Crisis*, 13; from Brecher, with Geist, *Decisions in Crisis*, 399.

18. Dowty, *Middle East Crisis*, 12; from Brecher, with Geist, *Decisions in Crisis*, 399. Ultimately derived from H. B. Shapiro and M. A. Gilbert, *Crisis Management: Psychological and Sociological Factors in Decision-Making* (Arlington, Va.: Office of Naval Research, 1975), 19,

20; J. W. Moffitt and R. Stegner, "Perceptual Rigidity and Closure as a Function of Anxiety," *Journal of Abnormal and Social Psychology* 52 (1956): 355; and Holsti, *Crisis, Escalation, War*, 15, 19.

19. See de Rivera, *Psychological Dimension of Foreign Policy*, 19–104; Alexander George and Richard Smoke, *Deterrence in American Foreign Policy: Theory and Practice* (New York: Columbia University Press, 1974), 580–86; Dina A. Zinnes, Robert C. North, and Howard E. Koch, "Capability, Threat, and the Outbreak of War," in James N. Rosenau, ed., *International Politics and Foreign Policy* (New York: Free Press, 1961), 469–82; Barton Whaley, *Codeword Barbarossa* (Cambridge, Mass.: MIT Press, 1973), passim; Graham T. Allison, *The Essence of Decision: Explaining the Cuban Missile Crisis* (Boston: Little, Brown, 1971), passim.

20. Dowty, *Middle East Crisis*, 13; from Brecher, with Geist, *Decisions in Crisis*, 375, 399. Hypothesis 1 is ultimately derived from Glenn Paige, "Comparative Case Analysis of Crisis Decisions: Korea and Cuba," in Hermann, ed., *International Crises*, 52. Hypothesis 2 is derived from Paige, *Korean Decision*, 288, and Janis, *Victims of Groupthink*, 4–5. Hypothesis 3 was put together by Dowty from two hypotheses in Brecher, with Geist, *Decisions in Crisis*, 399.

21. Hypotheses 4 and 5 are worded by Dowty, *Middle East Crisis*, 14; from Brecher, with Geist, *Decisions in Crisis*, 399.

22. Dowty, *Middle East Crisis*, 14; from Brecher, with Geist, *Decisions in Crisis*, 376. Hypothesis on greater need for leadership is ultimately derived from Paige, "Comparative Case Analysis," 52, 305, and *Korean Decision*, 289. Hypothesis on conflict is ultimately based on Paige, "Comparative Case Analysis," 52, and H. H. Lentner, "The Concept of Crisis as Viewed by the United States Department of State," in Hermann, ed., *International Crises*, 133.

23. Dowty, *Middle East Crisis*, 14; from Brecher, with Geist, *Decisions in Crisis*, 376. Taken from Shapiro and Gilbert, *Crisis Management*, 56; Paige, "Comparative Case Analysis," 52; and R. L. Frye and T. M. Stritch, "Effects of Timed versus Non-timed Discussion upon Measures of Influence and Change in Small Groups," *Journal of Social Psychology* 63 (1964): 141.

24. Dowty, *Middle East Crisis*, 15; taken from Holsti and George, "Effects of Stress," 285–93.

25. Both of these hypotheses are taken by Dowty (*Middle East Crisis*, 15) from Holsti and George, "Effects of Stress," 296.

26. Dowty, *Middle East Crisis*, 15; taken from Holsti and George, "Effects of Stress," 297.

27. One case where such nonbureaucratic behavior was thought to have beneficial results was the 1962 Cuban missile crisis, as handled by the Kennedy administration. See Allison, *Essence of Decision*, 124–26, 131–32, and Robert Kennedy, *Thirteen Days* (New York: New American Library, 1969), 30–33, 37–38, 44–46. Another case that may be relevant is described in Paige, *Korean Decision* (especially p. 290).

28. Dowty, *Middle East Crisis*, 16; taken by Brecher, with Geist, *Decisions in Crisis*, 377, from Shapiro and Gilbert, *Crisis Management*, 83; derived from Paige, "Comparative Case Analysis," 51.

29. Dowty, *Middle East Crisis*, 15–17. Hypothesis 1 is taken from Brecher, with Geist, *Decisions in Crisis*, 399. Hypothesis 2 is taken from Brecher, with Geist, 377. It is derived from Ole Holsti, "The 1914 Case," 365; Holsti, *Crisis, Escalation, War*, 14–17, 200; G. Allison and M. Halperin, "Bureaucratic Politics: A Paradigm and Some Policy Implications," in R. Tanter and S. Ullman, eds., *Theory and Policy in International Relations*, 50. Hypothesis 3 is taken from Holsti and George, "Effects of Stress," 279. The fourth hypothesis is worded by Dowty, *Middle East Crisis*, 16, and taken from Brecher, with Geist, *Decisions in Crisis*, 378. It is derived from Charles Hermann, "Threat, Time and Surprise: A Simulation of International Crises," in Hermann, ed., *International Crises*, 210; and Holsti, *Crisis, Escalation, War*, 121.

30. Dowty, *Middle East Crisis*, 16: taken from Brecher, with Geist, *Decisions in Crisis*, 377. Derived from Shapiro and Gilbert, *Crisis Management*, 36; Milburn, "Management of Crisis," 264; Holsti and George, "Effects of Stress," 278.

31. Dowty, *Middle East Crisis*, 16; taken from Brecher, with Geist, *Decisions in Crisis*, 399.

32. Dowty, *Middle East Crisis*, 16; taken from Holsti and George, "Effects of Stress," 279.

33. Dowty, *Middle East Crisis*, 16; taken from Brecher, with Geist, *Decisions in Crisis*, 402.

34. The way the "hostility" variable is used here is derived from Dina Zinnes, "A Comparison of Hostile Behavior of Decision-Makers in Simulated and Historical Data," *World Politics* 18 (1966): 481; Dean G. Pruitt, "Definition of the Situation as a Determinant of International Action," in Herbert C. Kelman, ed., *International Behavior* (New York: Holt, Rinehart and Winston, 1965), 394–97; and David C. Schwartz, "Decision-Making in Historical and Simulated Crises," in Hermann, ed., *International Crises*, 170. On the subject of foreign policy actions being the result of different goals held by different decision-makers and the factions or organizations they represent, see Allison, *Essence of Decision*, 76, 144–84.

Bibliography

UNPUBLISHED SOURCES

Galbraith, J. K. Letter to the author, dated 2 Dec. 1988.

Lamb, Alastair. Letters to the author, 7, 17 May 1984, 11 Apr. 1989.

Mehta, J. S. Letters to the author, dated 22 May and 5, 11 Dec. 1984.

Nehru, Jawaharlal. "Fortnightly Letters" to the Chief Ministers of the Indian States. Private collection, 1959–1963.

Palit, D. K. Chapters on "Seventh Brigade" and "Director of Military Operations." In untitled memoir, 1985–1986.

Singh, Umrao. Annotations to personal copy of Niranjan Prasad's *Fall of Towang*, 1981.

INTERVIEWS

Listing of interviews includes name; highest-ranking post held between 1959 and 1962; and number and dates of interviews.

Chaudhuri, Joyoti Nath. Lt. Gen., Chief of Army Staff (COAS). Three interviews: Oct. 1969, Jan. 1970, July 1970. 3

Desai, M. J. Foreign Secretary, Secretary-General, Ministry of External Affairs (MEA). One interview Feb. 1966. 1

Desai, Morarji. Minister of Finance. Five interviews: three interviews Mar.–Aug. 1966; one interview Aug.–Sept. 1967; one interview 10 May 1983. 5

Dhillon, Joginder S. Major General, Deputy Chief of General Staff. Three interviews: 5, 13, 29 Apr. 1983. 3

Dutt, Subimal. Foreign Secretary. Four interviews: two interviews Mar.–June 1966; one interview Sept. 1967; one interview 23 Apr. 1983. 4

Galbraith, John K. U. S. Ambassador to India. One interview 7 Jan. 1985. 1

Gopal, Sarvepalli. Director, Historical Division, MEA. Twelve interviews: four interviews Mar.–Aug. 1966; two interviews Sept. 1967; and interviews on 24 Mar., 1, 8, 12 Apr., 23 May 1983, and 10 Jan. 1986. 12

29

Gopalachari, K. Deputy Director, Historical Division, MEA. Four inter-   4
views: three interviews Mar.–Aug. 1966; one interview Aug.–Sept. 1967.

Kaul, B. M. Lt. Gen., Chief of General Staff (CGS), Commander of IV Corps.   3
Three interviews: two interviews Mar.–Aug. 1966; one interview
Aug.–Sept. 1967.

Krishna Menon, V. K. Minister of Defense. Four interviews: three interviews   4
Mar.–Aug. 1966; one interview Aug.–Sept. 1967.

Krishna Rao, K. MEA official. Three interviews: one interview Mar.–Aug.   3
1966; two interviews Aug.–Sept. 1967.

Krishnamachari, T. T. Minister for Economic and Defense Coordination.   2
Two interviews: one interview Mar.–Aug. 1966; one interview Sept. 1967.

Lamb, Alastair. Historian. Two interviews, 21 May 1983; 12 Jan. 1989.   2

Mahatab, H. K. Deputy Leader, Congress Parliamentary Party. Two inter-   2
views: 25 Apr. 1983, 12 Jan. 1986.

Maxwell, Neville. New Delhi correspondent, *The Times* (London). Three   3
interviews: one interview Mar.–Apr. 1966; one interview 17 May 1983;
one interview 18 May 1983.

Mehta, J. S. Director, China Division, MEA; leader of Indian delegation to   8
1960 officials' talks. Eight interviews: two interviews Mar.–Aug. 1966;
one interview Aug.–Sept. 1967; one interview June 1970; and interviews
on 26 Mar. 1983, 10 Apr. 1983, 6 Jan. 1986, and 7 Jan. 1986.

Menon, K. P. S. Ambassador to the Soviet Union. One interview Mar.–Aug.   1
1966.

Menon, Lakshmi. Deputy Minister of External Affairs, Minister of State for
External Affairs. Two interviews: one interview Mar.–Aug. 1966; one   2
interview Aug. 1967.

Menon, N. B. Director, China Division, MEA. Seven interviews: two inter-   7
views Feb.–Aug. 1966 and interviews on 20, 21, 22 Apr. 1983, 15 Jan. 1986,
and 31 Aug. 1986.

Murty, T. S. Political officer, Tawang; adviser to Indian delegation at   6
officials' talks of 1960; MEA official. Six interviews: two interviews
Mar.–Aug. 1966; two interviews Aug.–Sept. 1967; one interview 11 June
1983; one interview 12 June 1983.

Nehru, R. K. Secretary-General, MEA. Four interviews: three interviews   4
Apr.–Aug. 1966; one interview Sept. 1967.

Palit, D. K. Brigadier, Commander of 7 Brigade, Director of Military   11
Operations (DMO). Eleven interviews: 25 Mar., 12 Apr., 4 May 1983; 25,
29 June, 31 Dec. 1985; 17 Jan., 20, 26 Aug. 1986; 2, 3 Sept. 1988.

Pant, K. C. Son of Pandit G. B. Pant. Two interviews May–June 1966.   2

Parthasarthi, G. Ambassador to China, Ambassador to Pakistan. One   1
interview March 1967.

Pillai, N. R. Secretary-General, MEA. Seven interviews: three interviews   3

Mar.–Aug. 1966; one interview Aug.–Sept. 1967; and interviews on 16, 23 May 1983 and 4 July 1985.

Prasad, Niranjan. Major General, Commander of 4 Division. Three inter-   3
views: one interview Aug.–Sept. 1967; one interview 23 Mar. 1983; one interview 7 May 1983.

Rao, G. N. Research Officer, Historical Division, MEA; adviser to Indian   6
delegation at officials' talks of 1960. Six interviews: two interviews Mar.–Aug. 1966; two interviews Aug.–Sept. 1967; one interview 15 Mar. 1983; one interview 11 Apr. 1983.

Sarin, H. C. Joint Secretary, Additional Secretary, Ministry of Defense. Two 2
interviews: 28 Apr. 1983 and 29 Apr. 1983.

Sen, L. P. Lt. Gen., Chief of General Staff; Commanding Officer for Eastern   1
Command. One interview Sept. 1967.

Singh, Harbakhsh. Lt. Gen., Officiating Commander of IV Corps. One   1
interview 30 Dec. 1985.

Singh, Umrao. Lt. Gen., Commander of XXXIII Corps. Three interviews: 17,   3
18 Mar., 18 Apr. 1983.

Sinha, Sumal. Director, China Division, MEA. One interview Mar.–Aug.   1
1966.

Subrahmanyam, K. Deputy Secretary, Budget, Ministry of Defense. Two   2
interviews: 29 Sept. 1983; 29 Dec. 1985.

Tyabji, Badruddin. Special Secretary (MEA). One interview 4 Apr. 1983.   1

Tyagi, Mahavir. Member of Executive Committee of Congress Parliamen-   1
tary Party. One interview Mar.–Aug. 1966.

21

NEWSPAPERS AND MAGAZINES

Far Eastern Economic Review   1
The Hindu (Madras)   21
Hindustan Times (New Delhi)   68
Hindustan Times Weekly Review (New Delhi)   29
India Today
New Republic   118
New York Times
Peking Review
The Statesman (Calcutta)
Sunday Times (London)
Times (London)
Times of India (Bombay and New Delhi)

PUBLISHED SOURCES

Allison, Graham. "Conceptual Models and the Cuban Missile Crisis." *American Political Science Review* 63 (1969): 689–718.

————. *The Essence of Decision: Explaining the Cuban Missile Crisis.* Boston: Little, Brown, 1971.

————, and Richard Neustadt. "Afterword" to Robert Kennedy, *Thirteen Days.* New York: Norton, 1971.

Avedon, John F. *In Exile from the Land of Snows.* New York: Knopf, 1984.

Bandhyopadyaya, J. *The Making of India's Foreign Policy.* Calcutta: Allied Publishers, 1970.

Barpujari, H. K. *Problem of the Hill Tribes: North-East Frontier,* vol. 3. Gauhati: Spectrum Publications, 1981.

Baybrooke, David, and Charles E. Lindblom. *A Strategy of Decision: Policy Evaluation as a Social Process.* New York: Free Press, 1963.

Benner, Jeffrey. *The Indian Foreign Policy Bureaucracy.* Boulder, Colo.: Westview Press, 1985.

Bhargava, G. S. *The Battle for NEFA.* New Delhi: Allied Publishers, 1964.

Bhat, Sudhakar. *India and China.* New Delhi: Popular Book Services, 1967.

Bowles, Chester. *Promises to Keep.* New York: Harper and Row, 1971.

Bozeman, Adda. "India's Foreign Policy Today: Reflections upon Its Sources." *World Politics* 10 (Jan. 1958): 256–73.

Brass, Paul. *Factional Politics in an Indian State.* Berkeley and Los Angeles: University of California Press, 1965.

Brecher, Michael. *The Foreign Policy System of Israel: Setting, Images, Process.* New Haven, Conn.: Yale University Press, 1972.

————. *India and World Politics: Krishna Menon's View of the World.* London: Oxford University Press, 1968.

————. "India's Decision to Remain in the Commonwealth." *Journal of Commonwealth and Comparative Politics* 13 (Mar. 1974): 62–90.

————. *Nehru: A Political Biography.* London: Oxford University Press, 1959.

————. "Nonalignment under Stress: The West and the India-China Border War." *Pacific Affairs* 52, no. 4 (1979–80), 612–30.

————. *Succession in India: A Study in Decision-Making.* London: Oxford University Press, 1966.

————. "A Theoretical Approach to International Behavior." In Michael Brecher, ed., *Studies in Crisis Behavior.* New Brunswick, N.J.: Transaction Books, 1978, 5–24.

————. "Toward a Theory of International Crisis Behavior." *International Studies Quarterly* 21 (Mar. 1977): 39–74.

————, with Benjamin Geist. *Decisions in Crisis: Israel, 1967 and 1973.* Berkeley and Los Angeles: University of California Press, 1980.

Chakravarti, P. C. *India's China Policy*. Bloomington: Indiana University Press, 1962.

Chaudhuri, J. N. *Arms, Aims, and Aspects*. Bombay: Manaktalas, 1966.

———, with B. K. Narayan, *General J. N. Chaudhuri: An Autobiography*. New Delhi: Vikas, 1978.

Cohen, Stephen P. *The Indian Army*. Berkeley and Los Angeles: University of California Press, 1971.

———. "India's China War and After." *Journal of Asian Studies* 30 (1971): 847–57.

———, and Richard D. Park. *India: An Emergent Power?* New York: Crane, Russak, 1978.

Dalvi, J. P. *Himalayan Blunder*. New Delhi: Thacker, 1969.

Dawisha, Karen. *The Kremlin and the Prague Spring: Decisions in Crisis*. Berkeley and Los Angeles: University of California Press, 1984.

de Rivera, Joseph. *The Psychological Dimension of Foreign Policy*. Columbus, Ohio: Merrill, 1968.

Desai, Morarji. *The Story of My Life*. 2 vols. New Delhi: Macmillan, 1974.

Dowty, Alan. *Middle East Crisis: U.S. Decision-Making in 1958, 1970, and 1973*. Berkeley and Los Angeles: University of California Press, 1984.

Dutt, Subimal. *With Nehru in the Foreign Office*. Calcutta: Minerva, 1977.

Edwardes, Michael. *Nehru: A Political Biography*. New York: Praeger, 1971.

Embree, Ainslie. *India's Search for National Identity*. New Delhi: Chanakya Publications, 1980.

Fairbank, John K., ed. *The Chinese World Order*. Cambridge, Mass.: Harvard University Press, 1968.

Finlay, D., O. Holsti, and R. Fagen. *Enemies in Politics*. Chicago: Rand McNally, 1967.

Fisher, Margaret W., Leo E. Rose, and Robert A. Huttenback. *Himalayan Battleground: Sino-Indian Rivalry in Ladakh*. New York: Praeger, 1963.

Galbraith, John K. *Ambassador's Journal*. Boston: Houghton Mifflin, 1969.

———. *A Life in Our Times: Memoirs*. New York: Ballantine, 1981.

George, Alexander, and Richard Smoke. *Deterrence in American Foreign Policy*: Theory and Practice. New York: Columbia University Press, 1974.

Gopal, Sarvepalli. *Jawaharlal Nehru: A Bibliography*. 3 vols. Cambridge, Mass.: Harvard University Press, 1976–1984.

———. "Sino-Indian Relations: Neville Maxwell's Misapprehensions." *The Round Table* 245 (Jan. 1972): 113–18.

Government of the People's Republic of China. *The Sino-Indian Boundary Question*. Peking: Foreign Languages Press, 1965.

Gundevia, Y. D. *Outside the Archives*. London: Sangam Books, 1984.

Gupta, Karunakar. *The Hidden History of the Sino-Indian Frontier*. Calcutta: Minerva Associates. 1974.

———. *India in World Politics*. Calcutta: Scientific Book Agency, 1969.

———. "In Quest of Source Materials, I–IV." *Frontier*, 13 Mar.–3 Apr. 1982.

———. "A Note on Source Material on the Sino-Indian Border Dispute— Western Sector." *China Report* 17 (May–June 1981): 51–55.

———. "Sino-Indian Relations: Getting the Facts Straight." *The Statesman*, 11 May 1981.

Gurtov, M., and B. M. Hwang. *China under Threat*. Baltimore: Johns Hopkins University Press, 1980.

Hangen, Welles. *After Nehru Who?* London: Hart-Davis, 1963.

Hermann, Charles F. *Crises in Foreign Policy: A Simulation Analysis*. Indianapolis: Bobbs-Merrill, 1969.

———, ed. *International Crises: Insights from Behavioral Research*. New York: Free Press, 1972.

Hilsman, Roger. *To Move a Nation: The Politics of Foreign Policy in the Administration of John F. Kennedy*. New York: Doubleday, 1967.

Hoffmann, Steven A. "Ambiguity and India's Claims to the Aksai Chin." *Central Asian Survey* 6 (1987): 37–60.

———. "Faction Behavior and Cultural Codes." *Journal of Asian Studies* 40 (1981): 231–54.

———. "Perceived Hostility and the Indian Reaction to China." *India Quarterly* 26 (1973): 283–99.

Holsti, Ole. *Crisis, Education, War*. Montreal: McGill-Queen's University Press, 1972.

———. "The 1914 Case." *American Political Science Review* 59 (June 1965): 365–78.

———. "Time, Alternatives, and Communications: The 1914 and Cuban Missile Crises." In C. F. Hermann, ed., *International Crises: Insights from Behavioral Research*. New York: Free Press, 1972. Pp. 58–80.

Hudson, Geoffery. "The Aksai Chin." *St. Anthony's Papers* 14 (1963): 9–22.

Janis, I. L. *Victims of Groupthink*. Boston: Houghton Mifflin, 1972.

Jervis, Robert. "Hypotheses on Misperception." *World Politics* 20 (1968): 454–79.

Jetly, Nancy. *India-China Relations, 1947–1977*. Atlantic Highlands, N. J.: Humanities Press, 1979.

Johri, S. R. *Chinese Invasion of Ladakh*. Lucknow: Himalaya Publishers, 1969.

———. *Chinese Invasion of NEFA*. Lucknow: Himalaya Publishers, 1968.

Jukes, Geoffrey. *Hitler's Stalingrad Decisions*. Berkeley and Los Angeles: University of California Press, 1985.

Kaul, B.M. *Confrontation with Pakistan*. New York: Barnes and Noble, 1972.

———. *The Untold Story*. New Delhi: Allied Publishers, 1967.

Kaul, T. N. *Reminiscences, Discreet and Indiscreet.* New Delhi: Lancers, 1982.

Kavic, Lorne. *India's Quest for Security: Defense Policies, 1947–1965.* Berkeley and Los Angeles: University of California Press, 1967.

Khera, S. S. *India's Defence Problem.* Bombay: Orient-Longmans, 1968.

Kunhi Krishnan, T. V. *Chavan and the Troubled Decade.* Bombay: Somaiya Publications, 1971.

Lall, Arthur. *The Emergence of Modern India.* New York: Columbia University Press, 1981.

Lamb, Alastair. *The China-India Border: The Origins of the Disputed Boundaries.* London: Oxford University Press, 1964.

———. "The Indo-Tibetan Border." *Australian Journal of Politics and History* 6 (May 1960): 28–40.

———. *The McMahon Line.* 2 vols. London: Routledge and Kegan Paul, 1966.

———. *The Sino-Indian Border in Ladakh.* Columbia: University of South Carolina Press, 1975.

———. "Studying the Frontiers of the British Indian Empire." *Royal Central Asian Journal* 53 (Oct. 1966): 245–54.

———. "War in the Himalayas." *Modern Asian Studies* 5 (1971): 389–97.

Macmillan, Harold. *At the End of the Day, 1961–1963.* London: Macmillan, 1973.

March, James G., and Herbert A. Simon. *Organizations.* New York: Wiley, 1968.

Mankekar, D. R. *The Guilty Men of 1962.* Bombay: Tulsi Shah Enterprises, 1968.

Mathai, M. O. *Reminiscences of the Nehru Age.* New Delhi: Vikas, 1978.

Maxwell, Neville. "China and India: The Un-negotiated Dispute." *China Quarterly* 43 (July–Sept. 1970): 47–80.

———. *India's China War.* New York: Doubleday, 1972.

Mehra, Parshotam. "India-China Border: A Review and Critique." *Economic and Political Weekly,* 15 May 1982, 831–38.

———. *The McMahon Line and After.* New Delhi: Macmillan, 1974.

———. *The North-Eastern Frontier.* 2 vols. New Delhi: Oxford University Press, 1979–1980.

Mellor, John W., ed. *India: A Rising Middle Power.* Boulder, Colo.: Westview Press, 1979.

Menon, K.P.S. *The Flying Troika.* London: Oxford University Press, 1963.

———. *Many Worlds: An Autobiography.* London: Oxford University Press, 1965.

Menon, N.B. "The Integrity of Frontiers as a Function of State Power." In *The State against People.* Bangalore: Ecumenical Christian Centre Publications, 1982.

Ministry of External Affairs, Government of India. *Notes, Memoranda and Letters Exchanged and Agreements Signed between India and China: White Papers.* 8 vols. New Delhi: Ministry of External Affairs, 1959–1966. (Referred to in notes as *White Papers.*)

———. *Prime Minister on Sino-Indian Relations: Parliament.* 2 vols. New Delhi: Government of India Press, 1961–1962. (Referred to in notes as *PMSIR: Parliament.*)

———. *Prime Minister on Sino-Indian Relations: Press Conferences.* 2 vols. New Delhi: Government of India Press, 1961–1962. (Referred to in notes as *PMSIR: Press Conferences.*)

———. *Report of the Officials of the Governments of India and the People's Republic of China on the Boundary Question.* New Delhi: Ministry of External Affairs, 1961. (Referred to in text and notes as Officials' Report.)

Moraes, Frank. *Jawaharlal Nehru: A Biography.* New York: Macmillan, 1956.

Mullik, B. N. *The Chinese Betrayal.* New Delhi: Allied Publishers, 1971.

———. *My Years with Nehru, 1948–1964.* New Delhi: Allied Publishers, 1972.

Murty, T. S. *Frontiers: A Changing Concept.* New Delhi: Palit and Palit, 1978.

Nehru, Jawaharlal. *The Discovery of India.* New Delhi: Oxford University Press, 1981. (Originally published in 1946.)

———. *Toward Freedom: The Autobiography of Jawaharlal Nehru.* New York: John Day, 1941.

Nayar, Kuldip. *Between the Lines.* New Delhi: Allied Publishers, 1969.

———. *India: The Critical Years.* New Delhi: Vikas, 1973.

Paige, Glenn. *The Korean Decision.* New York: Free Press, 1968.

Palmer, Norman D. *The United States and India.* New York: Praeger, 1984.

Pandey, B. N. *Nehru.* London: Macmillan, 1976.

Pandit, Vijayalakshmi. *The Scope of Happiness.* New York: Crown Publishers, 1979.

Panikkar, K. M. *Asia and Western Dominance.* New York: John Day, 1954.

———. *In Two Chinas: Memoirs of a Diplomat.* London: Allen and Unwin, 1955.

Patterson, George. *Peking versus Delhi.* New York: Praeger, 1964.

Prasad, Niranjan. *The Fall of Towang.* New Delhi: Palit and Palit, 1981.

Pruitt, Dean G. "Definition of the Situation as a Determinant of International Action." In Herbert C. Kelman, ed., *International Behavior.* New York: Holt, Rinehart and Winston, 1966. Pp. 392–432.

Raina, Ashoka. *Inside RAW: The Story of India's Secret Service.* New Delhi: Vikas, 1981.

Rao, G. Narayana. *The India-China Border: A Reappraisal.* New York: Asia Publishing House, 1968.

Rau, Chalapathi. *Govind Ballabh Pant: His Life and Times.* New Delhi: Allied Publishers, 1981.

Richardson, Hugh. *Tibet and Its History.* Boston: Shambhala Publications, 1984.

Saigal, J. R. *The Unfought War of 1962.* New Delhi: Allied Publishers, 1979.

Sharma, Surya. *India's Boundary and Territorial Disputes.* New Delhi: Vikas, 1971.

Shlaim, Avi. *The United States and the Berlin Blockade, 1948–1949: A Study in Crisis Decision-Making.* Berkeley and Los Angeles: University of California Press, 1983.

Singh, Sukhwant. *Defence of the Western Border.* New Delhi: Vikas, 1981.

Tharoor, Shashi. *Reasons of State.* New Delhi: Vikas, 1982.

Thomas, Raju G.C. *The Defence of India.* New Delhi: Macmillan of India, 1978.

———. *Indian Security Policy.* Princeton, N. J.: Princeton University Press, 1986.

Tyabji, Badruddin. *Indian Policies and Practice.* New Delhi: Oriental Publishers, 1972.

Van Eekelen, W. F. *India's Foreign Policy and the Border Dispute with China.* The Hague: Martinus Nijhoff, 1964.

Vertzberger, Yaakov. *Misperceptions in Foreign Policymaking: The Sino-Indian Conflict, 1959–1962.* Boulder, Colo.: Westview Press, 1984.

Whiting, Alan. *The Chinese Calculus of Deterrence.* Ann Arbor: University of Michigan Press, 1975.

Wohlstetter, Roberta. *Pearl Harbor: Warning and Decision.* Stanford, Calif.: Stanford University Press, 1962.

Woodman, Dorothy. *Himalayan Frontiers: A Political Review of British, Chinese, Indian, and Russian Rivalries.* New York: Praeger, 1969.

Zinnes, Dina A., Robert C. North, and Howard E. Koch. "Capability, Threat, and the Outbreak of War." In James N. Rosenau, ed., *International Politics and Foreign Policy.* New York: Free Press, 1961. Pp. 468–82.

Index

322

INDEX

Nepal, 66, 121
New Zealand, military aid to India, 216
Nonalignment, 48–50, 58–59; effect of crisis on policy of, 166–67, 176–77, 210, 215–17, 218, 266; U.S. policy toward, 122
North and North-Eastern Border Defense Committee, 24, 31
North-East Frontier Agency (NEFA): becomes state of Arunachal Pradesh, 9, 231; British policy toward, 16–22; Chinese campaigns in, 117, 128, 163, 177–80, 183–93; Chinese policy toward, 66, 80–81; and forward policy, 96, 99, 100–102, 108–11; Indian policy toward, 25, 31, 67–74, 78–82, 127, 239–40; map 9, 189; troop movement in, 79
Nu, Prime Minister U, 72

Officials' Report: as basis for talks, 107, 142, 149, 255–56; Chinese attitude toward, 91; findings of, 108, 111, 255; origins of, 90
Officials' Talks (1960), 88–90, 112–13
Onkar, Operation, 108
Operational code, Indian, 253

Pakistan: and China, 121; and Kashmir dispute, 23–24, 51, 217; Krishna Menon's image of, 56, 125; talks with India, 217; threat to India, 127–29, 133, 169–70, 180–81, 223, 239; troops transferred from front in, 177, 180–81; and U.S., 123, 166
Palit, Brigadier D. K., 96, 119; and decision-making, crisis, 134, 148, 244; and decision-making, wartime, 168, 178–79, 182, 188, 247–48, 251; and forward policy, 96–99, 103–4, 110–11
Panikkar, K. M., 31, 33, 52
Pant, K. C., 232
Pant, Pandit Govind Ballabh: appointed Minister of Home Affairs (1955), 000; death of, 97; and decision-making, 44, 46–47, 87–88, 249, 253, 254; and forward policy, 95; and 1959 White Paper, 67; view of border dispute, 58–59

Pan Tzu-li, Chinese ambassador, 35, 60, 65, 108, 244
Paranjpe, V. V., 89
Patel, Vallabhai, 31
Pathania, A. S., 186–93, 210, 252, 257–58
Pathania, M. S., 183, 184, 186, 188–94
People's Daily, 35, 60, 61, 238, 239
People's Liberation Army (China), 121
Philippines, 60
Poshing La, 178, 188
Prasad, Captain Mahabir, 110–11
Prasad, Major General Niranjan: and decision-making, pre-crisis, 110; and decision-making, wartime, 177–79, 182, 251; and Operation Leghorn, 131, 135, 136–38, 145–47; opposition to Kaul, 153, 158–59; replacement of, 170
Prasad, President Rajendra, 64, 204
Punjab, decision to withdraw from, 176, 180–81, 239, 252

Radhakrishnan, President Sarvepalli, 87–88, 205
Rao, G. N., 89
Rawlly, Brigadier N. C., 184, 185
Reddy, O. Pulla, 97
Reid, Sir Robert, 22
Rhodesia, military aid to India, 216
Rupa, 194
Rusk, Dean, U.S. secretary of state, 209

Sandys, Duncan, 217
Sarin, H. C., 144, 148, 157–58, 180
Satisficing, 253
Saunders, Trelawney, 12
Se La (Pass): British policy toward, 16, 22; Chinese attack on, 181, 185–93; defense strategy for, 170–72, 176, 177–80, 187, 210, 251, 252, 292n40; location of, 16; retreat from, 174, 176, 185–93
Sen, Lieutenant General L. P.: and decision-making, pre-crisis, 100–101, 247; and decision-making, crisis, 153–54, 157–58, 242–43; and decision-making, wartime, 172, 177, 188–89, 190, 248, 251; and Operation Leghorn, 130–38; 140; and Umrao Singh, 147–48, 289n20

Compositor : Thomson Press India Ltd.
Text : 11/13 Sabon
Display : Sabon and Helvetica Bold Condensed
Printer : Braun-Brumfield, Inc.
Binder : Braun-Brumfield, Inc.